RIGHTEOUS ANGER AT THE WICKED STATES

This book is a history that explains the adoption of the U.S. Constitution in terms of what the proponents of the Constitution were trying to accomplish. The Constitution was a revolutionary document replacing the confederation mode with a complete three-part national government supreme over the states. The most pressing need was to allow the federal government to tax to pay off the Revolutionary War debts. In the next war, the United States would need to borrow again. The taxes needed to restore the public credit proved to be quite modest, however, and the Constitution went far beyond the immediate fiscal needs. This book argues that the proponents' anger at the states for their recurring breaches of duty to the united cause explains both critical steps and the driving impetus for the revolution. Other issues were less important.

Calvin H. Johnson is the Andrews & Kurth Centennial Professor of Law at the University of Texas School of Law. He received his undergraduate degree from Columbia College (Philosophy) and his law degree from Stanford. Before entering teaching, he was a tax lawyer with Paul Weiss Rifkind Wharton & Garrison in New York and with the U.S. Treasury Department.

RIGHTEOUS ANGER AT THE WICKED STATES

THE MEANING OF THE FOUNDERS' CONSTITUTION

Calvin H. Johnson
University of Texas School of Law

CAMBRIDGE
UNIVERSITY PRESS

CAMBRIDGE UNIVERSITY PRESS
Cambridge, New York, Melbourne, Madrid, Cape Town, Singapore, São Paulo

Cambridge University Press
40 West 20th Street, New York, NY 10011-4211, USA

www.cambridge.org
Information on this title: www.cambridge.org/9780521852326

First published 2005

Printed in the United States of America

A catalog record for this publication is available from the British Library.

Library of Congress Cataloging in Publication Data
Johnson, Calvin H., 1944–
Righteous anger at the wicked states : the meaning of the founders'
Constitution / Calvin H. Johnson.
p. cm.
Includes bibliographical references and index.
ISBN 0-521-85232-3 (hard cover)
1. Constitutional history – United States. 2. United States – Politics and
government – 1789–1797. I. Title.
KF4541.J64 2005
342.7302'9 – dc22   2004027950

ISBN-13 978-0-521-85232-6 hardback
ISBN-10 0-521-85232-3 hardback

Contents

Acknowledgments

The law of large numbers and the law of offsetting errors say that you best correct errors with a very large sample. This history of our Constitution has tried to reduce error by casting out a large net into the sea of documents that survive from the period so that the catch for inspection will be as large as possible. This work could not have been possible without the digital searches available through the wonderful Library of Congress website, *A Century of Lawmaking for a New Nation*.[1] Two generations ago a serious historian of the constitutional period had to visit dozens of small archives spread north and south along the east coast. Forrest McDonald says he put 100,000 miles on his car when he got started.[2] A generation ago, the scattered letters and documents started to get collected in scholarly editions, with learned commentary, so that a scholar with access to a research university could see the core of the important sources with months' instead of years' worth of work. Now much of the original documentation is becoming available on the Internet. When this revolution is completed, one will find the same quotes that used to take years to collect in minutes from your desk terminal, or, for that matter, from your handheld wireless computer. Every researcher will have thousands of volumes of original sources available any time. One will be able to search, play, recheck quotes, run down ideas at any time of day or night with no lead or preparation time. With digital searches, one can follow how a word is used, or how an actor changes his mind simply by searching for a word or a cluster of related words. One can copy and paste to get quotes and cites right the first time, and take accurate notes by boiling down the original material, without ever having

---

[1] Word and phrase searches can be made from <http://memory.loc.gov/ammem/hlawquery.htm>

[2] Forrest McDonald, *Review*, Documentary History of the Ratification of the Constitution, vol. 3, 14–16 (Merrill Jensen, John Kaminski, et al., eds. 1978–1984), *in* 3 WM. & Mary Q. 643 (3d Series 1987).

to use a quill pen. The digital archives available on the Internet are bringing the papers and letters of the founding of the democracy out to the democracy.

I am also thankful to the generation of editors and historians who have made the Papers of Madison, Hamilton, Washington, Jay, Mason, and Jefferson so readily available. I thank especially the *Documentary History of the Ratification of the Constitution*, which is seeking to collect and publish all the available evidence of the ratification.[3] I thank my home library, the University of Texas Law School Library, which has been of so much service with such good cheer in getting the newest books and the oldest Assembly minutes available to me. I am, of course, thankful for the grand histories that I gratefully remember teaching me so much, including (without meaning to slight anyone) nine I can think of warmly: Jack Rakove, ORIGINAL MEANINGS (1996) and his THE BEGINNINGS OF NATIONAL POLITICS (1979); Forrest McDonald, ALEXANDER HAMILTON (1979) and his WE, THE PEOPLE (1958); E. James Ferguson, THE POWER OF THE PURSE (1961); Stanley Elkins and Eric McKitrick, THE AGE OF FEDERALISM (1995); Norman Risjord, CHESAPEAKE POLITICS, 1781–1800 (1978); Gordon Wood, CREATION OF THE AMERICAN REPUBLIC 1776–1787 (1969); and Richard B. Morris, THE FORGING OF THE UNION, 1781–1789 (1987). These are all great books for different reasons.

Many people have critiqued various chapters, including Walter Dean Burnham, Brenda Clayton, Jane Cohen, Sandy Levinson, Doug Laycock, Lino Graglia, and Scot Powe. Jim and Shelley Fishkin have heard these arguments in rehearsal enough times to break the patience of Job. I am deeply appreciative of them for their affection and support. Dennis Drapkin read the entire manuscript with wonderful comments to every chapter. I am thankful for the comments I received when I presented various chapters at the University of Texas Law School, where I teach, and at the Vanderbilt Law School. I am very grateful to Kristin Konschnik, Yvette Piggush, and Calvin E. Johnson for assisting in the research for the manuscript. Carolynn Johnson and Matthew Johnson checked cites. Jolyn Piercy was given a bounty of a nickel an error for the version of the manuscript she read and corrected, and I trust she will retire handsomely on her earnings. I take all the credit for the errors that remain, sometimes maintained in the face of hard but constructive advice. My family has had to live through my monomaniacal obsession with 1787–1788 for more than the time that it took to write the Constitution. To Maria, for her love and support, I dedicate this book.

3   DOCUMENTARY HISTORY OF THE RATIFICATION OF THE CONSTITUTION (Merrill Jensen, John Kaminski, et al., eds. 1978–).

Having finished this book and sent it out into the world, I want to continue to discuss its conclusions and implications. I will maintain a website at http://www.utexas.edu/law/faculty/calvinjohnson/RighteousAnger/ where I will post news, discussions, and related articles. I invite you to join in the discussion at that site.

Frequently Cited Sources

Short cite	Full cite
Short cite	*Full cite*
ANNALS	ANNALS OF CONGRESS (Joseph Gale, ed. 1834–1856)*
BASIC WRITINGS OF TJ	BASIC WRITINGS OF THOMAS JEFFERSON 683 (Philip Foner, ed., 1944)
BEARD	CHARLES A. BEARD, AN ECONOMIC INTERPRETATION OF THE CONSTITUTION OF THE UNITED STATES (1913)
BEYOND CONFEDERATION	BEYOND CONFEDERATION: ORIGINS OF THE CONSTITUTION AND AMERICAN NATIONAL IDENTITY (Edward Beeman, et al., eds., 1987)
BROWN	ROGER H. BROWN, REDEEMING THE REPUBLIC: FEDERALISTS, TAXATION, AND THE ORIGINS OF THE CONSTITUTION (1993)
CORNELL	SAUL CORNELL, THE OTHER FOUNDERS: ANTI-FEDERALISM AND THE DISSENTING TRADITION IN AMERICA, 1788–1828 (2000)
DEBATE	THE DEBATE ON THE CONSTITUTION: FEDERALIST AND ANTIFEDERALIST SPEECHES, ARTICLES, AND LETTERS DURING THE STRUGGLE OVER RATIFICATION (Bernard Bailyn, ed., 1993)

* Available for digital search on the Internet.

DHFFC	DOCUMENTARY HISTORY OF THE FIRST FEDERAL CONGRESS OF THE UNITED STATES OF AMERICA (Linda Grant De Pauw, ed., 1972–), 17 volumes
DHFFE	THE DOCUMENTARY HISTORY OF THE FIRST FEDERAL ELECTIONS, 1788–1790 (Merrill Jensen & Robert A. Becker, eds., 1975–1989), 4 volumes
DHRC	DOCUMENTARY HISTORY OF THE RATIFICATION OF THE CONSTITUTION (Merrill Jensen, John P. Kaminski & Gaspare J. Saladino, eds., 1976–), 24 volumes
E. WAYNE CARP	E. WAYNE CARP, TO STARVE THE ARMY AT PLEASURE: CONTINENTAL ARMY ADMINISTRATION AND AMERICAN POLITICAL CULTURE, 1775–1783 (1984)
EDLING	MAX M. EDLING, A REVOLUTION IN FAVOR OF GOVERNMENT: ORIGINS OF THE UNITED STATES CONSTITUTION AND THE MAKING OF THE AMERICAN STATE (2003)
ELKINS & McKITRICK	STANLEY ELKINS & ERICK McKITRICK, THE AGE OF FEDERALISM (1993)
ELLIOT	DEBATES IN THE CONVENTIONS OF THE SEVERAL STATES ON THE ADOPTION OF THE FEDERAL CONSTITUTION (Jonathan Elliot, ed., 1907), 5 volumes*
FARRAND	RECORDS OF THE FEDERAL CONSTITUTION OF 1787 (Max Farrand, ed., rev. ed., 1937), 4 volumes.* Citations are to Madison notes unless otherwise noted.
FEDERALIST	THE FEDERALIST (Jacob E. Cooke ed., 1961). Dates cited are to first appearance in New York newspapers.*
FERGUSON	E. JAMES FERGUSON, THE POWER OF THE PURSE: A HISTORY OF AMERICAN PUBLIC FINANCE, 1776–1790 (1961)

FOUNDERS' CONSTITUTION	THE FOUNDERS' CONSTITUTION (Philip B. Kurland & Ralph Lerner, eds., 1987)
JCC	JOURNALS OF THE CONTINENTAL CONGRESS, 1774–1789, ED. (Worthington C. Ford, et al., eds., 1904–1937), 34 volumes*
JENSEN, ARTICLES	MERRILL JENSEN, THE ARTICLES OF CONFEDERATION; AN INTERPRETATION OF THE SOCIAL-CONSTITUTIONAL HISTORY OF THE AMERICAN REVOLUTION 1774–1781 (1940)
JENSEN, NEW NATION	MERRILL JENSEN, THE NEW NATION: A HISTORY OF THE UNITED STATES DURING THE CONFEDERATION (1950)
JM	PAPERS OF JAMES MADISON (William T. Hutchinson & William M. E. Rachal, eds., 1962–1991), 17 volumes
KAMINSKI, CLINTON	GEORGE CLINTON KAMINSKI: YEOMAN POLITICIAN OF THE NEW REPUBLIC (1993)
KETCHAM	RALPH KETCHAM, JAMES MADISON: A BIOGRAPHY (1971)
LDCC	LETTERS OF DELEGATES TO THE CONTINENTAL CONGRESS, 1774–1789 (Paul H. Smith, et al., eds., 1976–2000), 25 volumes*
LMCC	LETTERS OF MEMBERS OF THE CONTINENTAL CONGRESS (Edmund C. Burnett, ed., 1921–36), 8 volumes
MADISON WRITINGS	THE WRITINGS OF JAMES MADISON (Gaillard Hunt, ed., 1900–1910
MAIN	JACKSON TURNER MAIN, THE ANTIFEDERALISTS: CRITICS OF THE CONSTITUTION, 1781–1788 (1961)
McDONALD, HAMILTON	FORREST McDONALD, ALEXANDER HAMILTON: A BIOGRAPHY (1979)
McDONALD, WE THE PEOPLE	FORREST McDONALD, WE, THE PEOPLE: THE ECONOMIC ORIGINS OF THE CONSTITUTION (1958)

Morris	Richard B. Morris, The Forging of the Union, 1781–1789 (1987)
Onuf	Peter S. Onuf, The Origins of the Federal Republic: Jurisdictional Controversies in the United States, 1775–1787 (1983)
PAH	The Papers of Alexander Hamilton (Harold C. Syrett, ed., 1961–87), 27 volumes
Pamphlets	Pamphlets on the Constitution of the United States (Paul Leicester Ford, ed., 1888, reprint 1968)
PGM	The Papers of George Mason, 1725–1792 (Robert A. Rutland, ed., 1970), 3 volumes
PGW:CS	The Papers of George Washington. Confederation Series (W. W. Abbot & Dorothy Twohig, eds., 1992–), 6 volumes
PJJ	The Correspondence and Public Papers of John Jay (Henry P. Johnson, ed., 1890), 4 volumes
PTJ	The Papers of Thomas Jefferson (Julian P. Boyd, ed., 1950–), 21 volumes
Rakove, Beginnings	Jack N. Rakove, The Beginnings of National Politics: An Interpretative History of the Continental Congress (1979)
Rakove, Original Meanings	Jack N. Rakove, Original Meanings: Politics and Ideas in the Making of the Constitution (1996)
RDCUS	The Revolutionary Diplomatic Correspondence of the United State (Francis Wharton, ed., 1888), 6 volumes
Reluctant Pillar	The Reluctant Pillar: New York and the Adoption of the Federal Constitution (Stephen Schechter, ed., 1985)

RISJORD	NORMAN K. RISJORD, CHESAPEAKE POLITICS, 1781–1800 (1978)
RUTLAND	ROBERT ALLEN RUTLAND, THE ORDEAL OF THE CONSTITUTION; THE ANTIFEDERALISTS AND THE RATIFICATION STRUGGLE OF 1787–1788 (1966)
RUTLAND, MADISON	ROBERT ALLEN RUTLAND, JAMES MADISON: THE FOUNDING FATHER (1987).
STORING	THE COMPLETE ANTI-FEDERALIST (Herbert Storing, ed., 1981), 5 volumes
WAH	THE WORKS OF ALEXANDER HAMILTON (John C. Hamilton, ed., 1851).
WOOD	GORDON S. WOOD, THE CREATION OF THE AMERICAN REPUBLIC, 1776–1787 (1969)
WTJ	WORKS OF THOMAS JEFFERSON (Paul Leicester Ford, ed., 1904–05), 12 volumes
WRITINGS OF GW	WRITINGS OF GEORGE WASHINGTON FROM THE ORIGINAL MANUSCRIPT SOURCES (John C. Fitzpatrick, et al. eds., 1931–1944), 39 volumes.
WRITINGS OF JM	THE WRITINGS OF JAMES MADISON (Gaillard Hunt, ed., 1900–1910), 9 volumes.

Introduction

To determine the original meaning of any historical document, including the Constitution, one must determine what the authors and proponents were trying to accomplish. Every historical document has a meaning derived from its goals that gives life to the literal or logical meaning of the words. One can understand what the Founders meant by their writing of the Constitution only if one knows their programs. Words are deeds, Wittgenstein tells us.[1] The Constitution was once a weapon in a hard-fought war and its weapon-like characteristics are core to its historical meaning.

The most pressing need for the historical Constitution was to give the federal government a source of revenue to restore its ability to borrow. Under the Articles of Confederation, which preceded the Constitution, the federal government had the responsibility for the common defense, but it had no power to raise money except by requisitions upon the states. When the Revolutionary War ended, the states stopped paying their requisitions. The Requisition of 1786, the last before the Constitution, "mandated" payments by the states, mostly to make current payments to avoid default on the Revolutionary War debts. The requisition required payments of $3.8 million, but collected only $663. The federal government was destitute – "impotent" and "imbecilic" in the wording of the times.

There had been proposals in 1781 and in 1783 to give the federal government its own tax, a 5 percent "impost," or tax on imports. The impost

---

[1] Ludwig Wittgenstein, Philosophical Investigations, 146 (2d ed. 1958). *See also* 1 Quentin Skinner, Visions of Politics: Regarding Method 3 (2002) (saying that "we need to make it one of our principle tasks to situate the texts within such intellectual contexts as enable us to make sense of what their authors were doing in writing them"); Quentin Skinner, *Meaning and Understanding the History of Ideas* in Meaning and Understanding: Quentin Skinner and his Critics 55–65 (James Tully, ed., 1988).

proposals required an amendment to the Articles of Confederation, however, and that in turn required unanimous confirmation by the states. The 1781 impost proposals were vetoed, however, first by Rhode Island and then by Virginia, and the 1783 impost proposal was vetoed by New York.

The Founders were desperate. When war came again the federal government would need to borrow again. Without a source of revenue, the federal government could not borrow. This coastline nation was vulnerable to attack by sea by any of three rapacious empires and it could pay for neither a sloop nor a gun to defend itself.

The Constitution was first a pro-tax document, written to give the federal government revenue to pay enough of the war debts to restore the public credit so that the federal government could borrow again in the next emergency. The Constitution, as the first listed power, gave the federal government a power to tax "to pay for the debts and to provide for the common Defence and general Welfare."

Giving the federal government the power to tax proved to be sufficient to restore the public credit with surprisingly modest federal taxes. Alexander Hamilton as first Secretary of the Treasury proposed taxes, amounting per capita to only a day and a half's worth of a workingman's wages. His taxes were imposed only on imports and hard liquors, which were considered things properly suppressed. The taxes that cured the fiscal crisis and restored the public credit could have been enacted within the confederate mode. Indeed, Hamilton's tax proposals were considerably less burdensome than the 1783 impost proposal that failed, and the 1783 proposal retained state sovereignty and was fully consistent with the confederation form of government. The Constitution effected radical changes that need to be explained by more than just the pressing need for federal taxes.

The historical Constitution is a revolutionary act that went far beyond the minimally necessary fiscal reforms. Under the confederation system that preceded the Constitution, the federal government was merely a "firm league of friendship." The Congress was a mere assembly of diplomats and an agent of sovereign states. After the Constitution, the Congress was no longer an agent of sovereign states and the states were no longer supreme. The Constitution created a complete three-part national government, able to raise revenue on its own in perpetuity, able to operate independently of the states, and able to enact federal law that was supreme over the states. Under the Constitution, the national government rests for its legitimacy not on sovereign states, but directly on the sovereignty of the people.

It is the thesis of this book that the Constitution was a radically nationalizing vector compellingly explained by the righteous anger of the Founders at the misdeeds of the states. The anger explains both key steps in the transformation and also the strength of the drive for the change.

The Founders were angry at the states for their defaults on the requisitions and for their vetoes of the federal impost. The Founders believed that the failure of requisitions was due to evil and shameful acts by the states. Rhode Island's veto of the 1781 impost was the "quintessence of villainy." Rhode Island was a detestable little corner of the Continent that injured the United States more than the worth of that whole state. Both Rhode Island and New York, it was said at the time, should rest in Hell.

The Founders expressed their anger at the states in immoderate, even religious terms. "United, we stand, divided we fall" had been the motto that held together the drive for independence and made victory possible. The states were betraying the sacred cause of the United States. The states had betrayed George Washington's army at Valley Forge and they were continuing their betrayal of the common cause. The action of the states in their defaults of requisitions and in veto of the impost was sin, disease, wickedness, and vice, not easily forgiven.

The anger allowed the revolution to go forward at key points in the Framers' logic. The delegates to the Philadelphia Convention had been given authority only to propose amendments to the Articles of Confederation, and amendments, under the rules of the Articles, had to be confirmed by all the states. The Framers did not think, however, that the wicked states that had vetoed the impost would ratify giving the federal government any power to tax. A federal impost was the least controversial federal tax and the Framers reasonably assumed that the states that had failed to ratify the impost – Rhode Island, New York, and Virginia – would veto again on any federal tax. The Framers were angry enough at the vetoing states that they were willing to go forward without their consent. Rhode Island was a pariah, out of the family, and it could not be allowed, once again, to do more damage to the Union than the detestable little state was worth.

Since the Framers did not think they could satisfy the Articles' requirement for unanimous confirmation by the states, they ignored the unanimous ratification requirement, ripped up the Articles of Confederation, and ended the confederation system of government. If the Articles of Confederation had not required unanimity or the Framers had not been so angry, the Framers might well have tried to find a solution to the fiscal crisis within the confederate mode in a way that preserved state sovereignty. Once they had to pass beyond the Articles, the Framers had freedom to be more radical in their changes. Starting from scratch, they abandoned the Articles and the old confederation framework.

The Framers ended the sovereignty of the states on the authority of the sovereignty of the people. The Framers sent the Constitution for ratification by the people meeting in conventions and bypassed the states because they did not think they could get ratification from the "local demagogues" who controlled the state offices. The Framers used the people as a weapon against the states. The Constitution was legitimate although it was not ratified by unanimous consent of the state legislatures, Alexander Hamilton argued, because the consent of the people is that "pure original fountain of legitimate authority."[2] Had the Framers trusted the states to ratify a reasonable solution, they might well have drafted a Constitution more appealing to the states. The decision to bypass the states and appeal directly to the people allowed the document to be a more revolutionary, anti-state act.

The shift from a general government resting on the sovereignty of the states to a national government resting directly on the sovereignty of the people also followed logically from the states' shameful failure to pay their requisitions. A radical vice of the requisition system, Madison wrote, was its assumption that the states would respect the Republican cause and pay their requisitions, without opposition. The failure of voluntary payments meant that the federal government would have to collect requisitions by military compulsion. Collecting tax from states by compulsion was a doomed project, however, because the states would resist payment by force as they would "a foreign tribute, or the invasion of an enemy." Far better not to risk civil war and to allow the federal government to collect its own tax directly from the people, by the ordinary process by which governments enforce the law.

Once the federal government could collect its tax directly from people, rather than from the states, there was no longer a need for the federal government to be considered an agent of the states. Under the political thinking of the time, a government properly represented those who contributed to it. The source of revenue determined sovereignty. The failure of requisitions ended state supremacy. The states had forfeited their supremacy by failing to pay their dues.

The principal architect of the constitutional revolution, replacing the confederate model, was James Madison. Madison's anger at the states emerged while trying to get the states to pay their requisitions, but it had also been nurtured in the Virginia Assembly in the years immediately before the Constitution. In the Virginia Assembly, Madison had lost repeatedly to a coalition

---

[2] *Federalist* No. 22, at 146 (Hamilton) (Dec. 14, 1787).

led by Patrick Henry. Henry gave tax holidays that made Virginia's quota of a requisition impossible to pay, Henry had violated the treaty that ended the war by denying foreign and out-of-state creditors access to Virginia courts, and Henry had sought state subsidies to Episcopal clergy. Madison's Constitution can reasonably be viewed as his revenge against Patrick Henry for all of the issues that Madison had lost to Henry in the previous decade.

Madison in preparation for the Philadelphia Convention concluded that state sovereignty was inconsistent with the general welfare and he sought "a due supremacy of the national authority." Madison's older mentors, George Washington and Governor Edmund Randolph, told Madison that revisions of the government would have to be grafted on the confederate mode.[3] Madison was too radical for that. "It has been shown," Madison wrote, "that the existing Confederation is founded on principles which are fallacious; that we must consequently change this first foundation, and with it, the super-structure resting upon it."[4] "The general authority [must] be defended against encroachments by the subordinate authorities."[5] Madison's theory of the "extended republic," represented by *Federalist* Number 10, explained why the federal government would protect individual rights, whereas the states would abuse them. Madison first concluded privately that state sovereignty had to be replaced by a strong national government. He then carried his Virginia colleagues, then the Philadelphia Convention, and finally the nation to agree with him.

The program that gives the original meaning to the Constitution is also the proponents' program, rather than the opposition's. The Anti-Federalists did not write the Constitution, they opposed what they saw, and they lost in the only purpose that organized them – defeating ratification of the Constitution. Their goals explain the Constitution only by silhouetting it. A normative history organized around the idea that the Constitution should not have been adopted is of no use to explain the programmatic meaning of the document. It is the Federalists' goals that give the Constitution its purposive meaning, even if the Federalists' goals had been wrong goals. The Founders had a strong political agenda that they were not shy about articulating. There is no need to posit some secret or conspiratorial motives beyond their righteous

---

3 Washington to Madison (Mar. 31, 1787), *in* 9 JM 342 (saying that many considered that "the only Constitutional mode by which the defects can be remedied" was the revision of Federal system); Randolph to Madison (Mar. 27, 1787), *in* 9 JM 335 (saying that remedies would need to be "grafted on the old confederation").

4 *Federalist* No. 37, at 233 (Madison) (Jan. 11, 1788).

5 Madison to Jefferson (Oct. 24, 1787), *in* 10 JM at 209.

goals. They have left a great deal of evidence as to their true rationale in surviving letters and debates because they needed to persuade each other, and then the nation, of why this Constitution was so desperately needed.

Anti-Federalists in different states had little in common, except that they opposed the shift in power from their state government to the new national government. The Anti-Federalists represented the interests of continuing state power – the feudal barons and local demagogues – and they never came to grips with the desperate needs that made the Constitution so necessary. The mission of preserving the power of the state governments was not especially progressive. When they had to choose, the Anti-Federalists commonly chose state power over individual rights and the most important leaders were hostile to democracy as well. By ratification of the Constitution creating the new government, in any event, the Anti-Federalists lost. Once the new government began to operate, Anti-Federalist opposition to the Constitution shrank to an insignificant minority and then ceased to operate as a viable political force. On all the important issues, the strongly nationalist vision won the field and explains the original intent of the document.

Understanding the purposive meaning of the Constitution does require inquiry beyond the words of text to reach the historical context. Any interpretation of the Constitution certainly needs to be consistent with the words. The words are like laboratory data, the final test for any theory and never to be fudged. Still reading the words over and over again in the twenty-first century is by nature a limited tool. With each reading a modern reader tends to interject familiar modern controversies into a text written with the dreads and assumptions of a strange other age.[6] One can never understand the Constitution out of its context. One cannot reproduce the battlefields for which the Constitution was a weapon without knowing enough history to understand the battle.

Other factors often cited as causes of the Constitution do not carry nearly as much weight as the Founders' high anger at the misdeeds of the states. Giving Congress the power of "regulation of commerce" is commonly considered a substantial motive for the Constitution. All the programs seriously proposed under the cover of the words, "regulation of commerce," were mercantilist programs restricting or channeling deep-water shipping. None of the programs seriously espoused under the cover of "regulation of commerce" amounted to much, however, other than tax on commerce for

[6] *See, e.g.,* Calvin H. Johnson, *Purging out* Pollock: *The Constitutionality of Federal Wealth or Sales Taxes,* 97 TAX NOTES 1723 (2002) (arguing that a Supreme Court 1896 decision misunderstood 1787 purpose of apportionment of direct tax).

revenue, even once Congress was given the authority to regulate commerce. The subsequent failure to adopt the "regulation of commerce" programs is good evidence that "regulation of commerce" was not an important cause of the Constitution.

The Constitution is sometimes portrayed as a contest between paper money and sound money, but neither Federalists nor Anti-Federalists spoke up for paper money in the ratification debates. The collapse of the Continental dollar had left too many scars. Another argument points to Shays's Rebellion, which had upset the country in the year before the Philadelphia Convention. The Massachusetts state government, however, had defeated the rebellion and scattered the rebels, and then promptly lost in the next election. Shays's Rebellion did not challenge state competency or justify national taxes or the movement to national power. The Constitution is also sometimes now thought of as tilted in favor of slaveholders, but at the time, the slaveholders themselves were not sure whether the Constitution was favorable or adverse to their interests. The Constitution supports the republican ideal that the people are the source of all legitimacy, without significantly affecting whether the nation would in fact be less or more democratic than it was.

It is common to see the Constitution described as written to limit the federal government and to protect states rights.[7] Indeed, the Supreme Court in recent years has been creating new doctrines to restrict the federal government and to protect the states[8] and the justification for the new anti-federal

---

[7] See, e.g., EDLING 219 (2003) (saying that "[t]he mainstream interpretation of the Federalist argument presents it as a call for limited government and protection of minority rights").

[8] The Supreme Court has found, for example, that the federal government may not prohibit guns on school property (Lopez v. New York, 514 U.S. 549 (1995) (holding that Congress could not make carrying firearms on school property a federal crime)), may not create federal civil damages remedy for rape (United States v. Morrison, 120 S.Ct. 1740 (2000) (holding that Congress could not create a federal civil remedy for rape)), and may not demand that local sheriffs check arrest records for federal gun control laws. Printz v. United States, 521 U.S. 898 (1997) (Congress could not require local police to check arrest records of prospective gun purchasers). See also New York v. United States, 505 U.S. 144 (1992) (federal government may not force states to take responsibility for nuclear waste). The states are newly immune from federal labor standards (Alden v. Maine, 119 S.Ct. 2240 (1999)) and federal trademark and patent remedies (College Savings Bank v. Florida Prepaid Postsecondary Educ. Peens Bd., 119 S.Ct. 2219 (1999)). See Seminole Tribe v. Florida, 517 U.S. 44 (1996), which is the seminal (as well as Seminole) case holding that the Eleventh Amendment gives the states substantive immunity that Congress can not abrogate. State agencies are immune from federal administrative process of an adjudicative nature. Federal Maritime Commission v. South Carolina State Ports Authority, 535 U.S. 743 (2002)(state sovereign immunity extends to federal administrative adjudication brought by private party because administrative adjudications were "walked and squawked" like litigation in federal

restrictions is based heavily on a "jurisprudence of original intention."[9] The Supreme Court is also going beyond the words of the document to find that the unstated overall structure or design of the Constitution favors the states and hobbles the national level.[10] The Court is relying on an abstract "plan of the convention,"[11] or "the system of federalism established by the Constitution"[12] to restrain the federal government, even in the absence of any explicit restriction in the constitutional text.

Limitation of the federal government, however, does not describe the crisis for which the Constitution was written. As James Wilson said to the Convention, "[i]t has never been a complaint agst. Congs. that they governed overmuch. The complaint has been that they have governed too little."[13] Or as Madison had to explain to Jefferson, when Jefferson returned to America, "[t]he evils suffered and feared from weakness in Government . . . have turned the attention more toward the means of strengthening the [government] than of narrowing [it]."[14] The 1787 Constitution was written to take sovereignty or supremacy away from the states because of their wickedness, and to create and empower a complete national government. The historical Constitution was written to end the impotence or imbecility of the federal level. Restoration of the historical Constitution with a purified understanding of its original meaning or its deep structure would not be friendly to Anti-Federalist principles, even the new ones.

Sometimes it is argued that the original purpose of the Constitution was to limit the federal government to protect individual rights. The core of the Constitution is thus said to rest in the ten amendments of the Bill of Rights. Madison's theory of the extended republic, however, considered the federal government the best protector of individual rights. Madison's presumption that states would inevitably abuse individual rights was consistent, Madison

court barred by the Eleventh Amendment) (over dissent of Breyer, J, arguing that federal administrative agency can use adjudications to decide whether to bring constitutionally allowed enforcement proceedings).

9 Edward Meese, Speech to American Bar Association, July 9, 1985, *reprinted in* 2 BENCHMARK 1 (1986) (calling for a "jurisprudence of original intention").

10 *See, e.g.*, Alden v. Maine, 527 U.S. 706, 729 (1999) (Kennedy, J.) (arguing that states have immunity from federal fair labor standards because of the "fundamental postulates implicit in the constitutional design"); Printz v. United States, 521 U.S. 898, 936 (1997) (O'Connor, J. concurring) (concluding that federal plans "utterly fail to adhere to the design and structure of our constitutional scheme"). Note also the subtitle of RAOUL BERGER, FEDERALISM: THE FOUNDERS' DESIGN (1987).

11 Alden v. Maine, 527 U.S. 706, 730 (1999).

12 *Id.*

13 Wilson, Federal Convention (July 14, 1787), *in* 2 FARRAND 10.

14 Madison to Jefferson (Feb. 4, 1790), *in* 16 PTJ 150.

believed, with his experience in opposition to Patrick Henry in the Virginia Assembly in the prior decade. The Constitution, before any amendment, protected the right to trial by jury in criminal cases and judicial review by writ of habeas corpus of the legality of any imprisonment. Madison viewed Anti-Federalists' calls for a further Bill of Rights as just an excuse offered to defeat the structural shift from state to federal power. There is nothing friendly to the evil states in Madison's motives in creating the 1787 Constitution.

The Bill of Rights, consisting of the first ten amendments to the Constitution, is best understood in historical context as a symbol or sop, with little substantive meaning. The Anti-Federalists tried to make ratification of the Constitution contingent on prior approval of a Bill of Rights, adding rights beyond what was in the Constitution already, but they failed. Instead, the Bill of Rights was drafted and debated in the first Congress, in which Anti-Federalists held only 15% of the voting power. Madison filtered the rights proposals to remove anything he considered unsafe or anti-federal. Anything the Anti-Federalists wanted that the proponents of the Constitution did not was defeated, without serious contest. The Virginia Anti-Federalists voted against the Bill of Rights because they considered it a sop. Indeed, in context, the Bill of Rights looks like a sop. It was written to give something to the two states, North Carolina and Rhode Island, which had not yet ratified. Not much would be given, however, especially not to wicked Rhode Island.

The Tenth Amendment, which provides that Congress shall have only the powers delegated to it, is especially to be understood as a sop. Article II of the Articles of Confederation provided that Congress would have only the powers expressly delegated to it. The Framers took out the "expressly delegated" limitation. When challenged by the Anti-Federalists, the Founders said that the "expressly delegated" limitation had proved to be "destructive" to the Union and that they wanted the federal passport system, although it had not been expressly authorized.[15] The absence of the word "expressly" under that history should be understood to mean that the federal government has implied or unexpressed powers, particularly the passport power.

The Constitution is sometimes described as if it were a timeless document written to establish eternal verities. That is probably not a helpful way to understand the original intent. The most intensely felt needs in 1787–1788 were desperate but short-term needs. The most pressing need, to restore the federal credit, was accomplished with the new federal taxes, adopted by 1791.

---

[15] Randolph, Virginia Convention (June 24, 1788), *in* 3 ELLIOT 600–601. *See* Madison, U.S. House of Representatives (Aug. 18, 1789), *in* 1 ANNALS 790 (successfully resisting the insertion of the word "expressly" into what became the Tenth Amendment).

Any serious program beyond tax in the "regulation of commerce" power was finally abandoned by the time of the negotiation of the Jay Treaty in 1794, which prevented retaliatory imposts against the British. The Constitution had effect beyond the concrete programs, but like the ripples in a lake, all of the energy of the Founders was in the rock and first ripple, and the ripples beyond that had rapidly decreasing energy. The Founders were willing to claim grand principles to persuade and support their programs, but the grand principles should be understood as servants to the immediate programs, used to persuade the fence sitters. Madison, for instance, quickly abandoned his grand theory of the superiority of the extended republic within a decade when the politics of the principle changed. A politician must first settle the political problems of his or her own time. Six months is a long time in politics. It is, in any event, very hard to write eternal verities when that is not an especially important part of what one is trying to do.

The strict end of the Constitutional movement is best marked by the adoption of the Eleventh Amendment to the Constitution in 1796. The Eleventh Amendment granted immunity to the states from suits by creditors from the Revolutionary War and allowed the states to refuse to pay their just war debts, not long after the Supreme Court had explicitly held that the Constitution made the war debts enforceable against the states. Payment of the war debts and anger at the states for dereliction of their duties was core to the Constitution. Enforcement of state debts, however, was not a necessary part of the purpose because it was the destitution of the federal government, and not of the states, that was the mortal danger to Republic. It was the federal government that would borrow again to defend the nation in the coming war. Payment of state debt was primarily just a moral issue that seems not to have been settled by the constitutional debates. By 1796, moreover, the Constitutional movement had achieved its purposes, an energetic three-part government on the national level, supreme over the states and able to borrow again. The programs under "regulation of commerce" had either been adopted or abandoned. By 1796, the Founders had split into two partisan camps – one Hamiltonian and one Jeffersonian – which were never able to cooperate again. The movement for the Constitution had splintered and diffused and the polity had moved on to other issues.

The anger at the states also dissipated and the pendulum swung back in their favor. Jefferson was elected in what he called the Revolution of 1800,[16] and the policy of his Administration was to favor the states and restrict the

---

[16] Jefferson to Spencer Roane (Sept. 16, 1819), *in* 10 WTJ 140.

federal government. Jefferson argued that the states gave "the surest bulwarks against anti-republican tendencies."[17] Jefferson consistently wanted the federal government to confine its power to foreign affairs and to stay out of domestic affairs.[18] The federal government had infinite powers within the foreign sphere, implied without need for a writing, but domestically, Jeffersonian doctrine would have held the federal government to petty little powers, without a unifying grand principle. Whether the federal government would be confined to enumerated powers, Jefferson said, became the landmark dividing the Jeffersonian from the Federalist party.[19] Jefferson had had little influence or understanding of the constitutional debates at the time, because he was abroad in Paris as Ambassador to France, but his view of a proper role of a national government ultimately prevailed as a matter of politics.

By electing Thomas Jefferson, the people put the federal government into a far smaller corral than required by the original constitutional document. That the federal government occupies less than its maximum scope is, of course, quite routine, at least in peacetime. The Constitution may set the full potential scope, but there is no requirement that the government occupy its possible range. Indeed, in absence of emergency, the government should have a cushion of power that it does not use. By the political process, the people decide the actual scope. In any event, by the time of the schism between Hamilton and Jefferson – much less by the time of the election of Jefferson – the Constitution as a text had been written and ratified and the ink was dry.

The structural part of the Constitution endures, however, long after the original anger at the states has dissipated. The three-part national government able to tax on its own, operate independently of the states, and enact supreme federal law has survived. That revolution, replacing the weak assembly of sovereign states that Congress was before, seems best explained as the righteous anger at the wickedness of the states.

---

[17] Jefferson, First Inaugural Address (March 4, 1801), in BASIC WRITINGS OF TJ 641.

[18] Jefferson to Madison (Dec. 16, 1786), in 9 JM 210, 211 (saying that the proper division between the general and state governments is that national government would have power over foreign concerns and the states would have power over the domestic ones); Jefferson to Gideon Granger (Aug. 13, 1800), in 7 WTJ 451 (saying that the true theory is that states are independent as to everything within themselves and general government is reduced to foreign concerns only).

[19] Jefferson to Albert Gallatin (June 16, 1817), in 10 WTJ 91 (saying that "the tenet that Congress has only the power to provide for enumerated powers, and not for the general welfare is almost the only landmark which now divides the federalists from the republicans").

☆ PART ONE ☆

THE NECESSITY OF THE CONSTITUTION

CHAPTER ONE

The Rise of the Righteous Anger

A. THE FAILURE OF REQUISITIONS

Under the Articles of Confederation, the national-level government could raise funds for the national needs only by requisitions on the states. Each state was required to pay its quota of the total requisition into the federal treasury by raising revenue under its own tax system and collecting it with its own tax officials.[1] Requisitions were mandatory in theory under the Articles – "sacred & obligatory," as James Madison put it.[2] With the end of the war, however, the state legislatures began treating requisitions as "mere recommendations,"[3] even as "pompous petitions for charity"[4] and they did not pay. In the requisition of 1786 – the last before the Constitution – Congress mandated that states pay $3,800,000,[5] but it collected only $663.[6]

---

[1] ARTICLES OF CONFEDERATION, art. VIII, 9 JCC 217 (March 1, 1781).

[2] Madison, Continental Congress (Feb. 21, 1783), *in* 25 JCC 908: *See also* ARTICLES OF CONFEDERATION, art. XIII, 9 JCC at 221 (providing that every State shall abide by the determination of the United States Congress and that the Articles "shall be inviolably observed by every State"); Robert Morris to President of the Congress (Mar. 8, 1783), *in* 6 RDCUS 278 ("The Right of Congress is perfect and the Duty to pay is absolute[.]"); Madison, Continental Congress (Jan. 28, 1783), *in* 25 JCC 875 (saying that a "requisition of Congress on the states . . . is as much a law to them as their revenue acts when passed are laws to their respective citizens").

[3] *Federalist* No. 15, at 93 (Dec. 1, 1787). (Hamilton) (arguing that the states treated requisitions as mere recommendations although requisitions were mandatory in theory).

[4] Robert Livingston, New York Convention (June 27, 1788), *in* 2 ELLIOT 342. *See also* Randolph, Virginia Convention (June 7, 1788), *in* 9 DHRC 1017 (saying that the states treated requisitions as earnest entreaties, humble supplications, and solicitations).

[5] Report of the Board of Treasury (Aug. 2, 1786), *in* 31 JCC 462.

[6] *See* BROWN 26. The Board of Treasury reported zero receipts from the Requisition of 1786 just after the close of the Constitutional Convention. (Sept 29, 1787), *in* 33 JCC 572. Brown relies on Treasury Reports ending earlier, March 31, 1787, and the difference is

Some states simply ignored the requisitions. Some sent them back to Congress for amendment, more to the states' liking.[7] New Jersey said it had paid enough tax by paying the tariffs or "imposts" on goods imported through New York or Philadelphia and it repudiated the requisition in full.[8] Congress's Board of Treasury had concluded in June 1786 that there was "no reasonable hope" that the requisitions would yield enough to allow Congress to make payments on the foreign debts, even assuming that nothing would be paid on the domestic war debt.[9] George Washington reported,

> Requisitions are a perfect nihility, where thirteen sovereign indepen-
> dent disunited States are in the habit of discussion and refusing com-
> pliance with them at their option. Requisitions are actually little better
> than a jest and a bye word throughout the land.[10]

Almost all of the money called for by the 1786 requisition would have gone to payments on the Revolutionary War debt. French and Dutch creditors were due payments of $1.7 million, including interest and some payment on the principal. Domestic creditors were due to be paid $1.6 million for interest

apparently a judgment about credit given for prior state expenditures. The bridge between $663 and zero, in any event, can be comfortably spanned by rounding.

7 *See, e.g.* Madison to Pendleton (Feb. 24, 1787), *in* 9 JM 295 ("No money is paid into the public Treasury; no respect is paid to the federal authority. Not a single state complies with the requisitions, several pass them over in silence, and some positively reject them").

8 Votes and Proceeding of the General Assembly of the State of New Jersey, 10th Sess. 2d sitting, at 12 (1786). *See* RUTH BOGIN, ABRAHAM CLARK AND THE QUEST FOR EQUALITY IN THE REVOLUTIONARY ERA, 1774–1794, at 127–131 (1982).

9 Report of the Board of Treasury (June 3, 1786), *in* 30 JCC 354–64. The report cataloged the state shortfalls: Connecticut, New Jersey, Delaware, and North Carolina had not passed any act for the 1785 Requisition. Virginia had relied on a tax that was expected to yield only about half of its quota. New York had just agreed to accept payment of its taxes in state paper money and so it could not expect to collect any specie for its quota. Pennsylvania gave $86,000 of its quota for specie in indents (Treasury notes paid out in lieu of interest) instead of specie. The New Hampshire tax had not been efficacious for the 1785 requisition, so would probably not be dependable for the 1786 requisition. Massachusetts committed its taxes first for state programs and state debt, so any shortfall in revenue would come from the federal requisition. South Carolina claimed credits offsetting her full quota. Rhode Island claimed that its aid to invalids and an unpaid bill for an oxen team offset her quota in full. The Board did not have a copy of Georgia's Revenue Act so it could not ascertain how much, if anything, it would pay.

10 Washington to Jay, (Secretary of Foreign Affairs) (Aug. 1, 1786), *in* 28 WRITINGS OF GW 503. *See also* Charles Pinckney, South Carolina House of Representatives (Jan. 16, 1788), *in* 4 ELLIOT 255 (saying that for the last six or eight years, not one state had completely complied; but a few had even paid up their specie proportions; others very partially; and some, he had every reason to believe, had not to this day contributed a shilling to the common treasury since the Union was formed).

only.[11] Express advocacy of repudiation of the federal debt was rare,[12] but with the failure of requisitions, payment was not possible. Virginia postponed its taxes for 1787 and Madison wrote to his father, "We will [cut] a sharp figure, after our declarations [supporting the] Continental debt if we wholly omit the means of fulfilling them."[13]

Beyond the repayment of the war debts, the federal goals were quite modest. The operating budget was only about $450,000 and half of that was for the small military detachments posted on the frontiers to protect against the Indians.[14] The requisitions had to pay for the clerks and other expenses of the Congress itself, and the federal government maintained a small office for surveying and mapping.[15] Without money, however, the handful of troops on the frontier would have to be disbanded and the Congress' offices shut. "The payments . . . of late fall short even of the pittance necessary for the civil list of the Confederacy," wrote Madison.[16] Congress had to declare their "utter inablility to make [a] pitiful advance" of $1,000 to transport ammunition to American posts along the Ohio River.[17] In the wording of the time, the federal government was "imbecilic" and "impotent."[18]

---

[11] Proceedings of the Continental Congress (Aug. 2, 1786), *in* 31 JCC 462. In the Treasury's 1789 inventory of the debt, the U.S. owed $12 million to France and to Dutch investors and $40 million to domestic creditors. Hamilton, Report on Public Debt to the House of Representatives, *in* 6 PAH 86.

[12] *But see* PELATIAH WEBSTER, POLITICAL ESSAYS ON THE NATURE AND OPERATION OF MONEY, PUBLIC FINANCES, AND OTHER SUBJECTS 362–363, 372 (1791) (suggesting that federal revenue system was so delicate, young, and tender that the fiscal crises needed to be solved by reducing the federal debt by docking it).

[13] Madison to James Madison, Sr. (June 15, 1784), *in* 8 JM 80.

[14] Consideration of the Requisition of 1786, *in* 31 JCC 462.

[15] *Id.* (allocating $4000 of the failed 1786 requisition to geographer). The "present reduced state of our finances," meant that the Congress could not pay for a "much desired" map of the middle states. Report of a Committee (Oct. 23, 1783), *in* 25 JCC 711.

[16] Madison to Pendleton (Feb. 24, 1787), *in* 9 JM 295

[17] Letter of Rufus King to Washington (June 18, 1786), *in* 8 LMCC 393.

[18] Hamilton, The Defence of the Funding System (July 1795), *in* 19 PAH 22, 27 (arguing that requisition from the states was a system of "imbecility" and "impoten[ce]"). *See also, e.g.,* Randolph, Federal Convention (May 29, 1787) 1 FARRAND 25 (McHenry notes) ("Imbecility of the Confederation"); Randolph, Federal Convention (June 16, 1787), *in* 1 FARRAND 255 (painting "in strong colours, the imbecility of the existing Confederacy"); Madison, Federal Convention, July 7, 1787, 1 FARRAND 551 ("impotent . . . as the old" government); Madison, House of Representatives (April 8, 1789), *in* 12 JM 65 (calling for a retaliatory tariff on British shipping because the union has recovered from the "state of imbecility, that . . . prevented a performance of its duty"); Christopher Gore to Rufus King (June 28, 1787), *quoted in* BROWN at 261 (saying our government is "weak, languid, and inefficient to support the great objects of civil institutions," and that one "must invent some plan to increase the circulation at the heart"); ARCHIBALD MACLAINE, PUBLICOLA: ADDRESS TO THE FREEMEN OF NORTH CAROLINA, STATE GAZETTE OF NORTH CAROLINA (Mar. 20, 1788),

The failure to pay the war debts was dangerous because when war came again the country would need to borrow again.[19] It will be necessary in emergencies to borrow, Hamilton told the New York Convention, and "it is impossible to borrow, unless you have funds to pledge for the payment of your debts."[20] "In the modern system of war," Hamilton argued, "even the wealthiest nations are obliged to have recourse to large loans."[21] "A nation without credit," Hamilton said, "would be in great danger of falling a victim in the first war with a power possessing a vigorous and flourishing credit."[22] Borrowing when the next war came meant that the government would need to raise only enough to pay the current interest and could avoid having to raise the whole funds of war immediately. Raising the entire funds of war without borrowing, would be "distressing to the people, [and to] our country perhaps overrun by the enemy."[23] "Our credit as a nation is sinking," wrote Roger Sherman, and "the resources of the country [can] not be drawn out to defend against a foreign invasion"[24]

The proponents of the Constitution thought war was inevitable. The United States was a coastal nation spread out along the Atlantic and vulnerable to attack by sea by any of three rapacious empires: France, Spain, or England. "It would be strange," said a proponent in Connecticut, if England or Spain did not force us into war within 15–20 years.[25] "We are circumscribed with enemies from Maine to Georgia"[26] The prospect of war, James Wilson told Pennsylvania, was "highly probable."[27]

The insolvency of the federal government would make it hard to defend the nation. This "wretched confederation," Edward Rutledge told South Carolina, is "unable to discharge of any part of our debts...Without a

reprinted in 16 DHRC 436 (saying Continental Congress without the power to "raise a single shilling" had been reduced to the "present state of imbecility"); James Wilson, Public Meeting in Philadelphia (Oct. 6, 1787), *in* 13 DHRC 343 (arguing that the imbecility of the Confederation left the states with great debt).

19 EDLING at 47, 207–208, 220, 228–29 (2003) argues that the Constitution was formed to create a military-fiscal state capable of defense, much as the European states were formed to pay for defense.

20 Hamilton, New York Convention (June 27, 1788), *in* 2 ELLIOT 352.

21 *Federalist* No. 30, at 192 (Hamilton) (Dec. 28, 1787).

22 Hamilton, Defense of the Funding System (July 1795), 19 PAH 57.

23 James Iredell, North Carolina Convention, July 30, 1788, 4 ELLIOT 220–221.

24 Letter of Roger Sherman to William Floyd, *in* 3 DHRC 353. *See also* Randolph, Virginia Convention (June 7, 1788), *in* 9 DHRC 1021 (saying that every nation must borrow during war); Madison, (June 6, 1788), *in* 9 DHRC 996–997 ("For all nations, debts come from war").

25 Republican VI, CONN. COURANT (MARCH 19, 1787) *in* DHRC MICROFICHE SUPPL. CONN.

26 Christopher Gore, Massachusetts Convention (Jan. 22, 1788), *in* 2 ELLIOT 67.

27 Wilson, Pennsylvania Assembly (Sept. 17, 1787), *in* 2 DHRC 58.

ship – without a soldier – without a shilling in the federal treasury, without a ... government to obtain one," he said, "we hold the property that we now hold at the courtesy of other powers."[28] "If a war breaks out, and our situation invites our enemies to make war," Oliver Ellsworth argued, "how are we to defend ourselves? Has government the means to enlist a man or buy an ox?"[29] "What is there to prevent an Algerine Pirate from landing on your coast, and carrying your citizens into slavery?" Hugh Williamson asked North Carolina. "You have not a single sloop of war."[30] The Congress was empowered to make war, John Jay told New York, "but [they] are not empowered to raise men or money to carry it on."[31] An imbecilic and impotent government could not defend the country.

In the *Federalist* the most important subject was war and the financing of it. The essays of the *Federalist* were written by Alexander Hamilton, James Madison, and John Jay, all under the single pseudonym of *Publius*, in order to convince the people to ratify the newly proposed Constitution. *Publius* said that "nations in general will make war whenever they have a prospect of getting any thing by it,"[32] and that therefore "to model our political systems upon speculations of lasting tranquillity, is to calculate on the weaker springs of the human character."[33] The Union under an efficient national government, *Publius* argued, affords "the best security that can be devised."[34] The national government could best defend the nation because it could apply "the resources and power of the whole to the defence of any particular part."[35] The national government would need to be able to call on the full resources of the continent. The power of providing for defense can "know no other bounds," *Publius* wrote, "than the exigencies of the nation and the resources of the community."[36] "The circumstances that endanger the safety of nations are infinite," *Publius* said, "and for this reason no constitutional shackles can wisely be imposed on the power to which the care of it is committed."[37]

---

[28] Edward Rutledge, South Carolina Legislature (Jan. 16, 1788), *in* 2 DEBATE 23.

[29] Oliver Ellsworth, Connecticut Convention (Jan. 4, 1788), *in* 2 ELLIOT 189.

[30] Hugh Williamson, Speech at Edenton, N.C., N.Y. DAILY ADVERTISER, (Feb. 26, 1788), *in* 25 DHRC 206.

[31] A CITIZEN OF NEW YORK (JOHN JAY), ADDRESS TO THE PEOPLE OF THE STATE OF NEW YORK (April 15, 1788), *in* 17 DHRC 109.

[32] *Federalist* No. 4, at 18–19 (Jay) (Nov. 7, 1787).

[33] *Federalist* No. 34, at 212 (Hamilton) (Jan. 5, 1787).

[34] *Federalist* No. 3, at 14 (John Jay) (Nov. 3, 1787).

[35] *Federalist* No. 4, at 21 (John Jay) (Nov. 7, 1787).

[36] *Federalist* No. 31, at 196 (Hamilton) (Jan. 1, 1787).

[37] *Federalist* No. 23, at 147 (Hamilton) (Dec. 18, 1787). *See also Federalist* No. 23, at 149 (Hamilton) (Dec. 18, 1787) (arguing that the Union must be empowered to pass all laws as guardian of the common safety); *Federalist* No. 26, at 164 (Hamilton) (Dec. 22, 1787)

The language the Framers used to describe the failure of requisitions was intensely moral, even religious. The requisitions were mandatory under the Articles, and "were as *sacred & obligatory* as the constitutions of the several States."[38] The failure of requisitions caused "repeated breaches of the public *faith*."[39] "American *faith*" was said to have become a bitter proverb in Europe by reason of American failure to pay its debts.[40] "The failure of the requisitions was a *vice* of the system[41] and not just an omission or error. "The deficiency by the states most capable of yielding their quotas was *shameful*.[42] The default on Revolutionary War debts was a "*humiliation*"[43] and "our *infamy*."[44] The fact that the government had to borrow money even to pay interest on its existing debt was "the most *humiliating* and *disgraceful* measure that a nation could take,"[45] the Federalists said, and "should strike us with *shame*."[46] All of Congress' efforts to keep the national vessel from sinking, Madison wrote Jefferson, "have been frustrated by the *selfishness* or *perverseness* of some part or other of [Congress'] constituents."[47]

(arguing that the idea of restraining the legislative authority over the means of providing for the national defense is "more ardent than enlightened"); *Federalist* No. 30, at 188 (Hamilton) (Dec. 28, 1787) (arguing that a regular and adequate supply of tax money is an "indispensable ingredient in every constitution"); Randolph, Virginia Convention (June 7, 1788), *in* 3 ELLIOT 115 (saying "[w]ars cannot be carried on without a full and uncontrolled discretionary power to raise money in an eligible manner").

38 Madison, Notes on Debates in the Congress (Feb. 21, 1783), *in* 6 JM 270, 271 (emphasis added).

39 James Bowdoin, Massachusetts Convention (Jan. 23, 1788), *in* 2 ELLIOT 82 (saying noncompliance with congressional requisitions caused "breaches of public faith") (emphasis added).

40 Aristedes, *Remarks on the Proposed Plan of a Federal Government* (Jan. 31, 1788), *in* 15 DHRC 538 (emphasis added).

41 Madison, Vices of the Political System of the United States (April 1787), in 9 JM 348 (emphasis added); Madison, Notes on Ancient and Modern Confederacy (1786 or 1787), *in* 9 JM 6, 8,11,16,22.

42 Madison (member of Congress representing Virginia) to Jefferson (Governor of Virginia) (April 16, 1781), *in* 3 JM 71 (emphasis added).

43 *Federalist* No. 15, at 91 (Hamilton) (Dec. 1, 1787) (identifying national humiliation from failure to pay Revolutionary War debts as part of the situation forcing the need for change of the weak Confederation) (emphasis added).

44 The North American No. 1, PENNSYLVANIA JOURNAL AND WEEKLY ADVERTISER (Sept. 17, 1783), *reprinted in* 3 WM. & MARY Q. 569, 580 (1946) (attributed to Richard Peters of Philadelphia by *Editorial Note, in* 7 JM 319–363) (saying that Dutch and French seizure of American shipping to pay debts will record our *infamy* as well as our *impotence*) (emphasis added).

45 William Davie, North Carolina Convention (July 24, 1788), *in* 4 ELLIOT 19 (emphasis added).

46 Hamilton, New York Convention (June 28, 1788), *in* 2 ELLIOT 366 (emphasis added).

47 Madison (serving in Virginia Assembly) to Jefferson (Ambassador in Paris) (Oct. 3, 1786), *in* 8 JM 373 (emphasis added).

"[R]equisitions were rendered nugatory," John Jay told New York, "not by their want of propriety, but by their want of power."[48] Partial performance of requisitions reversed "the first principle of all Government," Madison wrote to Jefferson, because "the requisition system punishes not the *evildoers*, but those that do well."[49]

The failure of requisitions was also inconsistent with the highest ideals for which the Revolutionary War had been fought. The debts had been "fairly contracted" to fight the war and "justice and good faith demand that [they] should be fully discharged."[50] The "public debt rendered so sacred by [the] cause in which it had been incurred remained without any provision for its payment."[51] The war debt was "the price of liberty" for which "the faith of America has been repeatedly pledged."[52] The failure to pay public debt was "horrid," Madison said, "the erecting of our independence on the ruins of public faith and national honor."[53] The defaults exposed "the friends and patrons of the Republic ... to insult by ... the votaries of tyranny."[54] The prospective break up of the Union would lead "the minds of men every where [to] become alienated from republican forms."[55] The defaults prevented the nation from securing "the fruits of the Revolution" despite "the blood, the toils, the cares and the calamities" of the War.[56] The defaults dishonored the "great cause," he said, "the last and fairest experiment in favor of the right of human nature."[57]

The Congress pleaded pathetically with the states to pay their quotas:

> The Crisis is arrived when the People of these United States, by whose
> Will and for whose Benefit the Federal Government was instituted,

---

[48] A CITIZEN OF NEW YORK (JOHN JAY), ADDRESS TO THE PEOPLE OF THE STATE OF NEW YORK (April 15, 1788), *in* 17 DHRC 107.

[49] Madison to Jefferson (Oct. 3, 1785), *in* 3 JM 72 (emphasis added).

[50] Madison, Address to the States, by the United States in Congress Assembled (April 26, 1783), *in* 24 JCC 277, 282.

[51] Madison, "Preface to the Constitution" (circa 1820s), *in* 3 FARRAND 547. *See also* James Wilson, Pennsylvania Convention (Nov. 24, 1787), *in* 2 DHRC 360 (saying that "the commencement of peace was the commencement of every disgrace and distress" and that "devoid of national credit, ... our public securities melt in the hands of holders").

[52] Hamilton, Report Relative to a Provision for the Support of Public Credit (Jan. 9, 1790), *in* 6 PAH 51, 69.

[53] Madison, Notes on Debates in Congress (Jan. 28, 1783), *in* 6 JM 142–149.

[54] *Id.*

[55] A CITIZEN OF NEW YORK (JOHN JAY), ADDRESS TO THE PEOPLE OF THE STATE OF NEW YORK (April 15, 1788), *in* 17 DHRC 120. FORREST MCDONALD, NOVUS ORDO SECLORUM: THE INTELLECTUAL ORIGINS OF THE CONSTITUTION 185 (1985) collects additional expressions on the vulnerability of the democratic form of government because of the fiscal crisis.

[56] Madison, Address to the Nation (April 26, 1783), *in* 24 JCC 281.

[57] *Id.*

must decide whether they will support their Rank as a Nation by maintaining the Public Faith, at home and abroad; or whether for want of a
timely exertion in Establishing a General Revenue and giving Strength
to the Confederacy, they will hazard, not only the existence of the
Union, but of those great and invaluable privileges, for which they
have so arduously and honorably contended.

(February 8, 1786)[58]

Whilst the United States in Congress, are denied the means of satisfying those Engagements which they have constitutionally entered
into for the common Benefit of the Union; they cannot be responsible
for those fatal Evils which will inevitably flow from a breach of Public
faith, pledged by solemn contract, and a violation of those principles
of Justice, which are the only solid Basis of the honor and prosperity
of Nations.

(February 13, 1786)[59]

"[Failure of the states to pay their requisitions denied Congress] the
Means of satisfying these Engagements, which they had constitutionally entered into for the Common Benefit of the Union, it was their duty
to warn their Constituents, that the most fatal Evils would inevitably
flow from a breach of Public Faith, pledged by solemn Contract, and
a violation of those principles of Justice which are the only solid Basis
of Honor and Prosperity of Nations."

(August 13, 1786)[60]

It is with the most painful anxiety that [the Congress] are compelled to
declare, that, having been denied the means of satisfying the engagements which they have constitutionally made for the common benefit
of the Union it is now their duty solemnly to warn their constituents
that the most fatal evils will speedily and inevitably flow from a breach
of public faith and a violation of the principles of justice, which are the
solid basis of the honor and prosperity of Nations.

(October 6, 1786)[61]

Reminding the states of the consequences of delay in taxes, Robert Morris
said in 1782, "was like preaching to the dead."[62]

---

[58] Report of the Board of Treasury (Feb 8, 1786), *in* 30 JCC 57.
[59] Report of the Committee, consisting of Rufus King, Charles Pinckney, et al. (Feb. 13, 1786),
in 30 JCC 67–68. The Virginia Assembly cited this language as the first reason to appoint
delegates to the Philadelphia Convention. Resolution of the Virginia Assembly, Nov. 23,
1786, 8 DHRC 540.
[60] An Address from the United States in Congress Assembled to the Legislatures of the several
States (Aug. 31, 1786), *in* 31 JCC 613, 614.
[61] An Address from the United States in Congress Assembled to the Legislatures of the several
States (Oct. 6, 1786), *in* 31 JCC 747–748.
[62] Erna Risch, "Supplying Washington's Army" 257 (U.S. Army Center of Military History
1981), <http://www.army.mil/cmh-pg/books/RevWar/risch/chpt-8.htm>

The nationalists attempted to persuade the states of their duty by reminding them to whom they owed the duty: The money was owed to France, Madison said, who "to the exertion of his arms . . . [were] added the succours of his treasure,"[63] and to the Dutch who were "first to give so precious a token of their confidence in our justice . . ."[64] It was owed to individual creditors "in commercial States, attached to the American cause," who "obeyed the public call" and trusted the new Republican government with their loans.[65] "[T]he individuals who lent us money in the hour of our distress are now reduced to indigents."[66] Money was owed to the soldiers of the Revolution, "whose blood and whose bravery have defended the liberties of their country."[67]

The failure to pay the soldiers had been especially shameful. "[The soldiers] ask for no more than such a portion of their dues as will enable them to retire from the field of victory and glory, into the bosom of peace and private citizenship."[68] "The war-worn veteran whose reward for toils and wounds existed in written promises," said John Jay to New York, "found Congress without the means, and too many States without the disposition to do him justice."[69]

---

[63] Madison, Address to the States, by the United States in Congress Assembled (April 26, 1783), *in* 24 JCC 277, 282. The identified author of the Address is a committee consisting of Madison, Hamilton, and Oliver Ellsworth, but the manuscript was in Madison's handwriting (24 JCC 283) and Madison claimed to have written it. *Editorial Note, in* 6 JM 498. *See also* Madison, Virginia Convention, June 6, 1788, 3 ELLIOT 136:

> How have we dealt with that benevolent ally? Have we complied with our most sacred obligations to that nation? Have we paid the interest punctually from year to year? Is not the interest accumulating, while not a shilling is discharged of the principal? The magnanimity and forbearance of that ally are so great that she has not called upon us for her claims, even in her own distress and necessity.

[64] Madison, Address to the States, by the United States in Congress Assembled (April 26, 1783), *in* 24 JCC 282.

[65] THE NORTH AMERICAN NO. 1, PENNSYLVANIA JOURNAL AND WEEKLY ADVERTISER (Sept. 17, 1783), *reprinted in* 3 WM. & MARY Q. 569, 574–75 (1946) (attributed to Richard Peters of Philadelphia by *Editorial Note, in* 7 JM 319–363). *See also* Madison, Address to the States, by the United States in Congress Assembled (April 26, 1783), *in* 24 JCC 277, 282–283 ("The remaining class of public creditors is composed partly of such of our fellow-citizens as originally lent to the public the use of their funds, or have since manifested most confidence in their country, by receiving transfers from the lenders; and partly of those whose property has been either advanced or assumed for the public service").

[66] William Davie, North Carolina Convention (July 24, 1788), *in* 4 ELLIOT 19.

[67] Madison, Address to the States (April 26, 1783), *in* 24 JCC 277, 282.

[68] *Id.*

[69] A CITIZEN OF NEW YORK (JOHN JAY), ADDRESS TO THE PEOPLE OF NEW YORK (April 15, 1788), in 17 DHRC 107.

"Hard necessity," Jay said, compelled the veterans "to sell their honest claims on the public for a little bread."[70]

An unpaid army, moreover, was dangerous. In 1783, unpaid soldiers drove the Congress out of Philadelphia and the Congress fled to Princeton, New Jersey, where it held a session in exile.[71] When Virginia repudiated a proposal to give Congress power to impose taxes on imports, Madison wrote home that

> Virginia could never have cut off this source of public relief at a more unlucky crisis.... The deputies of the Army are still here.... But what can a Virginia Delegate say to them, whose constituents declare that they are unable to make the necessary contribution to establish the funds for the obtaining of their pay?[72]

The failure of the requisition left the founders "despondent as to the present System."[73] "Payments to the federal Treasry. are ceasing every where," Madison wrote his father, "and the mind of people losing all confidence in our political System."[74] Rufus King of Massachusetts was "more agitated for Country than he could express," and he "conceived that [the Constitutional Convention] to be the last opportunity of providing for [the Country's] liberty & happiness."[75]

"[S]omething must be done, or the fabrick must fall," Washington wrote in 1786, "for it certainly is tottering ... From the high ground we stood upon, from the plain path which invited our footsteps, to be so fallen! so lost! it is really mortifying...."[76] "In a word, it is at an end," Washington declared in 1787, "and, unless a remedy is soon applied, anarchy and confusion will inevitably ensue."[77] "General Government is now suspended by a Thread,"

---

[70] *Id.*

[71] RAKOVE, BEGINNINGS at 334–335.

[72] Madison to Randolph (Jan. 22, 1783), *in* 6 JM 55–56. *See* discussion in KETCHAM 171–173.

[73] Madison to Pendleton (Feb. 24, 1787), *in* 9 JM 294.

[74] Madison to Madison, Sr. (Feb. 25, 1787), *in* 9 JM 297. *See also* Letter of Madison to Ambrose Madison (Aug. 5, 1786), *in* 9 JM 89 (saying that "[n]o money comes into the public treasury, ... and the States are running mad after paper money, which among other evils disables them from all contributions of specie for paying the public debts, particularly foreign ones").

[75] Rufus King (Massachusetts), Federal Convention (June 30, 1787), *in* 1 FARRAND 490.

[76] Washington to Secretary of Foreign Affairs (John Jay) (May 18, 1786), *in* 28 WRITINGS OF GW 430, 431–2. Accord, Letter of Madison to Randolph (Feb. 25, 1787) 9 JM 299 (saying that lacking money and respect for its authority, the Confederation was tottering on its foundation).

[77] Washington to Jefferson (May 30, 1787), *in* 3 FARRAND 31.

he wrote in a 1788 letter, "I might go further . . . *it is really at an End.*"[78] "We may indeed with propriety be said to have reached almost the last stage of national humiliation," *Publius* said. "We have neither troops nor treasury nor government."[79] Things had fallen apart; the center could not hold.

For the Framers of the Constitution, the failure of requisitions was a matter of state willfulness and not of incapacity. "[W]e labour under one sad Evil," John Jay wrote, "the Treasury is empty tho' the Country abounds in Resources, and our people are far more unwilling than unable to pay Taxes."[80] The times were prosperous, the founders believed.[81] "Population is encreasing," John Jay reported, "new houses building, new lands clearing, new settlements forming and new manufacturing establishing with a rapidity beyond conception."[82] The country, Franklin said, was on the whole so

---

[78] Extract of a Letter, of a late Date, from the illustrious President of the late Federal Convention [Washington], to his Friend in Fredericksburg, Virginia – extracted from Mr. Green's Virginia Herald, Maryland Journal (Jan. 1, 1788), *in* 15 DHRC 136 (emphasis in original).

[79] *Federalist* No. 15, at 91 (Hamilton) (Dec. 1, 1787).

[80] Jay to John Adams (Feb. 27, 1787), *quoted in* BROWN at 260. *See also* BROWN, at 157–167 for other descriptions of the Federalists' view that failure of requisitions was the result of "an unvirtuous people." Brown himself is a dissenter from that view, considering the failure of requisitions to be an unavoidable result of lack of specie in the rural communities and economic depression, but given the prosperity and commodity exports of the nation, the failure to tap any of the considerable wealth of the nation or to create viable mechanisms for collection has to be understood as a failure of will and institutions, and not an act of God or force of nature. *See, e.g.*, Charles W. Calomiris, *Institutional Failure, Monetary Scarcity, and the Depreciation of the Continental*, 48 J. OF ECON. HISTORY 47, 60 (1988).

[81] It is quite surprisingly still unclear as to whether the economy should be considered overall as booming or in depression in 1787. Proponents of prosperity include RISJORD at 156 (finding economic prosperity in Virginia. with state tax receipts increasing by 15% between 1785–1786 and 1786–1787); JENSEN, NEW NATION 214–18, 245–57 (describing booming trade and economy); MCDONALD, HAMILTON at 89 (saying that New York revenues burgeoned from $95,000 in 1784 to $450,000 in 1785, mainly thanks to import duties, but also good 1785 harvest and recovery from the ravages of the war); 167–168 (Pennsylvania prosperous as computed from import and export data); 186 ("boom" in Mass). Arguing for depression, John P. Kaminski, *New York: The Reluctant Pillar, in* RELUCTANT PILLAR 48, 54; JOHN J. MCCUSKER & RUSSELL R. MENARD, THE ECONOMY OF BRITISH AMERICA, 1607–1789 at 373–77 (1985) (arguing that something truly disastrous happened to American economy from 1775 to 1790). MORRIS at 130–148 (1987) has an excellent discussion arguing in favor of depression on the grounds of drop in prices and increasing trade deficits.

A great deal does not ride on whether the country was prosperous or not, but I come down on the side of prosperity. Price drops that Morris points to were a monetary phenomenon attributable to the withdrawal of state paper money. Trade deficit figures also show steadily increasing exports and also a trend to increasing imports, although not steadily. Morris gives credence to mercantilists who decry increasing imports, but increasing imports are in fact not a sign of bad economic health. In the end, it is the perceptions of the Framers that count, and their letters are filled with optimism.

[82] Charles Thomson to Jefferson (April 6, 1786), *in* 9 PTJ 380.

prosperous that there was every reason for profound thanksgiving.[83] "Our country is fertile, abounding in productions in demand and bearing a good price," wrote John Jay to Jefferson.[84] The harvests were good ones and the states were recovering from the ravages of war and then deflation.[85]

The states were using their increasing revenues to purchase debt held by citizens of their own state, rather than paying the requisition that would extinguish the debt for the benefit of the whole union.[86] The purchases benefited local voters, at least to the extent of the depreciated value of the debts, without reducing the federal burden. New York bought the federal debt held by supporters of Governor George Clinton as part of a program to garner political support for the governor. New York also acquired enough securities that interest due to New York on the federal debt was more than New York's quota under a requisition, so that the State could afford to ignore requisitions, as it did.[87] Clinton was supposed to come in as co-debtor helping to extinguish the debts. Instead he came in as a creditor pushing to the head of the line. The debts held by New York would have priority even over the Dutch creditors because New York payments under requisitions and its collections as creditor would cancel each other out. Virginia did not pay her quota of requisition, but she did purchase federal debt at their depreciated value in 1787, speculating that a new Constitution would allow payments on the federal debt that would enrich Virginia.[88] Virginia and New Jersey paid off their state debts, without paying the requisition quotas that would have allowed the federal government to pay off the general debts.[89] Those same payments should have gone to extinguish the federal debt under the mandatory provisions of the Articles of Confederation.

B. VETO OF THE IMPOST

In 1781 Congress had proposed that it be granted its own tax, a 5% tax on imports called the "impost" so that it did not have to rely entirely on

---

[83] *Quoted in* BEARD 49.

[84] Letter of Jay to Jefferson (Dec. 14, 1786), *in* 3 PJJ 224.

[85] On deflation, *see* discussion Chapter 6, pp. 218–220.

[86] FERGUSON at 228–234 (saying that Pennsylvania, Massachusetts and New York began buying federal debt from their own citizens at a fraction of the face value, replacing the federal debt with state paper money and state debts).

[87] MCDONALD, HAMILTON at 88–89; EDMUND BURNETT, CONTINENTAL CONGRESS 540–46 (1941); FERGUSON at 189, 230, 233. *Cf.* KAMINSKI, CLINTON 102 (1993) (saying that Clinton bought 28% of the federal securities owned by New Yorkers but not those of the wealthy New York City residents, who had little sympathy for Clinton).

[88] JENSEN, NEW NATION at 397.

[89] *Id.* at 34, (Virginia), at 392–393 (New Jersey).

requisitions. The impost proposal required an amendment of the Articles of Confederation, however, and, under the Articles themselves, amendment required the endorsement by all thirteen states.[90] Rhode Island vetoed the impost of 1781, saying that a federal tax was inconsistent with the sovereignty and independence of the State.[91]

When Rhode Island vetoed the impost, the rest of America was unforgiving. Because of its veto of the impost, Rhode Island was "an evil genius" whose veto "injured the United States more than the worth of that whole state."[92] Rhode Island was "shameful" and a "perverse sister."[93] "Cursed State ought to be erased out of Confederation, and . . . out of the earth, if any worse place could be found for them."[94] A poem of 1782 showed Mother Columbia, the symbol of all America, protecting all her thirteen children, when the Devil comes to her and says he must take one state. Fair Columbia protests, but then she remembers Rhode Island's veto of the 1781 impost. She smiles, consents, and lets the devil have Rhode Island.[95]

As the states came together for the Constitutional Convention, the newspapers were filled with attacks on Rhode Island. Selfish "Rogue Island" was said to be responsible for the poverty of the Revolutionary soldiers, for the high taxes on land, and for the embarrassment of public finances.[96] Rhode Island was the "Quintessence of Villainy."[97] It was governed by "miscreants void of even the appearance of Honor or Justice."[98] "The small district of Rhode Island put a negative upon the collected wisdom of the continent."[99] Even to a talented, moderate Anti-Federalist, Melancton Smith, Rhode Island was an

---

[90] ARTICLES OF CONFEDERATION, art. XIII, para. 1, 9 JCC 221 (March 1, 1781).

[91] Congressman David Howell to Gov. Wm. Greene (July 30, 1782), in 18 LDCC 678. See also Congressman David Howell to Gov. Wm. Greene (Feb. 5, 1784), in 21 LDCC 340 (saying that if the "States give up to Congress the power of raising money . . . , their sovereignty will in fact be absorbed into one mighty sovereignty"). See IRVIN H. POLISHOOK, RHODE ISLAND AND THE UNION, 1774–1795, at 82 (1969) (collecting arguments that impost violated state sovereignty). See id at 53–88 for a description of Rhode Island's decision to veto the impost.

[92] STATE GAZETTE OF SOUTH-CAROLINA (CHARLESTON) (June 1, 1786) and "A FABLE," EXCHANGE ADVISER (BOSTON) (Feb. 11, 1786), quoted in IRVIN H. POLISHOOK, RHODE ISLAND AND THE UNION, 1774–1795, at 96 (1969).

[93] Madison to Randolph (Nov. 19, 1783), in 5 JM 289.

[94] John Montgomery to Edward Hand (July 26, 1784), in 6 LMCC 575.

[95] PHILADELPHIA COLUMBIAN MAGAZINE (1782), described in JOHN K. ALEXANDER, THE SELLING OF THE CONSTITUTIONAL CONVENTION at 24 (1990).

[96] Id. at 23 (1990) (quoting SALEM (MASSACHUSETTS) MERCURY, 1787).

[97] Id. at 23. For additional expressions of anti-Rhode Island sentiments in the press, see id. at 23–24, 71–74, 158–169.

[98] Francis Hopkinson to Jefferson (July 8, 1787), in 11 PTJ 561.

[99] D. Thatcher, Massachusetts Convention (Feb. 4, 1788), in 2 ELLIOT 142 (complaining that Rhode Island had prevented repaying Massachusetts for her disproportionate contribution to the war).

illustration of "political depravity," "genuine infamy," and "a wicked administration."[100] Rhode Island, according to the scholarly Noah Webster, was that "little detestable corner of the Continent."[101]

Rhode Island was not, however, alone in its veto of the impost. Once Rhode Island vetoed the 1781 impost proposal, Virginia revoked its prior ratification, saying that giving any body other than the Virginia General Assembly power over taxation was "injurious to [Virginia's] Sovereignty."[102] Nathaniel Gorham of Massachusetts reacted that Virginia not only refused to contribute the necessary requisitioned funds, but at the same moment repealed her concurrence in the only scheme that promised to make up the deficiency of contributions.[103] "How all these sovereign People will agree in the Establishment of National Security," Oliver Wolcott reacted, "is difficult to say."[104]

In 1783 Congress proposed again that it be given a 5% impost, this time limiting the impost to 25 years and to the payment only of past debts.[105] New York vetoed the 1783 impost. [106] By 1783, New York State had a state impost, exploiting New York harbor to pay for New York government, in part by taxing imports destined for neighboring states.[107] The state was reluctant to give up the advantage of its impost in favor of the nation.[108] New York, like Rhode Island and Virginia, also claimed that federal tax would swallow up

---

[100] Melancton Smith, New York Convention (June 27, 1788), *in* 2 ELLIOT 335.
[101] "AMERICA" (NOAH WEBSTER), NEW YORK DAILY ADVERTISER (Dec. 31, 1787), *reprinted in* 15 DHRC 201.
[102] XI Statutes of Virginia 171 (William Waller Henning, ed., Oct. 1782).
[103] Nathaniel Gorham, Continental Congress (Jan. 27, 1783), 25 JCC 868.
[104] Oliver Wolcott to Oliver Wolcott, Jr. (Feb. 19, 1783), *in* 19 LDCC 715.
[105] 24 JCC 258 (April 18, 1783).
[106] In form, the New York resolution on the 1783 impost merely required that the federal impost be collected in New York paper money and by New York officers, but those conditions prevented the Congressional resolution from becoming effective. *See* Report of a Committee of William Johnson, Rufus King, Charles Pinckney, James Monroe, and William Grayson (Aug. 22, 1786), *in* 31 JCC 532, 535; Letter of Rufus King to Elbridge Gerry (May 14, 1786) *reprinted in* 23 LDCC 284 (saying that New York's grant of impost to pay in paper money to be collected by officers amendable and removable by New York will have the consequence of Congress not having the power to put the impost into operation and no money will come into the federal Treasury). The federal government needed not more paper money but specie to pay its foreign debts. According to Hamilton, New York's Governor Clinton argued to defeat the impost that "Congress might misapply it" and that Clinton did not care how the impost was collected so long as Congress did not get it. H.G.VIII, NEW YORK DAILY ADVERTISER (Feb. 28, 1789), *reprinted in* 5 PAH 277–278.
[107] John P. Kaminski, *New York: The Reluctant Pillar*, *in* RELUCTANT PILLAR at 48, 52–53, 56–58; MAIN at 76 (1961).
[108] *See, e.g.*, KAMINSKI, CLINTON at 91 (discussing the attitude that the New York harbor was a "privilege Providence has endowed us with" that should not be surrendered to Congress).

entirely "the sovereignty of the particular states."[109] When New York vetoed the impost, it was said, every "liberal good man [wished] New York [should rest] in Hell."[110]

The Congress had also used up its credit. Toward the end of the Revolutionary War, Congress had borrowed from France and on Dutch financial markets with French guarantees. With the end of the war, however, France had stopped both the loans and the guarantees.[111] By 1787, Congress was in default on interest and principal, and the foreign debt had depreciated to about a sixth of its face value.[112] In 1783, Rhode Island gave Congress the useless advice that it should keep requisitions low and borrow the rest of any funds that were needed in Europe.[113] By vetoing the impost, Rhode Island simultaneously denied to Congress "the only fund that would be satisfactory to lenders."[114] Late in 1786, Congress attempted to float a loan for $500,000, but attracted not a single subscriber.[115] Congress had no revenue nor prospects that could justify further lending.[116] "Our own experience will shew," the Superintendent of Finance Robert Morris had told Congress, that the nation's "want of honesty is severely punished by the want of credit."[117]

C. FRAGMENTATION?

Professor E. James Ferguson has argued that the states might have paid off the Revolutionary War debts without a national government, with each state assuming part of the total debt.[118] *Publius* did not find that plan viable.

---

[109] A Rough Hewer, New York Journal (Mar. 17, 1785), *quoted in* Kaminski, Clinton at 90 (1993).

[110] Henry Jackson to Henry Knox (April 23, 1786), *quoted in* Robert A. Feer, *Shays's Rebellion and the Constitution: A Study in Causation*, 42 New Eng. Q. 388, 398 (1969).

[111] *See, e.g.*, Robert Morris to the President of the Congress (Mar. 17, 1783), *in* 6 RDCUS 309 (saying that there is no hope of any further pecuniary help from French court; even if she was inclined to assist us, "it is not in her power").

[112] Jensen, New Nation at 38 (giving evidence that debt was worth 1/6th of face value – $67 million borrowed, specie value of $11.5 million – by 1780).

[113] Madison to Randolph (Nov. 19, 1783), *in* 5 JM 289.

[114] *Id.*

[115] Report of the Board of Treasury (Feb. 7, 1787), 32 JCC 33.

[116] Brown at 17–21 (1993).

[117] Robert Morris, Report of the Office of Finance (July 29, 1782), *in* 22 JCC 429, 435 (Aug. 5, 1782).

[118] E. James Ferguson, *The Nationalists of 1781–1783 and the Economic Interpretation of the Constitution*, 56 J. of Am. Hist. 241, 246, 252 (1969) argues that there was good chance that the states could come to hold all the federal debt. *See also* E. James Ferguson, *Book Review of Forest McDonald, E Pluribus Unum*, 23 Wm. & Mary Q. 149 (3rd Series, 1966) (arguing that federal taxation to pay the debt was merely a "gambit" of those who wanted to strengthen

Some states, *Publius* argued, would feel an indifference, even repugnance to paying the debt, because they were less impressed with the importance of national credit, or because their citizens held little, if any, of the debt. Other states, however, would be "strenuous for some equitable and effective" distribution of the burden. The "procrastinations of the former would excite the resentments of the latter" and the states would collide.[119] In the period before the Constitution, the states were not buying the debt held by the crucial foreign creditors in the Netherlands. They were buying only the domestic debt held by their own citizens. Even for the domestic debt, they were buying only some of it.[120] The states were also not extinguishing the federal domestic debt upon purchase of it, but demanding payment of it, or at least offsets for their payments under a requisition.

The suggestion that each state would voluntarily pay off a portion of the war debt is, indeed, not very credible in the terms of modern analysis. Paying off the war debt was what is now called a "collective action" problem.[121] No state could be excluded from the benefits of a healthy national credit when war came again, even if they had not helped restore the public credit. Defense for one state would generally be tantamount to defense for all. A state paying just its fractional quota of the debts, when other states defaulted, would not have done any good. Thus each state had no separate advantage to paying and every motive to default and free ride on other states. In any event, the states did not pay the war debt, even when it was mandatory that they make contributions to do so via requisitions. Why should anyone think that the states would pay more if the mandate disappeared?

The Framers treated the prospect of a breakup of the Union into fragments as frightening.[122] Separate states or coalitions would inevitably have "frequent and violent contests with each other," Hamilton argued.[123] Disunited

---

the Union and that "[a]s the states began to assume the federal debt during the 1780's this bond of union decayed, bringing on a crisis, not of the country, which was in pretty good shape, but of the nation's political future").

[119] *Federalist* No. 7, at 41 (Hamilton) (Nov. 17, 1787).

[120] New York, for instance, was acquiring only the debt held by supporters of Governor George Clinton. McDONALD, HAMILTON at 88–89; KAMINSKI, CLINTON at 102.

[121] *See, e.g.*, TODD SANDLER, COLLECTIVE ACTION: THEORY AND APPLICATIONS 5–6 (1992); KEITH DOUGHERTY, COLLECTIVE ACTION UNDER THE ARTICLES OF CONFEDERATION 8–10 (2001).

[122] *See, e.g.*, *Federalist* No. 13, at 80 (Hamilton) (Nov. 28, 1787) (discussing how states might clump into separate confederacies in lieu of one union). *Cf. Federalist* No. 1, at 7 (Hamilton) (Oct. 27, 1787) (saying that opponents whisper of the necessity to "resort to separate confederacies of distinct portions of the whole").

[123] *Federalist* No. 6, at 28 (Hamilton) (Nov. 14, 1787); *generally*, *Federalist* No. 8 (Hamilton) (Nov. 20, 1787).

states of America, Hamilton wrote, would have the same inducements that all nations in the world have shown to deluge themselves in blood.[124] Disunion in America would require a state of constant preparation and standing armies, he said, just as disunion did in Europe.[125] Great Britain, when once separated into three countries, Jay said, was constantly embroiled in quarrels and wars among the three countries.[126]

The proponents of the Constitution also thought that solutions to the crisis required loyalty to the united cause. The governing maxim for the Revolutionary War had been, "United we stand, divided we fall."[127] The union represented the ideals of independence and the republican form of goverment. The prospect of fragmentation, Madison thought, should rouse all "real friends of the Revolution to exert themselves ... to perpetuate the Union and Redeem the Honor of the Republican name."[128] America, according to John Jay, was

> one connected, fertile, wide spreading country, ... one united people, descended from the same ancestors, speaking the same language, professing the same religion, attached to the same principles of government, very similar in their manners and customs, and who by their joint counsels, arms and efforts, fighting side by side throughout a long and bloody war, have nobly established their general Liberty and Independence.[129]

America was a single nation: "[T]he kindred blood which flows in the veins of American citizens, the mingled blood which they have shed in defence of their sacred rights, consecrate their union, and excite horror at the idea of their becoming aliens, rivals, enemies."[130]

---

[124] *Federalist* No. 7, at 36 (Hamilton) (Nov. 17, 1787).
[125] *Federalist* No. 8, at 49 (Hamilton) (Nov. 20, 1787).
[126] *Federalist* No. 5, at 24 (Jay) (Nov. 10, 1787).
[127] John Adams to Henry Murchant (June 1, 1790), *in* 4 DHFFE 402 (saying "United we stand but divided we fall. Join or die. Those were our Maxims twenty-five or thirty years ago, and they are neither less true or less important now than they were then"); Courtland Canby, *Robert Munford's "The Patriots,"* 6 Wm. & Mary Q. 437, 459 (3rd. Ser. 1949) (character in Virginia play of 1775 or 1776 describes "United We Stand, Divided We Fall" as the American motto).
[128] Madison to Pendleton, (Feb. 24, 1787), *in* 9 JM 294–295. *See also* A Citizen of New York (John Jay), Address to the People of the State of New York (April 15, 1788), *in* 17 DHRC 120 (saying that fragmentation would lead "the minds of men every where [to] become alienated from republican forms").
[129] *Federalist* No. 2, at 9 (Jay) (Oct. 31, 1787). *See also Federalist* No. 14, at 88 (Madison) (Nov. 30, 1787).
[130] *Federalist* No. 14, at 88 (Madison) (Nov. 30, 1787).

D. TO STARVE THE ARMY AT THEIR PLEASURE

The Founders' anger at the states for the states' failure to pay requisitions and for the veto of the impost stood on top of a swelling anger at the states carried over from the Revolutionary War. The states had repeatedly betrayed the army and the cause of independence by their failure to provide financial support. Washington was a committed Federalist because he had seen first hand the effect of the state's starvation of the army[131] and Hamilton became a nationalist at the start of his career as George Washington's smart young aide. The officers of the Continental Army were disproportionately supporters of the Constitution.[132]

The national Congress, to whom requisitions were due, embodied the cause of the Revolutionary War. As resistance to British policies intensified into war, the cause held on to its moderates, who preferred a settlement with Britain, as well as its radicals, who wanted quick independence, under the principle that everyone should defer to the Continental Congress. If the sides could not agree to what steps of resistance to undertake, they could nonetheless unite under the principle of supporting whatever steps the Congress would agree on. "Allegiance to Congress became the primary test of the right to participate in the emerging Revolutionary polity."[133] A united stand by all the colonies was at the core of the Revolution: Virginia and the other colonies would support Boston's resistance to Great Britain[134] and a Virginia general would command New England troops at Bunker Hill to make it a Continental Army, embodying the common mission of resistance and independence.[135] The Union was then worshipped with "as much fervor

---

[131] See, e.g., Letter of Washington to Hamilton, <http://lcweb2.loc.gov/cgi-bin/query/r?ammem/mgw:@field(DOCID+@lit(gw260324))> (March 31, 1783) (saying that no man in the United States had felt the bad effects of the want of powers in the Congress more than himself). See GLENN A. PHELPS, GEORGE WASHINGTON AND AMERICAN CONSTITUTIONALISM 47–53 (1993) for a more extended discussion of Washington's bitterness at the failure of the states to support the war effort.

[132] See HUGH GRIGSBY, THE HISTORY OF THE VIRGINIA FEDERAL CONVENTION OF 1788, 160 (1890, 1969 reprint) (attributing ratification in Virginia to ex-military officers); McDONALD, WE THE PEOPLE 261–262 (finding ex-officers of the continental line to be heavily but not exclusively pro-ratification in Virginia). Cf. FORREST McDONALD, NOVUS ORDO SECLORUM: THE INTELLECTUAL ORIGINS OF THE CONSTITUTION 187 (1985) (saying the Framers at the Philadelphia convention were "court-party" nationalists who shared a complex of experiences including service for a considerable time as officers in the Continental Army).

[133] RAKOVE, BEGINNINGS at 66.

[134] See John W. Blassingame, American Nationalism and Other Loyalties in the Southern Colonies 1763–1775, 34 J. OF S. HIST. 50, 63 (1968) (describing Southern support for united stand against the British).

[135] JAMES THOMAS FLEXNER, WASHINGTON: THE INDISPENSABLE MAN 60 (1969).

as pagans...implored the protection of titular deities."[136] Loyalty to the Union defined the Revolutionary cause.

In 1776, Congress had instructed the revolutionary assemblies and conventions of the Colonies to take the powers of government as representatives of the people away from the Crown and to adopt a government that was most conducive to the happiness and safety of America.[137] Congress supervised the revolutionary committees spread across the full nation in the resistance and then the war. The provincial authorities were, in many ways, subordinate officials of Congress who were expected to implement its directives and policies.[138] The Articles of Confederation contained no provision empowering Congress to use coercive authority against the states because, quite simply, in 1776–1777 when they were drafted, "it was difficult to believe they would willfully defy its decisions."[139] The authors of the existing Confederation, John Jay told New York in 1787, "were led to flatter themselves that the people of America only required to know what ought to be done, to do it."[140]

Congress throughout the Revolutionary War had tried every tool and trick at its disposal to fund the army. In the early years, the war was financed just by issuing paper money, the Continental dollar. By the time the emissions of the Continental dollar ended, in 1780, Congress had issued $220 million. The states were required, in theory, to redeem their share of the Continental dollars with tax revenue.[141] The states, however, did not set up any mechanism for redemption and the paper depreciated. Continental dollars would have held their value if the states had imposed taxes to absorb the excess

---

[136] A Citizen of New York (John Jay), Address to the People of the State of New York (April 15, 1788), in 17 DHRC 107.

[137] Preamble (May 15, 1776), in 4 JCC 357–358; Resolution (May 10, 1776), in 4 JCC 342. See Morris at 76 (1987) (concluding that the states may rightly be considered a creation of the Continental Congress, which preceded them and brought them into being); Rakove, Beginnings at 173n (endorsing Morris' analysis on "one of the oldest and most contentious issues of Constitutional history").

[138] Rakove, Beginnings at 197.

[139] Id., at 172–173. See also id., at 145 (saying the extent of Congressional authority was *not* a subject of major political concern, because Congress already had authority over the conduct of the war and diplomacy).

[140] A Citizen of New York (John Jay), Address to the People of the State of New York (April 15, 1788), in 17 DHRC 101, 108.

[141] Jefferson, Notes on Debates on the Continental Congress (July 29, 1775), in 2 JCC 221 (resolving that "each colony provide ways and means to sink its proportion of the bills ordered to be emitted by this Congress, in such manner as may be most effectual and best adapted to the condition and circumstances, and usual mode of levying taxes in such colony"). See Edmond Burnet, The Continental Congress 215–20 (1941); Rakove, Beginnings at 205–15.

of dollars beyond the amount needed for trades,[142] but the states were not willing to tax. There was wealth to tax, but states did not try to protect the dollar.[143] By September 1779, Congress had issued $160 million of Continental dollars, whereas the states had contributed a trivial $3 million from taxes for redemption.[144] The Congress itself concluded that too much paper had been issued: "Where the quantity of money of any quality or denomination exceeds what is useful as a medium of commerce," Congress said, "its comparative value must be proportionately reduced [by tax]."[145] In 1779, John Jay, the president of the Continental Congress, wrote a circular to the states telling them that their failure to redeem the Continental dollars would "appear among reputable nations like a common prostitute among chaste and respectable matrons."[146] Fail, however, they did.

In 1780, Congress devalued the Continental dollar to 1/40th, renouncing any attempt to redeem anything but 2–1/2% of its value. Even then the dollar could not hold its new value, in absence of any creditable commitment from the states.[147] By 1780 when Congress stopped printing the Continental dollar, it had dropped in value to about a penny of specie and had ceased to circulate as acceptable currency.[148] The Congress's Office of Finance concluded that the government, by issuing the dollar but failing to redeem, had "committed injustice."[149] The depreciation of the Continental dollar stole from all who touched it, with the amount of the loss depending on how long the currency was held. The soldiers and domestic suppliers who had accepted the Continental dollar as currency, either absorbed the loss or passed the loss off to someone else.

---

[142] Charles W. Calomiris, *Institutional Failure, Monetary Scarcity, and the Depreciation of the Continental*, 48 J. OF ECON. HISTORY 47, 59 (1988) (states refused to accept Continental dollars at par but only at depreciated value, thus providing no backing).

[143] *Id.* at 59–60 (arguing that failure to support the Continental dollar was institutional failure or failure of will). *Accord*, FERGUSON at 29 (1961) (saying that the states could have been taxing to withdraw Continental dollars from circulation, but they were compounding the problem by issuing too much of their own paper).

[144] Draft of Circular Letter from President of the Congress (Sept. 13, 1779), *in* 15 JCC 1052–1053. Overall, only about 6% of the war cost was raised by taxes during the war. Confiscation of Tory property, for example, raised almost three times as much. Calomiris, *supra* note 142 at 58. *See also* Robert A. Becker, *Evolution and Reform: An Interpretation of Southern Taxation, 1763 to 1783*, 32 WM. & MARY Q. 417, 433–439 (3d Series 1975) (describing taxes in the Southern states, which fell very far short even of the paper dollars the states issued).

[145] Nov. 22, 1777, *in* 9 JCC 954.

[146] John Jay, Draft of a Circular from the Congress to the States (Sept 13, 1779), *in* 15 JCC 1060.

[147] 16 JCC 262–267 (March 18, 1780). *See also* FERGUSON at 51–53.

[148] JENSEN, NEW NATION at 37–41.

[149] Robert Morris, Report of the Office of Finance *in* 22 JCC 435 (Aug. 5, 1782).

When Continental paper failed, Congress called on the states to deliver specific supplies to specific sites. The results of the specific requisition system were at no time satisfactory and were at times disastrous.[150] The requisition of specific supplies, Washington concluded, was "pernicious beyond description,"[151] and "the most uncertain, expensive, and injurious that could be devised."[152] "One state will comply with a requisition of Congress," General Washington complained, "another neglects to do it, a third executes it by halves, and all differ either in the manner, the matter, or so much in point of time, that we are always working up hill, and ever shall be."[153] Even the Continental dollar had been far better, while it lasted: "Whilst [Congress] exercised the indefinite power of emitting money on the credit of their constituents," James Madison wrote,

> [Congress] had the whole wealth and resources of the continent within their command, and could go on with the affairs independently and as they pleased. Since the resolution passed for shutting the press the power has been given up and they are always dependent on the states. They can neither enlist pay nor feed a single solder; nor execute any other purpose but as the means are first put into their hands.[154]

The winter camp of 1779–1780 at Morristown was miserable for the Continental Army. Hard snow and cold came early. Quartermaster-General Nathaniel Greene wrote bitterly in March 1780, "Perhaps this campaign is to be the Marvelous kind. We are to . . . exist without support."[155]

State laws to fund the specific requisitions gave the farmers the right to trial by jury, and lots of rights to delay the procedures.[156] Local magistrates were reluctant to impress supplies from their friends and neighbors.[157] The state legislatures deliberated on every measure and by their slowness "the Army has been fed only from day to day & at some times [was] almost entirely

---

[150] See Erna Risch, *supra* note 62, at 231–258 ; E. WAYNE CARP at 171–187 (1984); JENSEN, NEW NATION at 34.

[151] Washington to the President of Congress (April 3, 1780), *in* 18 WRITINGS OF GW 207,209.

[152] Washington to the President of Congress (Aug. 20, 1780), *in* 19 WRITINGS OF GW 402, 403; *See also* Committee at Headquarters (May 15, 1780), *in* 5 LMCC 142 (saying that to "Depend on the States for *effectual* Supplies . . . would be hazarding too much").

[153] Washington to Joseph Jones (Delegate to the Continental Congress from Virginia) (May 31, 1780), *in* 18 WRITINGS OF GW 453.

[154] Madison (member of Congress representing Virginia) to Jefferson (Governor of Virginia) (May 6, 1780), *in* 2 JM19.

[155] Nathaniel Greene to Jeremiah Wadsworth (Mar. 2, 1780), *quoted in* E. WAYNE CARP at 180.

[156] E. WAYNE CARP at 85–86.

[157] *Id.*, at 185–186.

destitute of any provision at all."[158] The Army officers, including Washington and Hamilton, "witnessed and daily felt the effect of the states' inability or unwillingness to provide for the army."[159] The system of specific requisitions allowed the states, as one Major J. Burnett put it, "to starve the army at pleasure."[160]

The Army was nearly always at the point, Washington wrote, where without immediate provisions it must "[s]tarve, dissolve, or disperse."[161] "The army must dissolve," Hamilton wrote in September 1780. "It is now a mob, rather than an army, without cloathing, without pay, without provision, without morals, without discipline. We begin to hate the country for its neglect of us, the country begins to hate us for our oppressions of them."[162] The Continental army, wrote Robert Morris in 1782, was "an army unfed, unpaid, unclothed, which would subsist of itself or disband itself."[163]

There was no serious lack of available provisions had Congress been able to pay for them. The French had no difficulty in obtaining flour with gold and when the Continental army had funds to pay specie, the supplies were available. What was lacking "was the means to draw out the resources – that is, the cash in hand to pay for the wheat, flour, cattle and other subsistence which farmers were otherwise reluctant to release."[164] Indeed, American farmers were willing to sell their produce to the British, who had hard currency with which to pay.[165]

The states sometimes appropriated for their own militias goods meant for the Continental Army.[166] In January 1777, for example, the New York militia had seized Washington's only supply of clothing in transit from New

---

[158] James Bowdoin to President of the Congress Samuel Huntington (Sept. 1780), *quoted in* RAKOVE, BEGINNINGS at 277 .

[159] E. WAYNE CARP at 198.

[160] Major J. Burnett to Jeremiah Wadsworth (Mar. 18, 1780), *quoted in* E. WAYNE CARP at 179.

[161] Washington to The President of Congress (Dec. 23, 1777), *in* 10 WRITINGS OF GW 192; *See also* Madison (then Representative to Congress from Virginia) to Jefferson (then Governor of Virginia) (Mar. 27, 1780), *in* 2 JM 5, 6 (saying that the army has the immediate alternatives of disbanding or living on free quarter, since the public credit is exhausted).

[162] Hamilton to James Duane (Sept. 3, 1780), *in* 2 PAH 403, 404–408, 409, 417.

[163] Robert Morris, Draft of Proposed Letter to the Governors of the States (May 16, 1782), *in* 5 DCAR 425.

[164] Erna Risch, *supra* note 62, at 419.

[165] Sung Bok Kim, *The Limits of Politicization in the American Revolution: The Experience of Westchester County, New York,* 3 J. OF AMER. HISTORY 868, 883–84 (1993). The American troops responded with plunder of the Westchester farmers. *Id.* at 885.

[166] June 17, 1777, *in* 8 JCC 472–473 (reporting Clothier-General James Mease's complaining that the states frequently appropriated clothing and necessaries, on their passage through the state, leading to "disorder and confusion" in his department).

England to the Continental Army. Washington wrote that "the troops in the field are now absolutely perishing for want of it."[167] In August 1780, Governor William Greene of Rhode Island flatly refused to send the food the Congress had ordered to be delivered to the army on the ground that the food was needed for the Rhode Island militia because he expected a British invasion.[168] "The contest among the different States now," Washington wrote in 1780, "is not which shall do most for the common cause, but which shall do least."[169]

With the end of the Continental dollar, the Army in the field survived primarily on impressments.[170] Impressments were involuntary seizures from civilians with the misfortune of living within reach of the army as it moved or camped.[171] The civilians would receive in return for their goods not cash or specie, but rather Quartermasters Certificates or Commissary Certificates or certificates of whatever department had authorized the seizure. Whenever possible the army would ask the regular civilian authorities to seize the goods to soften the confrontation between soldier and farmer. Originally the certificates were in handwriting. Printed certificates came later. Wherever the army passed or camped, the countryside was soon saturated with certificates. Ultimately the amount of certificates approximated the amount of outstanding Continental dollars. As Robert Morris, the Financial Superintendent for the Congress explained the system, "property has been wrested . . . by force to support the war," with certificates given in return "which are entirely useless."[172] In 1780 the certificates were restated in terms of the specie value of what was delivered. Interest was promised thereafter at 6%.[173] The certificates were ultimately settled when the Constitution gave the Congress a source of revenue, although with less interest than had been promised.[174] Still, at the time when they were given, the future payments were not known

---

[167] Washington to William Duer (Jan. 14, 1777), *in* 8 PAPERS OF GEORGE WASHINGTON: REVOLUTIONARY WAR 63–64.

[168] E. WAYNE CARP at 184.

[169] Washington to Fielding Lewis (July 6, 1780), *in* 19 WRITINGS OF GW 129, 132.

[170] *See, e.g.*, Washington to Mason (Oct. 22, 1780), *in* 2 PGM 677, 678 (saying that "[w]e are without money . . . without provision & forage except what is taken by Impress.")

[171] Impressments are described by E. WAYNE CARP at 77–98 and FERGUSON at 57–70 upon which this paragraph is based.

[172] Robert Morris, Report of the Office of Finance *in* 22 JCC 435 (Aug. 5, 1782).

[173] April 14, 1780, *in* 16 JCC 363 (adopting a new policy of paying interest at 6% on quartermaster and commissary certificates); May 26, 1780, *in* 17 JCC 463–464 (mandating that the certificates be accepted as state taxes and quota of requisitions if holder affirms that they were received for value given and had not been paid), Aug. 23, 1780, *in* 17 JCC 782–785 (mandating that the certificates be reduced to their specie value).

[174] *See* discussion, Chapter 7, pp. 232–238.

and were not very creditable. Impressments and certificates were "legal rob-
bery qualified by a promissory note."[175]

It was the misery of the specific requisition system and of impressment
of supplies that lead Congress to propose that the federal level be given the
power to tax on its own. In 1781 and again in 1783, Congress proposed
that the Congress be allowed to lay the "impost," which was a tax of 5% on
imports.[176] It was that solution that evil Rhode Island and then damnable
New York vetoed.

Over the years, many states had taken a turn as the chief assassin of the
general welfare. Maryland had single-handedly delayed the ratification of
the Articles of Confederation for four years.[177] Delaware had refused to join
an embargo on exports to Britain, and her merchants profited from trade,
while the other colonies sacrificed.[178] Rhode Island had vetoed the 1781
proposal for a federal-level impost and then Virginia joined and revoked its
ratification once Rhode Island had vetoed. New York had vetoed the proposed 1783 federal impost, to keep the high-yield impost for itself[179] and
New Jersey had renounced the 1786 requisition, saying it had paid enough
taxes already by paying the New York and Philadelphia imposts.[180] For
Georgia there was a rule of thumb that "Congress could make any emergency request and confidently expect that about three years later, Georgia
would agree to not quite what Congress had asked."[181] No state had paid its
quota of the 1786 requisition. The states had stabbed deeply into the federal
authority.

Publius was not only the name adopted by the authors of the *Federalist*,
but also the name of a virtuous Roman senator who watched as a helpless

---

[175] ALLAN NEVINS, THE AMERICAN STATES DURING AND AFTER THE REVOLUTION 1775–1789,
at 506 (1924).

[176] MAIN at 84–99 (1961) is a fine description of the fate of the impost proposals in the various
states; 1 BRANT, THE NATIONALIST at 209–231 describes the disputes from Congress's side.

[177] JENSEN, ARTICLES at 236–238 (describing Maryland's delay in the ratification of the Articles).
The Articles were adopted by Congress on Nov. 15, 1777, after fifteen months debate,
(9 JCC 928) but not ratified by Maryland until March 1, 1781 (1 DHRC 135–137).

[178] Madison to Jefferson (April 16, 1781), *in* 3 JM 71 (saying that at a time when all the
other states were submitting to the loss and inconveniency of an embargo on their exports,
Delaware absolutely declined the measure, and not only defeated the general object, but
enriched herself at the expense of those who did their duty); E. WAYNE CARP at 184 (1984)
(saying that Delaware lifted the embargo on British goods in May 1780).

[179] John P. Kaminski, *New York: The Reluctant Pillar*, *in* RELUCTANT PILLAR 48, 52–53, 56–58.

[180] *See* RUTH BOGIN, *supra* note 83 at 127–131 (1982).

[181] FORREST MCDONALD, E PLURIBUS UNUM: THE FORMATION OF THE AMERICAN REPUBLIC,
1776–1790, at 156 .

bystander while Brutus, Cato, Cassius, and the conspirators assassinated Caesar. "Publius," wrote Shakespeare, was "quite confounded with this mutiny."[182]

---

[182] WILLIAM SHAKESPEARE, JULIUS CAESAR, act 3, sc. 1.
    Identifying *Publius*, the author of *Federalist*, with Publius, the bystander who witnessed the assassination of Caesar, is a good fit, but a speculation. The New York newspapers had already published essays from a strident Federalist, *Caesar* (Oct. 1), and two assassins of Caesar, *Cato* (Sept. 27) and *Brutus* (Oct. 18), before *Publius* first appeared on October 27. 13 DHRC 287, 255, 411, 486. *Federalist* No. 1 shows a number of specific reactions to *Brutus'* arguments. There is an apt one-upmanship in taking the name *Publius*, in reaction to the already-published assassin. *Publius* is the fair and public-minded essayist. Douglas Adair speculates that *Publius* of the *Federalist* was the hero, Publius Valerius Poplicola, who helped found the Roman Republic, but the only reason given is that Plutarch, who discussed Poplicola, was familiar to Hamilton. Douglas Adair, *A Note on Certain of Hamilton's Pseudonyms*, 12 WM. & MARY Q. 282, 283–284, n. 4 (3d Series 1955). Identifying *Publius* of the *Federalist* with Publius Valerius Poplicola is possible, but Shakespeare's Publius, the bystander who witnessed the assassination of Caesar, is a better fit. *Publius* identifies himself in *Federalist* 1 as an outside observer, not unfriendly to the Constitution, and not as a Constitution *maker*, as Publius Valerius Popicola had been.
    Hamilton had used the pseudonym *Publius* in October 1778 to attack Congressman Samuel Chase of Maryland for overcharging the union for wheat (PUBLIUS LETTERS I–III (Oct. 1778), *reprinted in* 1 PAH562, 567, 580), and in that context as well, *Publius* is better understood as a fair observer than as a Constitution maker.

CHAPTER TWO

Madison's Vision: Requisitions and Rights

At the start of the Constitutional Convention in Philadelphia in May 1787, the Virginia delegation offered a plan, now called the Virginia Plan, which set the agenda for the deliberations. The Virginia Plan proposed a strong national government, "breathtaking," Gordon Wood has called it, in its contrast to the weak assembly of delegates from the states that preceded it.[1] Under the Virginia Plan, the government at the national level would be a complete government, able to raise taxes act on its own without approval of the states. National law would be supreme over state law. To Lord Dorchester, governor of Quebec, the Virginia Plan is the Constitution: When the Convention had finished, Lord Dorchester reported home that the delegates rejected the New Jersey Plan, which would have merely increased the powers of the present congress, on the ground that the powers it gave to the congress were insufficient. They had rejected Alexander Hamilton's plan, which, Dorchester claimed, would have established a monarchy. The Convention, he said, had adopted the Virginia Plan.[2]

Edmund Randolph, then governor of Virginia, offered the Virginia Plan to the Convention, but it had been largely written by James Madison.[3] Madison had to give up some provisions of his nationalism in the Virginia

---

[1] Gordon Woods, *Ideology and the Origins of Liberal America*, 44 WM. & MARY Q. 628, 633 (1987) (saying that "at the time of Independence no one, as far as I know, even conceived of America's having a strong central government resembling the one that emerged from the Constitutional Convention in 1787, not to mention the breathtaking government of the Virginia Plan that was the working model for the delegates in Philadelphia").

[2] Lord Dorchester to Lord Sydney (Oct. 14, 1788), *in* 3 FARRAND 353–354. Lord Dorchester liked any plan for a monarchy, falsely reporting that the Convention "looked to placing the crown upon the head of foreign prince" – in imitation of Great Britain's Glorious Revolution of 1688.

[3] KETCHAM 188–189 (1971).

Plan.[4] As the Convention continued, Madison lost on issues that were important to him. Still the important structural idea of a complete, independent,
and supreme national government would survive from Madison's private
studies, into his letters to mentors, into the Virginia Plan, into the document drafted at the Philadelphia Convention, to finally become the ratified
Constitution. Madison's solitary studies set the basic framework for the Constitution, but he operated in a social network, drawing support from, and
compromising with, his colleagues.

Madison was not a good writer. His sentences were too long and too
complicated. Hamilton's prose was cleaner and Jefferson wrote the most
memorable phrases. Madison's arguments, however, stand out as intelligently
adapted to his audience when other speakers seem happy to repeat standard
arguments. Fisher Ames of Massachusetts, who would soon become a hard
political enemy, would describe Madison almost in awe, as the new Congress
was getting started:

> He derives from nature an excellent understanding but I think he excels
> in the quality of judgment. He is possessed of a sound judgment, which
> perceives truth with great clearness, and can trace it through the mazes
> of debate, without losing it. As a reasoner, he is remarkably perspicuous
> and methodical. He is a studious man, devoted to public business, and
> a thorough master of almost every public question that can arise, or
> he will spare no pain to become so, if he happens to be in want of
> information. What a man understands clearly, and has viewed in every
> different point of light, he will explain to the admiration of others, who
> have not thought of it at all, or but little, and who will pay in praise for
> the pains he saves them.[5]

---

4 Madison had wanted Congress to be able to veto any and all state legislation to prevent
the frequent and flagrant encroachments of the states upon individual rights. Madison to
Jefferson (Oct. 24, 1787), *in* 10 JM 212. The Virginia Plan gave the federal government
power over national or common issues, where no one state could competently settle the
issue or where a state might interrupt the harmony of the United States, and it gave the
Congress the power to veto state law that contravened the "articles of the Union." Virginia
Plan, Resolution 6 (May 29, 1787), *in* 1 FARRAND 21. The apparent difference is that the
Virginia Plan did not give Congress as broad a power to protect individual rights as Madison
would have, where common harmony among the states did not require the protection. Also
contrast Madison, Federal Convention (July 14, 1787), *in* 2 FARRAND 8 (saying that votes
should be proportional to people) with Virginia Plan, 1 FARRAND 20 (saying that votes should
be proportional to fair market value of land and improvements in the states or number of
free inhabitants, "as one or the other rule may seem best in different cases").

5 Fisher Ames to George Minor (May 29, 1789), *in* 12 JM 53. *See also* Louis Otto, Liste des
Membres et Officiers du Congrés, 1788, French Archives: Ministère des Affaires Etrangères,
in 3 FARRAND 237 (describing Madison as "educated, wise, moderate, sweet-tempered, stu-
dious, perhaps more profound than Hamilton but not as brilliant, close friend of Jefferson's

William Pierce described him as,

> a character who has long been in public life; and what is very remarkable every Person seems to acknowledge his greatness. He blends together the profound politician, with the Scholar. In the management of every great question he evidently took the lead in the Convention, and tho' he cannot be called an Orator, he is a most agreeable, eloquent, and convincing Speaker. From a spirit of industry and application which he possesses in a most eminent degree, he always comes forward the best informed Man of any point in debate. The affairs of the United States, he perhaps, has the most correct knowledge of, of any Man in the Union. He has been twice a Member of Congress, and was always thought one of the ablest Members that ever sat in that Council. Mr. Maddison is about 37 years of age, a Gentleman of great modesty – with a remarkable sweet temper. He is easy and unreserved among his acquaintance, and has a most agreable style of conversation.[6]

Madison was more like a crafty lawyer, using arguments to achieve an end, than a philosopher drawing goals from an intellectual system. Even his most profoundly philosophical argument – the superiority of the extended republic – changed when the cause changed. Madison himself said he doubted that the problems could be solved by some "artificial structure and regular symmetry," by "an abstract view of the subject" or by a constitution, which "an ingenious theorist . . . planned in his closet in his imagination."[7] Madison indeed is so strong because he is so adaptable, so chameleon-like. More than other founders, Madison seems willing to shape an argument to fit the needs of the audience before him. Hamilton, Jefferson, Washington, and Adams were all men of principle, but they all seem far too proud to shape their arguments to persuade the middle. Madison commonly built his arguments on other people's premises. He was willing to stoop to conquer. Madison also commonly wrote for other speakers, using a more powerful speaker to make his arguments.[8] Indeed, the Virginia Plan was nominally offered to the

---

and deeply attached to France.... You need to study him at length to understand him properly"); ELKINS & MCKITRICK at 80 (1993) (saying Madison "would enter upon no question of policy or law without the most massive prior preparation, which meant that he would almost always know at least twice as much about it as anyone else present").

6 William Pierce, Character Sketches of Delegates (undated), *in* 3 FARRAND 94–95.

7 *Federalist* No. 37, at 238 (Madison) (Jan. 11, 1788) emphasized by Jack N. Rakove, Madison Theorizing at 5 (presented Nov. 13, 2000, The University of Texas).

8 ELKINS & MCKITRICK at 80 (1993) (saying that Madison functioned best under some kind of cover). One wonderful example of Madison's ghost writing is in the first session of the new Congress, where Madison charted the uncharted wilderness of protocol, by writing both the Address of the House of Representatives to the President (May 5, 1789), *in* 12 JM

Convention by Governor Randolph. Madison also commonly wrote under cover of pseudonyms, including most famously, the *Publius* of the *Federalist*. Tracing the roots of the Constitution back through Madison's thought is more rewarding than trying to find some sources in the debates in Congress or the states in the years before the Convention. Madison had served in the Continental Congress from 1780–1783 and had been a supporter of the nationalists, so he learned his nationalism in the Congress.[9] But the striking feature of the discussions in the last years of the Articles of Confederation, Jack Rakove has written, "is that they do not foreshadow the intensity, scope, and sophistication of the debates of 1787–88. . . . The search for specific antecedents of the Convention [in the Articles period] . . . proves disappointing."[10] It was Madison's work before the Convention, at first alone, that caused the Constitutional revolution.

A. THE IMBECILITY OF THE FEDERAL LEVEL

In the period before the Convention, Madison decided that all confederate systems of government, including that of the Articles of Confederation, would inevitably fail. The problem with all confederations was that the central or general-level government was too weak and the constituent states too strong and independent. The fault was the "state encroachments on the General authority."[11] The "radical infirmity" of the system created by the Articles of Confederation, he said, was the "dependence of congress" on the "voluntary and simultaneous compliance with its Requisitions" by

132 congratulating Washington on his election as "first Magistrate" and also the Reply of the President (May 8, 1789), *in* 12 JM 141–142, in which Washington replied by promising honest and ardent zeal.

9 Lance Banning, *James Madison and the Nationalists, 1780–1783,* 40 WM. & MARY Q. 227 (3d Series 1983), *republished as* LANCE BANNING, SACRED FIRE OF LIBERTY 43–75 (1995) argues that Madison was a consistent Virginia loyalist throughout his career including in the Confederation period. Banning's description of Madison's service in the Continental Congress, from 1780–1783, however, shows Madison as believing that Congress had surrendered too much power to the states and as supportive of Superintendent Robert Morris on all crucial questions of federal financing. Banning's description also shows Madison's enmity toward his fellow Virginians, Theodorick Bland and Arthur Lee, for their irresponsibility in undercutting the federal government. Except in Banning's summary, Madison appears to be properly categorized as a strong nationalist. JACK RAKOVE, BEGINNINGS 320–322 puts Madison as not a core nationalist in the 1783 impost proposal, by reason of concern that a federal internal tax would not be ratified, but supportive of the financing plan that was ultimately adopted.

10 RAKOVE, BEGINNINGS 387–388.

11 Madison to Jefferson (Oct. 24, 1787), *in* 10 JM 209.

so many independent states.[12] Madison convinced first himself and then an ever larger group that the United States needed not just a revision of the confederation, but an entirely new system.

Madison's thinking can be traced back, first, to two private memoranda, his *Notes on Contemporaneous and Ancient Confederacies*,[13] prepared in the spring of 1786 and then his *Vices of the Political Organization of the United States*,[14] prepared in the spring of 1787. Madison refined the arguments in the spring before the start of the Philadelphia convention in letters to his older Virginia mentors, George Washington,[15] Edmund Randolph,[16] Edmund Pendleton,[17] and Thomas Jefferson.[18] The ideas were then embodied in the Virginia Plan and Madison used the arguments in speeches to the Philadelphia Convention. He gave a thorough exposition of the mature arguments in a letter to Jefferson written soon after the Philadelphia Convention ended. Jefferson missed the convention, serving as the American ambassador in Paris, but Jefferson was an astute observer and Madison was very fond of him. The delegates had accepted a veil of secrecy over the convention's proceedings as they were going on, but when the proceedings were over Madison explained the whole Constitution to Jefferson for the first time.[19] Madison finally used the arguments in the *Federalist*, Numbers 18–20. With each reiteration of his argument, Madison became more confident about the inevitability of the failure of confederations.

Both the *Notes on Confederacies* and *Vices of the Political System* were private memoranda, written for Madison's own study and not to persuade anyone

---

[12] Madison, "Preface to the Constitution" (circa 1820s), *in* 3 FARRAND 539, 547.

[13] Madison, Notes on Contemporaneous and Ancient Confederacies (April–June, 1786), *in* 9 JM 3. The editors of the PAPERS OF JAMES MADISON place the writing of these notes in April–June, 1786, when Madison had an extended stay at home, although Madison's prior biographers put the studies in 1787 closer in time to the convention. Editorial Note, *id.*, at 22.

[14] Vices of the Political Organization of the United States (April 1787), *in* 9 JM 345.

[15] Madison to Washington (April 16, 1787), *in* 9 JM 382.

[16] Madison to Randolph (April 8, 1787), *in* 9 JM 369.

[17] Madison to Edmund Pendleton, (Feb. 24, 1787), *in* 9 JM 295 (saying that the prospect of fragmentation should rouse all "real friends of the Revolution to exert themselves . . . to perpetuate the Union and Redeem the Honor of the Republican name"); Madison to Pendleton (April 22, 1787), *in id.* at 394 (saying that the new Constitution would need ratification of the people and not just of the state legislatures, since the Constitution would encroach on state Constitutions). Pendleton had a long and distinguished public career in Virginia, including, for instance, his election as chair of the Virginia Ratification Convention. *See* Dennis J. Mahoney, *Edmund Pendleton*, 3 ENCY. OF THE AMER. CONST. 1373 (Leonard W. Levy, ed. 1986).

[18] Madison to Jefferson (Mar. 19, 1787), *in* 9 JM 368.

[19] Madison to Jefferson (Oct. 24, 1787), *in* 10 JM 205.

else. Madison, as Professor Rakove put it, "was trying to solve a set of problems for which he did not yet have answers. Theorizing was the prior private activity to which exercises in public persuasion would be the sequel."[20]
Madison's first self-study, *Notes on Ancient and Modern Confederacies*, was simply reading notes on the available treatises on ancient and contemporary
confederacies. Madison had given Jefferson an open commission to buy any
relevant books in Paris and ultimately Jefferson delivered more than two
trunks of "literary cargo."[21] Madison ended the discussion of each ancient and
modern confederation he looked at with a short discussion of the vices of their
constitutions. The Greek Amphyctionic League would never have yielded to
Philip of Macedonia and might even have proved a barrier to the expansion
of Rome, Madison concluded, had her confederation not been so loosely tied
together.[22] The Swiss confederation showed "proof of the want of authority in the whole over its parts,"[23] he said, and in the Germanic league, the
member states supplied their quotas of requisitions "very irregularly & de-
fectively."[24] Viewed retrospectively, Madison's conclusion that all confederations inevitably failed is contained in *Notes*, but the conclusion is fragmented
and scattered across his ending notes for each separate confederation.

In his second self-study, *Vices of the Political System of the United States*,
Madison applied his perception that confederations inevitably fail against
the American confederation. The first "vice" of the current system was the
"failure of the States to comply with the Constitutional requisitions:"[25]

> This evil has been so fully experienced both during the war and since
> the peace, results so naturally from the number and independent au-
> thority of the States and has been so uniformly examplified in every
> similar Confederacy, that it must be considered as not less radically and
> permanently inherent in, than it is fatal to the object of, the present
> System.[26]

A related "vice" was a mistaken confidence in "the justice, the good faith, the
honor, the sound policy," of the separate state legislatures.[27] The mistake was

[20] Jack N. Rakove, Madison Theorizing at 35 (presented Nov. 13, 2000, The University of Texas).
[21] Editorial Note, *in* 9 JM 3.
[22] 9 JM 6–7. Madison made the same argument in *Federalist* No. 18, at 113 (Madison) (Dec. 25, 1787).
[23] *Id.* at 11.
[24] Madison, *Notes on Confederacies, in* 9 JM 22.
[25] Vices of the Political Organization of the United States (April 1787), *in* 9 JM 348.
[26] *Id.*
[27] *Id.*, at 351.

in assuming that the states would pay their requisitions, that is, that the honor of the states would make it unnecessary to use any of the ordinary means "by which the laws secure the obedience of individuals."[28] The inevitable failure of requisitions was the hard fact behind the Constitution.

In letters to his Virginia mentors, Madison took another step and concluded that the state sovereignty, assumed under the Articles, must end. The difficulties of the coming convention, Madison told Jefferson, were "almost sufficient to dismay," but must be faced because of the "mortal diseases of the existing constitution."[29] The need was to "guard the national rights and interests against invasion" by the states.[30] Writing to George Washington and Edmund Randolph in the month before the convention, Madison explained that the "individual independence of the States is utterly irreconcilable with the idea of an aggregate sovereignty" so that he sought "a due supremacy of the national authority."[31] Madison viewed his supremacy of the national authority as a "middle ground" because he would "not exclude the local authorities wherever they can be subordinately useful" and because "a consolidation of the whole into one simple republic would be as inexpedient as it unattainable."[32]

Madison's Virginia colleagues thought that the coming convention could amend the existing confederation system, but not replace it. Washington told Madison barely two months before the Convention that many considered that "the only Constitutional mode by which the defects can be remedied" was the "revision of [confederal] system."[33] Governor Randolph told him that remedies would need to be "grafted upon the old confederation."[34] Madison was far more radical. He responded to Randolph that he thought it would be best to use the valuable parts of the old system in a new framework, rather than trying to engraft the new ideas onto the old framework. "Indeed my

[28] Id.
[29] Madison to Jefferson (Mar. 19, 1787), in 9 JM 318.
[30] Id.
[31] Madison to Randolph (April 8, 1787), in 9 JM 369. The language of Madison to Washington (April 16, 1787) in 9 JM 383 is similar.
[32] Madison to Washington (April 16, 1787), in 9 JM 383. See also prior draft of same idea in Madison to Randolph (April 8, 1787), in 9 JM 369.
[33] Washington to Madison (Mar. 31, 1787), in 9 JM 342. Washington for himself, however, wanted "that the Convention may adopt no temporizing expedient, but probe the defects of the Constitution to the bottom, and provide radical cures, whether they are agreed to or not. Id. at 344. See also Washington to Mason (Oct. 22, 1780), in 2 PGM 677, 678 (calling in 1780 for an entirely new plan in which Congress would have power "adequate to all the purposes of War").
[34] Randolph to Madison (Mar. 27, 1787), in 9 JM 335.

ideas of reform strike so deeply at the old Confederation," he said, "and lead to such a systematic change that they scarcely admit of an expedient."[35]

Madison also used his studies to show to the Philadelphia Convention that the confederation mode inevitably failed:

> It is evident, if we do not radically depart from a federal plan, we shall share the fate of ancient and modern confederacies. The amphyctionic council, like the American congress, had the power of judging in the last resort in war and peace – call out forces – send ambassadors. What was its fate or continuance? Philip of Macedon, with little difficulty, destroyed every appearance of it. The Athenian had nearly the same fate – The Helvetic confederacy is rather a league – In the German confederacy the parts are too strong for the whole – The Dutch are in a most wretched situation – weak in all its parts, and only supported by surrounding contending powers.[36]

"The Defects of the Amphictionick League were acknowledged," he said, "but they never cd. be reformed."[37]

When the convention was over and the Constitution had been written, Madison explained the design to Thomas Jefferson, who had missed it while in Paris. Madison generalized to say that the want of control by the general government "seems to have been mortal to the ancient Confederacies, and to be the disease of the modern."[38] The Amphyctionic League and the Achaean League had been "destroyed by the predominance of the local over the federal authority," and in the modern Netherlands and Germany, the common interest was "not sufficient to secure the authority and interests of the generality, agst. the antifederal tendency of the provincial sovereignties."[39] The general authority [must] be defended against encroachments by the subordinate authorities."[40] "Encroachments of the States on the general authority, sacrifices of national to local interests," he wrote, "form a great part of the history of our political system."[41]

---

[35] Madison to Randolph (April 8, 1787), *in* 9 JM 369.
[36] Madison, Federal Convention (June 19, 1787) *in* 1 FARRAND 326–327 (Yates' Notes);
[37] Madison, Federal Convention (June 29, 1787), *in* 1 FARRAND 478 (Yates' Notes); *see also* Madison, Federal Convention (June 28, 1787), *in* 1 FARRAND 448 (Madison's Notes) (finding rivalry among the members of ancient & modern confederacies); Wilson, Federal Convention (June 6, 1787), *in* 1 FARRAND 143 (Yates' Notes) (saying that in every confederation, the individual states encroached on and dissolved the general government).
[38] Madison to Jefferson (Oct. 24, 1787), *in* 10 JM 210.
[39] *Id.*
[40] *Id.*, at 209.
[41] *Id.*, at 210.

Finally, the lessons that Madison took from other confederacies showed up in Madison's contribution to *Federalist*, even more confidently stated. The central governments of those other confederations were often strong on paper, but weak in practice because, Madison claimed, the constituent bodies retained their independent sovereignty in the councils of the central government.[42] Independent sovereignty of the constituent bodies meant that the central government was weak and incapable of regulation of its own members, "insecure against external dangers: and agitated with unceasing fermentations in its own bowels."[43] The independent sovereignty led to "weakness, the disorders, and finally the destructions of the confederacy."[44]

Madison's calls for an end to the "individual independence of the States" and for "supremacy of the national authority"[45] were resisted by the Anti-Federalists who opposed the Constitution. "Is it not possible to strengthen the hands of Congress so far as to enable them to comply with all the exigencies of the union," one Anti-Federalist asked, "without devolving upon that body the supreme powers of government in all its branches?"[46] For Madison, however, defense of the national sphere against encroachment by the states required that the national government be supreme.

Hamilton had earlier said much the same things, quite well. In 1780 at the age of 23, Hamilton had written his delegate to Congress, urging that Congress needed the power to tax without the states. The fundamental defect in the Confederation, he had said, is "a want of power in Congress" and "a want of sufficient means at [Congress'] disposal to answer the public exigencies."[47] "The particular states show a jealousy of all power not in

---

[42] *See, e.g., Federalist* No. 18, at 111 (Madison) (Dec. 25, 1787) (saying that the Amphyctionic Confederation was different in effect than in theory because deputies, like the present Congress, were appointed and controlled wholly by the Greek city states, acting in their sovereign capacities); *Federalist* No. 19, at 117–123 (Madison) (Dec. 8, 1787) (same point as to Germanic Empire); *Federalist* No. 20, at 126 (Madison) (Dec. 11, 1787) (United Netherlands was strong on paper but imbecilic in practice, and suffered from precarious existence in peace and special calamities in war). In his *Notes on Confederacies*, 9 JM 16, Madison had said similarly that the Netherlands union on paper gave enough authority to the general government to preserve harmony, but the sovereignty of each province rendered the practice very different from the theory.

[43] *Federalist* No. 19, at 119 (Madison) (Dec. 8, 1787) (Germanic Empire).

[44] *Federalist* No. 18, at 111 (Madison) (Dec. 7, 1787) (Amphyctionic League). *See also Federalist* No. 19, 119–121 (Madison) (Dec. 8, 1787) (Germanic Empire).

[45] Madison to Washington (April 16, 1787), *in* 9 JM 383; Madison to Randolph (April 8, 1787), *in* 9 JM 369.

[46] The Impartial Examiner, Virginia Independent Chronicle (March 5, 1788) *reprinted in* 8 DHRC 463.

[47] Hamilton to James Duane (Sept. 3, 1780), *in* 2 PAH 400, 401.

their own hands," Hamilton wrote, "and this jealousy has led them to exercise a right of judging in the last resort of the measures recommended by Congress, and of acting according to their own opinions of their priority or necessity."[48] Hamilton's radical remedy, like Madison's, was to give the power of taxation to the federal government, because "without certain revenues, a government can have no power." "[T]hat power," Hamilton said, "which holds the purse strings absolutely, must rule."[49] Hamilton also argued that the states could not even be given sovereign control over their "internal police" without enfeebling the general government because there were "instances without number, where acts necessary for the general good... must interfere with internal police of the states, and [because] the particular states by arrangement of internal police can effectually though indirectly counteract the arrangements of Congress."[50] Both Hamilton and Madison had argued in the early 1780s that the Congress had an implied power to coerce the states into paying their requisitions by military actions against the defaulting states.[51] Hamilton's 1780 work was consistent with opinions within the Continental Army.[52] Washington, for instance, had called for an "entirely new plan" in 1780, under which powers must be lodged in Congress "adequate to all the purposes of War."[53]

However, Madison and not Hamilton set the agenda for the 1787 convention. While abuse of the army contributed to the magma chamber of anger against the states that erupted in 1787, neither Washington nor Hamilton nor the plight of the army convinced the polity to adopt any remedy in 1780. Hamilton played a useful role in Annapolis Convention that called for a new constitution,[54] but he was ineffectual at the Philadelphia Convetnion.

---

[48] Id., at 402–403.

[49] Hamilton to James Duane (Sept. 3, 1780), in 2 PAH 400, 404.

[50] Hamilton to James Duane (Sept. 3, 1780), in 2 PAH 400, 402.

[51] Id., at 401, 417; Madison to Jefferson (April 16, 1781), in 3 JM 71–72; Report on Restoring Public Credit (Mar. 6, 1783), in 6 JM 312–313.

[52] See, e.g., Rakove, Beginnings 294 (arguing that Hamilton's views in 1780 reflected the concerns of the Army but were not sensitive to the political difficulties that Congress faced).

[53] Washington to Mason (Oct. 22, 1780), in 2 PGM 678.

[54] Hamilton is apparently the real author of the Annapolis Convention Resolution that called for a convention in May 1787 to examine the defects of the Articles of Confederation and to make recommendations adequate to "the exigencies of the Union," although he was not on the committee of five that were the nominal authors. Editorial note to "Address of the Annapolis Convention," 3 PAH 686. That service is not trivial. Still the Convention rejected the important constraint of the Annapolis Address that the Constitution once framed would need to be confirmed by every state legislature (id. at 686; Chapter 3, pp. 78–80), and it is Madison's Virginia Plan and not Hamilton's plan that is the main line for the framing of the Constitution.

Hamilton's speech to the Convention outlining his grand plan of government was conventionally Montesquieu and followed the model of the British
"mixed" constitution, but it was a side track, not sufficiently republican or
democratic to be taken seriously by the delegates, and it bore no fruit.[55]
Hamilton was commonly "praised by every body," but "supported by none."[56]
Votes at the convention were cast by state, with the majority of the delegation
determining how the vote should be cast, and Hamilton was always outvoted
within his own delegation. The other New York delegates, Robert Lansing
and John Yates, were loyal to Governor George Clinton and for keeping the
New York harbor impost in state hands[57] and they were on the anti-nationalist
side on the issues. Lansing and Yates left the convention when it became
clear that the convention was going beyond mere revision of the Articles
of Confederation, leaving Hamilton without a delegation in which to vote.
Lansing and Yates proved to be a "clog on their Colleague," as Madison had
predicted.[58]

While Hamilton was isolated and ineffective at the convention, Madison
was effective. Madison was a superb strategist and politician, who never acted
alone. It was Madison's work within a political network that created the
Virginia Plan and hence the radical Constitution.

B. PROTECTION OF INDIVIDUALS AGAINST THE STATES

When Madison explained his grand design to Jefferson, the first subject was
that the new system was to protect the national sphere from the states, but
a second object of the new general government was to protect the rights of
individuals against the same irresponsible states.[59] Madison sought

---

[55] Hamilton, Federal Convention (June 18, 1787), *in* 1 FARRAND 283–292 (Madison's Notes).

[56] William Samuel Johnson, Federal Constitution (Lansing notes), *in* 1 FARRAND 363. *See*
MORRIS, at 275 (1987) (saying that Hamilton was a "man of immense talent" and centralizing
drive, but he did not live up to the high expectations of his friends at Philadelphia and, if
anything, seemed to confirm the worst suspicions of his foes).

[57] KAMINSKI, CLINTON 91, 94 (1993). *See also* Madison, Unsent letter to John Tyler (1833), *in*
3 FARRAND 530–531 (saying that Yates and Lansing were representatives of the dominant
party in New York, which was opposed to the Convention and had refused even to grant
a duty of 5 percent on imports for the urgent debt of the Revolution, so as to tax the
consumption of her neighbors).

[58] Madison to Washington (Mar. 18, 1787), *in* 9 JM 315. LINDA GRANT DePAUW, THE
ELEVENTH PILLAR: NEW YORK STATE AND THE FEDERAL CONSTITUTION 55–58 (1966)
discusses the politics of appointment of Hamilton, Lansing, and Yates.

[59] *See* Madison to Jefferson (Oct. 24, 1787), *in* 10 JM 209–212 for the two "encroachments."

not only to guard the national rights and interests against invasion, but also to restrain the States from thwarting and molesting each other, and even from oppressing the minority within themselves by paper money and other unrighteous projects.[60]

The first rights of individuals in Madison's vision were creditors' rights and the primary creditors were British and out-of-state creditors. The need to protect individuals from the irresponsible states applied, however, well beyond the core case of out-of-state creditors.

The Constitution, in many important respects, arose out of Madison's experience with Virginia politics of the 1780s.[61] Madison returned to the Virginia Assembly in 1784 after serving for the maximum allowable three years in the Continental Congress.[62] The Virginia House of Delegates, before Madison's return, was a "kaleidoscope" of temporary alliances among leaders with a personal following. Decisions were reached as much by personal influence or antipathy as by principle or ideas.[63] Madison created a political program that organized the Virginia assembly by interests by uniting two issues: the collection of Virginia taxes to satisfy federal requisitions and the opening of the Virginia courts to British creditors. Madison was opposed on both issues by a coalition led by Patrick Henry. In the legislative battles in Virginia in the 1780s, Patrick Henry almost always won and Madison almost always lost. Patrick Henry can be understood as the personification of the vices that the Constitution was written to correct. The Constitution can be understood, on one level, as Madison's revenge against Henry on the Virginia issues of the prior decade.

Patrick Henry was the governor of Virginia from 1784 to 1787 and a dominating force in the Assembly both before and after his governorship. "The Edicts of [Patrick Henry]," Washington wrote, are like royal edicts: "[Patrick Henry] has only to say let this be Law – it is Law."[64] Henry's presence seems to have made a difference. In 1783, Henry Tazewell had attempted to convince the Virginia House to adopt a resolution that taxation should be sufficient to meet the needs of government, and indeed the resolution passed at first by

---

[60] Madison to Jefferson (Mar. 19, 1787), *in* 9 JM 318.

[61] Risjord at 120–138 is most responsible for this thesis.

[62] Articles of Confederation, art V (providing that "no person shall be capable of being a delegate for more than three years in any term of six years").

[63] Risjord at 71–73, 81.

[64] George Washington to Madison (Nov. 17, 1788), *in* 1 Papers of GW: Presidential Series 115 (Dorothy Twohig, ed., 1987); Risjord at 81–88, finds it impossible to measure Patrick Henry's strength in 1782–1784, because he participated in only ten roll calls.

30 votes. Patrick Henry arrived late, but gave a rousing speech against the measure, whereupon 61 delegates reversed their decisions and defeated the resolution. By the end of the session, the House eased Virginia's taxes for the year by allowing the whole state to pay taxes in commodities.[65] Madison did not like Henry's oratory – Madison said late in life that Henry was "a man of debate only," and not a "man of business."[66] But Henry was famous as an orator – the "son of thunder"[67] and it apparently had effect.

Patrick Henry was also not fond of Madison. In 1789, Henry successfully prevented Madison from being appointed to represent Virginia in the first U.S. Senate under the new Constitution. In the debate in Virginia Assembly, Henry said that Madison was "unworthy of the confidence of the people" and that his "election to office would terminate in producing revulets of blood throughout the land."[68] Madison might have been a prime mover for the Constitution, but Anti-Federalists William Grayson and Richard Lee got Virginia's first Senate seats.

Madison's private letters in turn are filled with barbs or worries about Henry.[69] Jefferson was Madison's ally against Patrick Henry and they shared secrets. In 1784, Jefferson wrote to Madison that "while Henry lives, [a bad constitution] will be saddled with us. What we have to do I think is devoutly prey for this death."[70] Had Patrick Henry offered Thomas Jefferson the famous choice of "Give me Liberty or give me Death!"[71] Henry might not have liked Jefferson's answer.

Virginia in the 1780s readily voted to delay Virginia taxes or to allow them to be paid in commodities, at the expense of Virginia's payment of its quota of federal requisitions. "Mr. Henry arrived yesterday," John Marshall

---

[65] RISJORD at 102. *See also id.* at 97–98 (describing 1780 episode in which Virginia Assembly could ratify devaluation of the Continental dollar only after Henry departed).

[66] KETCHAM 160. Patrick Henry also set up James Monroe to oppose Madison in what turned out to be a hard fought election in February 1789 to the House of Representatives. RUTLAND 43, 46–48.

[67] HENRY MAYER, A SON OF THUNDER : PATRICK HENRY AND THE AMERICAN REPUBLIC (1986).

[68] KETCHAM 275 (1971).

[69] *See, e.g.,* Madison to Jefferson (Mar. 19, 1787), *in* 9 JM 319 (saying that "Mr. Henry's disgust exceeded all measure and I am not singular in ascribing his refusal to attend the Convention to the policy of keeping himself free to combat or espouse the result of it according to the result of the Mississippi business"); Madison to Jefferson (June 6, 1787), *in* 10 JM 30 (saying the "appetite for paper money grows every day. Mr. Henry is an avowed patron of the scheme. . . . He is also said to be unfriendly to an acceleration of Justice. There is good reason to believe that he is hostile to the object of this convention").

[70] Jefferson to Madison (Dec. 8, 1784), *in* 7 PTJ 557, 558.

[71] Patrick Henry, Virginia Assembly (Mar. 23, 1775), http://www.yale.edu/lawweb/avalon/ patrick.htm (accessed Jan. 3, 2002).

told Monroe, "and appears as usual to be charged with the postponement of the collection of taxes."[72] Tax deferral benefited every planter in the state. Only a tiny band of Madison's allies saw any reason to complain and they were committed, not by self-interest but by ideology, to payment of the requisitions.[73] In fall of 1781, the House allowed residents of western counties to pay their taxes in tobacco, flour, or hemp. In spring of 1782, the House adopted a Patrick-Henry–sponsored bill to delay all taxes until December of 1782, and added deerskin to tobacco, flour, and hemp as the commodities that could be used to satisfy taxes.[74] In 1783, Henry convinced the House to allow the whole state to pay taxes with commodities.[75] In 1784, when Madison first returned to Virginia, Madison managed to convince the House not to postpone 1784 taxes.[76] In 1785, the House voted down a proposal supported by Henry to abolish all of Virginia's taxes for 1785, but by only the margin of 48–50.[77] In 1786, however, the House adopted a Patrick-Henry–sponsored proposal for a tax holiday for the 1786 taxes. The harvests were bountiful in 1786, and times were prosperous.[78] Madison opposed the tax holiday, but Henry prevailed.[79] In November 1787, the Virginia Assembly passed a bill permitting taxes to be paid in tobacco. Even Anti-Federalist George Mason considered payment in commodities a "foolish and injurious project," but the Virginia Assembly passed the bill by the ample margin of 88–27.[80] Virginia taxes, moreover, could be paid throughout the period by buying government interest indebtedness called "indents" at discounted market value as low as twenty cents on the dollar, and then trading the indents in for a full dollar of credit in payment of taxes.[81] Madison wanted to stop indents for taxes, but his proposal had too little support and was withdrawn.[82]

Madison and Henry also clashed on the issue of access by British creditors to Virginia courts, with Patrick Henry successfully blocking access. Before the Revolutionary War, the Virginia planters were perpetually in debt to

---

[72] John Marshall to James Monroe (May 15, 1784) *in* 1 PAPERS OF JOHN MARSHALL 123 (Herbert Johnson, ed., 1974).

[73] RISJORD at 103.

[74] *Id.*, at 102.

[75] *Id.*

[76] *Id.* at 149.

[77] *Id.* at 175–176.

[78] RISJORD at 156 (finding economic prosperity in Virginia with state tax receipts increasing by 15% between 1785–1786 and 1786–1787).

[79] 1 BRANT, THE NATIONALISTS at 358.

[80] RISJORD at 179, quoting Mason to Washington (Nov. 27, 1787), *in* 3 PGM 1019, 1021.

[81] FERGUSON 270 (citing the price of Virginia indents at 20–30 cents on the dollar in 1789).

[82] Madison to James Madison, Sr. (Nov. 16, 1786) in 9 JM 169.

British merchants. The planters borrowed to fund purchases of new land, as their old fields played out. They borrowed to buy slaves, to pay planting expenses, and to buy the goods to meet the accustomed standard of living of a planter household. Charles Beard has argued that avoiding British debt was a "powerful cause" for the Revolutionary War,[83] but the planters themselves would have denied it. "British Ministers and Tories have constantly accused us of engaging in the War to avoid Payment of our debts," George Mason said, "but every honest Man has denied so injurious a charge with indignity."[84] Madison's allies presumed that only a heretic like Patrick Henry could take the position that "wars between . . . nations [should] cancel every contract betwixt their citizens."[85] Patrick Henry was said to stand for the heretical position that "if we are now to pay the Debts due to British merchants, what have we been fighting for all this while?"[86] A gentleman paid his debts. Thomas Nelson, the Governor of Virginia in 1781, declared publicly, "By God, I will pay my debts like an honest man."[87]

Notwithstanding the indignation, payments on British debts effectively stopped when the fighting started in 1774.[88] Virginia attempted to "sequester" or confiscate debts owed to British merchants during the Revolutionary War as a means of financing the war effort.[89] In 1781, Virginia had formally adopted a moratorium on payment of both foreign and domestic debts.[90] In Virginia, collection of British debts was prohibited as a matter of law, but even in states like Maryland where collection was formally allowed, collection was hard. Counsel faced the implicit threat of violence when representing British creditors in court.[91]

The Treaty of Paris that ended the Revolutionary War required that the British creditors "shall meet with no lawful impediment to the recovery of the full value in sterling money of all bona fide debts."[92] If Virginians had received

[83] CHARLES BEARD, ECONOMIC ORIGINS OF JEFFERSONIAN DEMOCRACY at 270 (1915).

[84] Mason to Patrick Henry (May 6, 1783), *in* 2 PGM 771.

[85] Emory G. Evans, *Private Indebtedness and the Revolution in Virginia, 1776 to 1796*, 28 WM. & MARY Q. 349, 363 (3rd. Ser. 1971).

[86] Mason to Patrick Henry (May 6, 1783), *in* 2 PGM 171.

[87] Quoted in Emory G. Evans, *The Rise and Decline of the Virginia Aristocracy in the Eighteenth Century: The Nelsons, in* THE OLD DOMINION: ESSAYS FOR THOMAS PERKINS ABERNATHY 77 (Darrett B. Ruttman, ed. 1964).

[88] Evans, *supra* note 85 at 351.

[89] *Id.* at 354–356.

[90] RISJORD at 111.

[91] EDWARD C. PAPENFUSE, PURSUIT OF PROFIT: THE ANNAPOLIS MERCHANTS IN THE ERAS OF AMERICAN REVOLUTION, 1763–1805, at 170 (1975).

[92] The Paris Peace Treaty of September 3, 1783, Art. IV in http://www.yale.edu/lawweb/avalon/diplomacy/paris.htm (accessed May 30, 2001).

the furniture, they were supposed to pay for it, notwithstanding the war. The treaty, however, was wildly violated by the states. "If you tell the Legislatures they have violated the treaty of peace and invaded the prerogatives of the confederacy," George Washington wrote to John Jay in 1786, "they will laugh in your face."[93] In October 1786, John Jay gave the Congress a lengthy report detailing that many states had violated the treaty, and dismissed the defenses offered for the violations.[94] Congress responded by calling upon the states to repeal their impediments to collection and comply with the treaty of peace.[95]

Madison made a number of efforts in the 1780s to require Virginia to open its courts to British creditors in compliance with the Treaty of Paris. All failed.[96] In June 1784, Madison proposed to the Virginia Assembly that all acts of Virginia that prevented compliance with the treaty be repealed, but he lost by 37–57.[97] In December, Madison came back with a compromise under which Virginia courts would be open to British creditors, but also that payments on all outstanding debts would be stretched over seven years, without the consent of the creditor. The "compromise" passed both houses with small variations in the language. The bill was expected to pass, after reconciliation between the two versions. On the freezing night of January 5, 1785, however, the James River became blocked with ice, preventing delegates staying across the river from returning to Richmond to make a quorum for the final vote. Even the Virginia Courts could not determine whether the bill was effective so that the Virginia courts were open to British debts.[98] There were also serious attempts later in 1785 and again in 1787 to reopen the courts to British creditors; both attempts failed.[99] "The repeated disappointments I have sustained in efforts in favor of the Treaty," Madison wrote to Jefferson, "make me extremely averse to take the lead in the business again."[100]

British creditors would be denied real access to the Virginia courts for more than another decade. The denial of access in violation of the Treaty of Paris was a major irritant to the British.[101] Finally, in the Jay Treaty of 1796, the federal government agreed to pay the British creditors their just debt from federal funds, as determined by arbitration, out of despair that it

---

93 Washington to Jay (Aug. 15, 1786), *in* 4 PGW:CS 213.
94 Jay, Report of the Office of Foreign Affairs, Oct. 13, 1786, 13 JCC 781–874.
95 Madison, Notes on Debates in Continental Congress (March 21, 1787), *in* 9 JM 326–327.
96 *See* Evans, *supra* note 85, at 363–366; RISJORD at 109–116, 137–138, 150–151.
97 Evans, *supra* note 85, at 363; RISJORD at 114.
98 Evans, *supra* note 85, at 364–365. RISJORD at 114–115.
99 Evans, *supra* note 85, at 367.
100 Madison to Jefferson (Dec 4, 1786) *in* 9 JM 191.
101 ELKINS & MCKITRICK at 247, 252.

was possible to get collection of the debts enforced in Virginia and the other states.[102] In 1796, the United States Supreme Court held that the Treaty of Paris was paramount over Virginia law, that the treaty required the Virginia planters to pay their British creditors, and that Virginia wartime confiscation of the debts was invalid. That decision finally opened the Virginia courts to British creditors by 1797.[103]

Madison and his allies viewed Virginia's breach of the Treaty of Paris as a danger to public safety. The British might plausibly send a frigate or two in reprisals against Virginia trade.[104] The impediments to payment of British debt also stood in the way of attracting further British capital to Virginia, and Virginia planters were always desperately in need of loans.[105] State violation of the Treaty of Paris was among the reasons proponents cited for ratification of the Constitution. The Articles were a failure, James Iredell told North Carolina, because Congress had power to enter into negotiations with foreign nations, "but cannot compel the observance of treaties that they make."[106]

Professor Norman Risjord has argued that it was the association of the issue of payment of British creditors with the issue of the payment of the public war debts that organized Virginia politics into parties according to issues and principles, instead of personalities.[107] Risjord traces the earliest connection of public and private debts to a resolution drafted by James Iredell and adopted at a citizens' meeting in Edenton, North Carolina, in August 1783.[108] Laws

---

[102] CHARLES R. RITCHESON, AFTERMATH OF REVOLUTION: BRITISH POLICY TOWARD THE UNITED STATES, 1783–1795, at 334–338 (1969); JULIUS GOEBEL, HISTORY OF THE SUPREME COURT: ANTECEDENTS AND BEGINNINGS TO 1801, at 748–756 (1971).

[103] Ware v. Hylton, 3 U.S. (Dall.) 199 (1796). See JULIUS GOEBEL, supra note 102, at 748–756 (1971); Evans, supra note 85, at 372–373 (saying that British creditors began winning the federal court cases by 1794, but not the Virginia court cases until 1797).

[104] Mason to Henry Tazewell (May 6, 1783), in 2 PGM 774.

[105] See, e.g., RISJORD at 135–136 arguing that Madison opposed Henry's closing of Virginia courts to British suits because it would hamper the flow of foreign credit.

[106] James Iredell, North Carolina Convention (July 28, 1788), in 4 ELLIOT 146: See also Wilson, Pennsylvania Convention (Nov. 26, 1787), in 2 ELLIOT 431 (saying that "[d]evoid of national dignity, we could not, . . . perform our treaties, [nor] obtain nor compel the performance of them, on the part of others); Federalist No. 3, at 15–6 (Jay) (Nov. 3, 1787) (espousing the Constitution because the federal government will keep the peace by obeying treaties whereas the states have breached the British treaty).

[107] RISJORD at 126.

[108] Edenton Resolutions, reprinted in GRIFFITH McREE, LIFE AND CORRESPONDENCE OF JAMES IREDELL: ONE OF THE ASSOCIATE JUSTICES OF THE SUPREME COURT OF THE UNITED STATES 60, 62, 63, 64 (1857) (saying that it was "indispensably necessary that the requisition of Congress should be complied with for the payment of the public debts," that no more paper money be issued, and that suspension of suits enforcing payment of debt should end); see also RISJORD at 121 (quoting a December 1783 resolution from Shenandoah Valley demanding compliance with requisitions, opposing any further tax postponements, and

inhibiting payment of British debts, one resolution said, were "inconsistent with those principles of honesty and patriotism which we have uniformly avowed."[109] The connection of taxes and court access, Risjord says, was "the germ of a [coherent] political platform."[110]

Madison and Henry also clashed on debtor relief that was not expressly limited to British creditors. In late 1786, Henry sponsored a bill stretching all debts out over three years without creditor consent, "installing all debts now due, so as to make them payable in 3 annual portions."[111] Madison fought it, at least to try to require a tolling of the statute of limitations and to require that debtors post security.[112] Madison succeeded in requiring the consent of creditors, which destroyed the point of Henry's bill, and the installment of debts was later dropped in the Virginia legislature in favor of an act just to stay execution of the debts.[113]

To the extent that creditors were citizens of other states, anti-creditor measures were also considered by the nationalists to be aggressions by one state against its neighboring states. The Articles of Confederation prohibited a state from imposing duties or restrictions on a person from another state that it did not impose on its own inhabitants,[114] and even beyond the Articles, the principle of nondiscrimination against out-of-state Americans was strong.[115] Debtor relief violated that principle. In his *Vices of the Political System*, Madison concluded that the "emissions of paper money and kindred measures" were "trespasses" by the states upon each other, that is, "aggressions" by states whose citizens were debtors overall on states whose citizens were not creditors.[116] A Constitution without power over state debtor legislation, Madison told the Philadelphia Convention, would leave the states "as much at liberty as ever to execute their unrighteous projects agst. each other."[117] Violation of creditor's rights violated the respect that the states owed to each other.

declaring that any person who "obstructed the Treaty in America ought be considered as an enemy to his country").

[109] *Id.* at 125, quoting Resolution of Botetourt County, in Maryland Journal [Baltimore] (Nov. 23, 1784).

[110] *Id.* at 120.

[111] Madison to Washington (Dec. 7, 1786), *in* 8 JM 200.

[112] 1 Brant, The Nationalists at 358–359 (1948).

[113] *Editorial Note 4, in* 10 JM 246.

[114] Articles of Confederation, art. IV.

[115] *See, e.g., Federalist* No. 22, at 137 (Hamilton) (Dec. 14, 1787) (saying that the genius of the people of this country would not permit tolls on interstate commerce unless the United States were to break up).

[116] Vices of the Political System of the United States (April 1787), *in* 9 JM 349.

[117] Madison, Federal Convention (June 19, 1787), *in* 1 Farrand 318.

Madison was also outraged at the violation of morality inherent in debtor relief. "Defaulting debtors," as Gordon Wood well puts it, "were still thought to be more than unfortunate victims of bad times: they were moral failures, violators of a code of trust and friendship who deserved to be punished and imprisoned."[118] The greatest threat to liberty, Madison told the Virginia Ratification Convention, came from the "majority trampling on the rights of the minority."[119] In his *Vices of the Political System*, Madison listed as examples of vice, "paper money, installments of debts, occlusion of Courts, making property a legal tender."[120] In *Federalist* Number 10, he described the disease as "a rage for paper money, for an abolition of debts... or for any other improper or wicked project."[121] In *Federalist* Number 44, he said

> The loss which America has sustained since the peace, from the pestilent effects of paper money, on the necessary confidence between man and man[,]... on the industry and morals of the people, and on the character of Republican Government, constitutes an enormous debt against the States chargeable with this unadvised measure... which can be expiated no otherwise than by a voluntary sacrifice on the altar of justice, of the power [to issue paper money].[122]

At the Philadelphia Convention, Madison argued that one needed to consider the evils "which prevail within the States individually as well as those which affect them collectively" because both vitiate the political system of the United States,[123] and he criticized the plan offered by Patterson of New Jersey because it "contained no remedy for this dreadful class of evils."[124]

The states' legislative attacks on creditor rights had much in common with the failure of requisitions. In both, irresponsible states prevented payment

<hr>

[118] Gordon S. Wood, *Interests and Disinterested in the Making of the Constitution, in* BEYOND CONFEDERATION 106–107.
[119] Madison, Virginia Convention (June 6, 1788), *in* 11 JM 79.
[120] Madison, Vices of the Political System of the United States (April 1787), *in* 9 JM 349. Madison listed the vices of paper money, installments of debts, occlusion of the Courts, making property a legal tender as "tresspasses of the States on the rights of each other" in his April memorandum on vices, but by the October 24, 1787 explanation to Jefferson, issuance of paper money was a state encroachment upon the rights of individuals. The latter expression is an improvement because although creditors were often out of state or even out of country, they were not always states.
[121] *Federalist* No. 10, at 65 (Madison) (Nov. 23, 1787). In the original passage, omitted from the quoted portion, is "equal division of property," which Madison was also against. *See also* Madison to Randolph (April 8, 1787), *in* 9 JM 370 (saying that there has been no moment since the peace at which the federal assent would have been given to paper money).
[122] *Federalist* No. 44, at 300 (Madison) (Jan. 23, 1788).
[123] Madison, Federal Convention (June 19, 1787), *in* 1 FARRAND 318.
[124] *Id.*, at 319.

to legitimate creditors. Debtor relief was a "wicked"[125] and "serious evil."[126] Paper money destroyed the "confidence of man to man"[127] and "vitiat[ed] morals."[128] Paper money, like failure to pay Continental debts, "disgrace[d] Republican Govts in the eyes of mankind."[129] The injustice had been "so frequent and so flagrant as to alarm the most stedfast friends of Republicanism."[130] Failure of requisitions – like anti-creditor legislation – meant that debts were not paid and that creditors lost. Both "excite the disgusts agst the state governments."[131] Rhode Island was that "little detestable corner of the Continent" not only because of its behavior on the impost, but also because its paper money "so sacrilegiously violated" the "solemnity of contracts."[132] Both the failure of requisitions and the debtor relief were to be cured by a strong national government. "A reform therefore which does not make provision for private rights, must be materially defective."[133]

The payment of debts was viewed as a matter of honor, morality, and protection of the rights of creditors against the action of the majority, but payment of debts would also benefit the debtors in the long run. In the short term, payment of creditors was contrary to the interests of Madison and his Virginia planter class, just because payment represented a transfer of money from the planters to the British and out-of-state creditors. In the longer term, however, paying debts maintained the planter's creditworthiness and made it possible for desperately needed capital to return to Virginia. Stiffing creditors had certain short-term benefits, but also long-term detriments.

Madison's language on the need to prevent the trampling of individual rights covered not just the rights of creditors, but also the rights of religious minorities. Virginia imprisoned Baptists ministers because they preached outside of the aegis of the established Anglican church. Madison hated

---

[125] *Federalist* No. 10, at 65 (Madison) (Nov. 23, 1787).
[126] Madison to Jefferson (Oct. 24, 1787), *in* 10 JM 212.
[127] Madison, Notes for a Speech for the Virginia Assembly Opposing Paper Money (ca. Nov. 1, 1786), *in* 9 JM 158.
[128] *Id.*, at 159.
[129] *Id.*
[130] Madison to Jefferson (Oct. 24, 1787), *in* 10 JM 212. *See also* Randolph, Virginia Convention (June 17, 1788), *in* 3 ELLIOTT 478 (saying that "frequent interference by legislature with private contracts" produced calamities which have befallen our reputation as a people but that the corner stone of republicanism was in fact justice and honor).
[131] Madison to Jefferson (Sept. 6, 1787), *in* 10 JM 164.
[132] "America" (Noah Webster), NEW YORK DAILY ADVERTISER (Dec. 31, 1787), *reprinted in* 15 DHRC 201.
[133] Madison to Jefferson (Oct. 24, 1787), *in* 10 JM 212.

that.[134] Patrick Henry had championed a tax assessment in the Virginia leg-islature in 1784–1785 to support teachers of the Christian religion. The assessment would have supported not just the Episcopal Church, which had been Virginia's tax-supported church before 1779, but also the other de-nominations. The non-Episcopalian denominations eventually opposed the assessment. Madison, in alliance with the Presbyterians and Baptists, defeated the proposals but only with a grass roots campaign, sponsoring newspaper items and petitions to the legislature. Risjord describes Madison's efforts as reaching a "new level of sophistication in the art of political combat."[135] In his campaign against the assessment, Madison had written a pamphlet, *Memorial and Remonstrance Against Religious Assessments*, saying that in a true republic issues on which the society divides must be decided by the will of the majority, "but it is also true that the majority may trespass on the rights of the minority."[136] The church taxes were a perfect example to Madison of the state's inevitable encroachments upon the rights of the minorities, at their core just like the debtor-relief legislation.

Madison commonly wrote in grand abstractions and fundamental prin-ciples. What the debaters knew, however, which their abstractions do not relate, is that the abstractions arose out of the context of specific issues and recent events. Madison did not retell those recent events in his public debate or letters. He and his correspondents had a tendency to say, for example "a rage for paper money, for an abolition of debts . . . or for any other improper or wicked projects"[137] as if the details of the failure of the Continental dollar and the recent wicked projects were too well known to bear repeating. For Madison, the "wicked projects" would have included tax holidays, payment of tax in commodities, closing of the courts to out-of-state creditors, and tax assessments in favor of ministers. The specific issues from the context that drove Madison were the issues that Henry and Madison had fought over in the 1780s in Virginia.

---

[134] *See*, Editorial Note, 1 JM 107 n. 8 (half dozen Baptists ministers imprisoned in Virginia in 1773–1774 to Madison's consternation).

[135] RISJORD at 203–210. For another description, *see* Douglas Laycock, *Nonpreferential Aid to Religion: A False Claim About Original Intent*, 27 WM. & MARY L. REV. 875, 895–899 (1986).

[136] Madison, Memorial and Remonstrance Against Religious Assessments (ca. June 20, 1785), *in* 8 JM 298, 299.

[137] *Federalist* No. 10, at 65 (Madison) (Nov. 23, 1787).

CHAPTER THREE

The Superiority of the Extended Republic

A. MADISON'S GRAND THEORY

In preparation for the convention, Madison abstracted beyond the immediate events and his comparative studies to conclude that the general-level government – the extended republic – would inevitably be superior to state governments, as a matter of fundamental philosophy. The theory of the superiority of the extended sphere was developed first in his *Vices of the Political System*; was continued in letters to Washington, Randolph, and especially Jefferson, and in the Philadelphia Convention; and then was published in the famous *Federalist* Number 10.

Madison sought to "prove in contradiction to the concurrent opinions of theoretical writers," that the republican form of government must operate not within a small but within an extensive sphere.[1] In Madison's vision, republican passions and selfish interests within the smaller states had trampled the general or national welfare and individual rights. Diversification of interests, found only in an extended republic, would moderate the effect of passions and selfish interests. In any representative democracy, Madison argued, the elected officials properly represent the passions and the selfish interests of people. The interests of people are diverse:

> Those who contend for a simple Democracy ... operating within narrow limits, assume or suppose a case which is altogether fictitious. They found their reasoning on the idea, that the people composing the Society, enjoy not only an equality of political rights; but that they have all precisely the same interests, and the same feelings in every respect. Were this in reality the case, their reasoning would be conclusive. The interest of the majority would be that of the minority also, the decision

[1] Madison to Jefferson (Oct. 24, 1787), *in* 10 JM 212.

could only turn on mere opinion concerning the good of the whole. We know however that no Society ever did or can consist of so homogeneous a mass of Citizens, . . . In all civilized Societies, distinctions are various and unavoidable.[2]

People inevitably vary in interests. It would destroy liberty to suppress the diversity of those interests. Suppression of the inevitable diversity of interests would be a tyranny much worse than the disease of diverse interests.[3]

Given the diversity of interests, however, elected officials in a republic will inevitably organize into parties or factions at conflict with each other. The principle of a republican government is that the majority rules. The faction with a majority will vote according to its selfish interests or passions that it represents and in a republic, that majority will win the legislation. The majority faction will inevitably disregard the public good and decide legislation, "not according to rules of justice, and the rights of the minor party, but by the superior force of an interested and over-bearing majority."[4] "If two individuals are under the biass of interest or enmity agst. a third, the rights of the latter could never be safely referred to the majority of the three."[5] "The lesson we are to draw from the whole," Madison told the Convention, "is that where a majority are united by a common sentiment, and have an opportunity, the rights of the minor party become insecure."[6]

The inevitable evils of factions and passions could be moderated, Madison believed, when the sphere of a republican government was extended. People would still always have diverse interests and passions and republican representatives would mirror those interests.[7] As the sphere was enlarged, however, it would grow harder to organize a faction that would suppress minority interests. "Extend the sphere, and you take in a greater variety of parties and interests; you make it less probable that a majority of the whole will have a common motive to invade the rights of other citizens."[8] "In a large Society," Madison explained to Jefferson, "the people are broken into so many interests and parties, that a common sentiment is less likely to be felt, and the

---

[2] *Id.*, at 212–13.
[3] *Federalist* No. 10, at 58 (Madison) (Nov. 22, 1787).
[4] *Federalist* No. 10, at 57 (Madison) (Nov. 22, 1787).
[5] Madison to Jefferson (Oct. 24, 1787), *in* 10 JM 213.
[6] Madison, Federal Convention (June 6, 1787), *in* 1 FARRAND 136.
[7] *See, e.g.*, Madison, Vices of the Political System of the United States (April 1787), *in* 9 JM 356–357 (saying that enlargement of the sphere will lessen the insecurity of private rights, not because the impulse of common interest predominates, but because the common interest is less apt to fall prey to a faction because majority factions are harder to form in larger spheres).
[8] *Federalist* No. 10, at 64 (Madison) (Nov. 23, 1787).

requisite concert less likely to be formed by a majority of the whole . . . Divide et impera, [divide and rule], the reprobated axiom of tyranny, is under certain qualifications, the only policy, by which a republic can be administered on just principles."[9] "Ambition must be made to counteract ambition," Madison said in *Federalist* Number 51.[10] "[P]rivate rights will be more secure under the Guardianship of the General Government than under the State Governments," he said.[11] Under Madison's vision, the national government must function as guardian of the rights of individuals as against the states because the national government was an extended republic. Madison's argument for the superiority of the diversified extended republic was "a republican remedy to the diseases most incident to republican government."[12]

Madison knew specific cases in which, within small states, overbearing majorities had hurt individual rights:

> It can be little doubted, that if the state of Rhode Island was separated from the confederacy, and left to itself, the insecurity of rights under the popular form of government within such narrow limits, would be displayed by such reiterated oppressions of factious majorities, that some [form of government other than a republic] would soon be called for by the voice of the very factions whose misrule had proved the necessity of it.[13]

Virginia under Patrick Henry was another, quite sufficient, example of a state controlled by a passionate or interested faction. Under Madison's philosophy, the behavior of the Virginia Assembly under Patrick Henry was an inevitable product of the republican principle, working within too small a sphere. Patrick Henry's vices were what the Constitution was written to control.

The theory of *Federalist* Number 10 also makes sense as a generalization from diversification of religions. In *Federalist* Number 51, Madison tied religious rights into his theory of diversification, saying that "in a free government the security for civil rights must be the same as that for religious rights. It consists in the one case in the multiplicity of interests, and in the other in the multiplicity of sects."[14] Madison opposed Patrick Henry's proposal in

---

[9] Madison to Jefferson (Oct. 24, 1787), *in* 10 JM 214.

[10] *Federalist* No. 51, at 349 (Madison) (Feb. 8, 1788).

[11] Madison to Jefferson (Oct. 24, 1787), *in* 10 JM 212.

[12] Martin Diamond, *Democracy and the* Federalist, *in* CONFEDERATION AND THE CONSTITUTION: THE CRITICAL ISSUES 137 (Gordon Wood, ed. 1973).

[13] *Federalist* No. 51, at 352 (Madison) (Feb. 6, 1788).

[14] *Federalist* No. 51, at 351–2 (Madison) (Feb. 6, 1788). *See also* Madison to Jefferson (Oct. 24, 1787), *in* 10 JM 214 (arguing that the diversity of the extended sphere applies to both religious and civil rights).

1785 to tax for religious education, saying it was an instance in which "the majority may trespass on the rights of the minority."[15] If the Episcopal majority in Virginia abused the rights of minority Baptists,[16] the majority Baptists in Rhode Island could be expected to abuse a Quaker minority of Rhode Island.[17] Then too, a Quaker majority in Pennsylvania could be expected to abuse a Presbyterian minority in Pennsylvania, and the Presbyterians would abuse right back when they had voting control.[18] On the national level, however, neither Episcopal, Quaker, or Baptist would have a majority and the diversity of religions would allow an individual freedom of conscience. A particular state, Madison would tell Virginia, "might concur in one religious project. But the United States as a whole abounds in such a variety of sects" that there "cannot be a majority of any one sect to oppress and persecute the rest."[19] Madison is said to have been fond of Voltaire's quip that if only one sect were allowed, "despotism might be apprehended; if two only, they would seek to cut each other's throats; but as there are at least thirty, they live together in peace and happiness."[20]

Within the constitutional debates, Madison's extended-republic argument served to neutralize Montesquieu and the other "greatest and wisest men who have ever thought or wrote on the science of government."[21] The Constitution proposed a complete continental-level government, supreme over the states, and the Anti-Federalists opposed the shift in power, arguing that the state, legislatures should make the decisions because they were more

---

15 Madison, Memorial and Remonstrance Against Religious Assessments (ca. June 20, 1785), *in* 8 JM 298, 299.

16 JOHN MARTIN DAWSON, BAPTISTS AND THE AMERICAN REPUBLIC 90 (1956) (describing a wave of mobbings and jailings of Baptists on the eve of the Revolution); Editorial Note, 1 JM 107 n. 8 (saying a half dozen Baptists ministers were imprisoned in Virginia in 1773–1774).

17 Carla Gardina Pestana, *The Quaker Executions as Myth and History*, 80 J. OF AM. HIST. 441, 454. (1993) (describing that Rhode Island Quakers' used seventeenth century executions in their justifying histories of themselves).

18 *See* O. S. Ireland, *The Crux of Politics: Religion and Party in Pennsylvania, 1778–1789*, 42 WM. & MARY Q. 455–456 (3rd. Ser., 1985) (dominant ingredient in the acrimonious relations between Constitutionalists and Republicans was religion) and discussion, *infra* chapter 6, pp. 141–42.

19 Madison, Virginia Convention (June 12, 1787), *in* 3 ELLIOT 330–331. Patrick Henry's response was that Madison's arguments were grounded only on the powers of reason, but that there "is many a religious man who knows nothing of argumentative reasoning" and that this "sacred right ought not to depend on constructive logical reasoning." *Id.* at 317.

20 IRVING BRANT, JAMES MADISON: THE VIRGINIA REVOLUTIONIST 68 (1941). *See also* Paul F. Boller, *George Washington and Religious Liberty*, 17 WM. & MARY Q. 486 (1960) (arguing that Washington's deism made him tolerant of dissenting religions and that Washington worried about disruption caused by religious strife).

21 Brutus I, NEW YORK JOURNAL. (Oct. 18, 1787), *reprinted in* 13 DHRC 417.

"immediate representa[tives]" of the people.[22] The Congress was too distant to be trusted, they said.[23] The Anti-Federalists cited Montesquieu as proving that the republican form of government was possible only in a small territory, where all members joined together in common interest.[24] Only in a small republic was it possible to foster the self-sacrificing devotion to the public interest that was essential to the republican form. History proved, Anti-Federalist "Brutus" argued, that whenever small republics "extended their conquests over larger territories," their governments became "the most tyrannical that ever existed in the world."[25] The United States was too extensive to be governed except by a despotic monarchy, argued Anti-Federalist James Monroe.[26] Under Montesquieu's theory, republican states might form leagues or alliances to defend themselves against the exterior enemies, but not for internal governance. A federal-level government, under a Montesquieuian system, was formed for the limited purpose of defending the whole against external enemies. "If a republic be small, it is destroyed by a foreign force; if it be large, it is ruined by internal imperfections."[27] Madison's argument in *Federalist* Number 10 repudiated Montesquieu, however, and

---

[22] A Virginia Planter, WINCHESTER VA. GAZETTE (Mar. 7, 1788), *reprinted in* 8 DHRC 469, 470–71. *See also* Federal Farmer, *Letters to the Republican* IX (Jan. 4, 1788), *reprinted in* 17 DHRC 288, 295 (arguing that "in the state legislatures the body of the people will be genuinely represented, and in congress not"); A Georgian, *Letter to the Editor*, GAZETTE OF THE STATE OF GEORGIA (Nov. 15, 1787), *reprinted in* 3 DHRC 236, 240 ("[O]ur own legislature is the only body politic to whose management it can be trusted").

[23] John Tyler, Virginia Convention (June 21, 1788), *in* 10 DHRC 1527–1528.

[24] *See, e.g.,* Brutus I, NEW YORK JOURNAL (Oct. 18, 1787), *reprinted in* 13 DHRC 417; Cato III, NEW YORK JOURNAL (Oct. 25, 1787), *reprinted in* 13 DHRC 473, 474; Dissent of the Minority to the Pennsylvania Ratification Convention (Dec. 18, 1787), *in* 15 DHRC 30–31; Luther Martin, *Genuine Information IV*, BALTIMORE MARYLAND GAZETTE (Jan. 8, 1788), *reprinted in* 15 DHRC 296; Curtiopolis, NEW YORK DAILY ADVERTISER (Jan. 18, 1788), *reprinted in* 15 DHRC 399, 400; James Bowdoin Jr., Debate in Massachusetts Ratification Convention (Feb. 1, 1788), *in* 2 ELLIOT 126. The same argument is made without specific reference to Montesquieu in An Old Whig IV, PHILADELPHIA INDEPENDENT GAZETTEER (Oct. 27, 1787), *reprinted in* 13 DHRC 497, 499 ("all political writers agree that Republican government can exist only in a narrow territory); Agrippa IV, MASSACHUSETTS GAZETTE (Dec. 4, 1787), *reprinted in* 4 DHRC 381 ("ablest writers" say that no extensive empire can be governed upon republican principles); Federal Farmer, *Letters to the Republican I* (Oct. 18, 1787) *reprinted in* 14 DHRC 18, 24 (argued that a free elective government cannot be extended over large territories); Mason, Virginia Convention (June 4, 1788), *in* 9 DHRC, 937 (saying that people have never retained their liberties with a general national government over so extensive a nation); Patrick Henry, Virginia Convention (June 9, 1788), *in* 3 ELLIOT 163–64 (government over such an extensive territory was impossible job for human wisdom).

[25] Brutus I, NEW YORK JOURNAL (Oct. 18, 1787), *reprinted in* 13 DHRC 417.

[26] James Monroe, Virginia Convention (June 10, 1788), *in* 3 ELLIOT 215.

[27] MONTESQUIEU, SPIRIT OF THE LAWS, Book 9, Chapter 1, *reprinted in* 1 FOUNDERS' CONSTITUTION 247.

reversed the superiority. According to *Federalist* No. 10 the small republics have inevitable internal faults that the diversity of the extended republic will fix. The Constitution is more than just an intellectual debate, but within the intellectual debate, Montesquieu is important. Cecelia Kenyon has argued that the Montesquieuian philosophy of the superiority of small republics was at the core of Anti-Federalist opposition to the Constitution.[28] If Madison's theory neutralized Montesquieu in the core intellectual contention in the ratification debate, that is no small prize.

Douglas Adair has argued that Madison's argument came from David Hume's essay, *Idea of Perfect Constitution*.[29] Hume indeed says some *Federalist*-10-like things on opposition of interests:

> The chief support of British government is the opposition of interests; but that though serviceable, breeds endless faction. In [my] plan, it does all the good without any of the harm. The competitors have no power of controlling the senate.[30]

Hume's thinking, however, and his essay on the Perfect Constitution were overall consistent with Montesquieu and inconsistent with an extended republic. Hume wrote, for instance, that

> [a] small commonwealth is the happiest government in the world within itself, because every thing lies under the eye of the rulers. But it may be subdued by great force from without.[31]

Hume was quite hostile to a government over large expanse. He condemned requisitions, for example, not because they failed but because the central ruler would overuse them, tolerating arbitrary levies because the ruler could not feel the burden of the requisitions directly.[32] Even when he sounds like *Federalist* Number 10, Hume used the theory of opposing interests to justify a confederation of small commonwealths that join together just for defense, as Montesquieu would allow. Madison was using the theory of opposing

---

[28] Cecelia M. Kenyon, *Men of Little Faith: The Anti-Federalists on the Nature of Representative Government*, 12 WM. & MARY Q. 3 (1955).

[29] Douglas Adair, *That Politics May be Reduced to a Science, in* FAME AND THE FOUNDING FATHERS 93, 98–104 (Trevor Colbin, ed. 1974).

[30] David Hume, *The Idea of a Perfect Constitution, in* HUME'S POLITICAL ESSAYS 221, 229 (Knud Haakonssen, ed. 1994).

[31] David Hume, *id.* at 230.

[32] David Hume, *Of Taxes in from Part II of Essays: Moral, Political, and Literary* II.VIII.11 (1752), http://www.econlib.org/library/Hume/HumeEssTax.htm (accessed Aug. 22, 2001) (using the example of the Turkish emperor, who could raise taxes only by requisitions upon the bashaws and governors who then oppress and abuse their subjects).

interests as an argument to replace such a confederation with a strong central government.[33] If Hume had ever seen Madison's work, Hume would have treated Madison as a failing student, who obviously had failed to pick up the purpose of the opposition of interest argument and had quoted it out of context.

Hamilton was a strong nationalist, but he was initially skeptical about the validity of Madison's proof of the superiority of the extended republic. Hamilton in his private notes to Madison's speech to the Philadelphia Convention conceded that Madison's point "is in some degree true, but not so generally as may be supposed." Even the federal level might be dominated by passions, he thought. The legislature "will meet in one room [even] if they are drawn from half the globe – and be liable to all the passions of popular assemblies." The national legislature might be enthralled by a demagogue, Hamilton wrote, who would "give an impulse to the whole. . . . [Even p]atricians were frequently demagogues."[34]

In the Convention, Hamilton's articulated ideal for the new government emulated the British system, a "mixed constitution" balancing the interests of "the few & the many."[35] In the British mixed constitution, the Commons represented the people, the House of Lords represented property, and the Crown represented the nation. Madison's theory of offsetting factions, by contrast, worked squarely within the norms of a representative democracy, with no room for special representation for the peerage, Crown, or for the few. Hamilton was an articulate ally of Madison on the need for a strong national government, but he was not predisposed to agree with Madison on a theory of faction balancing faction that might justify a democratic government or to make a democratic congress be consistent with individual rights.

---

[33] The point is well made by Edmund S. Morgan, *Safety in Numbers: Madison, Hume, and the Tenth Federalist*, in Huntington Lib. Q. 49 (1986) (saying that Hume's scheme bears a striking resemblance to the Articles of Confederation, the system that Madison worked so assiduously to replace).

[34] Notes at the Federal Convention (June 6, 1787), *in* 4 PAH 165–66.

[35] Hamilton, Federal Convention (June 18, 1787), *in* 1 Farrand 288. *See also*:

> Give all power to the many, they will oppress the few. Give all power to the few, they will oppress the many. Both therefore ought to have power, that each may defend itself agnst. the other. To the want of this check we owe our paper money, instalment laws &c.

Madison notes for a speech on representation also called for a balance between representatives of property and representatives of the people. Madison, Note to his Speech on the Right of Suffrage (undated), 3 Farrand 450–55. Madison, however, never became a target of Jefferson's fury, so he kept his good republican name.

By the time the *Federalist* was published, however, Hamilton had abandoned his mixed constitution and came around to the ideal of the extended republic. Gordon Wood has argued that the conventional wisdom in the period before the Constitution was that a "mixed" government on the model of the English constitution was ideal. John Adams, Wood convincingly argues, was irrelevant to the Constitution because he believed in the mixed British Constitution, whereas in the Philadelphia Convention, the consensus was the strictly republican principle that all branches of government were agents of the people.[36] Hamilton, by contrast with Adams, benefited from the consensus building at the Convention and he adapted to the republican consensus. In *Federalist* Number 22, published in December of 1787, for example, Hamilton argued that the Constitution needed to be ratified by the people because the consent of the people is the "pure original fountain of all legitimate authority."[37]

Hamilton also came to endorse the theory of *Federalist* Number 10 with enthusiasm, notwithstanding his initial reservations. In *Federalist* Number 28, Hamilton argues that "the obstacles to usurpation . . . increase with the increased extent of the state."[38] Indeed, in *Federalist* Number 9, Hamilton calls Madison's extended republic idea a "great improvement upon the science of politics." The dialogue between Madison's *Federalist* Number 10 and the Anti-Federalists who relied on Montesquieu's arguments for the inevitability of a small republic was a dialogue in which both ends were within the republican consensus.

Hamilton also undercuts Montesquieu quite effectively on his own. In *Federalist* Number 9, he argues that the states had already grown far too large to be homogenous enough to fit Montesquieu's ideal. Reducing the size of government down to the Montesquieu ideal, Hamilton argues, would leave us with "splitting ourselves into an infinity of little jealous, clashing, tumultuous commonwealths, the wretched nurseries of unceasing discord and the miserable objects of universal pity or contempt."[39]

James Wilson has a rival theory to *Federalist* Number 10, which is that representation is the "vital principle" which solves the Montesquieuan impossibility of large republics. The American states had diffused representation

---

[36] WOOD 567–592 (1968).

[37] *Federalist* No. 22, at 146 (Hamilton) (Dec. 14, 1787).

[38] *Federalist* No. 28, at 179 (Hamilton) (Dec. 28, 1787). *See also Federalist* No. 27, at 172 (Hamilton) (Dec. 25, 1787) (arguing that the general government will be "less apt to be tainted by the spirit of faction [than] smaller societies" and that factions "beget . . . injustice and oppression of a part of the community," and "distress, dissatisfaction, and disgust").

[39] *Federalist* No. 9, at 52–3 (Hamilton) (Nov. 21, 1787).

throughout all constituent parts of government, he said. "Representation is the chain of communication between the people and those to whom they have committed the exercise of the powers of government. This chain may consist of one or more links, but in all cases it should be sufficiently strong and discernible."[40] Wilson's argument, unlike *Federalist* Number 10, does not prove the superiority of the more extended republic, but it does say that the proposed government is so representative of the people, in all its parts, that it will not be a tyranny.

A young John Marshall was also effective against Baron Montesquieu in the Virginia Ratification debates, also using representation. Marshall said that the Montesquieuian objection that a large country could not have a republican government was a misunderstanding and misapplication: "To what does it owe its source?" Marshall asked. "To observations and criticisms on governments, where representation did not exist."[41]

Madison's diversity argument was part of a network of parallel nationalist argument against Montesquieu: Wilson's theory of representation said that tyranny was not inevitable on the national level and Hamilton said that we did not have and did not want the squabbling petty Lilliputian states that were supposedly the Montesquieuian ideal. Still, Madison's theory alone said that the national government would not be tyrannical, but would actually be superior to the state governments. Madison, moreover, is the organizing force for the Constitution and the other arguments are those of allies who were not the central force.

B. WHAT WEIGHT TO *FEDERALIST* 10?

Notwithstanding the importance of the offsetting-factions argument in neutralizing the great Montesquieu, one should also probably not take the Madisonian philosophy of offsetting factions too seriously. Professor Larry Kramer has recently shown that *Federalist* Number 10 went over poorly with Madison's audience, other than Hamilton. The delegates to the Convention who left us records, other than Madison himself, did not hear the theory, did not understand it, did not agree with it, or some mixture of all three.[42] Even Madison's allies on the various nationalist proposals used some other rationales. After writing *Federalist* Number 10, Professor Kramer argues, Madison stopped using the theory because it was not persuading anyone.

---

[40] Wilson, Pennsylvania Convention (Nov. 30, 1787), *in* 2 ELLIOT 424.
[41] John Marshall, Virginia Convention, (June 10, 188), *in* 3 ELLIOT 232.
[42] Larry D. Kramer, *Madison's Audience*, 112 HARV. L. REV. 611, 678 (1999).

Madison also had quite limited success in convincing his colleagues to put into effect the theory that the federal government was the better guardian of individuals rights. The Constitution does prevent the states from impairing contracts, passing ex post facto laws, or issuing paper money,[43] all of which were perceived as individual rights issues. But Madison wanted a federal government able to veto states' acts in any case to prevent their frequent and flagrant abuse of individual rights[44] and he did not get that plenary protection of individual rights.[45] A theory like *Federalist* Number 10 also works as an explanation of why the states did not pay their requisitions, and why they vetoed the impost: the states were pursuing their own fractious self-interests. In contrast, a recognition of the general welfare by the more extended republic would reach the conclusion that the war debts needed to be paid. An extended republic would give better attention to the pressing needs of the common defense than the rogue states were allowing. Still, Madison wanted the federal government with a plenary power to veto state legislation in protection of individual rights and that remedy is not in the Constitution.

Within four years, moreover, Madison himself had sloughed off the theory of *Federalist* Number 10 and adopted its opposite. When the new government under the Constitution began to function, Madison and Jefferson found that they profoundly disagreed with the administration of President Washington and of Secretary of the Treasury Alexander Hamilton. Jefferson was always a proper and conventional Montesquieuan, from long before the Constitution to long after its adoption. He espoused the superiority of a small republic over the larger ones so as to protect republican ideals.[46] When Madison went into

---

43 U.S. CONST., art. I, §10, cl. 1.
44 Madison to Jefferson (Oct. 24, 1787), *in* 10 JM 212.
45 To cite another failure, Madison wanted an amendment within the Bill of Rights to prevent the states from establishing a specific church or impairing the freedoms of conscience, press, or trial by jury, and the first and very Federalist Congress refused the amendment. *See, e.g.,* BERNARD SCHWARTZ, THE BILL OF RIGHTS: A DOCUMENTARY HISTORY 1032 (Madison espousing an unsuccessful amendment as a part of the Bill of Rights to provide that "no *states* shall violate the equal rights of conscience, or the freedom of the press, or the trial by jury in criminal cases," which Madison "conceived to be the most valuable amendment in the whole list").
46 Jefferson to Madison (Dec. 16, 1786), *in* 10 PTJ 603 (saying that the proper division of powers between the general and the particular governments is in making us "one nation as to foreign concerns and keep[ing] us distinct in Domestic ones," saying that Congress has reversed "the natural order of things" by making the Western states fewer and larger and saying that "[a] tractable people may be governed in large bodies, but in proportion as they depart from this characteristic the extent of their government must be less"); Jefferson, 1st Inaugural Address (March 4, 1801) *in* BASIC WRITINGS OF TJ 641 (citing as a principle of his administration "the support the State governments in all their rights, as the most competent administration of our domestic concerns and the surest bulwarks against anti-republican tendencies").

opposition to Hamilton, as Jefferson's lieutenant, Madison made quite traditional Montesquieuan arguments as well, directed now against Hamilton. By the fall of 1791, Madison was calling for small ideologically homogeneous states, such as Virginia, to be a check on the national government.[47] Madison's 1791 writings, espousing the superiority of the small homogeneous republic as the guardian of individuals, is at the opposite end of the spectrum from his 1787 "proof" of the inevitable superiority of the national level, where the interests were diverse and offsetting.[48] Madison thus should be viewed not as a philosopher who built consistent and eternal logical systems, but a politician who was willing to make philosophic arguments in service of a political cause.

For more than a generation, political science as a discipline has taken Madison's theory of offsetting factions very seriously as a legitimating norm of government.[49] Madison's law of offsetting factions has been used to explain why government can be expected usually to come out right, much as Adam Smith's invisible hand explains why economic results will usually come out right. Both are justifications by process, and neither worries much about specific, presumably anomalous, injustices. Yet the discipline of political science is now increasingly seeing problems with government, especially in extended republics, also on process grounds. For large republics, the stake of any one voter is very small – too small, for instance, to justify the work of becoming an educated voter. Organizing citizens with trivial stakes is difficult because no one cares enough, given the triviality of an individual stake, to join together for a result – or even to respond to someone else's organizing efforts. In a large republic, the chances of affecting an issue are too small even to give a rational justification for coming out to vote. Smaller groups and special interests will inevitably beat the general interest, under the new skeptical theories of collective action, because the special interests are easier

---

[47] See NATIONAL GAZETTE (Sept. 1791, Nov. 1791), reprinted in 6 WRITINGS OF JM 68, 81, 114. See Douglas Jaenick, Madison v. Madison: the Party Essays v. the Federalist Papers, in REFLECTIONS ON THE CONSTITUTION: THE AMERICAN CONSTITUTION AFTER TWO HUNDRED YEARS 116 (Richard Maidment & John Zvesper, eds. 1989) (contrasting the nationalism of Madison in the Constitutional period with the state focus after breaking with Hamilton).

[48] John Zvesper, The Madisonian Systems, 37 W. POL. Q.236, 250 (1984).

[49] See, e.g., DAVID F. EPSTEIN, THE POLITICAL THEORY OF THE FEDERALIST 59 (1984) (saying that Federalist 10 is today the most famous and highly regarded essay of the Federalist, perhaps even of all American political writings); David F. Epstein, Remarks on the Federalist Number 10, 16 HARV. J. OF LAW & PUB. POLICY 43 (1993); Isaac Kramnick, The "Great National Discussion": The Discourse of Politics in 1787, 45 WM. & MARY Q. 3 (3d Series 1988); ROBERT A. DAHL, PLURALIST DEMOCRACY IN THE UNITED STATES 5–5, 25, 41–32 (1966) (citing Federalist 10). See also paeans collected at Larry D. Kramer, Madison Audience, 112 HARV. L. REV. 611, 612–613 (1999).

to organize. If the republic is smaller, the individual's stakes get a bit larger and the organization problems are not so formidable.[50] Madisonian theory of the superiority of extended republics may not be completely dead within the discipline of political science, but it is of declining vigor.

Still, notwithstanding his audience's quite limited reception, Madison's later defections, and its drop in influence now, Madison's work in preparation for the Convention, including the theory of an extended republic, is an important contributory cause to the Constitution that was adopted. A small Constitution without Madison would have created a system to get the Revolutionary War debts paid, overriding Rhode Island and New York in their opposition to the federal impost. Hamilton and Jay, when they spoke as *Publius* in their part of the *Federalist*, relied primarily on war and taxes to justify the new Constitution and its new central government. But the Hamilton–Jay arguments for the new Constitution to be ready for war are perfectly consistent with a confederation, albeit one with better capacity to marshal resources for defense: Montesquieu and Hume both would have allowed small republics to join together for defense against external enemies. The war argument did not, hwowever, legitimate a supreme and self-sufficient national government in peacetime. The Constitution that was adopted went beyond the confederation joining together for defense and created the revolution of complete national government. The constitutional revolution replaced the sovereignty of the states with a new general government, free from interference by the states, supreme above them all, and able to tax and spend on its own. To go from a compact or league of friendship among small states to a powerful national government, one needs a philosophy, at least something like Madison's paean to the extended republic that repudiates the existing wisdom that democracy could occur only in smaller states. Madison's working out the theory first alone and then in private with his mentors produced the Virginia Plan that set the agenda for the Convention and the framework for the Constitution that was finally adopted. The theory of *Federalist* Number 10 supported the plan that set the agenda and that plan survived as the framework of the Constitution.

"In truth my ideas of a reform strike so deeply at the old Confederation and lead to such a systematic change," Madison had written to Edmund Randolph

---

[50] *See. e.g.*, Mancur Olson, Jr., The Logic of Collective Action: Public Goods and the Theory of Groups 35, 164–166 (Rev. ed. 1971) (saying the rational individual in the large group will not be willing to make any sacrifices to achieve the objects he shares with others, and that the larger the group the further it will fall short of providing the optimal amount of a collective good).

as the Philadelphia Convention drew near, "that they scarcely admit of the expedient."[51] "It has been shown," Madison said, "that the existing Confederation is founded on principles which are fallacious; that we must consequently change this first foundation, and with it, the superstructure resting upon it."[52]

The Copernican Revolution, which put the sun rather than the Earth at the center of the galaxy, was motivated, it is said, by aesthetic and metaphysical theories, rather than by strictly scientific evidence. Copernicus said, for instance, that the sun "as though seated on a throne . . . governs the circumgyrating family of planets."[53] Madison's theory similarly enthroned the federal government on the ground that an extended and diversified republic was superior and this theory justified a new, self-sufficient, government on the national level, supreme over the states. Madison's theory provided the theoretical underpinnings for the constitutional revolution that was adopted. Copernicus' theory did not become accepted wisdom until more than a hundred years after it was published.[54] Madison's theory of the inevitable superiority of the federal government went from drawing board to Convention to ratification in a matter of months.

---

[51] Madison to Randolph (April 8, 1787), *in* 9 JM 369.

[52] *Federalist* No. 37, at 233 (Madison) (Jan. 11, 1788).

[53] Nicolas Copernicus, *quoted in* A. R. HALL, THE SCIENTIFIC REVOLUTION 1500–1800, at 67 (1960).

[54] *See, e.g., id.* at 102 (saying that Copernicus's heliocentric theory (published in 1543) was rendered conclusively superior to an earth-centered theory only with Newton's *Principia* (published in 1687)).

CHAPTER FOUR

Shifting the Foundations from the States to the People

A. THE STEP-BY-STEP REVOLUTION

The new Constitution created a national government supreme over the states on a foundation of sovereignty of the people. The new government, the French reported home, would no longer need the consent of the states for any of it operations.[1] "The necessity of having a government which should at once operate upon the people, and not upon the states," Pinckney told South Carolina, "was conceived to be indispensable by every delegation present" at the Philadelphia Convention.[2] Madison described the new Constitution to Jefferson saying that the Philadelphia Convention had adopted "the alternative of a government which instead of operating, on the States, should operate without their intervention on the individuals composing them."[3] Jefferson responded that he liked the idea of a Congress that should go on of itself peaceably, "without needing continual recurrence to the state legislatures."[4]

---

[1] Antoine de la Forest to Comte de Montmorin (Sept. 28, 1787) *in* 13 DHRC 259.

[2] Charles Pinckney, South Carolina House of Representatives (Jan. 16, 1788), *in* 4 ELLIOT 256.

[3] Madison to Jefferson (Oct. 24, 1787), *in* 12 PTJ 271. *See also*, before the Convention, Madison to Randolph (April 8, 1787), *in* 9 JM 369 (calling for a federal system "which would operate without the intervention of the States"); Madison to Jefferson (Mar. 19, 1787), *in* 9 JM 318 (calling for "such augmentation of federal power as will render [the federal government] efficient without intervention of the [State] Legislatures"). *See also* later descriptions, Hylton v. United States, 3 U.S. 171 (1796) (Iredell, J.) (saying that the Constitution was particularly intended to affect individuals, and not states); Madison to Andrew Stevenson, March 25, 1826 in 3 FARRAND 473 (saying that the old government had "operated through requisitions on the states, and rested on the authority of State Legislatures." The government to take its place was "to operate directly & coercively on individuals.").

[4] Jefferson to Madison (Dec. 20, 1787), *in* 14 DHRC 482.

The new federal government, Jefferson wrote, would "walk upon its own legs."[5]

The core idea of forming an independent, complete government on the national level was accomplished early in the Convention at Philadelphia and stuck. On May 30, 1787, the fourth day of a quorum, the convention passed a resolution, derived from the Virginia Plan, stating "that a national governt. ought to be established consisting of a supreme Legislative Executive & Judiciary."[6] The Convention went on for another three and half months, but the most important issues in Philadelphia were settled without compromise on that day when the Virginia Plan was endorsed.[7]

The strength of the consensus for a complete and supreme national government should not belie its radical nature. The "congress of states assembled," which was the federal-level government under the Articles, was merely an assembly of delegates from sovereign states. The Constitution replaced the assembly with a new national government, having a "compleat and compulsive operation."[8] A minimal solution would have given the federal-level Congress enough revenue to avoid default on the Revolutionary debts, but paying off the war debts did not require abandonment of the confederation. Hamilton's tax package that restored the public credit was less intrusive than the vetoed 1783 impost package,[9] and the 1783 proposal would have left the confederation system intact. The Federalists relied heavily on beating the war drums, perhaps even exaggerating the immediate dangers of war,[10] but the existing confederation already gave the national government the exclusive

---

5 Jefferson to Richard Price (Jan. 8, 1789) *in* 14 PTJ 420.

6 May 30, 1787, *in* 1 FARRAND 33. Six states voted for the resolution (*id* at 35) and only Connecticut voted against it. Connecticut later ratified by a ratio of better than 3 to 1. 3 DHRC 562. New York was divided in the vote, but only by the accident Lansing was absent to leave Hamilton (pro) and Yates (against) in a tie. Ordinarily Lansing and Yates would have voted against the new government (*see* discussion accompanying *infra* notes 17–20). Rhode Island would also undoubtedly have voted against the resolution had it been present. *See* discussion, accompanying *infra* notes 25–30.

7 William E. Nelson, *Reason and Compromise in the Establishment of the Federal Constitution, 1787–1801*, 44 WM. & MARY Q. 458 (1987). *Accord*, Leonard Levy, *Introduction*, *in* THE FRAMING AND RATIFICATION OF THE CONSTITUTION xxv (Leonard W. Levy & Denis J. Mahoney, eds. 1987) (saying that the Convention reached its most crucial decision almost at the outset, namely the national government consisting of a supreme legislative, executive and judiciary); John P. Roche, *The Founding Fathers: A Reform Caucus in Action*, 55 AM. POL. SCI. REV. 799, 803 (1961) (arguing that the fundamental precepts were accepted by overwhelming consensus once Clinton's men, who did not share in the consensus, left).

8 Gouverneur Morris, Federal Convention (May 30, 1787), *in* 1 FARRAND 34.

9 *See* discussion, *infra* Chapter 10, pp. 227–28.

10 *See* discussion Chapter 1, pp. 18–19.

jurisdiction over war and foreign affairs.[11] Destitution of the old Congress in the face of war debts was thus a necessary element, but not sufficient for the radical new Constitution.

The delegates to Philadelphia were proud when they were through with what the Convention had produced. James Wilson told the Pennsylvania Ratification Convention,

> After a period of six thousand years has elapsed since the creation, the United States exhibit to the world the first instance, as far as we can learn, of a nation, unattacked by external force, unconvulsed by domestic insurrections, assembling voluntarily, deliberating fully, and deciding calmly, concerning that system of government under which they would wish that they and their posterity should live.[12]

Madison wrote to Jefferson that considering the natural diversity of human opinions on new and complicated subjects, "it is impossible to consider the degree of concord which ultimately prevailed as less than a miracle."[13]

The new national government, while revolutionary, did not need a miraculous intervention. The Convention has "given birth to a revolution," its proponents celebrated, but it was one "effected by good sense and deliberation."[14] The Constitution arose from a philosophy, Madison's own, that proved the natural superiority of the extended republic and the inevitable vices of all confederations, and from a background of deep anger at the irresponsible states. The Constitution also arose from specific arguments directed at the specific problems. Step by logical step the Framers threw off their old constitution and adopted a new one. Each step was considered common sense, even inevitable.

The Framers first threw off the existing constitution, the Articles of Confederation. They could not expect endorsement from Rhode Island or from New York for even the easiest step – the federal impost – so they could not stay within the unanimous endorsement requirement for amendment of the

---

[11] ARTICLES OF CONFEDERATION, art. IX, 19 JCC 217 (March 1, 1781) (giving Congress exclusive power of determining war and peace, treaties and alliances, ambassadors, capture and prizes); art. VI, *id* at 216 (prohibiting states from sending or receiving foreign ambassadors, without Congressional approval).

[12] Wilson, Speech to the Pennsylvania Convention (Nov. 26, 1787), *in* 2 ELLIOT 422. *See also,* RAKOVE, BEGINNINGS 388 (saying that the delegates were optimistic that "a rational reassessment of the republican experiment was still possible and it was this sense of possibility, rather than the skeptical predictions that were still being voiced well into 1787, that ultimately set the tone for the Convention's deliberations").

[13] Madison to Jefferson (Oct. 24, 1787), *in* 10 JM 208.

[14] DAILY ADVERTISER, NEW YORK (Sept. 24, 1787), *reprinted in* 1 DEBATE 13.

existing Articles. Because the states were not paying their requisitions voluntarily, the new constitution would have to allow coercion against recalcitrant states. But enforcement of requisitions by coercion was madness, tantamount to civil war. Far safer for the general government to collect its revenue peacefully by taxing things and individuals directly. Once the general government could raise revenue on its own without recourse upon the states, the general government would no longer need to be dependent on the states. Once the Congress was no longer dependent on the states for contributions, but on the people, the basis of legitimacy of the general government could shift from the states and on to the people directly. Under the new system, the people would be sovereign and Congress would represent people and not states. The new constitution would be ratified by people acting in conventions and not by state legislatures in their corporate capacity. Voting power would be determined by population. Federal law would be supreme over state law and even state constitutions. Each step was inevitable, rolling unstoppably to a new foundation.

To an extraordinary degree, the revolution is Madison's revolution. Key steps including ending state sovereignty and moving from coercive enforcement of requisitions to a direct federal tax were Madison's ideas, worked out beforehand and evident in the debates only in the structure of the original Virginia Plan. There are no precursors in Congress or among the states to lay the foundation for such a revolution. The instructions the delegates received from their home states and the Congress impeded the shift rather than helping it.[15] The Convention adopted its resolution for a three-part government supreme over the states on May 30, much too quickly to allow significant discussion or development within the Convention itself. The foundation work is Madison's by default. But many hands joined together, raised up the document, and carried it out to the people.

---

[15] The best description of the instructions to delegates is in the introduction and documents on Appointment of Convention Delegates, 1 DHRC 191–230. There are many very general instructions from the states. Virginia instructed its delegates just to "secure the great objects for which the Government was instituted and to render the United States as happy in peace as they have been glorious in war." *Id.* at 541. But there were also many specific instructions that were totally ignored. New York sent delegates for the sole purpose of amending the Articles of Confederation and told its delegates that it could not allow amendment of the Articles rule that Congressional delegates could be recalled by the state legislature on discretion (*id.* at 193). Delaware did not allow its delegates to change the rule that each state got one vote. Both Congress and many of the instructions called for the convention to report back to the state legislatures for approval, which was ignored, as discussed in text *infra* pp. 78–81.

B. THE FALL OF THE ARTICLES OF CONFEDERATION

1. End of the One-State Veto

The target of the constitutional revolution was the existing constitutional document, the Articles of Confederation. Under the Articles themselves, amendment of the Articles, even in a death crisis, required confirmation by the legislature of every state.[16] The Framers of the Constitution did not think they could get unanimous confirmation. The least controversial step toward solving the federal destitution was the 5 percent impost, and New York, Rhode Island, and Virginia had already vetoed the 1781 or the 1783 impost proposals. "The present advantage which N. York seems to be so much attached to, of taxing her neighbours," Nathaniel Gorham told the Convention, "makes it very probable" that New York would veto amendments to the Articles.[17] John Lansing and Robert Yates, who constituted the majority of the New York delegation, had been leaders in New York's veto of the 1783 impost proposal.[18] Lansing and Yates walked out of the Convention when the document went beyond mere amendment to the confederation to propose a general national government[19] and declared opposition to any "general Government, however guarded by declarations of rights or cautionary provisions."[20] Rhode Island also could be expected to "persist in her opposition to general measures."[21] Proposing again amendment of the Articles, under the one-state veto rules, would have been laughable futility, no matter how desperate the general-level destitution.

---

[16] ARTICLES OF CONFEDERATION, art. XIII, *in* 19 JCC 221.

[17] Nathaniel Gorham, Federal Convention (July 23, 1787), *in* 2 FARRAND 90. *Accord*, Madison, Unsent letter to John Tyler (1833), *in* 3 FARRAND 530–531 (saying that the "dominant party in New York had refused even a duty of 5 per Ct. on imports for the urgent debt of the Revolution, so as to tax the consumption of her neighbors").

[18] KAMINSKI, CLINTON at 91, 94 (1993); RAKOVE, BEGINNINGS 176–338 (saying that Yates had emerged as an effective public critic of the impost because he was bitter that Robert Morris had refused to appoint him receiver of federal taxes).

[19] *See, e.g.*, John Lansing (June 16, 1787), *in* 1 FARRAND 249 (arguing that the Convention was restrained to amendments of the Articles of a federal nature, and was not authorized to seek a consolidation of the states or a national government); Introduction on Appointment of Convention Delegates, 1 DHRC 191, 193 (New York delegates given instructions to seek amendments to the Articles of Confederation).

[20] Robert Yates and John Lansing, Jr., *to Governor George Clinton*, DAILY ADVERTISER (Jan. 14, 1788), *reprinted in* 2 DEBATE3, 4.

[21] Nathaniel Gorham, Federal Convention (July 23, 1787), *in* 2 FARRAND 90. *Cf.* Wilson, Speech at the Federal Convention (Sept. 10, 1787), *in* 2 FARRAND 562 (unsuccessfully opposing submitting the Constitution to Congress in part because it was "worse than folly to rely on the concurrence of the Rhode Island members of Congs. in the plan").

While the Framers did not expect to be able to satisfy the unanimity rule, they were also not willing to let that preclude changes "as may be necessary to the exigencies of the Union."[22] "If one State...should suppose that they can dictate a Constitution to the Union," George Washington would write in December 1787, "they will find themselves deceived."[23] "The very refractory conduct of Rhode Island, in uniformly opposing every wise and judicious measure," Spaight told North Carolina, "taught us how impolitic it would be to put the general welfare in the power of a few members of the Union."[24] "Everybody knows that, through the peculiar obstinacy of Rhode Island, many great advantages were lost," James Iredell told North Carolina. "Notwithstanding her weakness," he said, "she uniformly opposed every regulation for the benefit and honor of the Union at large.... The deputies from twelve states unanimously concurred in opinion the happiness of all America ought not to be sacrificed to the caprice and obstinacy of so inconsiderable a part."[25] Rhode Island's "apostasy from every moral, as well as political, obligation," Edward Carrington wrote to Jefferson, "has placed her perfectly [outside] the views of her confederates; nor will her absence, or nonconcurrence, occasion the least impediment in any stage of the intended business."[26] "Unanimity in public bodies," Hamilton wrote, "has been founded upon a supposition that it would contribute to security," but unanimity operated in reality just "to destroy the energy of the government, and to substitute the... caprice...of an insignificant, turbulent, or corrupt junto, [–Rhode Island–] [for] the regular deliberations and decisions of a respectable majority."[27]

Rhode Island's opposition meant that necessary changes could not operate within the framework of the Articles of Confederation. In the Convention, Lansing argued that the Convention should only amend the Articles.[28] James Wilson responded that a solution within the Articles "goes too far,

---

[22] Address of the Annapolis Convention in 3 PAH 686 (calling for the Constitutional Convention). *Accord*, Resolution of Congress (Feb. 21, 1787), *in* 32 JCC 74.

[23] Washington to Charles Carter, Virginia Herald (Dec. 27, 1787), *reprinted in* 1 Debate 612. Washington thought his comment was given in confidence, but it was published and republished in at least 49 newspapers. *Editorial Note*, *in* 6 DHRC 276–281; Washington to Charles Carter (Jan. 12, 1788), *in* 6 PGW:CS37 (saying that "it gives me pain to see the hasty, and indigested production of a private letter handed to the public"). Ultimately he forgave Carter. Washington to Charles Carter (Jan. 22, 1788), *in* 6 PGW:CS53 (saying "I am satisfied you had no agency in publishing the extract of my letter to you").

[24] R. D. Spaight, North Carolina Convention (July 30, 1788), *in* 4 Elliot 207.

[25] James Iredell, North Carolina Convention (July 31, 1788), *in* 4 Elliot 228–229.

[26] L. Edward Carrington to Jefferson (June 9, 1787), *in* 3 Farrand 37.

[27] *Federalist* No. 22 at 140 (Hamilton) (Dec. 14, 1787).

[28] John Lansing (June 16, 1787), *in* 1 Farrand 249.

as it cannot be completed, unless Rhode-Island assents."[29] "Rhode-Island," Edmund Randolph would say, who was "notorious for her uniform opposition to every federal duty, would then have it in her power to defeat the union."[30] *Publius* later said the view that the Convention should have simply proposed amendments to the Articles of Confederation failed by reason "of the absurdity of subjecting the fate of twelve States to the perverseness or corruption of a thirteenth."[31]

Rhode Island was beyond redemption, out of the family. Rhode Island, as noted, was the "Quintessence of Villainy" . . . "responsible for the poverty of the Revolutionary soldiers, for the high taxes on land and for the embarrassment of public finances."[32] "Nothing," said James Madison, "can exceed the wickedness and folly which continue to reign there."[33] Rhode Island had forfeited all claim to the confidence of the nation and of the whole world. Rhode Island was "a disgrace to the human race."[34]

The intransigence of wicked Rhode Island meant that a switching out of constitutions would be necessary. Without the anger at Rogue Island, the Convention could not have slipped so easily out of the old confederation and over to a new foundation. Ripping up the old document gave the Framers freedom to be more radical in their changes because the changes did not have to fit into an old framework. Rhode Island was not the only wicked state – every state had, at minimum, failed in its obligation to pay the mandatory requisitions – but Rhode Island was a good target because it was small, anti-federal, and absent, and because its veto was sufficient.

Both the Annapolis Resolution and the subsequent Congressional Resolution calling for the Constitutional Convention had said the Convention's product would be reported to Congress and then for confirmation by every state legislature.[35] Given wicked Rogue Island, the Convention could not operate under the aegis of those Resolutions. Indeed, when the Convention submitted the completed Constitution to Congress,[36] Madison argued – to

[29] Wilson (June 16, 1787), *in* 1 FARRAND 261 (Yates Notes).
[30] Randolph, Virginia Convention (June 4, 1788), *in* 3 ELLIOT 28.
[31] *Federalist* No. 40, at 263 (Madison) (Jan. 18, 1788).
[32] JOHN K. ALEXANDER, THE SELLING OF THE CONSTITUTIONAL CONVENTION 23 (quoting SALEM, MASSACHUSETTS MERCURY (1787)). *See also* other expressions of anger at Rhode Island in Chapter 1, pp. 27–28.
[33] Madison to Randolph (April 2, 1787), *in* 9 JM 362.
[34] Gov. Samuel Huntington, Connecticut General Assembly (May 11, 1787), *in* DHRC-MICROFICE SUPPL. CONN. 53.
[35] Address of the Annapolis Convention, *in* 3 PAH 686; Resolution of Congress (Feb. 21, 1787), *in* 32 JCC 74.
[36] Washington, Letter to Congress by Unanimous Order of the Convention (Sept. 17, 1787), *in* 2 FARRAND 666.

the considerable advantage of the proponents of the Constitution – that Congress could not amend the Convention's language, because the Constitution would then have had to go out under Congressional aegis as an Articles amendment to state legislatures and for unanimous approval. Submission of the Constitution to the Continental Congress, Madison tells us, was "intended merely as a matter of form and respect."[37] The old Congress acquiesced, in its way, to the revolution. Congress was unanimous, but only for the simple act of transmitting the revolutionary document to the state conventions.[38]

2. Dethroning the Articles

Madison argued that the Articles were no longer binding because they had been breached by the parties. The Articles were only a compact among the states. It therefore followed, Madison wrote, under "the doctrine of compacts, that a breach of any of the articles of the confederation by any of the parties to it, absolves the other parties from their respective obligations, and gives them a right if they chuse to exert it, of dissolving the Union altogether."[39] Because requisitions were mandatory, failure to pay was a material breach of the Articles. "[A] breach of the fundamental principles of the compact by a part of the Society would certainly absolve the other part from their obligations to it," Madison said. The violations of the Articles of Confederation had been "numerous & notorious."[40] As a matter of contract law, even today, a contract breached in a significant way by the other side is no longer binding.[41] The Articles had lost binding power, under the argument, because of the states' breaches of their requisition obligations. On this issue, Madison was more nationalist than Hamilton, who was "not yet prepared to admit the doctrine that the Confederacy could be dissolved by partial infractions of it."[42] Indeed no one but Madison seems to have given much weight to the breach of contract argument.[43]

---

[37] Madison to Washington (Sept. 30 1787), *in* 13 DHRC 276.

[38] Richard Henry Lee to Mason (Oct. 1, 1787), *in* 1 DEBATE 46.

[39] Madison, Vices of the Political System, *in* 9 JM 352–353.

[40] Madison, Federal Convention (June 19, 1787), *in* 1 FARRAND 315.

[41] 17A AMERICAN JURISPRUDENCE 2d §704 (1991) (saying that as a general rule, where one party to a contract repudiates or refuses to perform, the other party is not obligated to perform).

[42] Hamilton, Federal Convention (June 19, 1787), *in* 1 FARRAND 324. *See also* Oliver Ellsworth, Federal Convention, June 20, 1787, *in* 1 FARRAND 335 (opposing doctrine that a breach of any of the federal articles could dissolve the whole, because a convention is a dangerous thing, "better fitted to pull down than to build up Constitutions").

[43] *See* Bruce Ackerman & Neal Kumar Katyal, *Our Unconventional Founding*, 62 U. CHI. L. REV. 475, 540–551 (1995).

The Framers came to rely primarily on the argument that the Convention was not illegal, although it could not operate under the Articles, because the Convention was merely proposing a Constitution, and not giving authority to it. Lansing argued before he left that the Convention had exceeded its limited authority to offer only amendments "having for their basis the Confederacy in being."[44] The Federalists' counterargument was that the convention could propose anything because it had the power to conclude nothing.[45] "I have never heard before," Wilson told Pennsylvania, "that to make a proposal was an exercise of power."[46] As Madison put it, the Constitution was "merely advisory and recommendatory" and that it would be of "no more consequence than the paper on which it is written," unless ratified.[47] "The prudent enquiry, in all cases," Madison said, "ought surely to be, not so much from whom the advice comes, as whether the advice be good."[48] Thus if the advice for a new Constitution was good advice, it did not matter if the advice came from a non-authoritative source.[49]

Tom Paine, in his *Rights of Man*, captured the foundational myth:

> The convention, of which Benjamin Franklin was president, having met and deliberated, and agreed upon a constitution, they next ordered it to be published, not as a thing established, but for the consideration of the whole people, their approbation or rejections, and then adjourned to stated time. When time of adjournment was expired, the convention reassembled; and as the general opinion of the people in approbation of it was then known, the constitution was signed, sealed, and proclaimed

---

[44] *See, e.g.,* John Lansing (June 16, 1787), *in* 1 FARRAND 249 (arguing that the Convention was restrained to amendments of the Articles of a confederal nature, and was not authorized to seek a consolidation of the states or a national government). *See also* Robert Yates and John Lansing, Jr., *to Governor George Clinton, The Dissent of the Two New York Delegates to the Philadelphia Convention,* DAILY ADVERTISER (Jan. 14, 1788), *reprinted in* 2 DEBATE 3, 4 (arguing that convention had only the limited purpose of revising the Articles).

[45] Wilson, Federal Convention (June 16, 1787), *in* 1 FARRAND 266 (Yates Notes).

[46] Wilson, Pennsylvania Convention (Dec. 4, 1787), *in* 2 ELLIOT 469. *Accord,* Wilson, Pennsylvania Convention (Nov. 26, 1787), *in* 3 FARRAND 143 (saying that the federal convention proceeded upon original principles and not in reliance on the powers given to them by the states, "and having framed a constitution which they thought would promote the happiness of their country, they have submitted it to their consideration, who may either adopt or reject it, as they please").

[47] *Federalist* No. 40, at 264 (Madison) (Jan. 18, 1788).

[48] *Id.* at 267 (also saying that disapproval of the people would destroy the document while approval would blot out all antecedent error).

[49] *Accord,* William Davie, North Carolina Convention (July 24, 1788), *in* 4 ELLIOT 16–17 (saying that "the Federal Convention might recommend the concession of the most extensive powers, yet they could not put one of them into execution.").

on the authority of the people and the original deposited as a public record.[50]

Paine is a bit off on his facts: George Washington and not Ben Franklin was president of the convention, ratification did not have a set term, and the convention never re-met after breaking up. Still Paine captures the legitimating story that the Constitution was proclaimed on the authority of the people and was not illegitimate because the Convention had gone beyond its instructions.

Even beyond the technical argument that they were merely proposing the Constitution, the delegates who remained in the convention, after Lansing and Yates left, were ready to rip up the prior constitution. When the salvation of the Union was at stake, Edmund Randolph of Virginia said, it would be "treason to our trust, not to propose what we found necessary."[51] George Read of Delaware was

> agst. patching up the old federal System: he hoped the idea wd. be dismissed. It would be like putting new cloth on an old garment. The confederation was founded on temporary principles. It cannot last: it cannot be amended. If we do not establish a good Govt. on new principles, we must either go to ruin, or have the work to do over again.[52]

The Convention transformed the delegates against the Articles. Charles Pinckney told South Carolina that the Convention met with the thought of merely granting commercial powers and federal revenue to the confederation government, but "[t]hose who had seriously contemplated the subject were fully convinced that a total change of system was necessary" and "that the public mind was fully prepared for the change.... [T]he total want of government, the destruction of commerce, of public credit, private confidence, and national character, were surely sufficiently alarming to awaken their constituents to a true sense of their situation."[53]

---

[50] Tom Paine, Rights of Man, pt. II (1792) in Collected Writings 185 (Eric Foner, ed. 1995).

[51] Edmund Randolph, Federal Convention (June 16, 1787), in 1 Farrand 255 (Yates Notes) (also, Yates reports, painting "in strong colours, the imbecility of the existing Confederacy, & the danger of delaying a substantial reform"). Accord, Hamilton, Federal Convention (June 18, 1787), in 1 Farrand 283–292 (saying that "to rely on & propose any plan not adequate to these exigencies, merely because it was not clearly within our powers, would be to sacrifice the means to the end").

[52] George Read (Delaware), Federal Convention (June 6, 1787), in 1 Farrand 136–137.

[53] Charles Pinckney, South Carolina House of Representatives (Jan. 16, 1788), in 4 Elliot 255. Madison's fine restatement of all of the legitimate reasons why the Convention should strike to "fundamental principles" is in Federalist No. 40, at 261 (Madison) (Jan. 18, 1788).

While the Articles of Confederation was the fundamental constitutional document, moreover, it did not have much prestige. The Articles had not been ratified until the Revolutionary War was almost over, so the Articles had not helped the nation in the crucible of the war. "Our success, therefore, ought not to be imputed to the old Confederation;" Charles Cotesworth Pinckney told South Carolina.[54] The Articles were in need of serious amendment, even as they were ratified.[55] Congress, for example, offered the amendment for a national impost on February 3, 1781,[56] and offered an amendment to allow it to seize state merchandise to enforce its orders on March 16, 1781,[57] both within a month of the final ratification of the Articles on March 1, 1781.[58] The Articles were not venerable – from their ratification to the Convention was only a little over six years. The Articles also had inconsistencies in it, which meant that it had never been given careful draftsman's care.[59] Errors in the Articles could be excused, Charles Pinckney argued, because it had been drafted "in the midst of a dangerous and doubtful war, and by men, totally inexperienced in the operations of a system so new and extensive."[60] Most importantly, the Articles prevented self-correction because the single-state veto rule prevented their amendment. Ripping up the old constitution may have been a revolutionary act, but the Articles were ready to topple. The extent to which the revolution would go was not pre-ordained, but the single state veto and the power it gave to Rhode Island meant the old constitution had to be destroyed.

---

54 Charles Cotesworth Pinckney, South Carolina Legislature (Jan. 18, 1788), *in* 4 ELLIOT 301–302. The Articles were not ratified by all the states until March 1781, just seven months before the last major battle lead to the surrender of Cornwallis at Yorktown. Cornwallis surrendered on October 19, 1781 (Yorktown, Siege of, Encyclopedia Britannica, http://www.britanica.com/) and Maryland ratified the Articles of Confederation on March 1, 1781. 1 DHRC 136.

55 *See* RAKOVE, BEGINNINGS 164, 190 (saying that Articles when ratified "scarcely seemed adequate to the worsening problems Congress faced" and were considered to be "obsolete").

56 Congressional Resolution, 1 DHRC 140.

57 *Id.* at 141–143.

58 *Id.* at 136.

59 The preamble, for example, identifies the date at which the signing delegates assembled as Nov. 15, 1777, and the closing language right before the signature identifies the assembly as July 9, 1778. Neither date is true: the delegates from Maryland, the last state necessary to make the Articles effective, did not sign in Congress of the United States assembled until March 1, 1781. 1 DHRC 136. Another inconsistency is that the rule for apportionment of requisitions is set as according to value of land and buildings in Article VIII, but as according the white inhabitants in Article IX. Article IX reflects a prior draft never corrected. These inconsistencies are not very important in their own right, but they do illustrate the draft quality of the Articles.

60 Charles Pinckney, Observations on the Plan of Government Submitted to the Federal Convention, *in* 3 FARRAND 107.

C. COERCION BY ARMS OR BY LAW?

1. Tax by Military Force

The obligation of a state to pay its quota of a requisition was legally manda-tory, but not very serious. The Congress had no independent taxing author-ity; its revenue relied on requisitions.[61] Yet, the states ignored their obliga-tions and refused to pay their quotas, some with a thin bit of pretense for their avoidance and some without. Madison was bitter. The states them-selves, he argued, would never agree to voluntary tax: "If the laws of the States were merely recommendatory to their citizens, or if they were re-judged by the County authorities, what security . . . would exist that they would be carried into execution?"[62] A voluntary observance of the federal law by all the members could never be hoped for, Madison told Jefferson.[63] "We have probably had too good an opinion of human nature in forming our confederation," wrote George Washington.[64]

The right of coercion, Madison told Washington in preparation for the Convention, must be expressly declared.[65] "Coercion," Edmund Randolph would say, "is an indispensible ingredient."[66] The Convention must es-pouse the power of coercion by the general-level government, wrote Edward Carrington. The fault lay not in the American character, Carrington said, but in the defects of the Articles:

> Delinquencies of the States in their foederal obligations; acts of their legislatures violating public Treaties and private Contracts; and the universal imbecility in the public administrations, it is true, form the great features of our political conduct, but these have resulted rather from constitutional defects, . . . than the natural dispositions of the people.[67]

Coercion meant use of military force against the defaulting states. Madison had come into the Congress in 1781 arguing that the Confederation Congress should enforce requisitions with a small detachment from the army sent against the states or by sending two or three armed vessels against their

---

[61] ARTICLES OF CONFEDERATION, art. VIII.
[62] Id.
[63] Madison to Jefferson (Oct. 24, 1787), in 10 JM 207.
[64] Washington to Jay (Aug. 5, 1786) in 3 PJJ 208.
[65] Madison to Washington (April 16, 1787), in 9 JM 385.
[66] Randolph, Reasons for Not Signing the Constitution (Dec. 27, 1787), in 8 DHRC 260, 266.
[67] Edward Carrington to Jefferson (June 9, 1787), in 11 PTJ 408.

trade.[68] The vesting "of such a power in Congress," Madison had then written to Jefferson, "might [even] possibly supercede the use of it."[69] "General decrees must either remain without efficacy," William Samuel Johnson told Connecticut, "or be put in execution by a military force. When a Dutch province has neglected to furnish her quota for the national expense," he noted, "taxes have been levied by an army."[70] "No government shall be stable," wrote Randolph, "which hangs on human inclination alone, unbiassed by the fear of coercion."[71]

Although the federal right of coercion should be endorsed, collection of revenue by military force against the states was not a very good idea. "The difficulty & awkwardness of operating by force on the collective will of a State," Madison said, "render it particularly desirable that the necessity of it might be precluded."[72] Madison told the Convention early that he doubted the practicability or justice of using force against the states. The states attacked would probably consider violence a dissolution of all previous compacts by which they might be bound. A union containing an ingredient of coercion thus "seemed to provide for its own destruction."[73] The states would resist a compelled requisition, Robert Livingston would say, as they would "a foreign tribute, or the invasion of an enemy."[74] Enforcing requisitions by military force after default, Hamilton concluded, was "one of the maddest projects that was ever devised."[75]

---

[68] Madison to Jefferson (April 16, 1781), *in* 3 JM 71. In March 1781, the same month the Articles were finally ratified, the Confederation Congress had authorized an amendment to authorize it to seize state merchandise to enforce its orders. 1 DHRC 141–143.

[69] Madison to Jefferson (April 16, 1781), *in* 3 JM 71–2 (also saying that the power to coerce payments "is certainly a transcendent power, never to be used but in cases of absolute necessity and extremity").

[70] William Samuel Johnson, Connecticut Convention, *in* 3 DHRC 545. Oliver Ellsworth, Connecticut Convention (Jan. 4, 1788), *in* 3 DHRC 545 (saying that "a principle of coercion is absolutely necessary").

[71] Randolph, Reasons for not Signing the Constitution (Dec. 27, 1787), *in* 8 DHRC 266 (also saying that "coercion is an indispensable ingredient" but intrusion of troops would "shed kindred blood," so instead federal tax was needed and that Articles of Confederation prohibition on any but express powers prevented Congress from enforcing its mandates).

[72] Madison to Washington (April 16, 1787), *in* 9 JM 385. There is a possible transition from coercion to federal sovereignty in Washington's query: Washington had written Madison, in March, that the failure of public virtue and noncompliance of the states with requisitions meant that the federal government needed coercion or everything else would fail, but then asked, "But the kind of coercion you may ask? This indeed will require thought." Washington to Madison (Mar. 31, 1787), *in* 9 JM , 343.

[73] Madison, Federal Convention (May 31, 1787), *in* 1 FARRAND 53. *See also* Madison, (July 14, 1787), *in* 2 *id.* at 9 (saying that "[t]he practicability of making laws, with coercive sanctions, for the States as Political bodies had been exploded on all hands").

[74] Robert Livingston, New York Ratification Convention (June 27, 1788) *in* 2 ELLIOT 344.

[75] Hamilton, New York Convention (June 20, 1788) *in* 2 ELLIOT 232 (also saying that coercion would lead to a "nation at war with itself").

What was needed, Madison said, was a system that "would make use of force unnecessary."[76] If the Congress could operate directly on individuals, the Congress could enforce the law by the "mild and salutary coertion of the magistracy," instead of the "destructive coertion of the sword."[77] "The Radical vice in the Old Confederation," Hamilton would tell the New York ratifying convention, "is that the laws of the Union apply only to the states in their corporate capacity" and the Constitution fixed the vice by allowing the Union to operate directly on the people.[78] James Iredell told the North Carolina convention,

> Requisitions thus having failed of their purpose, it is proposed, by this Constitution, that, instead of collecting taxes by the sword, application shall be made by the government to the individual citizens. If any individual disobeys, the courts of justice can give immediate relief. This is the only natural and effectual method of enforcing laws.[79]

Even George Mason, who would become an ardent Anti-Federalist, agreed, saying that "punishment could not in the nature of things be executed on the States collectively, and therefore that such a Govt. was necessary as could directly operate on individuals, and would punish those only whose guilt required it."[80]

---

[76] Madison, Federal Convention (May 31, 1787), *in* 1 FARRAND 53.

[77] *Federalist* No. 20, at 129 (Madison and Hamilton) (Dec. 11, 1787); *See also Federalist* No. 16, at 103 (Hamilton) (Dec. 4, 1787) (saying that national government must carry its agency to the person of the citizens); *Federalist* No. 27, at 174 (Hamilton) (Dec. 25, 1787) (saying when the authority of the federal head extended to the individual citizens of the several states, the federal government could employ "ordinary magistracy" in the execution of its laws).

[78] Hamilton, New York Ratifying Convention (June 20, 1788), *in* 2 ELLIOT 231. *See also Federalist* No. 15, at 95 (Hamilton) (Dec. 1, 1787) (arguing that extending authority of the union to persons will avoid military execution as the sole instrument of civil obedience); *Federalist* No. 15, at 96 (Hamilton) (Dec. 1, 1787) (arguing that we must extend the authority of the union to the persons of the citizens because if the union has authority only over the states, then every breach and enforcement of law must involve a state of war, and "military execution must become the only instrument of civil obedience").

[79] James Iredell, North Carolina Convention (July 28, 1788), *in* 4 ELLIOT 146. Similarly see Charles Pinckney, South Carolina House of Representatives (Jan. 16, 1788), *in* 3 FARRAND 248 (saying that the Convention felt the necessity of establishing a government which, instead of requiring the intervention of thirteen different legislatures between the demand and the compliance, should operate upon the people in the first instance); Randolph, Reasons for not Signing the Constitution (Dec. 27, 1787), *in* 8 DHRC 266 (saying that coercion was indispensable ingredient, but troops to enforce requisitions would shed kindred blood, so a federal tax was needed instead).

[80] Mason, Federal Convention (May 30, 1787), *in* 1 FARRAND 34.

Professor Jack Rakove has argued that the Framer's response to the awkwardness of coercion against the states is the key to the Constitution.[81] The need for coercion, without civil war, led the Convention to adopt "a completely articulated government, capable of enacting, executing and adjudicating its own laws."[82] "Within the space of a single paragraph, paragraph 7 of Madison's *Vices of the Political System*," Rakove argues, Madison had moved from an empirical observation about the current situation to an abstract formulation about inevitable results. The Framers adopted a complete national government able to collect taxes from individuals so as to avoid military action that would amount to civil war.

2. Plenary and Perpetual Tax

The Framers' diagnosis was that the federal level needed a source of revenue for war that did not depend on the unreliable states. Madison had argued in 1783 that the establishment of a permanent and adequate fund for the federal level was "indispensably necessary for doing complete justice to the creditors of the United States, for restoring public credit and for providing for the future exigencies of the war."[83] "Wars have now become rather wars of the purse than of the sword," Oliver Ellsworth argued

> Government must therefore be able to command the whole power of the purse; otherwise a hostile nation may look into our Constitution, see what resources are in the power of government, and calculate to go a little beyond us; thus they may obtain a decided superiority over us, and reduce us to the utmost distress."[84]

A government that could command only some fraction of its resources for revenue, he argued was "like a man with but one arm to defend himself."[85]

---

[81] Jack N. Rakove, Madison Theorizing at 3–5 (presented Nov. 13, 2000 at the University of Texas Law School).

[82] *Id.*

[83] Madison, Motion in the Continental Congress (Jan. 28, 1783), *in* 25 JCC 870.

[84] Oliver Ellsworth, Connecticut Convention (Jan. 7, 1788), *in* 2 ELLIOT 191.

[85] Oliver Ellsworth, Connecticut Convention (Jan. 7, 1788), *in* 5 DHRC 274. *See also Federalist* No. 30, at 191 (Hamilton) (Dec. 28, 1787) arguing that a "government half supplied and always necessitous" cannot fulfill its purposes of security, advancement of prosperity, and reputation); *Federalist* No. 36, at 230 (Hamilton) (Jan. 8, 1788) (acknowledging his aversion "to every project that is calculated to disarm the government of a single weapon, which . . . might be usefully employed for the general defence and security"); *Federalist* No. 31, at 196 (Hamilton) (Jan. 1, 1788) (arguing that because the federal government had unlimited responsibilities in time of war or domestic unrest, it must be granted unlimited power to fund satisfaction of its responsibilities even in ordinary times).

The 1781 and 1783 proposals to give the national government the 5 percent impost would have limited use of the revenues collected to the payment of the debts of the Revolutionary War.[86] The Constitution did not earmark its revenue to the past debts, although that was the immediate crisis that generated the document. Under the Constitution, the new national government was given general funding – all taxes except for a tax on exports – to use "to provide for the common defence and general welfare."[87] "That power, which holds the purse strings absolutely, must rule," Alexander Hamilton had written in 1780,[88] and the Constitution gives Congress the absolute power to tax. Congress was given the "vital power of taxation exceeding those ever allowed by the Colonies to [Great Britain]," James Madison would later reflect. The Colonies had preferred "a bloody war, and final separation," he said, to giving Great Britain plenary power to tax them.[89]

The Constitution is a permanent empowerment on taxation, and not a temporary delegation. The British Parliament itself had granted temporary taxing power to the Crown for war, but not a permanent taxing power, so as to require the king to come back again for revenue for each new war.[90] The Constitution gave the new government the power to lay taxes directly without the "continual recurrence to the state legislatures"[91] and indeed without ever needing to go back to the states for revenue or reauthorization to tax.

The opponents of ratification of the Constitution treated the federal power to tax as crucial. "The celebrated Montesquieu establishes it as a maxim," said the Anti-Federalist Centinel, "that legislation necessarily follows the power of taxation."[92] The assumption of this power of laying direct taxes,

---

[86] Congressional Resolution (Feb. 3, 1781), *in* 19 JCC 112–113 (1781 impost limited to payment of principal and interest on the Revolutionary War debts); Congressional Resolution (April 18, 1783), *in* 24 JCC 258 (1783 impost similarly limited).

[87] U.S. CONST. Art. I, §8, cl. 1 (giving Congress the power to tax to provide for the common defense and general welfare), §9, cl. 5 (providing that no tax or duty shall be laid on articles exported from any state). *See also* Art. I, §8, cl. 1, §9 cl. 4 (requiring that direct taxes must be apportioned among the states according to population, counting slaves at three-fifths).

[88] Hamilton to James Duane (Sept. 3, 1780), *in* 2 PAH 400, 404.

[89] Madison to N. P. Trist (Dec. 1831), *in* 3 FARRAND 516. *See also* FERGUSON at 290 (1961) (arguing, unsympathetically, that "[n]othing testified more to the audacity of the founding fathers" than their demand that the people relinquish the power to tax, which they had fought the British to preserve).

[90] *See, e.g.*, Douglass C. North & Barry R. Weingast, *Constitutions and Commitment: The Evolution of Institutional Governing Public Choice in Seventeenth-Century England*, 49 J. OF ECON. HIST. 803, 816 (1989) (saying that Glorious Revolution of 1688 firmly re-established British Parliaments exclusive power to raise new taxes).

[91] Jefferson to Madison (Dec. 20, 1787), *in* 2 DHRC 482.

[92] "Centinel" [Samuel Bryan] I, INDEPENDENT GAZETTEER (PHILADELPHIA) (Oct. 5, 1787), *reprinted in* 1 DEBATE 53, 57.

Anti-Federalist George Mason argued, changed what was formerly a confederation into a consolidated government and allowed the general government to "annihilate totally the State Governments."[93] The Constitution gave the general government more powers than necessary for its purpose, Patrick Henry protested, and those powers could never be taken back except by revolution.[94] "Be careful then to give only a limited revenue, and the limited power of managing foreign concerns, 'Agrippa'," warned Massachusetts.[95]

The principle of state sovereignty had been used to veto the federal impost proposal in Rhode Island, Virginia, and New York,[96] and the Constitution would give the general government the impost. The Framers seem to have agreed with the syllogism that federal tax was inconsistent with state sovereignty. Monster sovereignty, Washington told John Jay, has taken hold of the states.[97] The Federalists then denied the conclusion that the federal government could not be given power over the impost and so rebutted the premise that the states should have sovereignty. If giving the general government any power to tax was a breach of state sovereignty, then so be it.

In the Pennsylvania Ratification Convention, opponents objected that giving the federal government the power to tax left no sovereignty in the state governments, and Wilson responded that he "should be very glad to know at what period the state governments became possessed of the supreme power . . . The principle of this Constitution [is that] the supreme power resides in the people."[98] Federal tax defeated the principle of state sovereignty.

Conversely, once it was decided that the federal government could collect its revenue directly, without using the states, then the states lost a critical argument that the Congress should be an agent of the states. It was widely believed, at the time, in both especially aristocratic and especially democratic circles that representation in government should follow contribution to the

---

93 Mason, Virginia Convention (June 4, 1788), *in* 9 DHRC 936.
94 Letter, Petersburg Virginia Gazette (June 19, 1788), *reprinted in* 10 DHRC 1653.
95 "Agrippa" (James Winthrop) IX, Massachusetts Gazette (Boston) (Dec. 28, 1787), *reprinted in* 1 Debate 630.
96 For Rhode Island *see, e.g.,* David Howell to Governor William Green (Feb. 5, 1784), *in* 21 LDCC 346 (saying that if the states give up to Congress the power of raising money from them and disposing of that money, their sovereignty will be absorbed into a single sovereignty). For Virginia see XI Statutes of Virginia 171 (William Waller Henning, ed., Oct. 1782) (saying that giving any entity other than the General Assembly of Virginia the power to levy taxes upon citizens of Virginia was injurious to Virginia's sovereignty); A Rough Hewer, N.Y. Journal. (Mar. 17, 1785), *quoted in* Kaminski, Clinton 90 (1993) (saying that federal tax would swallow up entirely "the sovereignty of the particular states").
97 Washington to Jay (March 10, 1787), *in* 3 PJJ 239.
98 Wilson, Pennsylvania Convention (Dec. 11, 1787), *in* 2 Elliot 502.

government in time of war.[99] If the contributions to war were to come from the people rather than from the states, then the national government under the principle would have to represent people rather than states. Having freed the Congress from dependence on the states on revenue, the Constitution shifted the legitimating foundation of the general government, so that it became an agent not of the states but a representative of the people directly. The states had forfeited their sovereignty by failing to pay their requisitions. Henceforth, "We the People" would be sovereign and the states would not be.

D. WE, THE PEOPLE

The legitimacy of the Articles of Confederation rested, on the face of the document, upon the states. The Articles, by its own description, created only "a firm league of friendship" among the states,[100] "nothing more," Madison wrote, "than a treaty of amity of commerce and of alliance, between . . . independent and Sovereign States."[101] The Articles themselves provided that each state entering into the league retained its "sovereignty, freedom and independence" and that Congress had no powers beyond those expressly delegated to it by the Articles.[102] The central organization for the friendship league was not a government at all, but rather an assembly of delegates of the states, called "the United States in Congress assembled."[103] The term, "congress", at the time meant an assembly of diplomats from sovereign nations, and not a governing body.[104] The actors who signed the Articles were designated "Delegates of the States" and in signing the Articles, the delegates

---

[99] *See, e.g.*, Pierce Butler (So. Carolina), Federal Convention (July 6, 1787), *in* 1 FARRAND 542 (arguing that property was the "only just measure of representations" because property was "the great means of carrying [war] on"); Gouverneur Morris (N.J.), Federal Convention (July 10, 1787), *in* 1 FARRAND 567 (arguing that voting should come from property in part, but that population should also come into the calculation because, although the South might provide its wealth in war, the Northern states "are to spill their blood"); Virginia Ratification Convention (June 7, 1788), *in* 9 DHRC 1048 n.11 (describing Franklin's 1753 plan for a union against the French and Iroquois in which colony would be represented according to its financial contribution to the general treasury).

[100] ARTICLES OF CONFEDERATION, art. I, *in* 19 JCC 214 (March 1, 1781).

[101] Madison, Vices of the Political System of the United States (April–June 1787), *in* 9 JM 351.

[102] ARTICLES OF CONFEDERATION, art. II, *in* 19 JCC 214.

[103] ARTICLES OF CONFEDERATION, arts. II, V, VI, VIII, IX. The first reference in Article II puts a comma in, so the reference is to "United States, in Congress Assembled."

[104] *See, e.g.*, Martin Diamond, *What the Framers Meant by Federalism*, *in* A NATION OF STATES 24 (Robert Goldwin, ed. 1961); Martin Diamond, *The Ends of Federalism*, *in* RELUCTANT PILLAR 16, 19–20 (both discussing the 1787 meaning of "federal" and "congress").

certified that the state legislatures they represented had approved the Articles.[105] Amendments to the Articles needed to be confirmed by every state,[106] and not just by majority or even super-majority of states, because the Articles did not create a single polity and each sovereign state had to consent to be bound by a change.

By contrast, the power of the Constitution, on its own terms, is derived from the people. While the preamble to the Articles identified the adopting actors as "Delegates of States," the parallel preamble to the Constitution identifies the adopting actors as, "We the people of United States" and says that they "do ordain and establish this Constitution."[107] "This...is not a government founded upon compact;" James Wilson told the Pennsylvania Ratifying Convention, "it is founded upon the power of the people. They express in their name and their authority – 'We, the people, do ordain and establish....'"[108] "Oft have I viewed with silent pleasure," Wilson declared, "the force and the prevalence through[out] the United States of this principle: that the supreme power resides in the people, and they never part with it."[109] The Anti-Federalists argued that twin sovereignties, one at the federal level and one at the state, was an impossible thing, a division of sovereignty. Sovereignty is absolute and cannot be divided, they said.[110] Wilson replied that there was only one sovereign – the people – and that both levels of government should report obediently to the sovereign people. "[I]n this government," James Wilson told Pennsylvania, "the supreme, absolute and uncontrollable power remains in the people."[111] The people were the supreme power "from which there is no appeal."[112]

[105] ARTICLES OF CONFEDERATION, preamble and Article XIII, *in* 19 JCC 214, 221.
[106] ARTICLES OF CONFEDERATION, art. XIII.
[107] U.S. CONST., preamble.
[108] Wilson, Pennsylvania Convention (Dec. 11, 1787), *in* 2 ELLIOT 497–498.
[109] Wilson, Pennsylvania Convention (Nov. 26, 1787), *in* 2 ELLIOT 433.
[110] Federalist No. 15, at 93 (Hamilton) (Dec. 1, 1787) (saying the Anti-Federalists seem to "cherish with blind devotion the political monster of imperium in imperio"). FORREST MCDONALD, NOVUS ORDO SECLORUM: THE INTELLECTUAL ORIGINS OF THE CONSTITUTION 277–81 (1985) (argues that popular sovereignty was a response to Anti-Federalists' argument that Constitution sought to divide sovereignty).
[111] Wilson, Pennsylvania Convention (Nov. 26, 1787), *in* 2 ELLIOT 432. *See also* Wilson (Dec. 1, 1787), *in id.* at 443 (saying that if there cannot be two sovereigns, then the people and not the states have the sovereignty); Wilson (Dec. 4, 1787), *in id.* 457–458 (saying "[m]y position is, sir, that, in this country, the supreme, absolute, and uncontrollable power resides in the people at large; that they have vested certain proportions of this power in the state governments; but that the fee-simple continues, resides, and remains, with the body of the people").
[112] Wilson, Pennsylvania Convention (Nov. 26, 1787), *in* 2 ELLIOT 432.

Wilson also dismissed the sovereignty of the states:

> Upon what principle is it contended that the sovereign power resides in the state governments? The honorable gentleman has said truly, that there can be no subordinate sovereignty. Now, if there cannot, my position is, that the sovereignty resides in the people; they have not parted with it; they have only dispensed such portions of power as were conceived necessary for the public welfare. This Constitution stands upon this broad principle. I know very well, sir, that the people have hitherto been shut out of the federal government; but it is not meant that they should any longer be dispossessed of their rights.[113]

In the Federal Convention, Wilson argued that the New Jersey Plan "flows from an illegitimate Sources [sic], the Legislative and Executive Powers of the States, and not the People at large."[114] If the New Jersey plan was illegitimate because it flowed from the legislatures of the states, then so were the Articles.

Other Federalists repeated the celebration of the shift from states to people. "No alterations in government should I think be made," John Jay had written in January 1787, "unless deducible from the only source of just authority – The People."[115] In preparation for the Convention, Madison had written Washington that "individual independence of the States is utterly irreconcilable with the idea of an aggregate sovereignty"[116] Ending state sovereignty was then a recurring theme at the Convention. Hamilton argued that "no amendment of the confederation, leaving the States in possession of their sovereignty could possibly answer the purpose."[117] Pinckney argued that if "the influence of the States is not lost in some part of the new Government we shall never have any thing like a national institution."[118] Even George Mason, who would later fight ratification of the Constitution, joined in the consensus at Philadelphia that that national sovereignty was derived from the people:

> Under the existing confederacy, Congs. represent[s] the States not the people of the States: their acts operate on the States, not on

[113] Wilson, Pennsylvania Convention (Dec. 1, 1787), *in* 2 ELLIOT 443.
[114] *See also* Wilson, Federal Convention (June 16 1787), *in* 1 FARRAND 279 (Yates Notes).
[115] Jay to Washington (Jan. 7, 1787) *in* 3 PJJ 224.
[116] Madison to Washington (April 16, 1787), *in* 9 JM383. *See also* prior draft of same language in Madison to Randolph (April 8, 1787), *in* 9 JM 369.
[117] Hamilton, Federal Convention (June 18, 1787), *in* 1 FARRAND 283.
[118] Charles Pinckney, Federal Convention (May 31, 1787), *in* 1 FARRAND 59 (William Pierce notes). *See also* Elbridge Gerry (June 29, 1787), *in* 1 *id.* 467 (saying that "[t]he States & the advocates for them were intoxicated with the idea of their sovereignty").

the individuals. The case will be changed in the new plan of Govt. The people will be represented; they ought therefore to choose the Representatives.[119]

In the final letter of the Convention transmitting the Constitution to Congress, George Washington said that it expected the states to give up some of "their rights of independent sovereignty" to "provide for the interest and safety of all."[120]

In *Federalist* Number 39, Madison wrote that "as the people are the only legitimate fountain of power, . . . it is from them that the constitutional charter . . . is derived."[121] The name "republic," he argued, is properly bestowed only on "a government which derives all its powers directly or indirectly from the great body of the people."[122] The consent of the people, Hamilton argued, is that "pure original fountain of legitimate authority."[123] The first Chief Justice, John Jay, would later say that by the preamble language "We the people of the United States," the people established their sovereignty and established a Constitution to which "the State Governments should be bound, and to which the State Constitutions should be made to conform."[124] The federal government, wrote Chief Justice John Marshall, proceeds directly from the people because it "is 'ordained and established' in the name of the people."[125]

The shift to "We the People" as a foundation for government drew support from republican norms arising from the Revolution. The movement leading to the Revolution had adopted the idea that the people were sovereign over all branches of government and all government was accountable to the people. The Congress had called upon Canada to join in the revolution in 1774 on the argument that "the first grand right, is that of the people having a share in their own government by their representatives chosen by

---

119 Mason, Debates in the Federal Convention (June 6, 1787), *in* 1 FARRAND 133.
120 Washington, Letter to Congress by Unanimous Order of the Convention (Sept. 17, 1787), *in* 2 FARRAND 666.
121 *Federalist* No. 49, at 339 (Madison) (Feb. 2, 1788). *See* also, *e.g.*, Benjamin Franklin, Debates in the Federal Convention (Aug. 7, 1787), *in* 2 FARRAND 204 (praising the virtue of our common people, whose public spirit contributed principally to the winning of the Revolution); Wilson, Continental Congress (Aug. 1, 1776), *in* 6 JCC 1105 (arguing that it is magic and not reason that "annexing the name of 'State' to ten thousand men, should give them equal right with forty thousand").
122 *Federalist* No. 39, at 251 (Madison) (Jan. 16, 1788).
123 *Federalist* No. 22, at 146 (Hamilton) (Dec. 14, 1787).
124 Chisholm v. Georgia, 2 U.S. (2 Dallas) 419, 471 (1793) (Jay, Chief Justice).
125 McCullough v. Maryland, 17 U.S. (4 Wheat) 316, 403 (1819) (Marshall, J.).

themselves."[126] The Declaration of Independence had justified the Revolution on the ground that governments "deriv[e] their just Powers from the consent of the governed."[127] Ratification by popular consent had also been established as an ideal during the war in the process of the adoption of the Massachusetts Constitution of 1780, where the town meetings had sought and achieved the power to ratify.[128] After the Revolution, the legitimacy of the government could rest directly on the people.

The Anti-Federalists opposed the new principle of resting the general government on the sovereignty of the people. "The plan before us... explicitly proposes the foundation of a new constitution upon the original authority of the people," Anti-Federalist John Smilie objected in Pennsylvania, "and not an association of states upon the authority of their respective governments."[129] Smilie asked,

> When it declared that 'We the people of the United States do ordain and establish this constitution' is not the very foundation a proof of a consolidated government, by the manifest subversion of the principle that [the confederation] constituted a union of States, which are sovereign and independent?[130]

"Who authorized them to speak the language of, We, the People, instead of We, the States?" Patrick Henry demanded. "States are the characteristics and the soul of a confederation. If the States be not the agents of this compact, it must be one great consolidated National Government of the people... The people gave them no power to use their name."[131] In Massachusetts, Samuel Nasson asked, "[If the phrase, 'We, the people'] does not go to an annihilation of the state governments, and to a perfect consolidation of the whole Union, I do not know what does."[132] The Constitution should show, Anti-Federalists argued, that the general government "depends for support upon the individual states as well as upon the sovereign

[126] Address of the Congress to the people of Canada [Quebec], *in* 1 JCC 107 (Oct. 26, 1774). *See* David Conway, *Development of a Revolutionary Organization, 1765–1775, in* JACK GREEN & J. R. POLE, THE BLACKWELL ENCYCLOPEDIA OF THE AMERICAN REVOLUTION 223, 229 (1991); DAVID F. EPSTEIN, POLITICAL THEORY OF THE FEDERALIST 119 (1984).
[127] Declaration of Independence, *in* 5 JCC 510 ¶2 (July 4, 1776).
[128] Oscar Handlin & Mary F. Handlin, *Introduction.* THE POPULAR SOURCES OF POLITICAL AUTHORITY: DOCUMENTS ON THE MASSACHUSETTS CONSTITUTION OF 1780, at 18–26 (1966) (describing successful demands by the townships to obtain the right to approve the Massachusetts state constitution).
[129] John Smilie, Pennsylvania Convention (Nov. 28, 1787), *in* 2 DHRC 408.
[130] *Id.*
[131] Patrick Henry, Virginia Convention (June 4, 1788), *in* 3 ELLIOT 22–23.
[132] Samuel Nasson, Massachusetts Convention (Feb. 1, 1788), *in* 2 ELLIOT 134.

people."[133] Anti-Federalist David Caldwell, in South Carolina, objected that the delegates to Philadelphia had no power from the people at large, but were representatives only of the state legislatures.[134] Even within the Convention itself, John Lansing had argued for the New Jersey Plan, because "the powers are exercised as flowing from the respective state governments," whereas the Virginia Plan, "deriving its authority from the people of the respective states[,] . . . must ultimately destroy or annihilate the state governments."[135] The Federalists might deny all the consequent horribles, but they did not deny that the Constitution replaced the sovereignty of the states with the sovereignty of the people.

E. RATIFICATION

Consistent with the shift in foundation for legitimacy from states to the people, the Framers also shifted the basis of ratification. The Articles of Confederation had been ratified by the legislature of each state, speaking throught agents, the delegates to Congress.[136] Ratification of the new Constitution, by contrast, bypassed the state legislatures and governors, who together acted for the state in its sovereign capacity. Ratification rested instead on ratification by the people directly, meeting in ratification conventions.

Ratification of the constitution was to occur in ratifying conventions, organized in each state. That the ratifying conventions organized the people by state was not meant to imply that the states would be the paramount, ratifying actors. Ratification was a measure of the people and not a measure of the state governments, said Justice John Marshall, even though the people assembled in conventions in the several states, which was the only way they could meet.[137] "No State, in its corporate capacity, ratified [the Constitution]," William Pinckney argued before the Marshall Supreme Court in 1819.[138]

Ratification by the people was necessary to achieve supremacy of federal law over state law. In his catalog of vices of the existing system under the

---

[133] George Len Trelvener to Madison (April 16, 1788), *in* 11 JM 24.
[134] David Caldwell, North Carolina Convention (July 24, 1788), *in* 4 ELLIOT 15–16.
[135] June 16, 1787, *in* 1 FARRAND 257 (Yates notes).
[136] 19 JCC 221 (March 1, 1781) (saying that the legislatures the signing delegates represented had approved the Articles and authorized ratification). Congress in passing the Articles of Confederation also said that the Articles "shall be proposed to the legislatures of all the united states to be considered, and if approved of by them they are advised to authorize their delegates to ratify the same in the Congress." 9 JCC 925 (Nov. 25, 1777).
[137] *See, e.g.,* McCulloch v. Maryland, 17 U.S. (4 Wheat.) 316, 403 (1819) (Marshall, J.).
[138] William Pinckney, Argument before the Supreme Court in McCullough v. Maryland, 17 U.S. (Wheat) 316, 377 (1819).

Articles, Madison has listed "want of ratification by the people" so that "the Union of States is to be regarded as a league."[139] The defect resulted in the "evil" that "[w]henever a law of a State happens to be repugnant to an act of Congress . . . it will be at least questionable whether the latter must not prevail."[140] Ratification by the people, by contrast, would establish a national government that was paramount over the states: Madison criticized the New Jersey Plan, on the grounds that under the plan, ratification was by the Legislatures of the states, "which could not therefore render the acts of Congs. [pursuant to the Constitution] even legally paramount to the acts of the States."[141] Madison proposed, as he explained to Jefferson, "to lay the foundation of the new system in such a ratification by the people themselves of the several States as will render it clearly paramount to their Legislative authorities."[142] "To give the System its proper validity and energy," Madison explained to Washington, "a ratification must be obtained from the people, and not merely from the ordinary authority of the Legislatures. This will be the more essential as inroads on the existing Constitutions of the States will be unavoidable."[143] Indeed the state legislatures could not be the ratifying actors, the Federalists argued, because the power resided in the people. It

[139] Madison, Vices of Political System 8, *in* 9 JM 352.

[140] *Id.* Madison was worried especially because the question of supremacy of state law over acts of Congress would be decided by the "Tribunals of the State, [which] will be most likely to lean on the side of the State." *Id.*

[141] June 19, 1787, *in* 1 FARRAND 317. Randolph made the same argument, apparently derived from Madison, identifying a defect of the Articles of Confederation that the Articles were not even paramount to the state constitution because the Articles were ratified by only the states. Federal Convention (May 29, 1787), *in* 1 FARRAND 24. *See also* Wilson (June 16 1787), *in id.* at 279 (Yates Notes) (arguing that the New Jersey plan "flows from an *illegitimate* Sources[sic], the Legislative and Executive Powers of the States, and not the People at large," but not about supremacy of federal law in specific).

[142] Madison to Jefferson (Mar. 19, 1787), *in* 9 JM 318; Jack Rakove, *Concept of Ratification, in* RAKOVE. ORIGINAL MEANINGS 94–108 (1996).

State legislatures (but not governors) have a possible or alternative role in ratification of subsequent Amendments to the Constitution. Amendments become valid when ratified by the Legislatures of three fourths of the several States, or by Conventions in three fourths thereof, as the one or the other mode may be proposed by Congress. U.S. CONST. art V. The states are invited in, however, by Congress. Congress gets to choose whether to have ratification by the state legislatures or by conventions of the people that by-pass the legislatures. A sovereignty that comes in only by invitation of Congress is not an ultimate source of legitimacy. For the ratification of the original Constitution, it was only conventions of the people and not the state legislatures as sovereign, who would ratify. U.S. CONST. art. VII.

[143] Madison to Washington (April 16, 1787), *in* 9 JM 385 (emphasis in the original deleted). *See also* Madison to Randolph (April 8, 1787), *in* 9 JM 370 (saying that "to give the new system its proper energy it will be desirable to have it ratified by the authority of the people, and not merely by that of the Legislatures").

would be "no less than treason in those to whom the people have delegated the exercise of the sovereign power," wrote one Federalist, "to attempt, without their constituents' express consent, fairly and fully given, to assign it over to others."[144]

Ratification by popular conventions rather than by the states also had a necessary tactical aspect to it because the Framers did not think that they could get ratification by the states acting in their sovereign capacity. In Philadelphia, Madison argued that the state legislatures would be disinclined to ratify, and would "devise modes apparently promoting, but really thwarting the ratification," for the simple reason that the Constitution would take power away from the states. The people, by contrast "were in fact, the fountain of all power, and by resorting to them, all difficulties were got over [because t]hey could alter constitutions as they pleased."[145] Hamilton argued, to start the *Federalist*, that the most formidable obstacles to ratification would be the state officeholders who will "resist all changes which may hazard a diminution of the power, emolument, and consequence of [their] offices. . . . "[146] Even men of consequence, Hamilton wrote privately, would oppose adoption from a "desire of playing a part in a convulsion for their own aggrandizement."[147] The opposition would come most likely, Governor Randolph said, from "the local demogagues who will be downgraded by it from the importance they now hold."[148]

The Framers tried to work around the established state powers by putting ratification of the Constitution to special conventions of the people convened only for the purpose of considering ratification. Consideration of ratification should be transferred away from the legislatures, where the local demogagues would "have their full influence, . . . to a field in which their efforts can be less mischievous."[149] The people at large were "not averse to a Genl. Govt," George Read of Delaware told the Convention. "The aversion lies among interested men. . . ."[150] The people will "follow us into a national Govt.," James Wilson predicted confidently, which was a good reason he said for submitting the Constitution to the people and not to the

---

[144] "Jonathan of the Valley" Boston Independent Chronicle (Oct. 20, 1785), *quoted in* Rakove, Beginnings 384.
[145] Madison, Federal Convention (Aug. 31, 1787), *in* 2 Farrand 476.
[146] *Federalist* No.1, at 4 (Hamilton) (Oct. 27, 1787).
[147] Hamilton's Conjectures About the New Constitution (Sept. 1787), *in* 1 Debate 9.
[148] Randolph, Federal Convention (July 23, 1787), *in* 2 Farrand 89.
[149] *Id.*
[150] George Read (Del.), Federal Convention (June 6, 1787), *in* 1 Farrand 137.

legislatures for ratification.[151] Thus ratification of the Constitution was not by the states, acting as sovereign entities, but rather by the people, organized for administrative ease, state by state. The people would support the Constitution.

[151] Wilson, Federal Convention (June 16, 1787), *in* 1 FARRAND 253.

CHAPTER FIVE

Partial Losses

The Constitution that was proposed by the Philadelphia Convention was less nationalistic than Madison's original plans expressed in his letters to his mentors. Madison's original vision for the Constitution would have required that votes in both houses of Congress be apportioned according to population. Congressmen would represent people and not states, and voting power in the Congress would depend on population. Madison, moreover, through the end of the Convention wanted a strong national government that would be able to veto any state law. He could not convince the Convention to grant the federal veto, however, and the scope of federal supremacy was not extended "to any case whatsoever." Madison was very unhappy about his losses, especially about the loss of the full-ranging federal veto. Still, what he accomplished of his nationalist vision was extraordinary and revolutionary.

A. PRINCIPLE OF REPRESENTATION

The shift in legitimating foundation from states to the people seemed to Madison to require a change in the rules of representation in Congress. Under the Articles, each state had equal vote in the Congress, no matter how many people were in the state. Thus a large state like Virginia and a tiny state like Rhode Island had the same voting power. A state could have as many as seven or as few as two delegates, but in determining questions in the Congress of states assembled, the delegates of the state altogether, no matter what their number, gave the state only a single vote.[1]

The new government was to represent people, not states. Since the new system, Madison explained to Washington, "would operate in many essential

---

[1] ARTICLES OF CONFEDERATION, art. V.

points without the operation of the state governments...,"[2] the change in the foundation of the government would require a "change in the principle of representation."[3] Madison proposed that representatives should be allocated according to population. The true principle, Madison explained to the Convention, was that "where the Genl. Governt. is to act on the people, let the people be represented and the votes be proportional [and] where the Governt. is to act on the States as such, in like manner as Congs. now act."[4]

From the norm that the government represents people, representation of states looked perverse. James Wilson had been savage in his condemnation of the principle, ultimately adopted in the Articles of Confederation, that votes and representation were by states. It was "magic and not reason," he said, that "annexing the name of 'State' to ten thousand men, should give them equal right with forty thousand."[5] Giving equal vote to the small states allowed a minority of the population to have the majority in Congress.[6]

Madison told Washington that he expected all of the states to go along with the shift in the representation formula from votes per state to votes according to population:

> A majority of the States, and those of greatest influence, will regard it as favorable to them. To the Northern States it will be recommended by their present populousness; to the Southern by their expected advantage in this respect. The lesser States must in every event yield to the predominant will. But the consideration which particularly urges a change in the representation is that it will obviate the principal objections of the larger States to the necessary concessions of power.[7]

Madison's prediction that small states would endorse the switch to votes by population turned out to be far too sanguine. The smaller states did not "yield to the predominant will" and forced a compromise reflected in the very different formulas for votes in the two houses of the new Congress. The Senate reflects the status quo principle of the Articles of Confederation, allocating votes by states, and only the House reflects the new principle of votes by population.

[2] Madison to Washington (April 16, 1787), *in* 9 JM 383.
[3] *Id.*
[4] Madison, Federal Convention, July 14, 1787, *in* 2 FARRAND 8.
[5] Wilson, Continental Congress (Aug. 1, 1776), *in* 6 JCC 1105.
[6] Madison, Federal Convention (July 7, 1787), *in* 1 FARRAND 554 (saying that the Senate will enable a minority to hold the majority).
[7] Madison to Washington (April 16, 1787), *in* 9 JM 383. The same argument is in Madison to Randolph (April 8, 1787), *in* 9 JM 371.

That Madison got his representation by population even in one house probably depended on the sentiment that governments should represent property. At the Philadelphia Convention there was a substantial block of delegates who were willing to give weight to the principle that contribution by tax should determine representation. Because wealth would determine tax paid, wealth should determine representation. Property was the "only just measure of representations," argued Pierce Butler of South Carolina, because property was the "the great object" of government and "the means of carrying [war] on."[8] Other delegates if not resting the government entirely on property, were willing to give the rich South some extra weight in the voting because of its wealth. Votes should reflect contribution to government and both wealth and the spilling of blood would contribute to the government in war.[9] The strength of the principle that votes should reflect contribution to government also meant that the most democratic spokesmen at the Convention argued that Congress should represent people, because they, like wealth, contributed to the winning of war.[10]

In one of the most interesting political moves in the Convention, the Federalists avoided the conflict between votes reflecting wealth and votes reflecting population by arguing that there was no need to distinguish between the two bases. James Wilson said he had seen the tax figures for Pennsylvania state tax and that there was no difference in outcome between Philadelphia and the rest of the state as to whether Pennsylvania taxes were apportioned by wealth or by population.[11] Nathaniel Gorham said there was no difference in Massachusetts: For Boston and the rest the state, he said, "the most exact proportion prevailed between the numbers & property."[12] Madison then generalized – and he was a generalizer – to argue that the proportion between wealth and population was inevitable, so long as migration was possible. Where intercourse among the states was easy and

---

[8] Pierce Butler (So. Carolina), Federal Convention (July 6, 1787), *in* 1 FARRAND 542. *See also* Pierce Butler (So. Carolina) (July 9, 1787), *in* 1 *id.* at 562 (Butler warmly urging the necessity of regarding wealth in the determination of representation).

[9] Gouverneur Morris (N.J.), Federal Convention (July 10, 1787), *in* 1 FARRAND 567 (arguing that voting should come from property in part, but that population should also come into the calculation because, although the South might provide its wealth in war, the Northern states "are to spill their blood"). *See also* Charles Pinckney (N. Carolina) (July 10, 1787), *in* 1 *id* 567 ("due weight" to property).

[10] *See, e.g.*, Benjamin Franklin, Federal Convention (Aug. 7, 1787), *in* 2 FARRAND 204 (praising the virtue of our common people, whose public spirit contributed principally to the winning of the Revolution).

[11] Wilson, Speech to the Federal Convention (July 11, 1787), *in* 1 FARRAND 587.

[12] Nathaniel Gorham, Speech to the Federal Convention (July 11, 1787), *in* 1 FARRAND 587.

free, then movement between the states would destroy any disproportion between population and wealth. Free labor would always migrate away from the poor land and into the cities or rich land. The value of labor, counting each hand the same, therefore, "might be considered as the principal criterion of wealth and ability to pay tax."[13] Thereafter, it was said, wealth and population were each "true and equitable rules of representation," but "the principles resolved themselves into one; population being the best measure of wealth."[14]

Having votes reflect wealth was as devastating as allocating votes according to population to the Articles' principle that each state should have an equal vote. Wealth deserved representation because votes should be proportional to the contribution to government reflected by tax paid. States would thus have to pay for their votes with taxes. If a small state was to have one-thirteenth of the votes, it would need to pay one-thirteenth of the taxes. Under that rule, Delaware, as Benjamin Franklin had quipped, could hardly afford the privilege of its votes.[15] Thus the aristocrats, believing that government properly represented wealth, and the democrats, believing that the people are the fountain of all sovereignty, were allies in opposition to the rule of the Articles, that each state should have equal votes.

Indeed, the aristocratic principle that votes should follow contribution to government condemns the Article's rule of the sovereignty of the states as well. The Anti-Federalists opposed to the Constitution wanted the document to affirm the sovereignty of the states, but without paying the requisitions by which they were to buy representation. Under the Articles of Confederation, the states had been sovereign, but they forfeited their sovereignty by failing to pay their dues.

Judiciously, the Virginia Plan took the position that "rights of suffrage in the National Legislature ought to be proportional to Quotas of contribution or number of free inhabitants, as one or the other rule may seem best in different cases."[16] Greater wealth could be allocated more votes if Congress

---

[13] Madison, Federal Convention (July 11, 1787), *in* 1 FARRAND 585.

[14] William Samuel Johnson (July 12, 1787), *in* 1 FARRAND 593. *Accord* Connecticut Land-holder, *Letter XI*, CONNECTICUT COURANT (Mar. 10, 1788), *reprinted in* 4 DHRC 367, 368 ("The population and fertility in any tract of country will be proportioned to each other"); Gaspard Joseph Amand Ducher to Comte de la Luzerne (Feb. 2, 1788), *in* 4 DHRC 11, 12 (wealth of a state was best calculated only by the work of its inhabitants).

[15] "Certainly if we vote equally we ought to pay equally; but the smaller states will hardly purchase the privilege at this price." Benjamin Franklin, Continental Congress (Aug 1, 1776), *in* 6 JCC 1102.

[16] Virginia Plan, 1 FARRAND 20. The Articles determined a states' quota of contribution by the relative value of land and improvements within the state, so that one of the alternatives

wanted that. This was a compromise that Madison was willing to give to his Virginia colleagues in order to get their assent to offer his designs as a Virginia Plan.[17] The distinction between a government based on people and a government based on property or contributions could be compromised, since both attacked voting by state. The important issue, in Madison's vision, was that the national government should not depend on the states.

Although Madison wrote that he expected the lesser states to "yield to the predominant will" and allow representation to be by population,[18] it turned out that the smaller states were not as willing to yield so quickly. The small states doggedly defended the status quo in the Articles, which gave them disproportionate weight by giving each state the same voting power, no matter what its population. Madison argued that small states would do best under the form of guardianship by the national government "which will most approximate the States to the condition of Counties,"[19] but the small states were not convinced.

The New Jersey Plan was put forward by William Patterson of New Jersey as an alternative to the Virginia Plan. The New Jersey Plan preserved the equal-state-votes principle of the Articles.[20] Under the New Jersey Plan, Congress had less plenary tax power: Congress would have had the power to lay stamp taxes and import duties, but otherwise would have had to raise its revenue by requisition.[21] It is quite plausible, that the impetus for the New Jersey Plan was for enlargement of small state votes within the national government, and not to challenge the consensus nationalism. "Give Jersey an equal vote," Pinckney argued, "and she will dismiss her scruples, and concur in the [national] system."[22] New Jersey did indeed endorse the final product

---

the Virginia Plan would allow, if it seemed best, was representation determined by value of real estate. ARTICLES OF CONFEDERATION, art. VII.

[17] To say that Madison compromised assumes, I think fairly, that Madison's personal views are consistent with his statement in *Federalist* No. 49, at 339 (Madison) (Feb. 2, 1788) that the people are the only legitimate fountain of power. Madison's pre-Convention statements are more concerned with taking sovereignty away from the states. Madison to Washington (April 16, 1787), *in* 9 JM 383 (saying that that "individual independence of the States is utterly irreconcilable with the idea of an aggregate sovereignty").

[18] Madison to Washington (April 16, 1787), *in* 9 JM 383. *Accord,* Madison to Jefferson (Mar. 19, 1787), *in* 9 JM 318–319; Madison to Randolph (April 8, 1787), *in* 9 JM 371.

[19] Madison, Federal Convention (June 28, 1787), *in* 1 FARRAND 449.

[20] Paragraph 1 of the New Jersey plan resolved that the Articles of Confederation ought to be revised and then says nothing more about representation. 1 FARRAND 242.

[21] *The New Jersey Amendments to the Articles of Confederation* 2–3 (June 15, 1787), *in* 1 DHRC 251, 1 FARRAND 242–245.

[22] Charles Pinckney, Federal Convention (June 16, 1787), *in* 1 FARRAND 255.

unanimously in its ratification convention, even with its broader federal tax.[23] In any event, the New Jersey Plan was rejected by the Convention, seven states against, three in favor, and one state divided.[24]

Although the New Jersey Plan did not have a majority of the states behind it, nonetheless the Framers compromised, at least halfway, in favor of the New Jersey Plan. Delaware's instructions for the Convention required that its delegates withdraw if the one state–one vote rule of the Articles was amended.[25] Gunning Bedford of Delaware threatened that if the large states dissolved the Articles, "the small ones will find some foreign ally . . . who will do them justice."[26]

The Senate equal-vote-per-state rule is also significantly a product of the decision-making machinery. The delegates to the Convention represented states, not equal populations, and voting was by state, not by how many people a delegation represented. One should not be surprised that the machinery of voting by states produced a result that, at least in half, allocated votes to per state.

Even then, however, the Convention compromised more with Delaware than Delaware's power would justify, even voting by states. The Framers at the Convention set the number of states necessary to ratify the Constitution at nine states of the thirteen, which was the level that the Articles had set even for quite routine governmental operations such as charging expenses to the general treasury. Under the nine of thirteen rule, the Framers could have let Rhode Island, Delaware, Connecticut, and New Jersey, the smallest states, dissent and still have its nine-state assent needed for ratification. Rhode Island, the state with the largest disparity between population and voting fraction in the Senate, was the despicable corner of the Continent, which the delegates in attendance were willing to ignore. Still, the Framers were willing to compromise toward the New Jersey Plan, apparently solely because the majority was supposed to compromise with a noisy minority, even a minority without justice, in the interests of consensus.

---

[23] 3 DHRC 184.

[24] June 19, 1787, *in* 1 FARRAND 313. The motion was to recommend the Virginia Plan and not the New Jersey Plan to the whole convention, when rising from the committee of the whole. New York, New Jersey, and Delaware opposed the motion to report the Virginia Plan rather than the New Jersey Plan, and Maryland was divided. *Id.*

[25] Instructions to the Delegates, 1 DHRC 191–230. *See* George Reed (Del.), Federal Convention (May 30, 1787), *in* 1 FARRAND 37 (telling the convention that Delaware delegates would need to withdraw if equal votes per state were changed).

[26] Gunning Bedford, Federal Convention (June 30 1787), *in* 1 FARRAND 492. Madison suggested that Delaware might avoid public embarrassment by defeating the equal-votes-per-state rule in Committee, but to no avail. Madison (May 30, 1787), *in* 1 *id.* at 37.

Under the "Great Compromise" of the Constitution, votes in the Senate follow the Articles, preserving the same vote per state rule.[27] A citizen of the smallest state gets weighted in the Senate at seventy times the weight of a citizen of the largest.[28] A Wyoming citizen who emigrates to California diminishes his worth on the Senate's scale to one-seventieth of what he was worth in Wyoming or, conversely, a Californian enhances his Senate weight by seventy times by moving to Wyoming. Under the Senate rules, the minority of the population, residing in the smallest states, holds the majority of the votes.[29] There is no principle of representative democracy that can legitimate voting by states. The malapportionment of the Senate is said to be perpetual.[30] Representation by population is, however, the principle in the House of Representatives.

Even in the Senate, however, the Constitution made senators less dependent on the states than the delegates to the Articles congress had been. Under the Articles of Confederation, delegates served at the pleasure of their home legislatures and could be recalled at will. The service-at-will rule gave the States legitimacy to review the daily deliberations of Congress, and that meant, Randolph complained, that the delegates had "no will of their own" and were "always obsequious to the views of the States, who are always encroaching on the authority of the U. States."[31] Senators were given long, fixed six-year terms,[32] and that ended the second guessing of senators on a daily basis. The New York delegates were instructed not to allow amendment

---

[27] U.S. Const. art, I, sec. 2. *See Federalist* No. 39, at 255 (Madison) (Jan. 16, 1788) (saying that "[t]he Senate on the other hand will derive its powers from the States, as political and co-equal societies . . . as they now are in the existing Congress").

[28] U.S. Census Bureau, Statistical Abstract of the United States 22 (2002). *See* Lynn A. Baker & Samuel H. Dinkin, *The Senate: An Institution Whose Time Has Gone?* 13 J.L. & Pol. 21, 25–30 (1997) (California population was 66 times Wyoming population in 1990 census).

[29] Madison, Federal Convention (July 7, 1787), *in* 1 Farrand 554 (saying that an equality of votes in the Senate will let a minority hold a majority). *See also* Madison, Federal Convention, June 28, 1787, 1 Farrand 446–447 (opposing giving small states equal votes by asking "Would 30 or 40 million of people submit their fortunes into the hands, of a few thousands?").

[30] U.S. Const. art. V (saying no State, without its Consent, shall be deprived of its equal Suffrage in the Senate). It is becoming time to reapportion the Senate to get rid of the injustice of it. A legal fiction may be available to help get over the perpetuity rule: a repeal of the existing Constitution and immediate replacement with a Constitution that has all the same provisions intact except for a reformed Amendment V, allowing some supermajority of the population to amend the Constitution without the consent of three-quarters of the states. The switch need not alter any other aspect of the existing Constitution.

[31] Randolph, Federal Convention (June 16, 1787), *in* 1 Farrand 256.

[32] U.S. Const. art. I, sec. 3, cl. 1.

of the Articles' rule that congressional delegates could be recalled by the state legislature on discretion.[33] When Lansing and Yates withdrew, however, the Convention ended the recall of senators on discretion.

Madison later emphasized what he saw as the good parts of the Senate. A bicameral legislature "doubles the security of the people, by requiring the concurrence of two distinct bodies in schemes of usurpation or perfidy."[34] Senators were supposed to use the longer terms, not only to acquire independence from their states, but also to acquire wisdom and the "cool and deliberate sense of the community."[35] The senators were supposed to be the best of the country, the guardian philosophers or "Solons" for the whole United States, who filtered the passions of the electorate.[36] Senators, unlike the delegates in the Continental Congress, had functions and justifications other than responsiveness to their state legislatures.

Although senators were given fixed terms, they remained appointees of the state legislatures, just as delegates had been under the Articles.[37] Popular election of senators, however, grew into an inevitable idea. Over time, senators stopped taking instructions from their home state legislatures, especially of course when party affiliation of the state legislature majority changed after the election of the senator.[38] By 1912, most states were requiring their state legislatures to follow the results of popular voting in appointment of their senators.[39] In 1913, the election of senators was formally changed, from the state legislators, over to popular election, completing the Constitution's revolution, by driving the states acting as sovereigns from out of any role in the federal government.[40]

The House of Representatives, by contrast with the Senate, had representation based on population. The adopted rule, however, showed its roots as ambiguously based on population as a fountain of legitimacy and on population as a proxy measure for wealth. The constitutional formula for population counted slaves, according to the "federal ratio" or three-fifths. Counting slaves at three-fifths was a tax formula, arising under the 1783 proposal to determine each state's quota under a requisition.[41] The function of the formula was to determine a state's quota by apportioning the requisition

33 1 DHRC at 193.
34 *Federalist* No. 62, at 418 (Madison) (Feb. 27, 1788).
35 *Federalist* No. 63, at 425 (Madison) (March 1, 1788).
36 *Id.*
37 U.S. Const. art. I, sec. 3, cl. 1; Articles of Confederation, art. V.
38 William H. Riker, *The Senate and American Federalism*, 49 Amer. Pol. Sci. Rev. 452, 456 (1956).
39 *Id.* at 468.
40 U.S. Const. amend. XVII.
41 Continental Congress (April 18, 1783), *in* 24 JCC 260.

according to the relative wealth of the states. Slaves were always included in the formula for representation because they contributed to wealth.[42] The pre-1783 formula, which had allocated taxes according to value of real estate, had proved inadministrable in absence of access to reasonable appraisals of the value of land and improvements. Population, with slaves counted at three-fifths, was chosen to be a proxy measurement for the wealth of a state that would be easier than assessments of real estate values. The debate was a tax debate on how much slaves contributed to wealth.[43] The 1783 formula was not adopted because New York vetoed it on the ground that it provided for a federal impost. Its acceptance in Congress and everywhere but New York, however, made it a legitimate formula in the constitutional debates. The 1783 proposal is a tax proposal only, and that tax ratio became the constitutional formula for representation in the House. Population-counting slaves at three-fifths was a legitimate way to apportion requisitions and then votes because it measured the relative wealth of the states, and taxes should be apportioned to reach wealth.

After the Civil War, however, the fractional count of slaves ended and the House came to represent the people as people and not as proxies for their contribution to war or their wealth. When popular sovereignty in fact came to mean resting the government upon the people, counting each person equally, the House formula unambiguously served to describe popular sovereignty, rather than wealth, whatever its original intent.

B. SUPREMACY OF THE NATIONAL

The new national government, with a legitimacy secured from a base independent of the states, was, in Madison's view, then to be made unambiguously superior to the states. As the Convention got under way, Edward Carrington wrote to Jefferson to explain that a revolution was afoot: "The ideas here suggested are as far removed from those which prevailed when you were amongst us, [that] it is probable that you may not be prepared to expect them."[44] But those ideas had "arisen with the most able from an actual view of events: I am certain that nothing less than what will give the foederal

---

[42] *See, e.g.* Charles Pinckney, U.S. House of Representatives (Feb. 14, 1820) *in* 3 FARRAND 442 (arguing that slaves were included in determining representation of Southern states because they contributed to wealth).

[43] *See* Calvin H. Johnson, *Apportionment of Direct Taxes: The Foul-Up in the Core of the Constitution,* 7 WM. & MARY BILL OF RTS. J. 84–96 (1998).

[44] Edward Carrington to Jefferson (June 6, 1787), *in* 11 PTJ 409–410.

controul over the State Governments will be thought worthy of discussion."[45]
It is essential, Madison wrote to Washington and to Randolph, to establish
a "due supremacy of the national authority."[46]

Under Madison's system, the states could have a subordinate role akin
to counties. "Consolidation of the whole into one simple republic would
be as inexpedient as it is unattainable," Madison wrote Washington, so he
would not "exclude the local authorities wherever they can be subordinately
useful."[47] The states would be useful reduced to "approximate the States to
the condition of Counties."[48] Madison, like a good politician, labeled the
new role the states might have as a "middle road," but middle road for him
was only an issue of efficacy or strategy, and the efficacious role of the states
was to be "subordinately useful" and like counties.

The national government would be supreme over the states. The Virginia
Plan, adopted by the May 30 resolution, said that a national government
ought to be established consisting of a *supreme* legislative, executive, and
judiciary.[49] Edmund Randolph's draft of the preamble to the Constitution
for the Committee of Detail in August 1787 said that the "present foederal
government is insufficient to the general happiness [and] the only effectual
means which [the convention] could devise, for curing this insufficiency, is
the establishment of a *supreme* legislative[,] executive and judiciary."[50]

1. The Negative

Madison's original system included what he called the "negative," which was
a power of Congress to veto state legislation. Madison wanted the Congress
to have the negative in any case. The states were inevitably irresponsible and
trampled individual rights, under Madison's vision. The extended republic
of the national government was the guardian of those individual rights. The
only mechanism by which the federal guardian could act, before damage was

---

45 *Id.*
46 Madison to Washington (April 16, 1787), *in* 9 JM 383. *Accord,* Madison to Randolph (April
    8, 1787), *in* 9 JM 369.
47 Madison to Washington (April 16, 1787), *in* 9 JM 383. *See also* prior draft of same language
    in Madison to Randolph (April 8, 1787), *in* 9 JM 370.
48 Madison, Federal Convention (June 28, 1787), *in* 1 FARRAND 449 (arguing that small states
    would be best protected by the guardianship of the national government).
49 May 30, 1787, *in* 1 FARRAND 33 (emphasis in original).
50 Randolph, Committee of Detail, *in* 2 FARRAND 138 (emphasis added) (notes for the preamble
    for a first draft of the Constitution).

done, according to Madison, was by vetoing objectionable state laws before they came into effect and no matter what the subject matter.[51]

Madison explained to Washington in preparation for the Convention that, in addition to its present powers, the national Government should be armed with positive and complete authority in all cases which require uniformity and that Congress should also have a veto or "negative" on legislative acts of the states, "in all cases whatsoever."[52] "Without this defensive power," he told Washington, "every positive power that can be given on paper will be evaded & defeated. The States will continue to invade the national jurisdiction, to violate treaties and the law of nations & to harrass each other with rival and spiteful measures dictated by mistaken views of interest." This prerogative would "controul the internal vicisitudes of State policy: and the aggressions of interested majorities on the rights of minorities and of individuals."[53] To Jefferson, Madison wrote that the effects of the negative would be not "only to guard the national rights and interests against invasion, but also to restrain the States from thwarting and molesting each other, and even from oppressing the minority within themselves by paper money and other unrighteous measures which favor the interest of the majority."[54] With the negative in place the national government would be "an essential branch" of the government of each state.[55]

The negative, with direct taxes, would serve as the replacement for violent coercion of recalcitrant states. At the Convention, Madison urged the negative to prevent the states from impairing rights. Given the "ingenuity of the Legislatures" to evade the prohibition on impairment of contracts, Madison argued, a negative on state laws would alone secure the protection.[56] "[R]ecurrance to force [on the states] which in the event of disobedience would be necessary, is an evil which the new Constitution meant to exclude as far as possible."[57] In this respect, the negative is parallel to giving Congress the power to tax people directly, bypassing the states, especially for the area in which the federal government was protecting against state encroachments

[51] See Charles F. Hobson, *The Negative on State Laws: James Madison, the Constitution, and the Crises of Republican Government*, 36 WM. & MARY Q. 215 (3d Ser. 1979), which also provides a critical commentary on other historians' descriptions.

[52] Madison to Washington (April 16, 1787), *in* 9 JM 383. *See also* earlier versions: Madison to Randolph (April 8, 1787), *in* 9 JM 370 and Madison to Jefferson (Mar. 19, 1787), *in* 9 JM 318.

[53] Madison to Washington (April 16, 1787), *in* 9 JM 3845.

[54] Madison to Jefferson (Mar. 19, 1787), *in* 9 JM 318.

[55] Madison, Federal Convention (June 28, 1787), *in* 1 FARRAND 447.

[56] Madison, Federal Convention (Aug. 28, 1787), *in* 2 FARRAND 440.

[57] Madison to Jefferson (Oct. 24, 1787), *in* 10 JM 211.

of individual rights. The negative would allow the federal government to use the "mild and salutary coertion of the magistracy" instead of the "destructive coertion of the sword,"[58] or "point of the bayonet"[59] to protect individual rights, just as direct tax instead of requisitions allowed the federal government to collect revenue without violence.

The idea for the negative came from the royal prerogative, that is, the right of the English crown to review and strike down acts of the colonial legislatures. "Nothing could maintain the harmony & subordination of the various parts of the empire," Madison told the Convention, "but the prerogative by which the Crown, stifles in the birth every Act... tending to discord or encroachment."[60] The only distinction Madison offered between the prerogative of the British king and the negative in his system was that the national legislature would be an extended republic and hence, wise. The Crown sometimes misapplied its prerogative, Madison conceded, but "we have not the same reason to fear such misapplications in our System."[61] Madison was willing to enforce the negative with a nationwide administration, much like the British had sent out to the royal governors: In order to render the exercise of such a negative prerogative convenient, "an emanation of it must be vested in some set of men within the several States so far as to enable them to give a temporary sanction [or veto] to laws of immediate necessity."[62]

Madison had some support for his negative. At the Convention, James Wilson called the negative the "key-stone wanted to compleat the wide arch of Government, we are raising."[63] Outside of the Convention, James Monroe, who would oppose the Constitution overall, nonetheless liked the negative as "the best way of introducing uniformity [to state laws] that can be devis'd."[64]

---

[58] *Federalist* No. 20, at 129 (Madison) (Dec. 11, 1787).

[59] *Id.* at 126.

[60] Madison, Federal Convention, July 17, 1787, 2 FARRAND 28. *See also* Madison to N. P. Trist (Dec. 1831), *in* 3 FARRAND 516 (saying that the negative and judicial review reflect "[t]he opinion that the States ought to be placed not less under the Govt. of the U.S. than they were under that of G. B").

[61] July 17, 1787, *in* 2 FARRAND 28. *See also* Charles Pinckney, Federal Convention (June 8, 1787), *in* 1 FARRAND 167 (making what is apparently Madison's argument, that the "universal negative was in fact the corner stone of an efficient national Govt.; that under the British Govt. the negative of the Crown had been found beneficial, and that the States are more one nation now, than the Colonies were then").

[62] Madison to Jefferson (Mar. 19, 1787), *in* 9 JM 318. *See also* Madison, Federal Convention (June 8, 1787), *in* 1 FARRAND 168 (arguing that Congress could send delegation, just as the Crown had sent out governors to the royal colonies).

[63] Wilson, Federal Convention (Aug. 23, 1787), *in* 2 FARRAND 391.

[64] James Monroe to Jefferson (July 27, 1787), *in* 3 FARRAND 65.

The Convention, nonetheless, rejected Madison's negative. Early on, the Convention unanimously approved the narrower version of the negative in the Virginia Plan, which provided that Congress could negate all laws passed by the states that in its opinion contravened the new Constitution.[65] Madison had wanted the negative "in any case," which was even a broader reach.[66] The Convention returned to the issue on July 17, however, and at that time defeated the negative in full, three states in favor and seven states against.[67] When Madison brought it up again in late August, it was defeated again, although more narrowly, by five states to six.[68]

The objections to the negative were partly procedural. Anti-Federalist John Lansing complained that Congress would never find the time for review: "On the most moderate calculation, [there will] be as many Acts sent up from the states as there are days of the year."[69] Madison's suggestion that Congress might appoint some group of agents to veto state legislation, just as the British governors had when the states were royal colonies, was not considered persuasive.[70]

The defeat, however, was more than just procedural. Lansing argued that the states "will never feel a sufficient confidence in a general Government to give it a negative on their laws,"[71] and Gunning Bedford of Delaware complained the negative would allow a small state like Delaware to be "injured at pleasure without redress."[72] The venerable Benjamin Franklin told the Convention that the Crown's governor constantly used the negative to "extort money" from his Council.[73]

Jefferson, from Paris, also reacted against Madison's negative, saying that "prima facie I do not like it." The negative proposed "to mend a small hole by covering the whole garment," whereas a patch should be commensurate with

---

[65] Virginia Plan 6, *in* 2 FARRAND 226; 1 FARRAND 21, 54.

[66] Madison to Washington (April 16, 1787), *in* 9 JM, 383 (recommending the negative for any case whatsoever); Madison to Jefferson (Mar. 19, 1787), *in* 9 JM 318. *See also* June 8, 1787, *in* 1 FARRAND 162–163 (motion to extend the negative to all cases defeated by three states to seven states against).

[67] July 17, 1787, *in* 2 FARRAND 28 (defeating the negative three states to seven states).

[68] Aug. 23, 1787, *in* 2 FARRAND 382.

[69] John Lansing, Federal Convention (June 20, 1787), 1 FARRAND 337.

[70] Madison, Federal Convention (June 8, 1787), *in* 1 FARRAND 168; Madison (July 17, 1787), *in* 2 FARRAND 28 (saying that problem of sending up all laws to the national legislature might be avoided by "some emanation of the power into the States, so far at least, as to give a temporary effect to laws of immediate necessity"); Charles Pinckney (Aug. 23, 1787), *in* 2 FARRAND 391 (declared that he thought executives ought to be so appointed with control over state enactments).

[71] John Lansing, Federal Convention (June 16, 1787), *in* 1 FARRAND 250.

[72] Gunning Bedford, Federal Convention (June 8, 1787), *in* 1 FARRAND 167.

[73] Benjamin Franklin, Federal Convention (June 4, 1787), *in* 1 FARRAND 98–99.

the hole.[74] Under the negative, Jefferson argued, British creditors would be able to go to Congress if the Virginia Assembly were unjust, but where, he asked, could an individual go if the Congress was unjust?

The negative, however, was too crucial for Madison to let it go easily. Without it, he told Jefferson, "I hazard an opinion that the plan should it be adopted will neither effectually answer its national object nor prevent the local mischiefs which every where excite disgusts agst the state governments."[75] In October 1787, Madison wrote a long letter to Jefferson explaining his vision and especially the negative.[76] The passages on the negative in the October letter are far too long – "an immoderate digression" Madison himself described it – and too passionate for a practical politician like Madison to spend on a lost cause. Madison marshaled for the defense of the negative the whole of this theory of the extended republic, in its fullest statement. He explained his studies showing that, in every confederacy, ancient or contemporary, the center had been too weak and he explained his grand philosophy proving the superiority of an extended republic. Madison's explanation of the extended republic became *Federalist* Number 10, except that by the time of its publication, Madison returned to being political enough that he knew not to organize his theory around the lost-cause negative.

Jefferson, in rejecting the negative, had suggested that judicial review, striking down state legislation that was inconsistent with the plan of union, would be sufficient. There is some evidence that opposition to the negative within the Philadelphia Convention also relied on judicial review and supremacy of national law. Gouverneur Morris, an ardent nationalist, had said that the negative would disgust the states, but that "[a] law that ought to be negatived will be set aside in the judiciary department; and if that security should fail, may be repealed by a National law."[77] Madison responded that the "States can pass laws which will accomplish their injurious objects before they can be repealed by the Congress or national tribunals."[78] To Jefferson, he argued that it was better to prevent the passage of a law than to declare it void after it is passed because a state that would violate the rights of the Union would not be very ready to obey a judicial decree in support of them. The Union would then need to resort to force to enforce its law, he argued, although the Constitution meant to exclude force, "as far as possible."[79] Jefferson had written that the negative "in every case" would overreach the crime, because

---

[74] Jefferson to Madison (June 20, 1787), *in* 11 PTJ 480–481.
[75] Madison to Jefferson (Sept. 6, 1787), *in* 10 JM 163–64.
[76] Madison to Jefferson (Oct. 24, 1787), *in* 10 JM 205.
[77] Gouverneur Morris, Federal Convention (July 17, 1787), *in* 2 FARRAND 27.
[78] Madison, Federal Convention (July 17, 1787), *in* 2 FARRAND 27.
[79] Madison to Jefferson (Oct. 24, 1787), *in* 10 JM 212.

99 out of 100 state acts had nothing to do with the confederacy. Madison responded that the negative was needed, not just to guard the national government needs, but also to secure individuals against encroachment of their rights. The state's injustices were a serious evil, he told Jefferson, and had been "frequent and flagrant."[80]

Drawing support for the negative from the Crown's prerogative, exercised through the royal governors, was not the best way to sell his idea to Jefferson nor to the revolutionary generation. Jefferson's draft of the Declaration of Independence, for example, had started his list of charges against the Crown by saying that the king had attempted to establish tyranny by putting his "negative" on wholesome laws the colonial legislatures had adopted.[81] George Mason claimed in the Virginia Ratification Convention that the royal government's negative (on a tax discouraging the importation of slaves) was "one of the great causes of our separation from Great-Britain."[82]

For that matter, Madison's language made the negative a very hard sell to the generation before him that had come to intellectual maturity in the gathering storms before the Revolution. To say as Madison did, that the purpose of the negative and of judicial review was that "the States ought to be placed not less under the Govt. of the U.S. than they were under that of G. B,"[83] does show a certain insensitivity to revolutionary ideals. The Crown's exercise of the prerogative veto over acts of the colonial assemblies had been a continuing irritation in the period leading up to the war.[84] Madison's language to allow the negative "in all cases whatsoever" was exactly the language of the Declaratory Act of 1766, which Parliament passed right after the Stamp Act crisis to claim full sovereignty by the Parliament over its colonies, and the Declaratory Act was among the most despised acts in America.[85] For once,

---

[80] *Id.* at 212.

[81] PAULINE MAIER, AMERICAN SCRIPTURE: MAKING THE DECLARATION OF INDEPENDENCE 107 (1997). Maier argues that Jefferson talked in such abstractions that it is not clear what he is talking about, but that the Crown governors had blocked import duties that the colonies of New Jersey, Massachusetts, and Virginia would have wanted to impose to discourage the slave trade. *Id.* at 111–13.

[82] Mason, Virginia Convention (June 17, 1788), *in* 3 ELLIOT 452. One should not take this seriously as a cause: The Committee supervising Jefferson for the Declaration of Independence took out Jefferson's claim that the king imposed slavery upon us. *See* MAIER, *supra* note 81, at 146.

[83] Madison to N. P. Trist (Dec. 1831), *in* 3 FARRAND 516.

[84] Jack P. Greene, *Ongoing Disputes over the Prerogative, 1767–1776, in* JACK GREEN & J. R. POLE, THE BLACKWELL ENCYCLOPEDIA OF THE AMERICAN REVOLUTION 171–176 (1991). *See also* text accompanying *supra* note 73 (saying that Benjamin Franklin told the Convention that the colonial governor used the negative to extort money from his Council).

[85] Great Britain Parliament, The Declaratory Act of March 18, 1766, <http://www.yale.edu/lawweb/avalon/amerrev/parliament/declaratory_act_1766.htm>. *See* WOOD at 348.

Madison's political ear failed him, apparently because the negative was so important to his overall philosophy.

Notwithstanding how strongly he felt about it, Madison did not get the negative. However, he did get the judicial remedy, which both Jefferson and Governeur Morris had supported as an adequate alternative. Article VI, Section 2, the Supremacy Clause, provides that the Constitution, and federal laws and treaties made under it, shall be the supreme law of the land binding on every state law judge, notwithstanding anything inconsistent in state law or the state constitution.[86] Article III allows Congress to create a full federal judiciary with jurisdiction over all controversies arising under the Constitution, federal laws, or federal treaties.[87] Madison also got a series of specific restrictions on the states in section 10 of Article I. The prohibitions reached many of the specifics that bothered him about the Patrick Henry program in Virginia in the 1780s, including a prohibition on impairment of contracts.

By the time of the Bill of Rights, Madison had adapted and he was then willing to treat the judicial remedy as a worthy guardian of individual rights.[88] The supremacy clause and judicial review of state legislation thus themselves became worthy successors of the negative, within the spirit of Madison's vision, even if bad state laws are allowed to get out of the gate. The ability of Congress to pre-empt a state law and the ability of the Supreme Court to strike down a state law are just as destructive of state law and hence state sovereignty as the negative would have been, although perhaps not as fast.[89]

Madison originally wanted a negative that would have extended to "all cases whatsoever" to cure the "frequent and flagrant abuses" by the states of individual rights. The judicial review meant that the scope of the federal government's authority was smaller than Madison would have wanted

---

86   U.S. Const. art. VI.

87   U.S. Const. art. III, secs. 1 and 2.

88   "If [the rights in the Bill of Rights] are incorporated into the constitution, independent tribunals of justice will consider themselves in a peculiar manner the guardians of those rights; they will be an impenetrable bulwark against every assumption of power in the legislative or executive; they will be naturally led to resist every encroachment upon rights expressly stipulated by the declaration of rights." Madison, Debate in the House of Representatives, 1 Annals 457 (June 8, 1789).

89   Indeed, judicial supremacy was a common ground for Anti-Federalist opposition. See, e.g., Mason, Virginia Convention (June 18, 1788), in 3 Elliot 521 (objecting that the judicial power, limited only by the judge's own determinations will have the effect, in operation, of utterly destroying the state government); Democratic Federalist, Pennsylvania Herald (Oct. 17, 1787), reprinted in 13 DHRC 386, 387 (opposing the Constitution on the ground that there is a material difference between the Constitution and the present federation for Congress in that the latter has no judicial jurisdiction).

as to protecting individual rights. Congress got direct taxes, to avoid state encroachment on the federal sphere – that is, default on requisitions – but it did not get the parallel strong remedy – the negative – to prevent state encroachment on individual rights. There are specific prohibitions upon the states in Section 10 of Article I of the Constitution against the states impairing contracts and issuing paper money, but no general authority to protect rights in "all cases whatsoever."

2. Defining the Federal Sphere[90]

Madison lost not only on the negative, but also on the general range over which the federal government would be able to operate. Madison wanted federal power, at least to veto, in all cases whatsoever. What he got instead was a federal government with power over issues appropriate to the national sphere. The national government had "every power requisite for general purposes," Madison told Jefferson, but it left "to the States every power which might be most beneficially administered by them."[91] Madison wanted plenary power for the national government to protect individual rights. The Constitutional prohibitions on state paper money and violations of contracts were all to the good, Madison told Jefferson, but he thought that Patrick Henry's mischief required federal supervision for every case.[92] He could not, however, convince the Convention.

The new government would, however, have power over the appropriate national issues. The Convention adopted supposedly binding resolutions to guide the drafting committees that actually provided the wording of the Constitution, and the resolution on the range of the federal government was a motion by Gunning Bedford. Bedford's motion provided that Congress would be able to "legislate in all cases for the common interests of the Union."[93] The drafting committees seem to have put the Bedford Resolution into effect by re-using language from the Articles of Confederation that Congress could provide for "the common Defence and general Welfare."[94]

---

[90] This section is a very short version of the arguments defended in Calvin Johnson, *The Dubious Enumerated Powers Doctrine,* – CONST. COMMENTARY – (forthcoming 2005).

[91] Madison to Jefferson (Oct. 24, 1787), in 10 JM 208. Madison says that the majority was "finally for a limited power without the negative" (*id.* at 209) and then went into an "immoderate digression" on the need for the negative, but even without the negative loss, he thought the drafted Constitution gave Congress every power for requisite general purposes.

[92] Madison to Jefferson (Oct. 24, 1787), *in* 10 JM 212.

[93] Gunning Bedford, Motion of July 17, 1787, 2 FARRAND 26.

[94] ARTICLES OF CONFEDERATION, art. VII, 19 JCC 217 (March 1, 1781).

The adopted standards of "*Common* interests of the Union," *common* defense, and *general* welfare exclude the purely particular and local issues that are left to the states, but give the new national government power in the national sphere.

The Articles of Confederation, in Article IX, listed a number of specific congressional powers including, for instance, the power to raise and support an army and navy, to fix weights and measures, and to coin money. The Constitution added some activities to the list including, for example, the power to regulate commerce, and to enact national legal regimes for bankruptcy, patents, copyrights, and naturalization of citizens. None of the added powers have any importance.

Table 5.1 compares the powers under Section 8 of Article I of the Constitution with the powers under the Articles and highlights the new powers in italics.

TABLE 5.1. *Powers of Congress*

Constitution	Articles of Confederation	Comments
Clause 2. To borrow money on the credit of the United States	Power to borrow implied by Article IX requirement that 9 of 13 states assent	
Clause 3. *To regulate commerce with foreign nations, and among the several states,* and with the Indian tribes	States allowed to impose imposts on foreigners, as their own citizens are subject to. Congress could regulate Indian trade and affairs under Article IX	Specific programs advocated under regulation of commerce never passed
Clause 4. *To establish a uniform rule of naturalization, and uniform laws on the subject of bankruptcies throughout the United States*		Permanent national bankruptcy law not passed until 1898
Clause 5. *To coin money,* regulate the value thereof, and of foreign coin, and fix the standard of weights and measures	States could coin money and Congress was allowed to regulate its value. Other powers in Article IX	
Clause 6. To provide for the punishment of counterfeiting	Article IX	
Clause 7. To establish post-offices *and post-roads*	Post offices only	

(*continued*)

TABLE 5.1 (*continued*)

Constitution	Articles of Confederation	Comments
Clause 8. *To promote the progress of science and useful arts, by securing for limited times to authors and inventors the exclusive right to their respective writings and discoveries*	No comparable prior provision	
Clause 9. *To constitute tribunals inferior to the Supreme Court*	Articles' courts were only for boundaries and high seas	
Clause 10. To define and punish piracies and felonies committed on the high seas, and *offences against the law of nations*	Article IX	
Clause 11. To declare war, grant letters of marque and reprisal, and make rules concerning captures on land and water	Article IX	
Clause 12. To raise and support armies, *but no appropriation of money to that use shall be for a longer term than two years*	Article IX	The limitation on appropriation to two years is new
Clause 13. To provide and maintain a navy	Article IX	
Clause 14. To make rules for the government and regulation of the land and naval forces	Article IX	
Clause 15. *To provide for calling forth the militia to execute the laws of the union, suppress insurrections and repel invasions*	Not mentioned	
Clause 16. To provide for organizing, arming and disciplining the militia, reserving to the states the appointment of the officers	States allowed to appoint officers of the army below the rank of general by Article VII	
Clause 17. *Create and govern a city for the seat of the national government*	No such power	
Clause 18. *Enact all laws which shall be necessary and proper for carrying out all other federal powers*	No comparable power	

The listed activities added by the Constitution are not important even all together. Post roads, bankruptcy, patents, copyrights, and naturalization are useful things for a general-level government to be able do, but they are not the kind of thing that required the revolutionary end of the confederation system, the dethroning of the supremacy of the states, a perpetual and plenary federal tax system, or a complete and independent national government. The bankruptcy power, for example, remained, a "mere dead letter," as Story's *Commentaries* put it,[95] until 1898,[96] and that is considerably too late for the bankruptcy to be considered to be a meaningful contributory cause to the Constitution. None of the nontax programs espoused under the heading of "regulation of commerce" ever amounted to much.[97] Programs not adopted, once the Constitution allowed them, cannot be used as major contributions to or justifications for the constitutional revolution.

There is much to be said for the position that the listed powers were not intended to be exclusive, even with the modest new powers. Article II of the old Articles of Confederation had limited Congress to the powers that were "expressly delegated" to it. The Framers, while taking language and structure from the Articles, left out the "expressly delegated" limitation. The Anti-Federalists objected to the deletion of the "expressly delegated" limitation.[98] In the Virginia Ratification Convention, however, Edmund Randolph defended the deletion because the "expressly delegated" limitation had been found to be "destructive" to the Union. Even the passport system, Randolph said, had been challenged under the Articles because it was not expressly authorized.[99] There had been a then-recent controversy over the federal

---

95 3 JOSEPH STORY, COMMENTARIES ON THE CONSTITUTION §§ 1105 (1833), *reprinted in* 2 THE FOUNDERS' CONSTITUTION 639, 641.

96 *See, e.g.*, Rhett Frimet, *The Birth of Bankruptcy in the United States*, 96 COM. L.J. 160 (1991) (describing the history of American bankruptcy legislation and proposals through the Bankruptcy Act of 1898).

97 *See* discussion in Chapter 8, The Modest and Mercantilist Commerce Clause.

98 *See, e.g.*, Cincinnatus I: *To James Wilson, Esquire*, NEW YORK J. (Nov. 1, 1787), *reprinted in* 13 DHRC 531 (saying that the Articles said at the outset that what is not expressly given is reserved, but the Constitution makes no such reservation, so the presumption is that the Framers of the proposed constitution did not mean to subject to the same exception); Centinel II, PHILADELPHIA FREEMAN'S J. (Oct. 24, 1787), *reprinted in* 13 DHRC 460 (objecting to the absence of "expressly delegated" and to fact that infinite federal law was made paramount over state law); A Democratic Federalist, PENNSYLVANIA HERALD (Oct. 17, 1787), *reprinted in* 13 DHRC 387 (objecting that limitation of the federal government should have been "clearly expressed in the plan of government"); *cf.* Brutus I, NEW YORK Journal (Oct. 18, 1787), *reprinted in* 13 DHRC 414 (necessary and proper power meant that "[t]his is as much one complete government as that of New York or Massachusetts [and] has as absolute and perfect powers to make and execute all laws . . .").

99 Randolph, Virginia Convention (June 24, 1788), *in* 3 ELLIOT 600–601. Randolph had served on the five-man Committee of Detail at the Philadelphia Convention (2 FARRAND 97),

passport that Pennsylvania citizens had seized goods from the ship *Amazon* intended for war prisoners and passing under George Washington's passport. The Pennsylvania legislature had decided that federal passport was supreme over the Pennsylvania statute on seizure of enemy goods.[100] The Federalists also defeated attempts to make the Tenth Amendment to the Constitution say that the Congress would have only the powers *expressly* delegated to it:[101] "The men who drew and adopted [the Tenth] amendment," Marshall wrote, had "experienced the embarrassments resulting from the insertion of this word ["expressly"] in the articles of confederation, and probably omitted it, to avoid those embarrassments."[102] The drafters apparently meant that there were to be some implied or unexpressed powers of uncertain scope in the Constitution, including especially the passport.

Limitation on the federal government was not the problem for which the Philadelphia Convention met. As James Wilson told the Convention, "It has never been a complaint agst. Congs. that they governed overmuch. The complaint has been that they have governed too little."[103] "The evils suffered and feared from weakness in Government," Madison told Jefferson, "have turned the attention more toward the means of strengthening the [government] than of narrowing [it]."[104] There does seem to have been a consensus that the new government would operate only within what was the national or general sphere, but the current Congress was so impotent

which been the committee that had taken the "expressly delegated" language out of the Constitution. Randolph's statement is also a kind of declaration against interest because it is not the kind of understatement of the Constitution's impact that the Federalists used to get the document ratified.

The proponents of the Constitution also wanted the Congress to have unexpressed or implied powers to enforce requisitions by force if necessary. *See, e.g.*, Randolph, Reasons for not Signing the Constitution (Dec. 27, 1787), *in* 8 DHRC 263 (saying that among reasons for the need for a Constitution was that the absence of implied federal powers to enforce requisitions prevented the federal government from enforcing the mandate).

100 Madison, Notes of the Continental Congress Debates (Jan. 24, 1783), *in* 19 LDCC, at 608 (reporting that a committee had concluded that the power of granting passports for the feeding of the prisoners was inseparable from the federal power of war); *id.* (Feb. 20, 1783), *in* 19 LDCC 719 n.4 (reporting that Madison had been told that Pennsylvania legislature had settled the business by deciding that Pennsylvania law was unconstitutional in so far as it interfered with passports).

101 Aug. 18, 1789, 1 ANNALS 790.

102 McCulloch v. Maryland, 17 U.S. 316, 406–407 (1819).

103 Wilson, Federal Convention, July 14, 1787, *in* 2 FARRAND 10.

104 Madison to Jefferson (Feb. 4, 1790), *in* 16 PTJ 146, 150; *see also* Roger Sherman & Oliver Ellsworth to Governor Samuel Huntington, *The Report of Connecticut's Delegates to the Constitutional Convention* (Sept. 26, 1787), *in* 13 DHRC 471 (saying that the states' principal object in authorizing the convention was to vest some *"additional* powers" in Congress) (emphasis added).

and imbecilic that stating the limits beyond which it might not grow was a speculative problem that could be solved on a future day.

The primary argument in the *Federalist* essays is that the border between the national and state sphere would be worked out in the future by competition between the levels for the loyalty of the people. Madison supposed that neither the local nor the general government would entirely yield to the other, " . . . and consequently that the struggle could be terminated only by compromise."[105] He argued that the people would become more partial to the federal than to the state governments, only if the federal level offered "manifest and irresistible proofs of a better administration."[106] Madison, moreover, explained the proposed Constitution to Jefferson in Paris by saying that in the new Constitution, there would be "a continual struggle between the head and the inferior members, until a final victory has been gained in some instances by one, in other by the other of them."[107] Hamilton in *Federalist* Number 31 said that it would be "vague and fallible" conjecture as to where politics would set the line.[108] Hamilton also told the New York Ratification Convention that it would be absurd to fix the division between federal and state objects in a Constitution both because the division would be too intricate and because alteration of circumstances must render a change of the division indispensable. "Constitutions should consist only of general provisions," he said, because "they cannot calculate the possible change of things. The states must have their resources," Hamilton said, but "it would be improper to point them out particularly in the Constitution."[109] Constitutions need to express principles and not just an enumeration of petty activities.

The general power given to the federal government also provoked opposition. Edmund Randolph initially announced his opposition to the Constitution that he had so importantly contributed to by saying that the Constitution wanted "a more definite boundary between the General & State

---

[105] *Federalist* No. 37, at 237 (Madison) (Jan. 11, 1788).

[106] *Federalist* No. 46, at 317 (Madison) (Jan. 29, 1788).

[107] Madison to Jefferson (Oct. 24, 1787), *in* 10 JM 210–211.

[108] *Federalist* No. 31, at 198 (Hamilton) (Jan. 1, 1788). Hamilton also argued that the states were protected because state issues were not worthy of ambition (*Federalist* No. 17, at 105–6 (Hamilton) (Dec. 5, 1787) (arguing that states are safe because the interesting issues of commerce, finance, and war are already federal issues and the domestic police and other state issues hold out only "slender allurement to ambition"), which is an argument that was not satisfying to the Anti-Federalists. *See* John Lansing, Federal Convention (June 16, 1787), *in* 1 FARRAND 249 (criticizing the Virginia Plan because the Congress "absorbs all power except what may be exercised in the little local matters of the States which are not objects worthy of the supreme cognizance").

[109] Alexander Hamilton, New York Convention (June 28, 1788), *in* 2 ELLIOT 364.

Legislatures"[110] and that the "lattitude of the general powers" allowed the Congress to swallow up the states.[111] Randolph eventually came around to support the Constitution quite effectively,[112] but at the end of Convention, he was an insider to the drafting who saw it as giving a general power to Congress. George Mason, who remained an opponent, also understood the text to give a general power because he wanted alterations so that "the object of the National Government, [would] be expressly defined, instead of indefinite power, under an arbitrary Constitution of general clauses."[113]

With the disappearance of the "expressly delegated" cap, the best legal maxim of interpretation for the list of powers in Article I, Section 8 of the Constitution is not *expressio unius est exclusio alterius* (expression of one excludes all others), but rather *ejusdem generic*, meaning that unstated items covered by a general standard must be of the same class as the enumerated items, but the enumerated items are not exclusive.[114] The list of powers is illustrative. Indeed they may be campaign promises of what the Framers really wanted to do quickly. But they are not exhaustive of what the Congress could do within the appropriately national sphere.

The broadest statement of the principle of federal jurisdiction is the power "to provide for the common Defense and general Welfare" in clause 1 of the Constitution's description of the powers of Congress.[115] Article VIII of the old Articles gave Congress the power to charge expenses for the common defense and general welfare to the common treasury. The Constitution continues the power by allowing Congress to tax "to provide for the

---

[110] Randolph, Federal Convention (Sept. 17, 1787), *in* 2 FARRAND 564.

[111] *See also*, Madison to Jefferson (Oct. 24, 1787), *in* 10 JM 215 (describing Randolph as opposing the Constitution because of "the latitude of the general powers"): Randolph, Reasons for Not Signing the Constitution (Dec. 27, 1787), *in* 8 DHRC 273 (saying that the the "cover of general words" allowed the Congress to swallow up the states).

[112] *See* discussion, Chapter 6, pp. 161–62.

[113] George Mason, Alterations Proposal (Aug. 31, 1787), *in* SUPPLEMENT TO MAX FARRAND'S THE RECORDS OF THE FEDERAL CONVENTION 25 (James H. Hutson ed., 1987).

[114] *See* 2A NORMAN J. SINGER, SUTHERLAND STATUTORY CONSTRUCTION §47.17, at 188–200 (5th ed. 1992). While *ejusdem generis* cases are often ones in which the general standard follows enumerated items, it applies as well to cases in which the general standards precede the enumerated items. *Id.* at 188.

 Ejusdem generis is said to accomplish "the purpose of giving effect to both the particular and the general words, by treating the particular words as indicating the class, and the general words as extending the provisions...to everything embraced in that class, though not specifically named by the particular words." National Bank of Commerce v. Estate of Ripley, 161 Mo. 126, 131, 61 S.W. 587, 588 (1901) cited in SINGER, SUTHERLAND at 189.

[115] U.S. CONST. art. I, §8, cl. 1.

common Defence and general Welfare." The change is simultaneously both a continuation of the status quo on paper and revolutionary in meaning. As Madison explained in *Federalist* Number 45,

> the change which [the new Constitution] proposes, consists much less in the addition of new powers to the Union, than in the invigoration of its original powers... The proposed change does not enlarge these powers; it only substitutes a more effectual mode of administering them. The change relating to taxation may be regarded as the most important: And yet the present Congress have as compleat authority to require of the States indefinite supplies of money for the common defence and general welfare....[116]

Madison's language describes a revolutionary change, albeit in terms meant to convey continuity. The Continental Congress' power to charge expenses was a paper power only. The Articles, for instance, required that charging expenses to the common treasury be approved by nine of the thirteen states and in the later days of the Confederation, Congress had trouble even making a quorum of seven states. Getting approval by nine states was a significant hurdle in practice.[117] The Constitution repealed the nine-state-vote requirement, allowing Congress to decide by mere majority that an expenditure was to provide for the general welfare or common defense, without the approval of any state. Even more importantly, the general treasury under the Articles was bare and with the failure of requisitions the Congress had no prospects of replenishing it. Congress was thus unable to turn an authorization into a payment under the Articles, even for expenses fairly justified by the common defense.[118] By giving Congress the power to collect tax on its own, and to collect revenue by the ordinary magistracy of the law and without recourse upon the recalcitrant states, the Constitution gave the federal government

---

[116] *Federalist* No. 45, at 314 (Madison) (Jan. 26, 1788) (capital letters for "new powers," "original powers," and "required" changed to lower case).

[117] *See, e.g.*, Motion of Jan. 30, 1786 appealing to the six missing states to send delegates given the "inconveniences arising from a want of a sufficient number of States to proceed on the business of the Union," 30 JCC 29. *See* RAKOVE, BEGINNINGS 355–356 (saying that in its weakened state, Congress could not command the regular attendance of many of its members, that it struggled almost constantly to maintain the quorum of seven states required by the Articles, and even minor business required passage by seven states, so that passage of any legislation in the 1780s required "a fair amount of luck and substantial level of consensus."); MORRIS at 91–93 (1987) (describing the difficulty of maintaining quorums).

[118] *See, e.g.*, Rufus King to Elbridge Gerry (June 18, 1786) in 8 LMCC 393 (regretting Congress's "utter inability to make [a] pitiful advance" of $1,000 to transport ammunition to American posts along the Ohio River).

"energy and consequence."[119] The revolution is both an identity of language on paper and a revolution in its meaning.

3. The Call of the "National"

The Convention was a transformative journey for many delegates, moving them from loyalty to the status quo, confederation system, to a new loyalty to a system with a national government. Madison's Virginia mentors had at first doubted that the Convention could do anything but amend the confederate mode, but by the time of the Virginia Plan they came around. The delegates to the Convention went through a similar shift. Early in the Convention, for example, Oliver Ellsworth of Connecticut offered a motion to strike the word "national" from the Virginia Plan's goal of creating a three-part national government, so as to keep the confederation mode: "It would be highly dangerous," he said, "not to consider the Confederation as still subsisting."[120] Edmund Randolph, in response, accepted Ellsworth's motion to strike "national" from his resolution, without accepting Ellsworth's rationale that ratification would be by legislatures and under the Articles.[121]

Thereafter, however, the Convention began to use the word "national" as a routine synonym for the general or Congressional level government, as if Ellsworth had never spoken.[122] By June 29, nine days after his motion to strike the word, "national," Ellsworth himself was saying that he wanted to establish a national legislature, executive, and judiciary to preserve peace and harmony.[123] A "national" government was often expressed as the object

[119] Phineas Bond to Lord Carmarthen (July 2, 1787), *in* 3 FARRAND 52.
[120] Oliver Ellsworth, Federal Convention (June 20, 1787), *in* 1 FARRAND 335. Ellsworth, at that point, wanted the Convention's proposal to go out to the state legislature for ratification as an amendment to the Articles of Confederation, and he worried that conventions of the people might not stop when they should. *Id.*
[121] Randolph, Federal Convention, *id.* at 336.
[122] *See, e.g.*, William Samuel Johnson, Federal Convention (June 21, 1787), *in* 1 ELLIOT 431 (saying while the New Jersey plan concentrates power in a distinct *national* government, it is not totally independent of that of the states); Wilson, *id.* at 432 (asking "How can the *national* government be secured against the states?"); Convention, June 23, *id.* at 226 (debating whether members of the *national* legislature should be paid out of the national treasury); Convention, July 22, *id.* at 216 (unanimously passing resolution that the legislative, executive, and judiciary powers of the *national* government, ought to be bound by oath to support the articles of the union); Convention, July 26, 1787, *id.* at 214 (passing resolution that a *national* executive be instituted to consist of a single person to be chosen by the national legislature); Convention (July 18, 1787), *in id.* at 210 (unanimously passing resolution that a national judiciary be established).
[123] 1 ELLIOT 465.

of the Constitution in the ratification debates. Randolph told Virginia he "intended to show the necessity of having a national government in preference to the Confederation"[124] Madison said that the "Southern States are, from their situation and circumstances, most interested in giving the *national* government the power of protecting its members."[125] John Jay told New York,

> The Convention concurred in opinion with the people, that a *national* government, competent to every *national* object, was indispensably necessary; and it was as plain to them, as it now is to all America, that the present Confederation does not provide for such a government.[126]

By the time of the Connecticut Ratification Convention, Ellsworth himself was saying that the Constitution was based on "the necessity of combining our whole force, and, as to *national* purposes, becoming one state."[127] We were to become a *nation* and not just a confederation.

C. WHAT DID MADISON ACHIEVE?

In the months before the start of the Convention, Madison set out his goals in letters to his Virginia mentors and allies. Madison's letters are a first draft of the Constitution and they are more radical and more nationalistic even than the Constitution that was ultimately adopted. But Madison did quite well if we follow his own checklist of goals.

In March of 1787, Madison explained to Thomas Jefferson four goals for the coming Convention:

(1) The new system would have to be ratified by the people of the several states so as to render the system paramount over state legislatures and state constitutions.

(2) The federal head would have to have a power to "negative" or veto state legislation in all cases whatsoever.

(3) Representation of a state in the federal system would have to be proportional to size of the state, ending the confederate system of one vote per state.

---

[124] Randolph, Virginia Convention (June 6, 1788), *in* 2 ELLIOT 71.
[125] Madison, Virginia Convention (June 16, 1787), *in* 3 ELLIOT 415 (emphasis added).
[126] A Citizen of New York, Address to New York, 1788, *in* 1 ELLIOT 496 (emphasis added).
[127] Oliver Ellsworth, Connecticut Convention (Jan. 4, 1788), *in* 2 ELLIOT 186 (emphasis added).

(4) Federal powers would have to be exercised by separate departments, so that, as Congressional powers and size increased, there was not further mismanagement.[128]

A fifth goal from Madison's April letter to George Washington is that the national government needed its own tax, so as to avoid violence in collecting requisitions from the states:

(5) The federal government should be given at least a limited tax power to avoid having to collect requisitions by coercive force against the states: "the difficulty & awkwardness of operating by force on the collective will of a State, render it particularly desirable that the necessity of it might be precluded."[129]

Madison did not win on all his issues, but he did quite well overall:

(1) The Constitution was indeed ratified by the people. State legislatures and governors were excluded. Valid federal law is paramount over state law.

(2) Madison did not get his negative, that is, pre-enactment of full discretionary review of state legislation, but he did get something very useful in post-enactment judicial review. Federal law does not govern in any case whatsoever to protect individual rights. But there are enforceable individual rights and there is a broad national power to protect the general interests on issues appropriately in the national sphere.

(3) Madison lost on the principle that voting power should follow population as to the Senate. But he won the principle as to the House. Even as to the Senate, Senators got insulation from the states in the form of long, six-year terms and because Senators could not be recalled.[130]

(4) Madison got a division of labor with a judicial, executive, and legislative branch, so that all of the business of government did not have to be conducted on the floor of the Congress.

(5) Madison wanted Congress to have a source of revenue sufficient to guard the Republic's cause by making payments on the war debts. He got it. Indeed, while Madison initially suggested only a limited source

---

[128] Madison to Jefferson (Mar. 19, 1787), *in* 9 JM 318.
[129] Madison to Washington (Apr 16, 1787) *in* 24 LDCC 231.
[130] *Cf.* Randolph, Federal Convention (June 16, 1787), *in* 1 FARRAND 256 (complaining that Congress under the Articles "was elected by Legislatures who retain even a power of recall" and complaining that the Congress has "therefore no will of their own, ... and [is] always obsequious to the views of the States, who are always encroaching on the authority of the U. States").

of taxes, the Constitution gives the Congress plenary and permanent power to provide for the common defense and general welfare, excepting only export taxes. With near plenary taxes, the Constitution is more nationalistic than in Madison's first draft.

Overall, Madison won on three issues of his list, did better than he hoped on taxes, and split on two, for something on the order of four-fifths or 80 percent overall. Except for the Senate compromise, loss of the general negative power to protect individual rights in any case whatsoever, and a vague limitation in the scope of Congress to the appropriately national sphere, the important parts of Madison's vision were included in the written Constitution. What Madison did accomplish was sufficient to create a revolution.

CHAPTER SIX

Anti-Federalism

When the writing of the Constitution was completed, it was sent out for ratification to conventions of the people, meeting by state.[1] The minimum necessary level of ratification for establishment of the Constitution was set at nine of the thirteen conventions (69%) by the new proposed Constitution itself.[2] Ratification by nine was a "respectable majority," made familiar by the existing Articles.[3] Nine of thirteen states had been the level required by the Articles of Confederation for reasonably routine actions, such as charging expenses to the common or federal treasury.[4] No state would be bound until both nine states and its own convention had ratified, but the new government would be formed when the ninth convention ratified. The Federalists, as noted, did not expect ratification in all states.[5] The nine-state minimum level for ratification meant that the states that had vetoed the impost – Rhode Island, New York, and Virginia – would not have to be brought in and another could be lost to spare. But the Federalists asked for ratification in all the states, and after delays and against their expectations, they got it.

---

[1] The grand narratives of the ratification include RUTLAND; MAIN; and RAKOVE, ORIGINAL MEANINGS 91–130 (1996) (discussing the "Concept of Ratification").

[2] U.S. CONST. art. VI. The governing resolution on this issue, adopted on July 12, 1787, called for "referring the new system to the people of the States for ratification." 2 FARRAND 214. The Convention debated and defeated a proposal that the Constitution be referred to the state legislatures on July 23, three states in favor and seven states against. 2 FARRAND 88–93.

[3] Randolph, Federal Convention (Aug. 30, 1787), *in* 2 FARRAND 469.

[4] ARTICLES OF CONFEDERATION, art. IX.

[5] *See, e.g.*, Washington, Letter to Congress by Unanimous Order of the Convention (Sept. 17, 1787), *in* 2 FARRAND 667 ("That it will meet the full and entire approbation of every State is not perhaps to be expected"). *See also* discussion in Chapter 4, pp. 78–81.

Table 6.1 lists the order by which the states ratified the Constitution and the percentage of the delegates to the state's convention that ultimately voted in favor of ratification.:

TABLE 6.1. *Ratification votes*

State (listed by order of ratification)	Date of Ratification	Population[6] (size rank in brackets)	Vote for Ratification[7]	Comments
1. Delaware	Dec 7, 1787	59,000 [13]	Unanimous	Without substantial debate
2. Pennsylvania	Dec 12, 1787	434,000 [3]	67%	First major state, and only early state with organized opposition
3. New Jersey	Dec. 18, 1787	184,000 [9]	Unanimous	
4. Georgia	Jan 2, 1788	83,000 [11]	Unanimous	
5. Connecticut	Jan. 9, 1788	238,000 [8]	76%	
6. Massachusetts	Feb. 6, 1788	476,000 [2]	53%	First close state, and first to recommend amendments
7. Maryland	April 28, 1788	320,000 [6]	84%	
8. South Carolina	May 23, 1788	249,000 [7]	67%	
9. New Hampshire	June 21, 1788	142,000[10]	55%	Ninth vote established the new government
10. Virginia	June 25, 1788	822,000 [1]	52%	Vetoed the 1781 impost
11. New York	July 25. 1788	425,000 [5]	54%	Vetoed the 1783 impost
12. North Carolina	Nov. 1789	430,000 [4]	72%	Ratification decision deferred in Aug. 1788
13. Rhode Island	May 1790	69,000 [12]	52%	Vetoed the 1781 impost, came in only after threat of facing U.S.
Weighted Total			65%	impost

Delegates representing 65 percent of the electorate (weighing states by population) ultimately voted to ratify the Constitution.[8] Opponents to

---

6   *U.S. Population by Official Census from 1790, in* HISTORICAL STATISTICS OF THE UNITED STATES: COLONIAL TIMES TO 1957 at 13 (1960) (1790 census, with Kentucky and West Virginia population included in Virginia, Tennessee's population included with North Carolina, Vermont's included in New York, and Maine's included in Massachusetts).

7   2 DHRC 105, 184, 278, 562 (Del., N.J., Ga., and Conn.); 3 DHRC 181 (Pa.); RUTLAND, at 158, 168, 212, 250, 264, 303, 305 (Md., S.C., N.H., Va. N.Y., N.C., R.I.): Robert Rutland, *Ratification of the Constitution, in* 2 ENCYCLOPEDIA OF THE CONSTITUTION 1512–1514 (Leonard Levy et al., eds. 1986).

8   The 65% figure is an average weighted by population. It is computed by multiplying the population of each state by the percentage of delegates in favor of ratification,

ratification garnered just over a third of the delegates. Enthusiasm was stronger in the seven smallest states (77% in favor of ratification) than it was in the six largest states (61% for ratification). New England (59% for ratification) was less enthusiastic than either the South (63% for ratification) or the mid-Atlantic states (66% in favor), but all regions supported the Constitution at nearly landslide levels. Although support for the Constitution was not overwhelming in all states, each state, north and south, large and small, eventually endorsed it. The opponents of ratification may well have been just as vigorous as the Federalists who pushed the Constitution through to ratification, but they were in the end less numerous.

Once the Constitution was ratified, the dominance of the friends of the Constitution increased. In the first elections under the new Constitution, with the people voting directly for their representatives in the House of Representatives, Anti-Federalists won only 20 percent of the seats (thirteen of sixty-six members).[9] In the first Senate, with Senators chosen by the state legislatures, only Patrick Henry's Virginia appointed opponents of the Constitution, so that only one of the eleven states represented or 9 percent was Anti-Federalist. Weighting Senate and House equally, Federalists controlled 85 percent of the voting power in the first Congress.[10]

Beyond the first elections, the opposition to the Constitution withered and disappeared. The Anti-Federalist–Federalist rivalry of 1787–1788, Madison would write, "expired with the regular and effectual establishment of the federal government"[11] In January 1790, Washington returned from a triumphant tour of New England, "luminous" at the "miracle that there should be so much unanimity, in points of such importance, among such a number of citizens, so widely scattered, and so different in their habits in many

then adding the products, then dividing the sum by the 3.9 million population as a whole.

9 The thirteen Anti-Federalists in the first House of Representatives were Grout and Gerry (Mass.); Floyd, Hathorn, Van Rensselaer (New York); Ashe and Bloodworth (North Carolina); Burke, Sumter, and Tucker (South Carolina) and Bland, Coles, and Giles (Virginia). On the Senate side, only Virginia appointed Anti-Federalists to the first Senate. 14 DHFFC at 489–932 (biographies of members).

10 The average of 20% in the House and 9% in the Senate is 15% for Anti-Federalist powers.

11 Madison (writing anonymously), *A Candid State of Parties*, National Gazette, Sept. 22, 1792, *reprinted n* 14 JM370, 371. *Accord*, RUTLAND at 305–314 (1966) (Anti-Federalist opposition to the Constitution dissolved after ratification). *See also* LINDA GRANT DEPAUW, THE ELEVENTH PILLAR: NEW YORK STATE AND THE FEDERAL CONSTITUTION 278 (1966) (saying that the rapid disappearance of Anti-Federalism in New York "points up the fundamentally insubstantial nature of the division in that state in the first place").

respects as the Americans were."[12] By April 1790, Thomas Jefferson, who was not overly sympathetic to the Constitution, could report to Lafayette, that "[t]he opposition to our new constitution has almost totally disappeared."[13] Anti-Federalists might well have been a majority before the ratification conventions,[14] especially if all skeptics are included, but after ratification the Anti-Federalists shrank into a tiny minority too small to affect policy. Anti-Federalism then ceased to exist as a policy to which electable politicians could attach themselves. The country liked the Constitution, once it had deliberated for a while and the new system did not seem so strange.

The level of support implies that the Constitution could have effected even more radical a change and still garnered majority support. If the Articles were in fact a nullity or a negative in the eyes of the people, then majority vote should plausibly have been the standard for writing a new constitution, starting from scratch. Majorities should govern, ordinarily, less a minority outweigh the more numerous. The vote was close in New York, Massachusetts, Rhode Island, and Virginia, and the Federalists started in the minority in those states. Still, the level of support that they ultimately achieved implies that the Federalists oversold their document, making claims that were more compromising with the pre-existing Articles of Confederation than was necessary. The level of support also implies that the Constitution was considered common sense at the time, at least once the people and their representatives got used to it.

[12] Washington to Catherine Macaulay Graham (Jan. 9, 1790) *in* 30 WRITINGS OF GW 496. The characterization of the letter as "luminous" is from ELKINS & McKITRICK 75 (1993).

[13] Jefferson to Lafayette (Apr 2, 1790) *in* 16 PTJ 293. Jefferson attributes the demise of Anti-Federalism to the Bill of Rights, saying that some Anti-Federalist leaders had gone to such lengths in their declarations of hostilities that they could not come over, he said, but the Bill of Rights had stripped them of almost all of their followers. That probably overstates the importance of the Bill of Rights. *See* discussion in text accompanying *infra* notes.

[14] MAIN at 249, footnote 1 argues that Anti-Federalists were in a majority by 52%–48% looking to the campaign positions of the delegates. *Cf.* John P. Kaminski, *New York: The Reluctant Pillar, in* RELUCTANT PILLAR, 99, 114 (Clinton in control of two-thirds majority).

The final votes were less ambiguous, would incorporate the deliberations of the convention, and probably most importantly would represent the change of events. The most important event for ratification in the last four states (N.Y., Va., N.C., and R.I.) was the *fait accompli* of a new government that won enough ratifying states to go into effect. The last four states could not keep the old Articles, but had to decide only whether they wanted to be in or out of the United States.

Opponents of the Constitution were called "Anti-Federalists," but they did not like the name. The opponents thought that they were the true "federalists" because they were defending the Articles of Confederation and the confederation form of government, whereas the Constitution effected not a federal form of government, but a "consolidation."[15] Anti-Federalist William Findley of Pennsylvania later said that the name "Anti-Federalist" had been applied to the true defenders of federal principles "from mistaken party spleen."[16] "Federal Farmer," an early and articulate opponent of the Constitution, chose his pseudonym because he thought "federal" applied to his side. Anti-Federalist Elbridge Gerry wanted the two parties to be called ratifiers and anti-ratifiers, or "Rats" and "anti-Rats" for short.[17]

It would, indeed, have been reasonable to call the proponents of the Constitution "nationalists" or "consolidationists," leaving the term, "federalists," to the opponents. "Federal" is just a shortened form of "confederal," the adjective form of "Confederation." Before "consolidation" was hurled at them as invective, the advocates of the Constitution were willing to describe the Constitution as effecting a "consolidation."[18] The advocates of the new Constitution were also willing, early on, to say that a union of the states "merely federal" was insufficient to accomplish the necessary objects and

---

[15] Federal Farmer, *Letters to the Republican* 1 (Oct. 8, 1787), *reprinted in* 14 DHRC 21 (saying that the Articles had a federal plan and a federal head and that the Constitution should have preserved the *"federal* form," whereas it was in fact primarily a *consolidation*); Patrick Henry, Virginia Ratification Convention (June 9, 1788), *in* 9 DHRC 1068 (asking "Is it not a Consolidated Government for every purpose almost?): Curtiopolis, New York Daily Advertiser (Jan. 18, 1788), *reprinted in* 15 DHRC 400 (arguing that "[b]y the new plan, the States will be politically *consolidated*, which is absolutely impossible, under a Republican form of Government . . . [as] Montesquieu has said so"); *Federalist* No. 39, at 253 (Madison) (Jan. 16, 1788) (saying that Anti-Federalists regard "the union as a *confederacy* of sovereign States" and accuse Federalists of framing "a *national* government, which regards the union as a *consolidation* of the States").

[16] William Findley, History of the Insurrection 43 (1796).

[17] Eldridge Gerry, House of Representatives, Aug. 15, 1789, 1 Annals 759.

[18] President of the Federal Convention to the President of Congress Transmitting the Constitution (Sept. 17, 1787), *in* Formation of the Union of the American States 1003 (Charles C. Tansill ed., 1927) (describing the document a consolidation of our Union) emphasized by Daniel A. Farber, *The Constitution's Forgotten Cover Letter: An Essay on the New Federalism and the Original Understanding: Reflections on United States v. Lopez*, 94 Mich. L. Rev. 615, 628 n. 73 (1995); Randolph, To The Speaker Of The Virginia House Of Delegates (Oct. 10, 1787), *in* 3 Farrand 123, 124 (saying that we "come, to the last, and perhaps only refuge in our difficulties, a consolidation of the union, as far as circumstances will permit"); Jefferson to Richard Price (Jan. 8, 1789), in 14 PTJ 420 (describing the big change in the country that had made a consolidation seem necessary).

that what was needed was a supreme "national" three-part government.[19] Still, in the period before the Constitution, the name, "federal," got attached to nationalists because they were champions of the central, then "Confederal" Congress[20] and "anti-federal" got attached to opponents of the central government.[21] "Federal complexion" meant loyalty to the central government.[22] Given the continuity of language, "Federalist" continued to describe nationalists in favor of more power for the central government, even when the nationalists ceased to be looking for a confederate system of government.

Anti-Federalists are sometimes called "Other Founders,"[23] but they did not draft the Constitution, nor influence its drafting, and they opposed the fixed written document when they got to see it. Even the Bill of Rights, while responding to some Anti-Federalist arguments, was drafted in the first Congress where 85 percent of the power was held by Federalists. The Anti-Federalists, at 15 percent, never had much influence on the Bill of Rights and as a party they opposed the Bill of Rights when it was completed. Pope Urban VIII, who prosecuted Galileo for heresy, participated in a dialogue at the time of the founding of the scientific method, but he was opposed to the method and its conclusion that the Earth revolved around the sun. Pope Urban's role in the dialog was to confine Galileo to house arrest for the duration of his life and tell him he would be burned at the stake if he

---

[19] Randolph, Federal Convention, May 30, 1787, *in* 1 FARRAND 33.

[20] Nathan Dane to Samuel Adams (Feb. 11. 1786) *in* 23 LDCC 143 (referring to "federal men [who] must urge for the purposes of amending & strengthening our Common Government"); Nathaniel Gorham to Caleb Davis (Feb. 23, 1786), *in* 23 LDCC 161 (saying "how necessary it is to send Men of good Federal ideas").

[21] Madison to Washington (March 18, 1787), *in* 9 JM 315 (describing Lansing and Yates as linked to "the antifederal party here"); Madison to Jefferson (April 23, 1787) *in* 11 PTJ 309 (saying that the "antifederal party" in Connecticut is "numerous and persevering"); Madison to Monroe (Aug. 7, 1785), *in* 8 JM 334–335 (saying that if states are blocked from remedy by "foedral means, I tremble at the anti-foedral expedients" they might be tempted by).

[22] Robert Livingston, New York Convention (June 27, 1787), *in* 2 ELLIOT 343 (saying that a state would not pay requisitions when the enemy was far away, but when the British appeared in any state, the state wore at once a "very federal complexion").

[23] Note the title of SAUL CORNELL, THE OTHER FOUNDERS: ANTI-FEDERALISM AND THE DISSENTING TRADITION IN AMERICA, 1788–1828 (2000). *See also* Gordon Wood, *Political Ideology of the Founders, in* TOWARD A MORE PERFECT UNION 1, 17 (Neil York, ed. 1988) (saying that Anti-Federalists must be counted among the Founders); Murray Dry, *The Anti-Federalists and the Constitution, in* PRINCIPLES OF THE CONSTITUTIONAL ORDER: THE RATIFICATION DEBATES 64 (Robert L. Utley, Jr., ed., 1989) (describing the Anti-Federalists as "junior partners" to the Constitution).

ever argued again that the sun was central.[24] Given their stance, the Anti-Federalists can be said to be the "Other Founders" of the Constitution in about the same sense that Pope Urban can be described as an "other founder" of the scientific method.[25]

The opponents groused that the Constitution was offered for ratification, as "this or nothing; ... urged with a most extreme intemperance."[26] Starting in Massachusetts, the sixth state to ratify, various amendments were offered to change the document as it came out of Philadelphia, but the amendments were offered as recommendations for amendment of the Constitution rather than as preconditions to ratification.[27] Madison argued that any state's adoption of the Constitution with preconditions would not work because "[p]articular States may view different articles as conditions."[28] Only the first Congress, Madison argued, could work out the differences and contradictions between many proffered amendments.[29] Massachusetts, the sixth state to ratify, was the first to offer any recommendations.

The all-or-nothing posture of the question to the state conventions undercut the quality of the ratification debate. Under all-or-nothing, details of the new government, even quite important ones, mattered only if they changed a delegate's mind on the single overall decision. In Philadelphia, delegates with opposing viewpoints could argue with vigor and perhaps move the consensus. In the this-or-nothing posture after Philadelphia, however, the debaters were rationally insincere. The private letters by prominent Federalists, including

---

[24] Giorgio De Santillana, *Galileo*, in 19 ENCY. BRITANNICA 640, 641 (15th ed. 1985) for the short version and GIORGIO DE SANTILLANA, THE CRIME OF GALILEO (1955, reprinted 1977) for the long version.

[25] *Accord, see* Paul Finkelman, *Turning Losers into Winners: What Can We Learn If Anything, from the Anti-Federalists?*, 79 TEX. L. REV. 877 (2001) (reviewing CORNELL) (arguing that Anti-Federalist interpretation of the Constitution was repudiated by the American people in 1787–1788).

[26] Richard Henry Lee to Mason (Oct. 1, 1787), *in* 3 PGM 996.

[27] Governor John Hancock, who was a fence sitter who ultimately supported the Constitution, suggested the procedure of recommending Anti-Federalist amendments to the Massachusetts ratification convention rather than insisting upon amendments as a precondition to ratification. Editorial Note, Massachusetts Convention, 16 DHRC 60–67.

[28] Madison to Randolph (Apr 6, 1787), *in* 9 JM 369.

[29] *See, e.g.*, Madison, Virginia Convention (June 24, 1788), *in* 3 ELLIOT 618–619 (arguing that every state will propose contradictory amendments and unable to agree on them); Madison to Hamilton (June 22, 1788), *in* 1 WAH 461 (explaining plan to accept preface of general truths that cannot effect the validity of the ratification and to attach recommended amendments): *See also* Madison to Hamilton (July 1788), *in* 1 WAH 465 (opposing any conditions or variances in New York's ratification of the Constitution because "compacts must be reciprocal").

Madison,[30] Hamilton,[31] Washington,[32] Robert Morris,[33] and others[34] are filled with statements that the proposed Constitution was imperfect. The Constitution had features, to quote Ben Franklin, "[of] which I do not at present approve."[35] In public, however, the Federalists were rationally insincere and they tended to argue, as Pinckney did, that "this is the best government that has ever yet been offered to the world." "Instead of being alarmed at its consequences," Pinckney declared, "we should be astonishingly pleased that one so perfect could have been formed from such discordant and unpromising materials."[36]

Anti-Federalists, on their side, having decided against this new general-level government resting on the sovereignty of the people, could not admit in public that the Confederation in place was bankrupt and in need of unachievable amendments. They did commonly admit that in private.[37] Having

---

[30] Madison to Jefferson (Sept. 6, 1787), *in* 10 JM 163–64 (saying that "I hazard an opinion . . . that the plan, should it be adopted, will neither effectually answer its national object, nor prevent the local mischiefs which everywhere excite disgusts agst. the State Governments").

[31] Hamilton, Federal Convention (Sept. 17, 1787), *in* 2 FARRAND 645 (saying that "no man's ideas were more remote from the plan than his," but he endorsed all delegates to sign it nonetheless because there was anarchy and confusion if it failed and a chance of good if it succeeded). In 1802 Hamilton called the Constitution a "frail and worthless fabric." Hamilton to Gouverneur Morris (Feb. 29, 1802), *in* 25 PAH 544.

[32] Washington to David Humphreys (Oct. 10, 1787), *in* 3 FARRAND 103–04 (saying that the "Constitution that is submitted, is not free from imperfections – but there are as few radical defects in it as could well be expected, considering the heterogeneous mass of which the Convention was composed"). *See also* Washington to Henry Knox (Aug. 19 1787), *in* 3 FARRAND 70 (saying that he was "fully persuaded it is the best that can be obtained at the present moment under such diversity of ideas as prevail"); Washington to Charles Carter (Dec. 14, 1787), *in* 29 WRITINGS OF GW 336, 340 (saying that "I am not a blind admirer (for I saw the imperfections) of the Constitution to which I have assisted to give birth but I am persuaded it is the best that can be obtained at this day").

[33] Robert Morris to a Friend (Jan. 1788), *in* 3 FARRAND 243 ("Faulty it must be, for what is perfect?").

[34] William Pierce to St. George Tucker (Sept. 28, 1787), *in* 3 FARRAND 100 ("To say, however, that I consider it as perfect, would be to make an acknowledgement immediately opposed to my judgment").

[35] Benjamin Franklin, Federal Convention (Sept. 17, 1787), *in* 2 FARRAND 641.

[36] Charles Pinckney, South Carolina House of Representatives (Jan. 16, 1788), *in* 4 ELLIOT 261. But see A CITIZEN OF NEW YORK (JOHN JAY), ADDRESS TO THE PEOPLE OF THE STATE OF NEW YORK (Apr 15, 1788), *in* 17 DHRC 113–115 (saying that the Constitution offered to New York was imperfect, the product of many compromises and accommodations).

[37] *See, e.g.*, FERGUSON at 242 (citing Anti-Federalists Arthur Lee, John Mercer, Richard Henry Lee, and James Monroe as being affected enough by the Congress' imbecility to call for adoption of the impost or for a federal convention).

decided under the all-or-nothing rule that the document should be defeated, the Anti-Federalists wildly exaggerated the dangers of the new government.[38] The contest over ratification was largely a contest of the insincere on both sides: there were wild exaggerations of the effects of the Constitution by the opponents and misleading understatements by the Federalist proponents.

The ratification debates were also inevitably cacophonous because of their structure. After Philadelphia, there was never again a single room in which everyone had even to pretend to reach a single meaning for the Constitution. In Philadelphia, the delegates argued from May to September to reach a single draft. They bickered over language, they delegated hard issues to one committee after another, and at the end they signed a single draft. The single room, long discussions, and single set of words may not mean that there was only a single understanding, common to all, but it does hedge in the understandings such that they are collected around a single document and words that had been discussed. By contrast, the ratification debate extended along the entire seaboard with a population of 3 million. There was, as Joseph Story said, "[n]o certainty either that different state conventions gave the same interpretation or that the same reasoning prevailed even within the majority of a single convention."[39] The ratifiers who published their views had a slightly different understanding of the significance of the words, even when they debated the fixed language clause by clause. Readers in the debates commonly missed the point, or came up with interpretations that we do not find as matching the words, although that was what they understood to be the meaningful point. Once the document left Philadelphia, there was also no longer any mechanism to force a single understanding. It is not coherent to say that the Federal Convention in Philadelphia misunderstood or made a mistake about the Constitution. What they understood is what the Constitution was. It is coherent to say that this or that ratifier, or even this or that state

---

[38] *See, e.g.*, "A Farmer and Planter," MARYLAND JOURNAL (April 1, 1788), *reprinted in* 5 STORING 76 (1981) (arguing that Congress would use its tax power to "destroy your plantation, abuse your wife, kill your infant, ravish your daughter and live in free quarters"); Henry Abbot, North Carolina Convention (July 30, 1788), *in* 4 ELLIOT 191–2, (reporting fears by "some people" that giving the federal government the power to make treaties would allow them to make a treaty to establish the Roman Catholic Church as the religion in the United States); Abraham Holmes, Massachusetts Convention (Jan. 30, 1788), *in* 2 ELLIOT 111 (arguing that if the federal government has power over crimes, they "are nowhere restrained from inventing the most cruel and unheard-of punishments. . . . [R]acks and gibbets may be amongst the most mild instruments of their discipline").

[39] JOSEPH STORY, 1 CONSTITUTIONAL COMMENTARY 388–389 (1833). *See also* Leonard Levy, *Ratifying Intent*, ENCYCLOPEDIA OF THE CONSTITUTION: SUPPLEMENT 40 (1991) (attacking the "utter looseness" of the argument that ratifier intent governs).

convention, made a mistake and misunderstood the Constitution.[40] In any event, if it is the writing that governs the interpretation of the Constitution, then the Philadelphia Convention governs the meaning, and not conventions of the states. The Constitution was written in Philadelphia and the writing was finished before any state saw it.

The best of the ratification debates for our needs are the essays in the *Federalist*, written by Hamilton, Madison, and John Jay under the single pseudonym of *Publius*.[41] Madison and Hamilton were in despair at the end of the Convention, both believing that the Constitution was inadequate to its desperate national mission,[42] but when it looked like the document might be not only inadequate but also defeated, they rallied to its cause. The essays in the *Federalist* have become famous retroactively because they give good rationales for specific provisions. Madison, Hamilton and Jay had been thinking about the national needs long and hard and they were as bright as existed on the continent. Madison and Hamilton heard the debates in Philadelphia, and they were willing to put aside their private reservations so as to praise the final document.

The *Federalist* essays were not as important at the time, however, as they are treated now. The essays appeared first as newspaper articles in the New York City papers to persuade the voters of New York to ratify, and they seem to have failed utterly for that purpose. There is no evidence, Linda De Pauw has concluded, that *Publius* converted a single Anti-Federalist, and indeed, he scared some fence-sitters toward the other side.[43] No one figured out who

---

[40] David McGowan, *Ethos in Law and History: Alexander Hamilton,* The Federalist, *and the Supreme Court*, 85 Minn. L. Rev. 755, 825 (2001) argues that to reach certainty under contract logic, the "[p]rivate understandings of the Philadelphia delegates are not relevant here for the same reason private understandings of contract terms are not relevant: giving weight to private meanings would make contracts uncertain and undermine the principle of assent on which the authority of the agreement is based." The difficulty with the argument is that the only meeting of the minds that could be said to be anything akin to a contract agreement occurred in Philadelphia. Once the document left Philadelphia there may well have been a million quite private understandings of what the Constitution meant and no obligation to reconcile the differences to come a single understanding. Looking to the million understandings in the ratification debate is not going to combat "uncertainty."

[41] *Accord*, Rakove, Original Meanings at xv (saying that nothing equals it in analytical breadth and conceptual power).

[42] Madison to Jefferson (Sept. 6, 1787), *in* 10 JM 163–64 (saying that "I hazard an opinion ... that the plan, should it be adopted, will neither effectually answer its national object, nor prevent the local mischiefs which everywhere excite disgusts agst. The State Governments"); Hamilton, Federal Convention (Sept. 17, 1787), *in* 2 Farrand 645 (saying that "no mans ideas were more remote from the plan than his").

[43] Linda Grant DePauw, The Eleventh Pillar: New York State and the Federal Constitution 278 (1966), at 106–117 (1966) (pointing specially at 114 to Hamilton's

Publius was at the time, or at least no one broke the code that there were three people behind this entity.[44] *Publius* thus did not get the full prestige at the time that the country was willing to give to great men. *Publius* was also too complicated and legalistic, "too learned and too long for the ignorant."[45] *Publius* has written a history, Anti-Federalist DeWitt Clinton scathingly snipped, "and [I shall] wait and buy one of his books when they come out."[46] If the value of the essays was in how it influenced the conventions, then the *Federalist* essays are of marginal value.

The ratification debates have a core coherence to them. The Anti-Federalists opposed the movement in power from state to national government, they were skeptical about the threat of war, and they uniformly opposed federal internal taxes, even in time of war. The fence-sitters came over, in the end, because of the pull of the united cause of independence and representative government for which the Revolutionary War had been fought, and also because each state decided it wanted to be part of the overall union, the United States.

A. THE FEUDAL BARONS

The Constitution created a new complete government at the continental level, drawing power for it from the states. The Framers meeting in Philadelphia "doubted much the practicability of annihilating the States," according to Rufus King, but they did think at least that much of the states' power "ought to be taken from them."[47] As Gouverneur Morris foretold at the end of the Philadelphia Convention, the "moment this plan goes forth all other considerations will be laid aside – and the great question will be, shall there be a national government or not."[48] The Anti-Federalists opposed the creation of the national government and stood in favor of maintaining the pre-existing power of the states. To the established state powers, the new national

---

Federalist 9, raising the specter of a standing army, as making enemies). *Accord*, John Kaminski, *New York: The Reluctant Pillar, in* RELUCTANT PILLAR 71–72.

44 *Editorial Note*, 13 DHRC 488.

45 Louis G. Otto, Liste des Membres et Officiers du Congrés. 1788, French Archives: Ministère des Affaires Etrangères, *in* 3 FARRAND 232, 234, 237.

46 NEW YORK JOURNAL (Jan. 7, 10, 1788), *quoted in* DEPAUW, *supra* note 43, at 115.

47 Rufus King (Massachusetts), Federal Convention (June 19, 1787), *in* 1 FARRAND 324. *Accord*, Gouverneur Morris to W. H. Wells (Feb. 24, 1815), *in* 3 FARRAND 421–422 (saying that discussion shortly after the Convention was on "the importance of arranging a national system of sufficient strength to operate, in despite of State opposition, and yet not strong enough to break down State authority").

48 Gouverneur Morris, Federal Convention (Sept. 17, 1787), *in* 2 FARRAND 645.

government created by the Constitution was an unknown and threatening monster. "This Government is so new it wants a name," said Patrick Henry. "I wish its other novelties were as harmless as this."[49]

The friends of the Constitution believed that the Anti-Federalists took up opposition to the Constitution in bad faith just to retain the power of their state offices. "The truth is it is a contest for power, not for liberty," said Hamilton at the Convention.[50] In *Federalist* Number 1, Hamilton starts the series saying that the most formidable obstacles to ratification would be the state office holders who will "resist all changes which may hazard a diminution of the power, emolument, and consequence of [their] offices."[51] The separate states might "aptly be compared with the feudal baronies,"[52] Hamilton said, and the barons could be expected to oppose the centralizing Constitution. Even men of consequence, Hamilton believed, would oppose adoption from a "desire of playing a part in a convulsion for their own aggrandizement."[53] "Whose opposition will be most likely to be excited agst. the System?" Edmund Randolph asked and then answered his own question pungently: "That of the local demogagues who will be degraded by it from the importance they now hold."[54]

Anti-Federalism was indeed represented most importantly by the officers who held power in the states. In New York, Governor George Clinton was "truly the leader of his party," and Clinton, Hamilton wrote, "is inflexibly obstinate, I count little on overcoming opposition by reason [Clinton] has declared his opinion of the *inutility* of the Union."[55] "The elections have gone wrong" Hamilton also wrote, "and Clinton has... declared the Union

---

49 Patrick Henry, Virginia Convention (June 9, 1788), *in* 9 DHRC 1058. *See, e.g.*, Stanley Elkins & Eric McKitrick, *The Founding Fathers: Young Men of the Revolution*, 76 POL. SCI. Q. 181, 202–203 (1961) (arguing that the proponents of the Constitution were deeply involved in the Continental war effort or were members of Congress serving on the war committees, while the Anti-Federalists were concerned primarily with state problems).

50 Hamilton, Federal Convention (June 29, 1787), *in* 1 FARRAND 466.

51 *Federalist* No. 1, at 4 (Hamilton) (Oct. 27, 1787). *See, also* DAILY ADVERTISER, NEW YORK (Sept. 24, 1787), *in* 1 DEBATE 13 (saying that perhaps the greatest difficulty against the adoption would come from "ambitious citizens in the different States, who either now are in power, or who will practice their political wiles on the ignorant and unsuspicious part of the people, in order to obtain their own private purposes"); A Landholder [Oliver Ellsworth], I, CONNECTICUT COURANT (Nov. 5, 1787), *in* 3 FARRAND 137 (saying that general Convention properly submitted their system to the people rather than the legislatures, whose decisions are often influenced by men "who have provided well for themselves and dread any change least they should be injured by its operation").

52 *Federalist* No. 17, at 109 (Hamilton) (Dec. 5, 1787).

53 Hamilton's Conjectures About the New Constitution (Sept. 1787), *in* 1 DEBATE 9.

54 Randolph, Federal Convention (July 23, 1787), *in* 2 FARRAND 89.

55 Hamilton to Madison (May 19, 1788), *in* 1 WAH 453.

unnecessary."[56] The New York delegates to the Federal Convention, Yates and Lansing, who represented Clinton, declared opposition to any "general Government, however guarded by declarations of rights or cautionary provisions."[57] The Anti-Federalists of New York, are "positively in favor of separation," the French Consulate wrote home.[58]

According to the Federalists, the high principle of New York Anti-Federalism was simply to retain for state purposes all of the revenue from the New York harbor imposts. The opposition in New York, said "Landholder" in Connecticut, is "not to this constitution in particular, but to the federal impost." The New York office holders whose salary is paid by the state impost, "Landholder" wrote, "are endeavoring to convince the ignorant part of the community that an annual income of fifty thousand pounds, extorted from the citizens of Massachusetts, Connecticut and New Jersey, is a great blessing to the state of New York."[59] "The dominant party in New York," Madison would say, "had refused even a duty of 5 per Ct. on imports for the urgent debt of the Revolution, so as to tax the consumption of her neighbors."[60]

---

[56] Hamilton to Gouverneur Morris (May 19, 1788), *in* 1 WAH 452.

[57] Robert Yates and John Lansing, Jr., *to Governor George Clinton, The Dissent of the Two New York Delegates to the Philadelphia Convention,* DAILY ADVERTISER (Jan. 14, 1788), *reprinted in* 2 DEBATE 3, 4.

[58] Comte de Moustier to Comte de Montmorin (June 25, 1787), *in* 18 DHRC 190 (saying also that the Anti-Federalists want fewer commercial ties with Europe, which only furnishes them with "luxuries that they must do without to live in the simplicity that befits a newborn State").

[59] The Landholder VIII (Oliver Ellsworth), CONNECTICUT COURANT (Dec. 24, 1787), *reprinted in* 15 DHRC 78). *See also* Oliver Ellsworth, Connecticut Convention (Jan. 7, 1788), *in* 2 ELLIOT 190–197 (saying that the people of Connecticut pay annually into the treasury of New York more than fifty thousand dollars by reason of the impost on New York harbor traffic); Nathaniel Gorham, Federal Convention (July 23, 1787), *in* 2 FARRAND 90 (pointing to the present advantage that New York seems to be so much attached to, of taxing her neighbors by the regulation of her trade); Timothy Pickering to John Pickering (Dec. 29, 1787), *in* 15 DHRC 177 (saying that "[New York] has long been acting a disingenuous part. They refused the impost to Congress – because half of New Jersey, a great part of Connecticut, the western part of Massachusetts & Vermont, received their imported goods thro' New York, who put into her *own* treasury all the duties arising on the goods consumed in [these] states").

[60] Madison, Unsent letter to John Tyler (1833), *in* 3 FARRAND 530–531. *See also* KAMINSKI, CLINTON at 91, 94 (1993) (saying that Lansing and Yates, the delegates from New York to the Philadelphia Convention, had been leaders in New York's veto of the 1783 impost proposal); RAKOVE, BEGINNINGS 176–338 (saying that Yates had emerged as an effective public critic of the impost, publishing a number of essays attacking the proposal, because he was bitter that Robert Morris had refused to appoint him receiver of federal taxes).

In Virginia, opposition was led by former Governor Patrick Henry.[61] Patrick Henry dominated Virginia[62] and Henry was said to prefer disunion to this Constitution.[63] Henry, it was said, was opposed to any system that would confirm the Union, were "it sent from heaven."[64]

Much of the ratification struggle was not seriously over ideas, but over power – answering the crucial question of politics: Do your people or my people get control? In Pennsylvania, for example, the fight over ratification was acrimonious, but only tangentially related to the issues. "Pennsylvania is divided," Jefferson observed, "& all the bitterness of her factions has been kindled anew on it."[65] Pennsylvania was rigidly divided along religious lines, with western Scotch-Irish Presbyterians forming one block, which decided against the Constitution, and eastern Quakers, Anglicans, and Mennonites the other, which decided in its favor. The religious blocks were tightly coherent. Professor Owen Ireland has shown that 92.5 percent of the members of the Assembly voted according to religion at least 80 percent of the time in the decade before the Constitution.[66] Madison noted that Pennsylvania was "split into two fixed and violent parties." In all questions, however unimportant in themselves, the same names invariably stood in opposite columns, he said, proving that "passion and not reason, must have presided over their decisions."[67] As Oliver Ellsworth put it,

> One of these parties happened to declare for the new federal constitution and this was a sufficient motive for the other to oppose it: the

---

[61] There are a number of lucid descriptions of the Virginia Ratification debates concentrating on the convention. MORRIS at 309–312 (1987); RUTLAND at 169–198, 218–234, 245–253 (1966); MAIN at 223–23; MCDONALD, WE THE PEOPLE 255–283 traces the economic interests of the delegates to make sense of what arguments influenced them.

[62] See, e.g., MCDONALD, WE THE PEOPLE at 262 (finding that Henry had at least two dozen delegates who had followed his lead on virtually every issue in the legislature).

[63] Edward Carrington to Madison (Feb. 10, 1788), in 8 DHRC 359 (saying that Patrick Henry's "views are a dismemberment of the Union"); Madison to Randolph (Jan. 10, 1788), in 8 DHRC 289 (saying that he considered Henry's politics as "driving at a Southern Confederacy"). Main collects statements on separate confederacies in Appendix A of his MAIN at 283 and concludes that other than Patrick Henry most comments on separate confederations came from the nationalist side. The Federalists were surer that Anti-Federalists wanted the break up of the union, than the Anti-Federalists were themselves.

[64] Henry Lee to Madison (Dec. 20, 1787), in 10 JM 339.

[65] Jefferson to William Carmichael (Dec. 15, 1787), in 14 DHRC 481.

[66] O. S. Ireland, The Crux of Politics: Religion and Party in Pennsylvania, 1778–1789, 42 WM. & MARY Q. 453, 456 (3rd. Ser., 1985). See more generally, OWEN S. IRELAND, RELIGION, ETHNICITY AND POLITICS: RATIFYING THE CONSTITUTION IN PENNSYLVANIA (1995) (dominant ingredient in the acrimonious relations between Constitutionalists and Republicans was religion).

[67] Federalist No. 50, at 345–6 (Hamilton or Madison) (Feb. 5, 1788).

dispute there is not upon the merits of the subject, but it is their old warfare carried on with different weapons. . . . [I]t was an even chance that the parties had taken different sides from what they have taken, for there is no doubt but either party would sacrifice the whole country to the destruction of their enemies.[68]

For the decade before the Constitution, the western Presbyterians had dominated Pennsylvania politics because the Quakers and Mennonites from the eastern part of the state refused for religious reasons to take the loyalty oaths, originally created to exclude British Loyalists from the electorate. The Presbyterians continued the loyalty oaths long after they functioned to exclude Tories and traitors, because the oaths excluded Quakers and other political enemies and that was considered a blessing. As the loyalty oath requirements were eased, the Quakers and Mennonites came back into the electorate and with a vengeance. By the time of the ratification convention, they were a two-thirds majority in favor of ratification and the Calvinist Presbyterians were a one-third minority. Being Calvinist, that is, Presbyterian or Dutch Reform, meant being against the Constitution, and being Quaker, Mennonite, Anglican, or anybody else meant being in favor. For the Pennsylvania Calvinists, the arguments they made against the Constitution were manifestations, but the underlying position was predestined.

The Pennsylvania Anti-Federalist Presbyterians are occasionally treated as populist heroes by sympathetic historians,[69] but they were no democrats. The loyalty oaths carried over from the Revolution excluded over half of the electorate from voting.[70] The Presbyterians also disenfranchised the mechanics and artisans of Philadelphia with new property requirements for voting because they held no land and also because they were voting against the Presbyterians.[71] On the important issue of slavery, it was the Federalist Quakers who had been in favor of emancipation in 1780 and the Calvinist Presbyterians and Dutch Reformers who were generally against it.[72]

---

[68] The Landholder VIII (Oliver Ellsworth), Connecticut Courant (Dec. 24, 1787), *reprinted in* 15 DHRC 78.

[69] *See, e.g.*, Robert Brunhouse, The Counter-revolution in Pennsylvania, 1776–1790, at 80 (1942).

[70] E. Bruce Thomas, Political Tendencies in Pennsylvania, 1783–1794, at 199 (1938) (unpublished dissertation, Temple University). *See* Editorial Note 9, *in* 15 DHRC 202 (saying that no one could vote in an election without a certificate proving he had taken an oath of allegiance before 1 June 1778, but all such laws were repealed by 1789).

[71] Brunhouse, *supra* note 69, at 192 reports the charge.

[72] In 1780 Pennsylvania passed a gradual emancipation act under which current slaves would remain enslaved, but their children would be freed when they reached age 28. Philadelphia and the East generally supported the emancipation, whereas the Calvinists in the West

There is evidence of clan reacting against clan in states other than Pennsylvania. A map of Virginia showing Federalist and Anti-Federalist delegates indicates alternating stripes as one moves inland: Tidewater is Federalist, the falls-line and Piedmont are Anti-Federalist, Shenandoah Valley and West Virginia is Federalist, and Kentucky is Anti-Federalist.[73] It looks as if each stripe is in part reacting to the power of the prior tier of settlement, so that Federalists and Anti-Federalists cycle their position in reaction to an earlier enemy.[74] Patrick Henry, the power in Virginia, seems motivated not so much by what he says, as by his enemies. The proposed Constitution not only created a whole new government that would pull power away from the Virginia he controlled, but even worse, it was to be run by his political enemies, Washington, Jefferson, and Madison.[75] The personal and clan animosities go a long way to explaining the positions, probably on both sides.

B. THE SCATTER-SHOT OPPOSITION

The Anti-Federalists were a diverse lot. In Virginia, New York, and Pennsylvania, there was a pre-existing faction that took up the cause of Anti-Federalism, but elsewhere the Anti-Federalists had trouble getting organized. They never formed an effective national organization. There were, for instance, letters of sympathy between the Virginia and New York Anti-Federalists, which, however, "did not constitute a political strategy in any practical sense."[76] Anti-Federalism was diffuse, which is arguably quite befitting a movement that was trying to avoid the centrifugal pull of a strong central government and trying to preserve the strength of the separate states.

---

generally opposed it. GARY NASH, FREEDOM IN DEGREES: EMANCIPATION IN PENNSYLVANIA AND ITS AFTERMATH 105–107 (1991). *See also* BRUNHOUSE, *supra* note 69, at 80 (saying that opposition to emancipation of the Pennsylvania slaves came from the Whig or country party and not Federalists).

73 *See* map of Virginia, *in* 8 DHRC, *inside cover and opposing pages*. Professor Risjord finds that Tidewater was disproportionately Federalist (14% more than the mean for the state as a whole), Piedmont was disproportionately Anti-Federalist (10% less Federalist than the state as a whole) and the West was again disproportionately Federalist (by 14%). RISJORD at 309.

74 *See also* RISJORD at 294 (saying that Western Virginia switched to pro-Constitution to provide the necessary votes for ratification because it was easy for them to transfer the blame for Indian raids from the British over to eastern planters).

75 *Cf.* The Landholder VIII (Oliver Ellsworth), CONNECTICUT COURANT (Dec. 24, 1787), *reprinted in* 15 DHRC 78 (arguing that in Virginia, the opposition wholly originated in enmity of the Lee faction to General Washington and the madness of Col. Mason).

76 RAKOVE, ORIGINAL MEANINGS at 122.

All the eleven states that remained represented in Philadelphia at the end of
the Convention supported the Constitution, but some individual delegates to
the convention were able to avoid the magnetism of the discussions to become
vocal opponents of the Constitution: George Mason of Virginia, Elbridge
Gerry of Massachusetts, Luther Martin of Maryland, and John Lansing and
Robert Yates of New York all attended the convention but opposed its results.
Governor Randolph of Virginia announced his opposition to the document
at the end of the Convention, but by the time of the Virginia Ratification
Convention had become an articulate defender of it.[77]

Within that small group of opponents, there was not a lot in common.[78]
The Virginia opponents of the Constitution – Patrick Henry, George Mason,
James Monroe, Richard Henry Lee, and William Grayson – were slaveholders, plantation owners, debtors, and land speculators, difficult to distinguish from their neighboring plantation owners, Madison, Washington,
Carrington, and Marshall, who led the constitutional revolution, nor from
the fence-sitters, Thomas Jefferson and Edmund Randolph, who eventually
supported the Constitution. The slaveholder Virginia opponents of the Constitution had far more in common with the Virginia proponents than they
did with fellow opponents, John Lansing of New York or Elbridge Gerry of
Boston, who were merchants and representatives of deep-water shipping.[79]
Congregationalist Anti-Federalist Elbridge Gerry had expressed deep hos-
tility to Anglican bishops[80] and Anglican Anti-Federalist Patrick Henry had
sponsored a tax to support the Anglicans in Virginia.[81] Western Pennsylvania Presbyterian Scotch-Irish Anti-Federalist leaders John Smilie and Robert
Whitehead opposed the Anglicans of Philadelphia on all issues, including on
the issue of the Constitution. Had Patrick Henry and Gerry or the Presbyterians been together in the same state, they could not have stayed on
the same side. Saul Cornell recently wrote a book dividing Anti-Federalist
spokesmen into Aristocrats, middling democrats, and levellers, but although
the schema brings some order to things, it does not help to explain what

---

[77] *See infra*, pp. 161–62.

[78] *See, e.g.*, THE LANDHOLDER [OLIVER ELLSWORTH] X, MARYLAND JOURNAL (Feb. 29, 1788),
reprinted in 3 FARRAND 271 (describing how Gerry and Luther Martin opposed each other
in their principles): Madison to Edward Pendleton, (Feb. 21, 1788), *in* 10 JM 533 (saying
that the grounds of objection among the dissenting members of the Convention were by
no means the same).

[79] David Gordon, *Eldridge Gerry*, *in* 2 ENCYCLOPEDIA OF THE AMERICAN CONSTITUTION 838–
9 (Leonard Levy, ed. 1986); Dennis J. Mahoney, *John Lansing, Jr.*, *in* 3 *id.* 1124.

[80] GEORGE BILLIAS, ELBRIDGE GERRY: FOUNDING FATHER AND REPUBLICAN STATESMAN 23–
24 (1976).

[81] *See, e.g.*, RISJORD at 203–210.

the very different Anti-Federalists had in common.[82] Madison's assessment of the opposition was that the various objections of the opponents were inconsistent with each other and that the views of the minorities, in states where the Constitution was not unanimously adopted, "are as heterogeneous as can be imagined."[83]

There is inconsistency even within the thinnest of ranks. George Mason, who was arguably the most important Anti-Federalist, is especially difficult to make consistent. Mason has many characteristics of a strong nationalist. Mason had been within Madison's party in Virginia in the 1780s organized against Patrick Henry and insisting on payment of public and private debt.[84] In November 1787, after the end of the Philadelphia Convention, Patrick Henry had sponsored legislation in Virginia, making its state taxes payable in tobacco. Mason called the legislation a "foolish and injurious project."[85] Mason had told Madison in the preparation for Philadelphia that he would take an active role in amending the Confederation.[86] At the Convention, he approved the core change that the Constitution would mean that Congress would represent not the states but the people directly, saying for instance, the new government would necessarily operate on individuals, because "punishment could not in the nature of things be executed on the States collectively."[87] At the end of the Convention, he told Madison that he did not object in general to the powers vested in the national government, and particularly wanted the Federal negative on state legislation and federal appointment of state governors.[88] But then Mason objected to supremacy of the federal judiciary, "which is so constructed & extended," he says, "as to absorb and destroy the Judiciariys of the several States."[89] To be in favor of the negative, but opposed to the more moderate remedy of judicial supremacy is hard to reconcile.

---

[82] SAUL CORNELL, THE OTHER FOUNDERS (2000).
[83] Madison to Edward Pendleton (Feb. 21, 1788), in 10 JM 533.
[84] See, e.g. RISJORD at 87.
[85] Mason to Washington (Nov. 27, 1787), in 3 PGM 1019, 1021.
[86] Madison to Jefferson (April 24, 1787), in 11 PTJ 310 (reporting that Mason had "renounced his errors on the subject of the Confederation" and meant "to take an active part in the amendment of it").
[87] Mason, Federal Convention (May 30, 1787), in 1 FARRAND 34. See also Mason, Federal Convention (June 6, 1787), in 1 FARRAND 133 (saying that Congress would represent the people not the states).
[88] Madison to Jefferson (Oct. 24, 1787), in 10 JM 216. Mason did tell Madison, however, on strategic grounds that he did not think that the public mind would now bear the negative and that it would have to await later amendments. Id.
[89] Mason, Objections to the Constitution of Government formed by the Convention (Oct. 7, 1787), in 8 DHRC 44.

Although Mason had been a staunch ally of Madison's in opposing Patrick Henry on paper money in Virginia in the 1780s,[90] in Philadelphia he fought for the states' power to issue paper money.[91] But Mason was opposed to "book debt," the tab that storekeepers use to let farmers have seed and supplies before the harvest comes, and he had tried to end the important institution of book debt by requiring that it be collected within six months of the time it arose.[92] Mason was no friend of easy credit or easy money.

In Philadelphia, Mason sometimes acted as an aristocrat, resisting democratic claims,[93] and sometimes as a democrat resisting aristocratic claims.[94] Mason objected to the Constitution on the ground that it had no Declaration of Rights in the Constitution, and that the national government with the supremacy of its laws might even take away the rights given to the people by state law.[95] The passage of the actual Bill of Rights did not reconcile him to the Constitution[96] and he did not become reconciled with his former ally, Madison, until Madison turned to become part of the Jeffersonian opposition to the Washington administration.[97] Mason, moreover, chose government over individual rights because he wanted state and national governments

---

[90] Risjord at 97–98, 153–154, 175, 177–78.

[91] Mason, Federal Convention (Aug. 16, 1787), *in* 2 Farrand 309 (saying that "though he had a mortal hatred to paper money, yet as he could not foresee all emergences, still he was unwilling to tie the hands of the Legislature because the late war could not have been carried on, had such a prohibition existed").

[92] A Bill for Discouraging Extensive Credit, Oct. 18, 1779, 2 PGM 578; Fairfax County Petition Protesting Repeal of the Act to Prevent Extensive Credit, 2 *id.* at 786–787. *See also* discussion in Chapter 9, pp. 206–07.

[93] Mason, Federal Convention (June 26, 1787), *in* 1 Farrand 428 (saying that needy persons should be ineligible for election to the Senate because one function of the Senate was to protect property).

[94] Mason, Federal Convention (Aug. 7, 1787), *in* 2 Farrand 201–202 (opposing a property requirement for voting in federal elections because of the embarrassment of disenfranchising voters eligible to vote in state elections). The two positions are not strictly inconsistent, because it is possible to believe that the Senate is the protector of property, while believing that the House and presidency elections should be at least as democratic as state standards. Ironically, his debating opponent on both days was conservative John Dickinson of Pennsylvania, who was for the people in denying a property requirement for Senators, but against the people in requiring property for federal voters. Dickinson's switch is harder to make consistent.

[95] Mason, Objections to the Constitution of Government formed by the Convention (Oct. 7, 1787), *in* 8 DHRC 45.

[96] Mason to John Mason (July 31, 1789) *in* 3 PGM 1164 (calling Madison's amendments a "farce").

[97] Elkins & McKitrick at 266 (Mason in January 1791 gestures reconciliation to Madison through Jefferson).

to be able to enact retroactive or ex post facto laws on the ground that "there never was or can be a Legislature but must & will make such Laws, when Necessity & the public safety require them."[98] Mason, like Hamilton but unlike the later southern states-rightsers, also supported governmental subsidies to promote American manufactures.[99]

Mason had alternative ideas for the House of Representatives, Senate, and Executive, some quite reasonable and some not very different from the system the Framers chose.[100] Still, Mason's alternatives should have left him far closer to the Constitution than he was to the Articles of Confederation and he should have swallowed his pride and moved into alliance with the Federalists. George Mason might be the most important opponent of the proposed Constitution and it is difficult to find a common agenda, even within him.

"Col. Mason," Madison relates, "left Philadelphia in an exceeding ill humour indeed. A number of little circumstances arising in part from the impatience which prevailed toward the close of the business, conspired to whet his acrimony."[101] Mason seems the plausible target of Madison's quip that one should not fail to abandon a condemned abode merely because the new one has no porch or the ceilings are higher than is fancied.[102] Madison also thought many of Mason's objections "were either not at all or very faintly urged at the time when alone they ought to have been urged."[103]

Mason's other colleagues were less indulgent of him. He was like the quarrelsome little French girl who "never found a person who was always in the right but herself."[104] George Nicholas thought that Mason held the vain opinion that "he has influence enough to dictate a constitution to Virginia,

---

98 Mason, Objections to the Constitution of Government formed by the Convention (Oct. 7, 1787), *in* 8 DHRC 43, 45.

99 Mason, Federal Convention (Sept. 13, 1787), *in* 2 FARRAND 606 (advocating association to discourage foreign superfluities and to encourage American manufactures). For the later controversies between Hamilton and Jeffersonians on government encouragement of American manufactures, see ELKINS & McKITRICK at 257–263, 276–282.

100 *See, e.g.*, Mason to Samuel Griffin (Sept. 8, 1789), *in* 3 PGM 1170, 1172 (saying he would have cheerfully supported the Constitution with following amendments: (1) confining federal judiciary to admiralty, (2) preventing Congress from moving election spots, (3) requiring two-thirds majority for navigation laws, and (4) giving the executive power to a council).

101 Madison to Jefferson (Oct. 24, 1787), *in* 10 JM 215–216.

102 *Federalist* No.38, at 246–7 (Madison) (Jan. 12, 1788).

103 Madison to Washington (Oct. 18, 1787), *in* 3 FARRAND 129.

104 Copy of a letter to Jefferson (in Jefferson's handwriting found in his papers) (Oct. 1787), *in* 3 FARRAND 105.

and through her to the rest of the Union."[105] Oliver Ellsworth thought that Mason should be left to vent his rage "to his own negroes and to the wind."[106]

The Anti-Federalists' attacks on the Constitution were often scatterblasts focusing on nothing specific, which carried the ratification debates into quite peripheral issues. The first state convention with a close vote was Massachusetts, and Massachusetts was a large, crucial state. Madison assessed the opposition in Massachusetts, saying "they had no plan whatsoever."[107] They "looked no further than to reject the Constitution in toto and return home."[108] That seems indeed a reasonable assessment in Massachusetts.

In the first three days of its substantive debate, the Massachusetts Convention debated whether failure to hold annual elections for Congressmen was tantamount to tyranny, and whether Congress could fix the outcome of an election by setting the time and place for voting.[109] With all due respect, the arguments over term of office or fixing the procedures for an election are not the telling issues as to whether a national government should replace the states.

The Framers were indeed concerned about giving Congressmen some operational independence. Under the Articles, Congressmen were elected by the state legislatures and they were subject to instant recall at the will of the state legislature.[110] The Framers thought subjecting Congressmen to instant recall would bind them to local prejudice instead of to the general welfare. Edmund Randolph complained

> Congs. are moreover not elected by the people, but by the Legislatures who retain even a power of recall. They have therefore no will of their own, they are a mere diplomatic body, and are always obsequious to the views of the States, who are always encroaching on the authority of the U. States."[111]

Robert Livingston told New York that with recall, a Congressman might be appointed one day and recalled the next by state legislature, "subject

---

[105] George Nicholas to Madison (April 5, 1788), *in* 3 FARRAND 296. *See also* Washington to Madison (Oct. 10, 1787), *in* 10 JM 215, 190 (saying that the groundwork of Mason's plan seems to be to "alarm the people").

[106] The Landholder (Oliver Ellsworth), CONNECTICUT COURANT (Dec. 24, 1787), *reprinted in* 15 DHRC 75, 78 (saying that if Mason had not been mad and the Lee faction had not been hostile to Washington, then Virginia would have ratified overwhelmingly and "Col. Mason would have vented his rage to his own negroes and to the wind").

[107] Madison to Jefferson (Feb. 19, 1788), *in* 10 JM 519.

[108] Madison to Edward Pendleton, (Feb. 21, 1788), *in* 10 JM 533.

[109] Massachusetts Convention (Jan. 14–15, 1788), *in* 2 ELLIOT 3–21.

[110] ARTICLES OF CONFEDERATION, art. V.

[111] Randolph, Federal Convention (June 16, 1787), *in* 1 FARRAND 256.

to fractious and irregular passions." "This would be a source of endless confusion," he said, because Congressmen "are not to consult the interest of any one state alone, but that of the union."[112] The pull from all the local prejudices, according to Hamilton, prevented the general welfare from prevailing.[113] The Framers might well have been conspiring, as the Massachusetts Anti-Federalists suggested, but the Anti-Federalists missed the point that the conspiracy was not against the people, but against the states. The Framers were using the people as a source of legitimacy against the wicked states. In any event, direct elections of any kind would have to be an improvement over the Articles' rule for appointment of Congress by state legislatures, as to responsiveness of Congressmen to the people. "The people have hitherto been shut out of the federal government," James Wilson told Pennsylvania, "but . . . they should not any longer be dispossessed of their rights."[114]

The Framers, on their part, considered the exact term of years for Congressmen to be an administrative detail. Both the Virginia Plan and the starkly different New Jersey Plan, when offered, had left blank the term of the legislators, as if it were a number to be filled in later.[115] The issue of length of term was debated at the Convention. Madison, in the Convention, favored three-year terms for representatives instead of two, to allow the representatives to form better knowledge of their job and to cut down on the burdensome travel between home and Congress.[116] Annual elections are plausibly a terrible idea, because they would distract the legislators, even more, with the demands of the perpetual campaign. If annual elections in fact increased turnover, that might well encourage more amateur Congressmen, who were less capable at their jobs and less skeptical than they should be about lobbying. But even if annual elections were a better idea, they were not the core issue in the Constitution.

As to the administration of elections, Article I, Section 4 of the Constitution gives the state legislatures the power in the first instance to prescribe the

---

[112] RR Livingston, New York Convention (June 24, 1788), *in* 2 ELLIOT 291.

[113] Hamilton, Federal Convention (June 18, 1787), *in* 1 FARRAND 287. *See also* Livingston, New York Convention (June 24, 1788), *in* 2 ELLIOT 296. (saying power of recall tended to bind Congressmen too strongly to the interests of their respective states).

[114] Wilson, Pennsylvania Convention (Nov. 30, 1787), *in* 2 ELLIOT 433.

[115] 1 FARRAND 20 (Virginia plan), 244 (New Jersey plan). Hamilton's plan would have let the Congress decide the length of its own term, although not more than three years. 3 FARRAND 620.

[116] Madison, Federal Convention (June 12 and 21, 1787), *in* 1 FARRAND 214, 361. On the Senate six-year terms see debate on June 26, 1787, *in* 1 FARRAND 421–426 (Convention rejects nine-year term in favor of six-year term for Senators).

times, places, and manner of holding elections, but then allows the Congress to take control and make or alter the state regulations. The power given to Congress to overrule the state decisions, once again, reflects a distrust of the states, and not of the people. The role of the general government was necessary, Madison told the Convention, because the state legislatures would sometimes choose local prejudice over the common interest.[117] The unfortunate aspect of deciding who will administer elections is that someone, on earth, has to make the administrative decisions. Whoever administers an election, there is a justifiable concern that personal convenience or favoritism will outweigh fairness. Still, the elected representatives of the people, that is the Congressmen, are a plausible choice to be the ultimate authority to decide the time, place, and manner of elections, among the possible candidates.

C. ANTI-FEDERALIST PHILOSOPHY: WAR AND TAX

Cecelia Kenyon has argued that the Montesquieuian philosophy that a democracy was possible only in a small republic was at the core of Anti-Federalist opposition to the Constitution.[118] From Kenyon's perspective, the major intellectual battle of the ratification debate was Madison's "proof" of the superiority of an extended republic, ultimately published as *Federalist* Number 10, and the Anti-Federalist "proof" of the superiority of the small republic by the authority of Montesquieu.[119] In the Montesquieu–*Federalist* 10 debate, each side makes arguments allied with its interests and germane to what it is trying to achieve. Montesquieu's proof supports state power and Madison's proof supports national power. Still the dispute, for all of its intellectual niceness, is only a skirmish in importance and not a major or telling battle. Madison seems only to have convinced Hamilton of the merits of *Federalist* 10, and beyond that neither Federalists nor Anti-Federalists were persuaded.[120] Montesquieu was mentioned by Anti-Federalists, but not always.[121] Without denying the intellectual niceness of the Montesquieu–*Federalist* 10 debate, power, taxes, and war seem to be the more concrete programs with considerable more power to persuade.

---

[117] Madison, Federal Convention (Aug. 9, 1787), *in* 2 FARRAND 240. Pinckney and Rutledge argued that the "[s]tates could & must be relied on in such cases," but their views "did not prevail." *Id.*

[118] Cecelia M. Kenyon, *Men of Little Faith: The Anti-Federalists on the Nature of Representative Government*, 12 WM. & MARY Q. 3 (1955).

[119] *See* Chapter 3, pp. 64–67.

[120] *See* Chapter 3, pp. 69–71.

[121] *See* Chapter 3, p. 65–66.

The most important fight in the ratification debate, according to contemporaneous witnesses, was over whether the federal government would have the power to impose direct or internal taxes in time of war. The purpose of the Constitution, from the proponents' point of view, was to restore the federal credit in preparation for the inevitable next war.[122] "[O]ur situation invites our enemies to make war," Oliver Ellsworth argued to Connecticut, and if war breaks out, "how are we to defend ourselves? Has government the means to enlist a man or buy an ox?"[123] The Federalists said that some power had to exist "capable of collecting and directing the national strength against foreign force, Indian deprecations [and] domestic insurrection."[124] The proponents wanted the Constitution so as to create a new central government able to restore the federal credit so as to be able to defend the nation.[125]

The Anti-Federalists opposed the strengthening of the federal level into a full government; they opposed tax, especially federal dry land or internal taxes; and they thought that the dangers of war were wildly inflated. The Anti-Federalists said, first, that the proponents' claims of war threats were overblown and that the difficulty did not in fact justify the cure. "What is the nature of our situation that imposes this disagreeable necessity upon us?" asked a Citizen in New York: "From abroad, we have nothing to fear – the interesting affair of the European powers will engage their attention beyond the atlantic – at home we are in a state of perfect tranquility."[126] "The truth is," said Anti-Federalist Brutus, "no such necessity exists."[127] The states could give the Continental government reasonable means for the common defense when the time came, Brutus said, according to the states' own more accurate estimates of the need. There was no need to give the Continental government unlimited revenue beforehand.[128] "We have no powerful nation in our neighborhood," he argued. "Some of the European nations, it is true, have provinces bordering upon us, . . . [but] if any of them should attack us, they will have to transport their armies across the atlantic, at immense expence, while we should defend ourselves in our own country."[129] "As to the danger

[122] See Chapter 1, pp. 18–19, for further illustrations of Federalists' argument on borrowing for war.
[123] Oliver Ellsworth, Connecticut Convention (Jan. 4, 1788), in 2 ELLIOT 189.
[124] Thomas McKean, Pennsylvania Convention (Nov. 28, 1787), in 2 DHRC 415.
[125] See, EDLING at 207–208, 220, 228–29 (arguing that the purpose of the Constitution was to create a military-fiscal state capable of defense).
[126] A Citizen, Reply to Medium, NEW YORK JOURNAL (Nov. 24, 1787) reprinted in 6 STORING 47.
[127] Brutus VII, NEW YORK JOURNAL (Jan. 3, 1788), reprinted in 15 DHRC 238.
[128] Id.
[129] Id.

arising from borders," Patrick Henry argued, "it is mutual and reciprocal. If it be dangerous for Virginia, it is equally so for them."[130] The Southern Anti-Federalists also opposed a navy, even to protect Amercian shipping: "The riches of America are not sufficient to bear the enormous expense [of] a Navy," said Anti-Federalist William Grayson.[131]

"The savage Indians [would] destroy us," Patrick Henry conceded, "but we have nothing to fear from them [because] our back settlers are considerably stronger than they are."[132] The aboriginal natives were unequal to a contest with this whole continent, Brutus argued. They were "rather to be dreaded for the depredations they make on our frontiers, than for any impression . . . on the body of the country."[133]

The Anti-Federalists saw even less threat from the outstanding Revolutionary War debts. "It is little usual for nations to send armies to collect debts," Patrick Henry reassured Virginia. "The House of Bourbon, that great friend of America, will never attack her for the unwilling delay of payment."[134] "We are in the next place frightened by dangers from Holland," Henry told Virginia sarcastically. "We must change our Government to escape the wrath of that Republic."[135]

The Anti-Federalists were especially sensitive to their constituents' hatred of tax. Anti-Federalist William Grayson wrote as the Convention was getting started that raising tax to pay requisitions was politically impossible:

> In Connecticut they have rejected the requisition for the present year decidedly, & no Man there would be elected to the office of a constable if he was to declare that he meant to pay a copper towards the domestic debt: . . . N Hampshire has not paid a shilling, since peace, & does not ever mean to pay one to all eternity: – if it was attempted to tax the people for the domestic debt 500 Shays would arise in a fortnight.[136]

Anti-Federalist "Cincinnatus" argued that the new government could not possibly raise the sum to pay the debts because the sum it would need to raise

[130] Patrick Henry, Virginia Convention (June 9, 1788), *in* 9 DHRC 1054.
[131] William Grayson, Virginia Convention (June 16, 1788), *in* 3 ELLIOT 428; *but see* Philadelphiensis VII (Anti-Federalist), PHILADELPHIA INDEPENDENT GAZETTEER (Jan. 10 1788), *reprinted in* 15 DHRC 338 ("if we mean to be a commercial people, we must endeavor to have a navy").
[132] Patrick Henry, Virginia Convention (June 9, 1788), *in* 9 DHRC 1054.
[133] Brutus VII, NEW YORK JOURNAL (Jan. 3, 1788), *reprinted in* 15 DHRC 234, 238.
[134] Patrick Henry, Virginia Convention (June 9, 1788), *in* 9 DHRC 1052.
[135] *Id.*
[136] William Grayson to James Monroe (May 29, 1787), *in* 3 FARRAND 30. "500 Shays" is a reference to Shays's Rebellion. *See* Chapter 9, pp. 213–22.

was more than twice the sum in specie raised in all the states.[137] Strengthening the Congress could not overcome the people's hatred of tax. "Will the vesting greater power in the federal council conquer the aversion which the people too generally seem to have to a strict government? Will it reconcile them to a more punctual payment of taxes?"[138] Anti-Federalist Melancton Smith of New York opposed the Constitution because paying the national debt would increase taxes. He revealed with shock that the Constitution would raise taxes:

> If then the capital embarrassment in our present government arises from the want of money, and this constitution effectually authorizes the raising of it, how are the taxes to be lessened by it? Certainly money can not be raised by taxes of some kind or other; it must be got either by additional imposition on trade, by excise or by direct taxes, or what is more probably, by all together. In either way, it amounts to the same thing, and the position is clear, that as the necessities of the nation require more money than is now raised, the taxes will be enhanced. This you ought to know, and prepare yourselves to submit to.[139]

Although wicked Rhode Island had vetoed only the federal impost in 1781, that should not be interpreted as a love of any other taxes. The impost, according to Rhode Island's representative, was

> ... but an entering wedge, others will follow – a land tax, a poll tax & an Excise. Is it not best to oppose the first in such a manner as to discourage application for the others? ... To draw a Revenue for their benefit out of our State and to collect it by their officers, [particularly when these revenues would injure] the morals of the community at large ... by nourishing in idleness and Luxury a numerous train of Collectors, Comptrollers, Searchers, tide-waiters, Clerks, etc, etc.[140]

---

[137] Cincinnatus V, *To James Wilson, Esquire*, NY J. (Nov. 29, 1787), *reprinted in* 14 DHRC 310 (saying that "with magnificent promises you have bought golden opinions of all sorts of people, and with gold you must answer them").

[138] Charles Thomson to John Dickerson (July 19, 1785), *quoted in* RAKOVE, BEGINNINGS at 367.

[139] Melancton Smith, *Address to the People of New York* (Apr 1787), *in* PAMPHLETS 87, 108.

[140] George Howell to Gov. Wm. Greene (July 30, 1782), *quoted in id.*, at 315. *See also* Arthur Lee (Congressional Delegate from Virginia), Continental Congress (Feb 13, 1783), Madison Notes of the Continental Congress, *in* 25 JCC 910 (saying it was an established truth that the purse ought not to be put into the same hands with the sword). The Articles of Confederation gave the Congress both the power to conduct the war and to raise mandatory requisitions, so that Lee is asking for a change in the Articles to treat the states like the British Parliament as having the power to reject requests for revenue. The states behaved as if they had the power to reject, but that was not the legal rule.

Rhode Island ratified the Constitution very late, in 1790, and only in reaction to the very real threat of an impost or embargo on goods coming from Rhode Island to any of the states of the Union.[141]

The Anti-Federalists opposed federal tax. "[Tax] is the most important of any power that can be granted," said Anti-Federalist John Smilie in Pennsylvania. Taxation for the common defense and general welfare, he said, meant that the federal government would have "unlimited power to drain the wealth of the people by every channel of taxation," leaving the states to supply their needs "from only the scanty gleanings of the harvest."[142] "Tax connects with . . . almost all other powers," said "Brutus," "and [tax] at least will in process of time draw all other after it."[143] Governments find a way to spend whatever revenue they can get, Anti-Federalist Melancton Smith told New York: "They will not be restrained from direct taxes by the consideration that necessity does not require them."[144] "We ought to be fully convinced of an absolute necessity existing before we entrust the whole power of taxation to the hands of Congress;" An Old Whig argued, "and the moment we do so, we ought by consent to annihilate the individual states; for the powers of the individual states will be as effectually swallowed as a drop of water in the ocean; and the next consequence will be a speedy dissolution of our republican form of government."[145] Section 8 of the Constitution gave the new Congress the power to tax "to provide for the common Defence and general Welfare" and the Anti-Federalists were sure that the Congress would construe every purpose to be for the general welfare and so seize on every object for revenue.[146]

The Anti-Federalists especially wanted to prevent Congress from laying "direct" or dry land tax. Denying Congress the power to lay direct tax seemed "to be the point most dear to the opposition,"[147] the "most popular topic

---

[141] *See* John Page (Va. Federalist), Speech to the House of Representatives (May 26, 1790), *in* 2 ANNALS OF CONGRESS 1673 (opposing Senate passed bill that would embargo all goods coming from Rhode Island); Bruce Ackerman & Neal Kumar Katyal, *Our Unconventional Founding*, 62 U. CHI. L. REV. 475, 538 (1995) (attributing Rhode Island's ratification heavily to Senate-passed bill that would prohibit Rhode Island ships in American harbors and American ships in Rhode Island harbors); John P. Kaminski, *Rhode Island: Protecting State Interests, in* RATIFYING THE CONSTITUTION at 385 (Michael Allen Gillespie & Michael Lienesch, eds. 1989) (same).

[142] John Smilie, Pennsylvania Convention (Nov. 28, 1787), *in* 2 DHRC 408.

[143] BRUTUS I, NEW YORK JOURNAL (Oct. 18, 1787), *reprinted in* 13 DHRC 415.

[144] Melancton Smith, New York Convention (June 27, 1787), *in* 2 ELLIOT 333.

[145] An Old Whig, PHILADELPHIA INDEPENDENT GAZETTEER (Nov. 24, 1787), *reprinted in* 14 DHRC 220.

[146] "Centinel [Samuel Bryan] I," INDEPENDENT GAZETTEER (PHILADELPHIA) (Oct. 5, 1787), *reprinted in* 1 DEBATE 57.

[147] Tench Coxe to Madison (July 23, 1788), *in* 11 JM 194.

among the adversaries,"[148] and "the chief object of [Anti-Federalist] per-suit."[149] Washington told Jefferson he would embrace any tolerable com-promise and would not much object to any of the suggested amendments except for the amendment that goes to the prevention of direct taxation and that one, he presumed, would be the amendment most strenuously insisted on.[150]

"Direct tax" in the debates refers usually to every tax except for the impost. The impost was an "external tax" and direct tax was the opposite, that is, "internal tax"[151] or "dry tax."[152] The Anti-Federalists usually acquiesced in giving Congress the 5 percent impost or custom duties, as had been proposed in 1781 and 1783,[153] although that acquiescence was not universal.[154] No

---

[148] Madison to Randolph (Dec. 2, 1787), *in* 12 DHRC at 332.

[149] Hardin Burnley to Madison (Dec. 5, 1789), *in* 12 JM 460.

[150] Washington to Jefferson (Aug. 31, 1788), 30 WRITINGS OF GW 82–83.

[151] For the uses of "direct tax" as a synonym for "internal tax," see Calvin Johnson, *Apportion-ment of Direct Taxes: The Foul-up in the Core of the Constitution*, 7 WM. & MARY BILL OF RTS. J. 1, 48–51 (1998).

[152] Amos Singletary, Massachusetts Convention (Jan. 25, 1788), *in* 2 ELLIOT 102 ("They tell us Congress won't lay dry taxes upon us, but collect all the money they want by impost."); Eliphalet Dyer to Jonathan Trumbull, Sr (April 3, 1783) *in* 20 LDCC 139 (saying that "[d]rye, forced & direct taxes for monies on the body of the people we fear will not answer [for the payment of interest to the several states], but [d]utys & Impost on Trade . . . must be paid in the first Instance by those through whose hands our moneys most frequently Circulate Viz the Merchants, and afterword by those only who Choose it, & without the disagreeable force of a Collector"). Sometimes, but not always, taxes on whiskey or luxuries, imposed to encourage good morals, were excluded from the definition of direct tax. Johnson, *supra* note 151, at 57–62.

[153] *See, e.g.*, Federal Farmer, *Letters to the Republican III* (Oct. 10, 1787), *reprinted in* 14 DHRC 35–36 (saying that imposts laid on imported goods are usually collected in a few seaport towns by a few officers and that the threat of smuggling limits how high they can go); Cato Uticensis, *To the Freemen of Virginia*, VIRGINIA INDEPENDENT CHRONICLE (Oct. 17, 1787), *reprinted in* 8 DHRC 73 (conceding imposts and allowing requisitions if imposts are not sufficient); An Old Whig, *Letter VI*, PHILADELPHIA INDEPENDENT GAZETTER (Nov. 24, 1787), *reprinted in* 14 DHRC 218 (arguing that the current misfortunes could be solved by allowing Congress to lay the impost, but that the Convention erroneously gave Congress revenue from any source in the continent); Brutus VII, NEW YORK JOURNAL (Jan. 3, 1788), *reprinted in* 15 DHRC 239 (saying that impost is the "one source of revenue, which it is agreed, the general government ought to have the sole controul of").

[154] John Smilie, Pennsylvania Convention (Nov. 28, 1788), *in* 2 DHRC 408–09 (arguing that if the federal government had unlimited power to drain the wealth of the people, *whether by imposts or by direct levies*, then the system was too formidable for states to break); "Agrippa," (James Winthrop) XII, MASSACHUSETTS GAZETTE (BOSTON) (Jan. 1, 15, 18, 1788), *reprinted in* 1 DEBATE 768 (arguing that imposts will oppress our foreign trade "for the benefit of other states"); James Wadsworth, Connecticut Convention (Jan. 7, 1788), *in* 15 DHRC 274 (arguing that impost is not a proper mode of taxation).

An impost was administrable on the federal level because most of it could be collected with just a few officers in the deep water harbors. State imposts, however, were neither fair

Anti-Federalist, however, could concede that Congress might have the power to lay a direct, internal, or dry tax.

Congress, the Anti-Federalists feared, would use the power to lay direct taxes to inconceivable excess, "swallowing up every object of taxation and consequently plundering the several states of every means [of support]."[155] "The power of direct taxation," Anti-Federalists argued, "is of that nature, that however oppressive, the people will have but this alternative, either to pay the tax, or let their property be taken, for all resistance will be in vain."[156] "[Direct taxes] take hold of every species of property," Brutus argued, "and come home to every man's house and packet. . . . [Direct taxes] are often so oppressive, as to grind the face of the poor, and render the lives of the common people a burden to them."[157]

Mason told the Virginia Ratification Convention,

> The assumption of this power of laying direct taxes does of itself, entirely change the confederation of the States into one consolidated Government. This power being at discretion, unconfined, and without any kind of control, must carry everything before it. The very idea of converting what was formerly a confederation, to a consolidated Government, is totally subversive of every principle which has hitherto governed us. This power is calculated to annihilate totally the State Governments.[158]

The future president, Anti-Federalist James Monroe, declared that to render the Congress "safe and proper, I would take from it one power only – I mean that of direct taxation."[159]

The Anti-Federalists offered an amendment, when they got organized a bit, that would have denied Congress the power to lay direct taxes, except within a state that was in default of paying its quota of a requisition[160] Absent

nor administrable because only some states had a deep water harbor and because porous borders between the states made smuggling too easy to maintain a viable state level tax. *See Federalist* No. 12, at 76 (Hamilton) (Nov. 27, 1787).
155 Robert Whitehill, Pennsylvania Convention (Nov. 28, 1787), *in* 2 DHRC 396.
156 The Address and Reasons of Dissent of the Minority of the Convention of the State of Pennsylvania (Dec. 18, 1787), *in* 15 DHRC 30–31.
157 Brutus V, NEW YORK JOURNAL (Dec. 13, 1787), *reprinted in* 14 DHRC 427.
158 Mason, Virginia Convention (June 4, 1788), *in* 9 DHRC 936.
159 James Monroe, Virginia Convention (June 10, 1788), *in* 9 DHRC 1109.
160 The New York Convention, for instance, adopted instructions to its Congressmen, as it ratified the Constitution, to pursue an amendment that would allow Congress to collect direct taxes only if import duties and excises were insufficient, and even then only if the state neglected or refused to pay its quota under a Congressional requisition. Upon delinquency of a state, Congress could itself collect that state's quota, including an added 6% annual interest, with its own agents and on the taxable objects that Congress set. 1 ELLIOT 329. The

default, the state government would have been able to choose the objects of tax and state officers would collect the tax. A majority of seven states endorsed the Anti-Federalist direct tax restrictions as they ratified the Constitution and instructed their Congressmen to seek the amendment.[161] The anti-direct tax amendment was explicitly defeated in only two early states – ordinarily not enough to block an amendment.[162] Quite plausibly, under another posture or procedure, eleven states would have endorsed the amendment, more than the nine states needed to effect the amendment. In the Virginia Ratification Convention, the Anti-Federalists offered a long list of proposed amendments to the Constitution. The Federalists challenged only the anti-direct tax amendment, but they lost on the challenge. The Federalists achieved a majority in Virginia for ratification of the document as a whole, but they were unable to garner a majority in favor of maintaining the federal direct tax in states that had not defaulted in paying requisitions.[163]

The Federalists, on their side, argued that Congress would need the direct tax in time of war. James Wilson argued that the impost would probably be sufficient for federal needs in ordinary times, but that Congress needed the power of direct tax within reach in case of emergency.[164] In time of war, an enemy with a powerful navy could cut off revenue from the impost by an effective blockade: "Take direct taxation from the list of Federal authorities," said Madison, and Virginia will be open to "surprize and devestation whenever an enemy powerful at Sea chuses to invade her."[165]

Virginia version of the amendment varied slightly: It required Congress to notify the state governor when it proposed a direct tax, and the amendment would suspend the collection of federal tax in the state if the state then passed legislation for collection of the state's quota of tax by state-chosen means. *See* Resolution in the Virginia Convention (June 27, 1788), *in* 10 DHRC 1553–54.

[161] In chronological order, the following states endorsed the Anti-Federalist amendment restricting federal direct tax: (1) Massachusetts (Feb. 7, 1788), *in* 1 ELLIOT 322, 323; (2) South Carolina (May 23, 1788), *in* 1 ELLIOT 325; (3) New Hampshire (June 21, 1788), *in* 1 ELLIOT 325, 326; (4) Virginia (June 27, 1788), *in* 10 DHRC 1556; (5) New York (July 26, 1788), *in* 1 ELLIOT 327, 329; (6) North Carolina (Aug. 1, 1788), *in* 4 ELLIOT 245; and (7) Rhode Island (May 29, 1790), *in* 1 ELLIOT 336.

Four more states ratified too quickly for the Anti-Federalists to get organized enough to offer their direct tax amendment into the debate: (1) Delaware (Dec. 7, 1787), *in* 3 DHRC 110; (2) New Jersey (Dec. 18, 1787), *in* 3 DHRC 184; (3) Georgia (Jan. 2, 1788), *in* 3 DHRC 275–276; and (4) Connecticut (Jan. 9, 1788), *in* 3 DHRC 560–562.

[162] Pennsylvania (Dec. 18, 1787), *in* 2 DHRC 618; Maryland (April 28, 1788), *in* 2 ELLIOT 552, 553.

[163] Virginia Convention (June 27, 1788), *in* 3 ELLIOT 661.

[164] Wilson, State House Yard, Philadelphia (Oct. 6, 1787), *in* 2 DHRC 171.

[165] Madison to George Thomas (Jan. 29, 1789), *in* 2 DHFFE at 344. *Accord*, Elisha Porter, *in* DEBATES IN MASSACHUSETTS 319 (saying that "to grant only an impost is to invite our

Even in peacetime, Hamilton argued, giving Congress the import duties, but not internal or direct taxes, would leave to the Union only one-third of the resources of the community, but the responsibility to pay for 90 to 95 percent of its expenses.[166] "Money," Hamilton argued, is "the vital principle of the body politic; as that which sustains its life and motion, and enables it to perform its most essential functions. A complete power therefore to procure a regular and adequate supply of [tax revenue], as far as the resources the community will permit, may be regarded as an indispensable ingredient in every constitution."[167] Hamilton also argued that if a state was going to be in default of its requisition, holding up the federal power would just allow the state to organize its armed opposition.[168] Why, in any event, the Federalists asked, would any man "choose a lame horse, lest a sound one should run away with him?"[169]

If the federal level had to rely on the impost alone, moreover, Madison argued, the South would be taxed disproportionately.

> The Southern States, from having fewer manufacturers will import and consume more. They will pay more of the imposts. The more commerce is burdened, the more the disproportion will be against them. If direct taxation be mixed with other taxes, it will be in the power of the General Government to lessen that inequality.[170]

enemies to attack us, for shuting our ports is to destroy us"); Jefferson to Washington (Nov. 4, 1787), *in* 14 PTJ 328 (saying that "[c]alculation has convinced me that circumstances may arise and probably will arise, wherein all the resources of taxation will be necessary for the safety of the state").

[166] *Federalist* No.34, at 214 (Hamilton) (Jan. 5, 1788). *See also* A CITIZEN OF PHILADEL-PHIA, THE WEAKNESSES OF BRUTUS EXPOSED (Nov. 8, 1787), *reprinted in* 14 DHRC 67 (arguing that union cannot be successful without power of raising money); Wilson, Speech in the State House Yard, Philadelphia (Oct. 6, 1787), *in* 2 DHRC 171 (arguing that delegation of the power of direct tax to the federal government was necessary given the broad federal duties to provide for national safety, dignity, and discharge of debts); Thomas McKean, Pennsylvania Convention (Dec. 10, 1787), *in* 2 DHRC 544 (arguing that Congress' power of direct tax was absolutely necessary for the salvation of the United States).

[167] *Federalist* No. 30, at 188 (Hamilton) (Dec. 28, 1787).

[168] *Id.*, at 367–368 ("After having passed through the empty ceremony of a requisition, the general government can enforce all its demands, without limitation or resistance . . . It is infinitely more eligible to lay a tax originally").

[169] A Citizen of Philadelphia, Remarks on the Address of Sixteen Members (Oct. 18, 1787), *reprinted in* 13 DHRC 301. *See also* Randolph, Virginia Convention (June 7, 1788), *in* 3 ELLIOT 122 (arguing that the power of imposing direct taxes "has been proved to be essential to the very existence of the Union").

[170] Madison, Virginia Convention (June 11, 1788), *in* 3 ELLIOT 252–253.

Hamilton made the same argument to the New York Ratification Convention, except that in Hamilton's argument, it would be New York who would be hurt by the impost by reason of New York's deficit in manufacture.[171]

In form the debate over the direct tax amendment was not about the level of federal tax, but only the objects of tax. Patrick Henry argued that the states would be better acquainted with the condition of the people so as to best accommodate tax to the convenience of the people. "The oppression arising from taxation is not from the amount, but from the mode."[172] Requisitions, he said, "secure to the States the benefit of correcting oppressive errors."[173] Still, the intensity of the debate does seem to come from Anti-Federalists hopes to deny federal internal taxes in total. Literally, the Anti-Federalist amendment would allow the states to pay just their quotas of a requisition, with taxes and tax officers of their own choosing, provided they paid the requisition when Congress asked. If a state were in default of paying its quota, then the federal system and federal officers could collect it, even under the Anti-Federalist amendment. In the South, it was plausible that the Anti-Federalists feared that the federal majority would tax slavery, when their local government would not.[174] Patronage was a plausible issue.[175] Still, given the state of the defaults, why did the Anti-Federalists think their amendment would make any difference? There was no apparent movement in any state to raise state taxes to pay the requisitions for the federal debts. If the states had not paid requisitions in the past, why would they so willingly find money to pay taxes in the future? The intensity of the debate seems to imply that the Anti-Federalists thought that their restrictive amendment could prevent the federal level from imposing internal tax, and not just delaying the tax, and would restrict the allowance given to the federal level to what it could get from the impost and sale of western land.[176] Even better,

---

[171] Hamilton, New York Convention (June 28, 1788), *in* 2 ELLIOT 369.

[172] Patrick Henry, Virginia Convention (June 12, 1788), *in* 3 ELLIOT 320.

[173] Patrick Henry, Virginia Convention (June 7, 1788) *in* 3 ELLIOT 148.

[174] *See, e.g.*, Patrick Henry, Virginia Convention (June 17, 1788), *in* 10 DHRC 1341–1342 (arguing that Congress might lay such heavy taxes on slaves, amounting to emancipation, such "that this property would be lost to this country"). *See also*, Patrick Henry, Virginia Convention (June 24, 1788), *in* 10 DHRC 1504 (arguing that "they can emancipate our slaves").

[175] *See, e.g.*, Madison, Notes on Debates in the Congress (Jan. 28, 1783), *in* 6 JM 143 (where Madison says that Hamilton let the cat out of the bag when he said that revenue officers deriving their office and pay from Congress would consequently be interested in supporting Congress).

[176] *See, e.g.*, Henry Lee to Madison (Nov. 25, 1789), *in* 12 JM 466–467, 454–455 (telling Madison that the impost and sale of western land would need to be made sufficient for federal needs, "for indeed if [they are] not I am at a loss to see what you will or can do").

many Anti-Federalists undoubtedly thought they could hold off federal tax entirely, maintaining the existing Garden of Eden forever, an allowance of $663 to cover the sum of federal needs. The proponents of the Constitution wanted to be able to call forth a bigger national-level government than that.

At least viewed retroactively, the taxes under consideration were modest, even trivial. The federal government would get the 5 percent impost, vetoed in 1781 and 1783, and it would adopt a whiskey tax. Alexander's Hamilton's 1790 tax package would total a day and half of laborer's wages per capita.[177] Perhaps the anti-tax rhetoric was overblown. The modest taxes were coming in, however, on a base line that was essentially zero. Almost no tax was collected from the American frontier before the Constitution.[178] The state whiskey taxes of the 1780s were a virtual dead letter in the West all along.[179] Not much would be collected from the frontier after the Constitution either. "[M]ost New Hampshireites had already achieved the tax-less, shiftless Utopia which most Americans cherished as a secret dream," Forrest McDonald tells us, "for which 'republicanism' and 'inalienable rights' were merely euphemisms"[180] Rhode Island's government expenses before the war averaged less than $5000 a year.[181] The modest taxes the new government would ultimately collect were on top of a base line of essentially zero tax.

D. WHY RATIFY?

Both New York and Virginia started with an Anti-Federalist majority, but both states decided by a close vote to ratify. The critical factor in both states was that the ninth ratification by New Hampshire meant that the new government would be formed, with or without the states that had not yet ratified. Once it was clear that they could not strike a better deal and that the choice

---

[177] *See* discussion, Chapter 10, pp. 225. *Compare* A LUNARIAN, NEW YORK DAILY ADVERTISER (Dec. 20, 1787), *reprinted in* 14 DHRC 310 n.7 (estimating that the new government would need $6 million per year, which translated into the sum of two dollars per year per capita).

[178] *See, e.g.*,, BRUNHOUSE, *supra* note 69, at 162 (1942) (saying that a great majority of the taxes had been collected from Federalist strongholds and the frontier towns had been very delinquent).

[179] ELKINS & McKITRICK at 469.

[180] FOREST McDONALD, E PLURIBUS UNUM, THE FORMATION OF THE AMERICAN REPUBLIC 1776–1790, at 199 (1965).

[181] IRVIN H. POLISHOOK, RHODE ISLAND AND THE UNION, 1774–1795, at 108 (1969).

was indeed between this Constitution or secession – this or nothing – then the fence-sitters were not willing to secede from the Union.[182]

In New York, the arguments that made the difference were appeals to the cause of the Union. Jay's Address to New York under the pseudonym, Citizen of New York, was described at the time as having an "astonishing influence in converting Antifederalists to a knowledge and belief that the New Constitution was their only political Salvation."[183] Jay's appeal was to the cause of the Revolutionary War: We are all Americans who have fought together a long and bloody war for the sacred cause of the Republican form of government.[184] Alexander Hamilton's appeal to the New York Convention for the Constitution and the Union called upon the ghosts of the patriots and living heroes of the Revolution to prevent fraternal strife and it brought tears to the eyes of many, the Anti-Federalist *New York Journal* reported.[185] Melancton Smith carried the deciding group of Anti-Federalists over to ratification in New York, it is said, because he saw the desperation of the situation and resolved to bring New York into the Union.[186]

In Virginia, it was Edmund Randolph, a fence-sitter who came to favor the Constitution, who expresses what made the difference. Randolph refused to sign the Constitution in September 1787 on the ground that the general power given to the federal government was too broad and too vague,[187] but he came around to support the Constitution nonetheless to preserve the Union. Randolph said he would rather have his arm lopped off than have the

---

[182] Bruce Ackerman & Neal Kumar Katyal, *Our Unconventional Founding*, 62 U. CHI. L. REV. 475, 533–536 (1995) is an excellent statement of the argument and collection of the sources.

[183] Samuel Webb to Joseph Barrell (April 27, 1788) quoted in *Editorial note*, 17 DHRC 103 and see other sources in *Editorial Note, id* at 101–104. The John Jay Address seems to have been far more important than the *Federalist* in getting New York to ratify. John Kaminski, *New York: The Reluctant Pillar, in* THE RELUCTANT PILLAR 72.

[184] *Federalist* No. 2, at 9 (John Jay) (Oct. 31, 1787) (saying that Americans "fighting side by side throughout a long and bloody war, have nobly established their general Liberty and Independence"); A CITIZEN OF NEW YORK (JOHN JAY), ADDRESS TO THE PEOPLE OF THE STATE OF NEW YORK (April 15, 1788), *in* 3 ELLIOT'S DEBATES 502 (saying that the people of America are a band of brothers who must avoid disorder and confusion to convince others that people can govern themselves).

[185] Robin Brooks, *Alexander Hamilton, Melancton Smith, and the Ratification of the Constitution in New York*, 24 WILLIAM & MARY Q. 339, 351 (3rd series, 1967).

[186] *Id.* at 357.

[187] Madison to Jefferson (Oct. 24, 1787), *in* 10 JM 215 (describing Randolph as opposing the Constitution because of the "latitude of the general powers"); Randolph, Reasons for Not Signing the Constitution (Dec. 27, 1787) in 8 DHRC 273 (arguing that the "cover of general words" in the Constitution allowed the Congress to swallow up the states).

Union be dissolved and he would support the Constitution when the single question was "union or no union."[188] When the choice was this Constitution or disunion, the fence-sitters chose the Constitution.

[188] *See, e.g.*, Randolph, Speeches to the Virginia Ratification Convention (June 4, 1788), *in* ELLIOT'S DEBATES 23, 26 (saying that he would rather have his arm lopped off than have the union be dissolved); June 6, 1788, *in* 3 ELLIOT'S DEBATES 65–71; June 9, 1788, *in* 3 ELLIOT 188–194 (speaking for the preservation of the union); June 10, 1788, *in* 3 ELLIOT 194–207 (speaking for the preservation of the union); June 25, 1788, *in* 3 ELLIOT 652 (supporting the Constitution when the single question is "union or no union").

CHAPTER SEVEN

False Issues: Bill of Rights, Democracy, and Slavery

The critical issues of the ratification debate were whether power would be taken from the existing state governments and transferred to the new complete national government and whether the national government would be given the power over internal taxes for national defense. In context, other issues seem less critical. The ratification debate was not seriously about individual rights, nor about democracy or slavery. Individual rights, democracy, and slavery are intensely important issues, but they are not seriously implicated in the disagreements between Federalists and Anti-Federalists.

A. THE BILL OF RIGHTS

The Anti-Federalists tried to beat the creation of the new national government by finding serious abuses implied by almost every clause of the proposed text. Give Congress the power to raise armies, the Anti-Federalists argued, and it will "keep armies continually on foot," and "billet them on the people at pleasure."[1] Give the federal government the power to make treaties and they would make a treaty to establish the Roman Catholic Church as the religion in the United States[2] and make the Pope of Rome our President.[3] Give the Congress the power to establish a Federal City, Anti-Federalists argued, and the federal government would make it a "sanctuary of the blackest crimes."[4] Give the federal government power over crimes and they "are nowhere restrained from inventing the most cruel and unheard-of

---

[1] Patrick Henry, Virginia Convention (June 16, 1788), *in* 3 ELLIOT 410.
[2] Henry Abbot, North Carolina Convention (July 30, 1788), *in* 4 ELLIOT 191–192 (reporting fears by "some people").
[3] James Iredell, North Carolina Convention (July 30, 1788), *in* 4 ELLIOT 195 (reporting pamphlet he had just read).
[4] Mason, Virginia Convention (June 16, 1788), *in* 3 ELLIOT 331.

punishments.... [R]acks and gibbets may be amongst the most mild instruments of their discipline."[5] Give the Congress power over direct tax, Anti-Federalists argued, and Congress would "cut your throats, ravage and destroy your plantations, drive away cattle and horses, abuse your wives, kill your infants, ravish your daughters and live in free quarters" to enforce the tax.[6] Anti-Federalist rhetoric had a "logic of escalation" to it. Any government power was presumed to be part of a larger conspiracy to abuse and destroy.[7]

Although proposals for a bill of rights had been circulating early among the Anti-Federalists, Madison interpreted them initially as mere excuses, aimed only at defeating the new government as a whole. Madison thought that the proposed amendments in Massachusetts were offered insincerely: "their objections being levelled against the every essence of the proposed Government."[8] For Madison, Patrick Henry was arch-abuser of individual rights, and his using rights against the Constitution was just hypocrisy. Henry had wanted to tax non-Anglicans to support a public religion and Patrick Henry had abused the just rights of out-of-state creditors. Madison had been the warm supporter of minority religious and creditor rights.[9] Under Madison's theory of *Federalist* Number 10, "[e]xtend the sphere [of the republican form of government] and you take in a greater variety of parties and interests; you make it less probable that a majority of the whole will have a common motive to invade the rights of other citizens."[10] The purpose of the extended republic, under Madison's fundamental theory, was to give better protection to the rights of individuals with a strong government on the general level.[11]

Protection of rights of individuals was also a Federalist idea first. The right to trial by jury, for instance, is said to be "one of our most vital barriers to governmental arbitrariness, ... embedded in our Constitution to secure

---

[5] Abraham Holmes, Massachusetts Convention (Jan. 30, 1788), *in* 2 ELLIOT 111.

[6] "A Farmer and a Planter," MARYLAND JOURNAL (April 1, 1788), *reprinted in* 5 STORING 74, 76. Federalist Robert Livingston satirized the Anti-Federalists as saying that federal direct taxation "will shut out the light of heaven, and will pick your pockets." (New York Convention (July 1, 1788), *in* 2 ELLIOT 363), but in this case, the satire does not go as far as the original.

[7] EDLING 67–68.

[8] Madison to Randolph (April 10, 1788), *in* 11 JM 18–19.

[9] Madison, Virginia Convention (June 12, 1787), *in* 3 ELLIOT 330–331 (saying that "I have warmly supported religious freedom").

[10] *Federalist* No. 10, at 64 (Madison) (Nov. 22, 1787).

[11] *Id.* (saying that a particular state might concur in one religious project, but that in the United States, there abounds such variety of sects, that no one sect will ever be able to outnumber or depress the rest). Henry's only response at the time was that although Madison might be perfectly satisfied by the powers of reason, still the "sacred right ought not to depend on constructive logical reasoning." Patrick Henry (June 12, 1787), *in* 3 ELLIOT 317.

their inviolateness and sanctity against the passing demands of expediency or convenience."[12] In the Constitutional debate, juries were said to be the "sacred barrier against injustice,"[13] the "palladiums of liberty,"[14] and the "surest barrier against arbitrary power."[15] Madison told Virginia that trial by jury was held "sacred."[16] The right to jury was said to be "an important reason for the adoption of the Bill of Rights."[17] But jury right for criminal cases was made part of the original Constitution by the Framers in Philadelphia, inserted long before the Anti-Federalists took up opposition.[18] The Constitution prior to amendment also prohibits the federal government from imposing retroactive or "ex post facto" laws and from suspending habeas corpus orders, except when public safety requires it.[19]

Except to defeat the new government, the Anti-Federalists were not very supportive of individual rights. The Anti-Federalists tellingly chose state power over individual rights in cases in which the unamended Constitution would protect the individual rights. The Constitution as it left Philadelphia prohibited the states from passing ex post facto laws and impairing contracts. The prohibitions, Randolph said, "announce to the world, the . . . apprehension that States may injure individuals in their property, their liberty, and their lives; may oppress sister States; and may act in derogation of the general sovereignty."[20] The Anti-Federalists opposed the restrictions. George Mason argued that retroactive or ex post facto laws were a necessary power of state government because "there never was or can be a Legislature but must & will make such Laws, when Necessity & the public safety require them."[21] Patrick Henry agreed, protesting that there

---

[12] Reid v. Covert, 354 U.S. 1, 9 (1957).

[13] Impartial Examiner I, Va. INDEPENDENT CHRONICLE (Feb. 27, 1788) *reprinted in* 8 DHRC 423.

[14] Luther Martin, *Genuine Information X*, BALTIMORE MARYLAND GAZETTE, Feb. 1, 1788, *reprinted in* 16 DHRC 9.

[15] *Id.*

[16] Madison, Virginia Convention, June 20, 1788, 3 ELLIOT 537.

[17] Reid v. Covert, 354 U.S. 1, 9 n. 13 (1957).

[18] U.S. CONST., art. III, §2, cl. 3 (also giving venue protection by requiring that the trial be held in the state where the crime was committed). The Sixth Amendment to the Constitution augments the Article III right to a jury by requiring a speedy and public trial, with rights of cross examination and the assistance of counsel, which are not trivial, but are still added upon the basic right to jury for criminal trials in Article III. The Seventh Amendment gives the right to jury in civil cases, but only as the common law then allowed it.

[19] U.S. CONST., art. I, §9, cl. 3 & 2.

[20] Randolph, Virginia Convention (June 20, 1788), *in* 3 ELLIOT 421–422.

[21] Mason, Objections to the Constitution of Government formed by the Convention (Oct. 7, 1787), *in* 8 DHRC 45.

are "thousands and thousands of contracts, whereof equity forbids exact literal performance."[22] Henry protested that the prohibition on ex post facto
laws was absurd because it would mandate payment of the old Continental dollars, in "gold and silver, shilling for shilling."[23] Virginia Anti-
Federalist William Grayson said that it was unfair to have the British creditors benefit from the prohibition on impairment of contracts, because
they probably contemplated the "procrastination and delays of our courts"
when they extended the loan.[24] Creditors' rights were individual rights that
the Federalists, but not the Anti-Federalists, wanted to protect from state
action.

The Anti-Federalists also had trouble with the system of checks and balances. They did not see checks and balance between the branches as securing
the rights of individuals, but rather as so complicating government as to throw
all into confusion.[25] "The complications of interests . . . will become intricate
and perplexed, and too mysterious for you to understand and observe," said
Cato in New York.[26] Checks and balances might work for England, said
Centinel in Philadelphia, but they are too complicated for here: "The only
operative and efficient check upon the administration [here] is the sense
of the people at large."[27] Checks and balances had been a major theme of
John Adams' work, but the Anti-Federalists embraced neither Adams nor his
checks and balances.[28] "Even the celebrated Mr. Adams, who talks so much
of checks and balances," Anti-Federalist Luther Martin argued, would not
need them if the confederation mode were kept.[29]

The Anti-Federalists were not tolerant civil libertarians in any modern
sense. A major attack on the Constitution was that it was too accommodat-
ing to "Roman Catholics, Papists, and Pagans."[30] Federal Farmer, perhaps
the most articulate of the Anti-Federalist essayists, expressed his shock that
the Constitution would allow federal office holders to be "Christians, Pagans,
Mahometans, or Jews; that they are of any colour, rich or poor, convict or

---

[22] Patrick Henry, Virginia Convention (June 12, 1788), *in* 3 ELLIOT 318–319.
[23] Patrick Henry, Virginia Convention (June 16, 1788), *in* 3 ELLIOT 461.
[24] William Grayson, Virginia Convention (June 21, 1788), *in* 3 ELLIOT 566.
[25] Rawlins Lowndes, South Carolina Legislature, Jan 18, 1788, *in* 4 ELLIOT 309.
[26] Cato III, NY JOURNAL (Fall 1787), reprinted *in* 2 STORING 111.
[27] CENTINEL I (Oct. 5, 1787), reprinted *in* 2 STORING 138.
[28] *See, e.g.*, Richard B. Morris, *Class Struggle and the American Revolution*, 19 WILLIAM & MARY
Q. 3, 7 (3d Series 1962) (characterizing John Adams' checks and balances as a "regal
system").
[29] Luther Martin, Federal Convention (June 27, 1787), *in* 1 FARRAND 439 (Yates notes).
[30] Thomas Rusk, Massachusetts Convention (Feb. 4, 1788), *in* 2 ELLIOT 148.

not."[31] Anti-Federalist Amos Singleton denounced the Constitution to the Massachusetts Convention because there was no requirement that men in power have any religion and because "a Papist, or an Infidel, was as eligible" as a Christian.[32] It was the Federalist defenders of the Constitution, for instance, Reverend Daniel Shute in Massachusetts, who argued that the absence of a religious test for office was a virtue of the proposed Constitution.[33] It was Anti-Federalist Patrick Henry who said that Jews, Mahometans, Deists, and pagans professed and practiced such abominations as rendered their persuasions unworthy the sanction of legal support.[34] It was the Anti-Federalists who denounced our Constitution because it allowed office holders who were "Quakers, Mahometans, Deists, abominable wretches, Negroes, Beggars and lastly Jews."[35]

The Anti-Federalists were also seeing abuses of the people, Federalists thought, when under the Constitution, the people themselves were in control. Representation by the people, Alexander Hamilton argued, was "the only efficacious security for the rights and privileges of the people which is attainable in civil society."[36] There was no need for explicit protection of the press, John Jay told New York because "[Congressmen] are to receive that business to manage, not for themselves and as their own, but as agent and overseers for the people to whom they are constantly responsible"[37] "Is it not astonishing that the gentleman who is so strenuous an advocate for the powers of the people, should distrust the people the moment that power is given to them?" Rutledge asked North Carolina, and should find "his

---

[31] Federal Farmer, *Letter to the Republican XII*, NEW YORK JOURNAL (Jan. 12, 1788), *reprinted in* 17 DHRC 310.

[32] Amos Singletary, Massachusetts Convention (Jan. 19, 1788), *in* 2 Elliot 44.

[33] Rev. Daniel Shute, Massachusetts Convention (Jan. 31, 1788), *in* 2 ELLIOT 118.

[34] James Monroe to Beverly Randolph (Nov. 26, 1784), *quoted in* RISJORD at 206.

[35] Curtiopolis, NEW YORK DAILY ADVERTISER (Jan. 18, 1788), *reprinted in* 15 DHRC 401 (also arguing that if a Jew were elected president, the army might be "ordered to rebuild Jerusalem").

[36] *Federalist* No. 28, at 178 (Hamilton) (Dec. 26, 1787); *Federalist* No. 57, at 387 (Madison) (Feb. 19, 1788) (asking "what is to restrain the House of Representatives.?" and answering: "the genius of the whole system; the nature of just and constitutional laws, and above all, the vigilant and manly spirit which actuates the people of America, a spirit which nourishes freedom, and in return is nourished by it"); *Federalist* No. 84, at 578–9 (Hamilton) (May 28, 1788) (saying that the preamble that 'We, The People establish this Constitution to secure the blessings of liberty' is a better recognition of popular rights, than volumes of those aphorisms of state bills of rights).

[37] A CITIZEN OF NEW YORK (JOHN JAY), ADDRESS TO THE PEOPLE OF THE STATE OF NEW YORK (April 15, 1788), *in* 17 DHRC 112–113. Also saying, *id.* at 112, that Congress will have no rights but such as the people commit to them.

objections . . . in the negligence of the people themselves?"[38] "To whom do we delegate these powers?" Pendleton asked Virginia, and answered, "To our own representatives." In the federal government, Pendelton said, "every branch [preserves] the representative, responsible character."[39] "Brutus seems grieved that congress should be the judges of this general welfare of the states," Federalist Pelatiah Webster related, "If [Brutus] will be kind enough to point out any other more suitable and proper judges, I will consent to have them admitted."[40]

The Federalists, however, had no immediate plans to imprison editors without the benefit of jury, establish the Roman Catholic church, impose punishment by rack and gibbits, or quarter troops on the people and they were ultimately willing to bind themselves on those issues with amendments to the Constitution, at least once it was no longer possible for a Bill of Rights to prevent ratification. Madison told the Virginia Convention that amendments that were "not objectionable, or unsafe" might be recommended in the first Congress[41] and indeed Madison offered and saw through to adoption the first ten amendments to the Constitution, constituting the Bill of Rights.

In 1785, Madison had favored a Bill of Rights in a proposal for a state constitution for Kentucky and his advice there turned out to be remarkably prescient about the federal Constitution:

> The [Kentucky] Constitution may expresly restrain [the Legislative power] from medling with religion – from abolishing Juries from taking away the Habeus corpus – from forcing a citizen to give evidence against himself, from controuling the press, from enacting restrospective laws at least in criminal cases, from abridging the right of suffrage, from seizing private property for public use without paying its full Valu[e] from licensing importation of Slaves, from infringing the Confederation &c, &c.[42]

Of Madison's 1785 list, the Constitution, without amendment, restrained Congress from abolishing criminal juries and habeus corpus, and prohibited

---

[38] Edward Rutledge, South Carolina Legislature (Jan. 16, 1788), *in* 2 ELLIOT 274–275.

[39] Edmund Pendleton, Virginia Convention (June 12, 1788), *in* 3 ELLIOT 300–301.

[40] "A Citizen of Philadelphia" (Pelatiah Webster), PHILADELPHIA (Nov. 8, 1787), *reprinted in* 1 DEBATE 178.

[41] *Ratification without Conditional Amendments* (June 24, 1788), *in* 11 JM 172, 177. Madison had previously identified Henry's aim as to offer amendments that would "strike at the essence of the system." Madison to Jefferson (Dec. 9, 1787), *in* 10 JM 312.

[42] Madison to Caleb Wallace (Aug. 23, 1785), *in* 8 JM 351.

retrospective laws in criminal cases.[43] "Infringing the Confederation" was a synonym, foremost, for the failure to pay requisitions, which the unamended Constitution fixed. "Infringing the Confederation" was also a rights issue for Madison, properly included in a list of constituitonal restraints on state legislatures. The Bill of Rights, in the First Amendment, added prohibitions on Congress' "medling in religion" and "controuling the press" and in the Fifth Amendment it added rights against giving evidence against oneself and rights for full payment upon government seizure of property. Two issues from Madison's list disappeared: The Convention after debate left the de-cisions on the rights of suffrage to the states.[44] When it took up the issue of "licensing of importation of slaves," the Convention decided to prohibit Congress from blocking importation of slaves for twenty years, rather than to restrain Congress from giving licenses for importation of slaves.[45] Nonethe-less, Madison's 1785 personal list for restraints on the legislature captures the core values of the Bill of Rights that was adopted, better than the Anti-Federalists' lists and long before the Bill of Rights became an issue in the ratification debate. Madison is the source for the Bill of Rights much as he is the source for the Constitution as a whole. Madison's movement in Virginia for a Constitution had been organized around the protection of the rights for out-of-state creditors and religious minorities, and against Patrick Henry. Madison's fundamental philosophy, the theory of *Federalist* Number 10, was that the federal government was the superior guardian of individual rights. The biggest shift was that Madison had to be willing to impose his restraints, listed in 1785, not just against legislatures of the wicked states, but also against the legislature of the extended republic. On the issues he listed, he was willing to tolerate the restraints, even against the extended republic.

In his inauguration address in April 1789, President Washington rec-ommended that the Constitution be amended to make certain that "the characteristic rights of freemen" might be "more impregnably fortified."[46] Washington also told Lafayette that the "[d]elegates to the Convention did not [really] object to their Bill of Rights or Tryal by Jury, they just did not see how to adopt a federal rule on right of trial in civil cases without intruding

---

43 U.S. CONST., art. I, §9, cl 2 (habeas corpus), cl. 3 (retrospective laws), art. III, §1, cl. 3 (juries in criminal cases).
44 Federal Convention (Aug. 10, 1787), *in* 2 FARRAND 201–206, 249. *See* discussion accompa-nying, *infra* note.
45 U.S. CONST., art. I, §9, cl.
46 Washington, Inaugural Address (April 30, 1789), *in* http://elsinore.cis.yale.edu/lawweb/avalon/presiden/inaug/wash1.htm) (accessed Oct. 16, 2002).

upon the modes of trial adopted in the various states."[47] A bill of rights was not seriously considered at the Federal Convention, James Wilson said, only because no one had thought it necessary.[48] Thus when Madison offered his Bill of Rights to the overwhelmingly Federalist House, the rights created were serious rights protecting individuals against the government, but only because and to the extent that protection of individual rights was a Federalist cause.

The venue for considering the Bill of Rights was in the first Congress, after recommendations from the state conventions. Taking up the proposed amendments in Congress rather than as a condition of ratification meant that the Bill of Rights amendments were taken up by an overwhelmingly Federalist Congress and only after the Constitution was safely ratified and the new government was in place.

The shift in venue from the ratification conventions to first Congress dramatically raised the votes needed for rights amendments. Before ratification, five states willing to precondition ratification on an amendment – a mere 38 percent of the thirteen states – could prevent the Constitution's achieving the nine-state minimum needed to take effect.[49] The Constitution would then need to be rewritten to serve demands of the five-state, 38 percent minority. But after ratification, three quarters were positively needed for amendment[50] and ten of the thirteen or 77 percent of the states would need to favor an amendment under Article V to make it effective. The "mere" change in venue upped the support required for amendment from five of thirteen states (38%) to ten of thirteen states (77%). The Anti-Federalists had held only 20 percent of the seats in the first House and 9 percent in the Senate, and under Article V, two-thirds of each house would be needed to bring an amendment to the states. Amendments favored by Anti-Federalists but opposed by friends of the Constitution had not a ghost of a chance of passage.

The Anti-Federalists did not like the shift in venue to the first Congress to consider amendments, but they did not have the votes to stop it. In New York

---

[47] Washington to Comte de Lafayette (April 28, 1788), *in* 4 DHRC 601–602. *Accord*, Wilson, Address to a Meeting of the Citizens of Philadelphia on October 6, 1787, *in* 3 FARRAND 101 (saying that the Convention discussed the issue and faced the difficulty that cases open to a jury, differed in the different states so it was impracticable to have made a general rule applicable to the whole nation).

[48] Wilson, Pennsylvania Convention (Nov. 28, 1787), *in* 3 FARRAND 143 (saying that the reason a bill of rights has not been annexed to the proposed plan is that it never struck the mind of any member in the convention until the last three days and then the idea was passed off in a short conversation, without formal debate or a motion).

[49] U.S. CONST., Art. VII.

[50] U.S. CONST., Art. V.

and in Virginia, the Anti-Federalists tried to insist on the amendments as a precondition to ratification, but lost.[51] Anti-Federalist Melancton Smith's pamphlet, *Address to the People of New York*, is primarily about not ratifying the Constitution until various amendments had been made,[52] but even he ultimately voted for the Constitution even without the prior amendments.[53] In Massachusetts, the amendments came to the floor only as recommendations for the first Congress.[54] Only North Carolina refused to ratify the Constitution, pending amendments to protect rights.[55]

In offering his Bill of Rights, Madison filtered the Anti-Federalist proposals, so that only amendments consistent with nationalist ideals were offered. The ratifying conventions had recommended some 100 diverse amendments to the Constitution. Madison generally included friendly amendments protecting the rights of individuals, like those on his 1785 list, while screening out amendments hobbling the new federal government or encroaching on its domain.[56] Various proposals requiring two-thirds approval by Congress were dropped from Madison's Bill. Federal law and the federal judiciary continued to be supreme over state law. The Anti-Federalists' favorite amendment, the

---

[51] *See, e.g.*, Virginia Convention (June 25, 1788), *in* 3 ELLIOT 653–655 (Convention rejects Anti-Federalist motion to have second convention for amendment prior to ratification, and then ratifies constitution with only recommended amendments); New York Convention (July 23, 1788), *in* 2 ELLIOT 412 (Convention replaces conditional ratification with recommended amendments instead).

[52] Melancton Smith, "Address to the People of New York" (April 1787), *in* PAMPHLETS 87, 89–109 (asking for amendments that were never adopted, *e.g.* an "expressly delegated" limitation on Congressional powers, a prohibition on federal direct tax, taking away from Congress the powers to supervise federal elections, as well as civil jury rights, which were adopted).

[53] New York Convention 2 ELLIOT 413.

[54] 2 ELLIOT 177.

[55] North Carolina Convention (Aug. 1, 1788), *in* 4 ELLIOT 248–251 (motion to ratify the Constitution before amendments fails 84–184).

[56] Madison, House of Representatives (June 8, 1789), *in* 12 JM 200 (saying that some opponents of the Constitution take that position because it grants more power than necessary to the federal government and controls the ordinary powers of the state government, but the great mass of the opponents just wanted more safeguards against encroachment of particular rights). *See* Donald Lutz, *The Pedigree of the Bill of Rights, in* THE BILL OF RIGHTS: GOVERNMENT PROSCRIBED 42, 47–52 (Ronald Hoffman and Peter J. Albert, eds., 1997) (Madison adopted twenty-six of the Anti-Federalists proposed amendments, but rejected seventy-one of them and screened out the proposals that would protect or strengthen the states). *Accord*, Kenneth R. Bowling, *"A Tub to the Whale": The Founding Fathers and Adoption of the Federal Bill of Rights*, 8 J. OF THE EARLY REP. 223–251 (1988); GORDON WOOD, *The Irrelevance of a Bill of Rights, in* WOOD 536–543; Paul Finkelman, *James Madison and the Bill of Rights: A Reluctant Paternity*, SUP. CRT. REV. 1990 at 344; ROBERT RUTLAND, THE BIRTH OF THE BILL OF RIGHTS 1776–1791, at 197–125 (1955).

restriction on direct tax, did not make it into his proposal.[57] Washington's inaugural address had called for amendments to fortify the characteristic rights of freemen, but he also said to avoid "every alteration which might endanger the benefits of an united and effective government."[58] Even after amendment, there would be a complete new government able to operate effectively without interference by the states.[59]

The Anti-Federalists wanted amendments that would enhance the power of the states and they considered the whole of Madison's Bill of Rights amendments to be a sop or diversion, "a tub thrown out to whale" to divert the whale and "secure the freight of the ship and its peaceable voyage."[60] Lansing and Yates had set a standard for Anti-Federalism that "the leading feature of every amendment ought to be the preservation of the individual States, in their uncontrolled constitutional rights,"[61] and the Bill of Rights generally protected not states but individuals. Abraham Yates termed the amendments to be "trivial and unimportant," and neglecting the more fundamental issues of structure of government.[62] The Amendments, Anti-Federalist William Grayson wrote to Patrick Henry, are "good for nothing" and "will do more harm than good." They "shall affect personal liberty alone," he whined, "leaving the great points of the Judiciary and direct taxation etc. to stand as they are."[63] The Bill of Rights amendments, Anti-Federalist Aedanus Burke argued, were "not those solid and substantial amendments which the

---

[57] *See* Madison to Washington (Dec. 5, 1789), *in* 12 JM 458, 459 (saying that Anti-Federalist opposition was reducible "to a single point, the power of direct tax"); Tench Coxe to Madison (July 23, 1788), *in* 11 JM 194 (saying that denying Congress the power to lay direct tax seemed "to be the point most dear to the opposition"); Hardin Burnley to Madison (Dec. 5, 1789), *in* 12 JM 460 (saying that denying Congress direct tax was "the chief object of [Anti-Federalist] persuit"). The Anti-Federalists offered their direct tax amendment separately from the floor of the House when it was not included in the Bill of Rights, but it was there defeated with nine votes for and thirty-nine against (1 ANNALS 431–42, 660–65, 773–77) which at 19% of the seats in favor is just below the level of 21% (14 of 66) which Anti-Federalist held in the House.

[58] Washington, Inaugural Address (April 30, 1789), *in* http://elsinore.cis.yale.edu/lawweb/avalon/presiden/inaug/wash1.htm) (accessed Oct. 16, 2002).

[59] Cf. Madison to Jefferson (Aug. 11, 1788), *in* 11 JM 226 (expressing fear of a second convention that might result "in alterations of the federal system which would throw *essential* powers into the State Legislatures").

[60] AEDANUS BURKE, GAZETTE OF THE UNITED STATES (Aug. 19, 1789), *reprinted in* CREATING THE BILL OF RIGHTS: THE DOCUMENTARY RECORD FROM THE FIRST FEDERAL CONGRESS 175 (Helen E. Veit, et al., eds. 1991).

[61] Robert Yates and John Lansing, Jr., to Governor George Clinton, DAILY ADVERTISER (NEW YORK) (Jan. 14, 1788), *reprinted in* 2 DEBATE 4.

[62] Staughton Lynd, *Abraham Yates's History of the Movement for the United States Constitution*, 20 WM. & MARY Q. 223, 227 (3d series 1963).

[63] William Grayson to Patrick Henry (Sept. 29, 1789), *in* CREATING THE BILL OF RIGHTS 248–249, 300 (Helen Veit et al., eds. 1991).

people expect: they are ... frothy and full of wind."[64] George Mason had announced he opposed ratification in part because the Constitution lacked a bill of rights but he was not mollified by this set. Madison's amendments, Mason claimed, were a "Farce."[65]

The Virginia Anti-Federalists also opposed adoption of the Bill of Rights when the amendments came to Virginia for ratification, preferring to try instead for a second convention to rewrite the Constitution.[66] Madison's source said that the opposition to the Bill of Rights was reducible "to a single point, the power of direct tax."[67] Because of Anti-Federalist opposition to the Bill of Rights, the Virginia assembly stalemated on ratification of the Bill of Rights in 1789.[68] Ironically, the delay meant that when Anti-Federalist Virginia revisited the Bill of Rights in 1791, it would be the tenth state that carried the Bill of Rights over the top to adoption.[69]

Madison remained skeptical that restraints were needed against the federal Congress. On the merits, Madison thought a Bill of Rights protecting individuals against the federal government was unhelpful and unnecessary – "superfluous," he called it.[70] His theory of the extended republic held that "[p]rivate rights will be more secure under the Guardianship of the General Government than under the State Government,"[71] because diversity protected liberty.[72] The only amendments that Madison had any enthusiasm for were restrictions he proposed against the states, which never made it into the final amendments. Madison proposed that "no states shall violate the equal rights of conscience, or the freedom of the press, or the trial by jury in criminal cases" and he conceived this restriction to be "the most valuable amendment in the whole list."[73] It was in the states, "the small communities where a mistaken interest or contagious passion, could readily unite a

---

[64] Aug. 15, 1789, *in* 1 ANNALS 774.

[65] George Mason to John Mason (July 31, 1789) *in* 3 PGM 1164; *accord*, Mason to Jefferson (March 16, 1790) *in* 3 PGM 1189 (saying that the Constitution was a "great danger to the Rights and Liberties of our Country" even after the Bill of Rights).

[66] *See* Edward Carrington to Madison (Dec. 20, 1789), *in* 12 JM 462, 463–465.

[67] Madison to Washington (Dec. 5, 1789), *in* 12 JM 458, 459. *See also* Hardin Burnley to Madison (Dec. 5, 1789), *in* 12 JM 460 (saying that adoption of the Bill of Rights at this time would be "an obstacle to the chief object of their persuit, the amendment on the subject of direct taxation").

[68] RISJORD at 356–357.

[69] *Id.* at 357.

[70] Madison to Jefferson (Oct. 17, 1788), *in* 11 JM 297–300 (saying tension between federal and state would make bill of rights unnecessary. A bill of rights was only needed to protect the people against a monarch).

[71] Madison to Jefferson (Oct. 24, 1787), *in* 10 JM 212.

[72] General Defense of the Constitution (June 12, 1788), *in* 11 JM 129, 130.

[73] BERNARD SCHWARTZ, THE BILL OF RIGHTS: A DOCUMENTARY HISTORY 1032 (1990).

majority of the whole under a factious leader, in trampling on the rights of the Minor party."[74] Madison avoided the merits of a bill of rights throughout the debates, but almost always argued for the Bill of Rights in terms of its political expediency.[75]

Robert Morris in Philadelphia did not like the Bill of Rights and he thought that Madison offered a Bill of Rights because he "got frightened in Virginia."[76] In his race for election for the first House of Representatives, Patrick Henry set Madison up against a formidable opponent, James Monroe, one of Virginia's delegates to Congress under the Articles and a future president.[77] Madison in that election had promised the Presbyterian and Baptist constituents that now that the Constitution was settled, he would offer amendments to protect the rights of conscience, freedom of the press, trials by jury, and security against general warrants.[78]

One difficulty with the theory that the Bill of Rights is a product of the Madison–Monroe congressional race is that the Bill of Rights is a misdirected remedy for the Virginia dissenting religious. The abuses that the Presbyterians and Baptists were afraid of were abuses by Patrick Henry's Virginia, and, at least as it turned out, the Bill of Rights gave them no protection from Virginia. For the Virginia Baptists and Presbyterians, the Bill of Rights restricted the federal government, which would be the protector of religious rights, while leaving untouched the prime abuser, the state of Virginia.

In introducing the Bill of Rights amendments, Madison said that he wanted to render the Constitution "as acceptable to the whole of the people of the United States, as it has been found acceptable to the majority of them."[79] He wanted to bring the people of good faith and talent who remained unreconciled, particularly in the two states, North Carolina and Rhode Island, which had not yet formally rejoined the union.[80] But there was not going to be much offered to the nonsigning states, especially not to Rogue Island.

The Tenth Amendment, which provides that the people or the states shall have powers not delegated to Congress seems especially written to be a symbol stripped of substance. As noted, the Articles of Confederation had provided that Congress would have only the powers "expressly delegated"

---

[74] Madison: Notes on his Speech on the Right of Suffrage to the Philadelphia Convention, *in* 3 FARRAND 454.

[75] Finkelman, *supra* note 56, at 343.

[76] Robert Morris of Pennsylvania, Aug. 18, 1788, *quoted in* RAKOVE at 334.

[77] RUTLAND, MADISON 44, 46–49 (1987).

[78] Madison to [Baptist Minister] George Eve (Jan. 2, 1789), *in* 11 JM 404–405.

[79] Madison, House of Representatives (June 8, 1789), *in* 1 ANNALS 448–449.

[80] *Id.* at 449.

to it.[81] The Framers used the Articles as a model for structure and language, but they had omitted the "expressly delegated" limitation. The Federalists defeated Anti-Federalist attempts to return the "expressly." We are to read from this history that while Congress has only delegated powers, it has some implied delegated powers, including especially the passport. Not all of the powers of Congress need to be written down.

Madison's first draft of the Tenth Amendment had even included an insult to the Anti-Federalists. His version was "That there be prefixed to the constitution a declaration, that all power is originally vested in, and consequently derived from the people."[82] In the Articles of Confederaton the powers not vested in Congress were left in the states, not with the people. Within the context of the debates, Madison's draft was a slap in the face of the Anti-Federalists, because the Anti-Federalists wanted Congress's power to depend upon the states, and not the people,[83] and the Federalists were using the sovereignty of the people as a weapon against the states. Congress was less confrontational than Madison was because the Tenth Amendment that it finally recommended provided that powers not delegated to the federal government are "reserved to the States *or* to the people,"[84] and that language avoids taking a position as to whether the powers of Congress originated from the states or the people. Still the reading that the Tenth Amendment is tautology, meaning that the Congress has whatever powers it has whether expressed or by implication, seems fair to the history.

B. DEMOCRACY

There is a long tradition interpreting the Constitution as a patrician document and as the Anti-Federalists as the defenders of democracy and the common man.[85] Merrill Jensen, for example, describes the Constitution as "the culmination of an anti-democratic crusade."[86] Gordon Wood describes

---

[81] *See also* discussion chapter 5, pp. 120–122.

[82] 1 ANNALS 451 (June 8, 1789).

[83] *See* discussion, chapter 3 4, 95–96.

[84] 1 Stat. 97 (Sept. 25, 1789) (emphasis added).

[85] *See, e.g.* BEARD 154, 324 (1913) (treating the Constitution as a conservative document written to suppress paper money); JENSEN, NEW NATION 424–25 (1950); FERGUSON at 241–245 (1961) (describing class warfare between paper and hard money interests). *See also* discussion, Chapter 6, accompanying nn. 2–49 on the subject of debates on paper money.

[86] JENSEN, ARTICLES at *xv.* (1940).

the Constitution as "an aristocratic document designed to check the democratic tendencies of the period."[87]

Interpreting the Constitution as anti-democratic does not work very well
because the most articulate democrats on the continent were Federalists and
the most articulate anti-democratic participants felt more comfortable as
Anti-Federalists. The times were not very democratic by modern standards,
and speakers unsympathetic to democracy can be found on both sides. Still,
overall the Constitution seems as democratic as the times allowed.[88]

The Anti-Federalists commonly dismissed the views of the people. Governor George Clinton, for example, warned New York about the "frenzy"
of the people, who could be guilty of "most imprudent and desperate measures." Clinton said he knew that "the people are too apt to vibrate from
one extreme to another."[89] Anti-Federalist "Federal Farmer" condemned
"levellers" and "little insurgents, men in debt, who want no law, and who
want a share of the property of others."[90] Federal Farmer expressed his
shock that under the Constitution neither the Congress nor the states could
constrict the qualifications for office holding.[91] Anti-Federalist Mercy Otis
Warren of Massachusetts denounced the "supple multitude" who were paying
a "blind and idolatrous homage" to false leaders.[92] In private, she expressed
her hope that a few virtuous men might rise and stand above the "absurd
enthusiasm that often spreads itself over the lower classes of life."[93] Anti-
Federalist Melancton Smith told the New York Convention that the "people
are frequently incompetent to deliberate discussion, and subject to errors
and imprudences."[94]

Elbridge Gerry of Massachusetts undoubtedly had the sharpest anti-
democratic tongue at the Philadelphia Convention. Gerry's analysis was that

---

[87] Wood at 513 (1969).
[88] *See* Cecelia M. Kenyon, *Men of Little Faith: The Anti-Federalists on the Nature of Representative
Government*, 12 Wm. & Mary Q. 3rd. Ser. at 33, 42 (Anti-Federalists little different from the
Federalists in distrust of majorities and profoundly distrustful of electoral and representative
process).
[89] George Clinton, New York Convention (June 28, 1788), *in* 2 Elliot 359.
[90] Federal Farmer, *Letters to the Republican V*, New York Journal (Oct. 13, 1787), *reprinted
in* 14 DHRC 50.
[91] Federal Farmer, *An Additional Number of Letters to the Republican XII*, New York Journal
(Jan. 12, 1788), *reprinted in* 17 DHRC 310, 311.
[92] A Columbian Patriot [Mercy Otis Warren], Observations on the New Constitution (Feb. 1788), *reprinted in* 16 DHRC 277.
[93] Mercy Otis Warren to Catherine Macaulay (July 1789), *quoted in* Cornell at 7.
[94] Melancton Smith, New York Convention (June 25, 1788), *in* 2 Elliot 312 (calling for a
recall of Congressmen by the state legislatures).

"the evils we experience flow from the excess of democracy"[95] and he told the Convention that he "had been taught by experience the danger of the levilling spirit."[96] Gerry opposed the Electoral College system for picking the president because it ultimately depended on votes by the people: "A popular election in this case is radically vicious," he said. "The ignorance of the people would put it in the power of some one set of men dispersed through the Union & acting in Concert to delude them into any appointment."[97] Gerry opposed popular election of Senators because "to draw both branches from the people will leave no security to the interest [of property]."[98] Gerry said that he was "as much principled as ever agst. aristocracy and monarchy," but that the representatives the people had in fact elected were "[m]en of indigence, ignorance & baseness, [who] spare no pains, however dirty to carry their point agst. men who are superior to the artifices practised."[99] Gerry has all the hallmarks of patrician anti-democrat and would work wonderfully as evidence that the Constitution was anti-democratic, except that Gerry chose the Anti-Federalist camp, opposed to the Constitution, as more in tune with his thinking.

Conversely, the best democrats in the nation placed themselves in favor of the new government. James Wilson consistently argued against votes depending on property and in favor of the people as the fountain from which all authority is derived. "[T]he supreme power resides in the people," he told the Pennsylvania Ratification Convention, "and they never part with it."[100] The legislature, Wilson said, "ought to be the most exact transcript of the whole Society."[101] Consistently, staunchly Federalist Benjamin Franklin was a good democrat, opposed to the Electoral College and in favor of the direct election of the presidency because "[i]n free Governments the rulers are the servants, and the people their superiors & sovereigns."[102] Tom Paine, whose *Common*

---

95 Elbridge Gerry, Federal Convention (May 31, 1787), *in* 1 FARRAND 48 (Madison's notes).
96 *Id.*
97 Elbridge Gerry, Federal Convention (July 25, 1787), *in* 2 FARRAND 114 (Madison's notes).
98 Elbridge Gerry, Federal Convention (June 7, 1787), *in* 1 FARRAND 151.
99 Elbridge Gerry, Federal Convention (June 6, 1787), *in* 1 FARRAND 132.
100 Wilson, Pennsylvania Convention (Oct. 6, 1787), *in* 2 ELLIOT 433.
101 Wilson, Federal Convention (June 6, 1787), *in* 1 FARRAND 132. *See also* MARK DAVID HALL, THE POLITICAL AND LEGAL PHILOSOPHY OF JAMES WILSON, 1742–1798, at 96 (1997) (quoting Wilson saying that the rights and duties of man belong equally to all).
102 Benjamin Franklin, Federal Convention (July 25, 1787), *in* 2 FARRAND 120. *See also* Benjamin Franklin, Federal Convention (Aug. 7, 1787), *in* 2 FARRAND 204 (praising the virtue of our common people, whose public spirit contributed principally to the winning of the Revolution). *See also* ERIC FONER, TOM PAINE AND REVOLUTIONARY AMERICA 34–35 (1976) (Franklin was hero of the artisans).

Sense had persuaded the Revolutionary generation that they needed neither aristocracy nor a king,[103] was also a staunch Federalist.[104] Wilson, Paine, and Franklin were Pennsylvanians, who might well have found some passion for both their democratic ideals and for federalism in the bitter Presbyterian-Quaker politics of the prior decade. In those fights, the Pennsylvania party that was to become Anti-Federalist was the party that was disenfranchising voters.[105]

By modern standards, the times were not very democratic. The conventional wisdom in the period before the adoption of the Constitution was praise for the "mixed" or checks-and-balances British system under which the Commons represented the people, the Lords represented property, and the Crown represented the nation.[106] Baron Montesquieu, the favorite source for the Anti-Federalists, praised the "beautiful system" of the English, including its protections for the privileges of the nobility.[107] There were certainly Federalists who trusted property more than they trusted people. John Jay, for instance, opined that "the people who own the country ought to govern it."[108]

Madison seems to be in the middle of the spectrum for his times. In 1788, he supported property requirements in state constitutions, at least as to one house.[109] Madison had worried in 1785 that extending the franchise "even to

---

[103] *See, e.g.*, Thomas Paine, Common Sense, Feb. 14, 1776, *in* Writings of Thomas Paine at 10 (Eric Foner, ed. 1995) (absurdity of the king checking the people). *See also* Thomas Paine, *Rights of Man* (1791), *in id.* 568 (praising American government as grafting representation upon democracy).

[104] *Id.*, at 433 (arguing that the powers vested in the states were too great and those vested in the federal government too little); *See* Eric Foner, Tom Paine and Revolutionary America 208–209 (1976) (Paine as supporter of the Constitution), at 217 (Paine as democrat).

[105] *See, e.g.*, James H. Hutson, *The Birth of the Bill of Rights: The State of Current Scholarship*, 20 Prologue: The Journal of the National Archives 143, 150 (1988) (arguing that Anti-Federalist support for disenfranchisement of the Quakers and German sects calls into question their commitment to liberty).

[106] Both John Adams and Alexander Hamilton praised the mixed British constitution, including its protections of nondemocratic privileges. Wood 567–592 (saying that Adams' espousal of a British mixed constitution was out of touch with the republican consensus at the convention); Hamilton, Federal Convention (June 4, 1787), *in* 1 Farrand 288 (saying that the few needed protection from the many). When Hamilton had gone through the discussions of the convention, he joined in the republic consensus, saying for instance in *Federalist* No.22, at 146 (Hamilton) (Dec. 18, 1787) (saying that the consent of the people is the "pure original fountain of legitimate authority").

[107] Montesquieu, *Of the Constitution of England*, Spirit of the Laws, book XI, ch. 6, 38 Great Books for the Western World at 74 (Encly. Britannica 1952).

[108] *Quoted in* Richard Hofstadter, *The Founding Fathers: An Age of Realism*, *in* The Moral Foundations of the American Republic 73, 84 (Robert H. Horwitz, ed. 1977).

[109] Madison, *Observations on Jefferson's Draft of a Constitution for Virginia* (Oct. 15, 1788), *in* 11 JM at 287.

those who possess a pittance may throw too much power into hands which will either abuse it themselves or sell it to the rich who will abuse it."[110] In private notes intended for a speech at the Convention, Madison asked for a balanced system in which both property and people were represented.[111] But Madison also said that limiting the vote to landholders would "exclued too great a proportion of citizens"[112] and that "[c]onfining the right of suffrage to freeholders ... violates the vital principle of free Govt. that those who are to be bound by laws, ought to have a voice in making them."[113] As *Publius* in the public constitutional debates, Madison said that "[t]he people are the only legitimate fountain of power."[114] Only the Republican form in which government represents the people, Madison said, is "reconcileable with the genius of the people of America [and] with the fundamental principles of the revolution."[115]

The Convention seriously considered a number of proposals that would have made voting dependent on property, but ultimately rejected them all. There were serious proposals to allocate votes in Congress according to wealth of the state, on the argument expressed, for instance, by Pierce Butler of South Carolina that property was the "only just measure of representation" because property was the great object of government and the great means of carrying on war.[116] The Convention ultimately did not make allocation of votes depend on wealth, albeit simply by ducking the issue.[117] The Convention considered requiring voters for representatives in the House to own property,[118] but it ultimately just adopted whatever the states did.[119] The Convention considered requiring that Congressmen hold property, but it ultimately rejected the proposal by voice vote.[120] As Gordon Wood has

---

[110] Madison to Caleb Wallace, Aug. 23, 1785 *in* 8 JM 353 (commenting on a constitution for Kentucky).

[111] Madison, Note to his Speech on the Right of Suffrage (undated), *in* 3 FARRAND 450–455.

[112] 8 JM at 353.

[113] 3 FARRAND at 453.

[114] *Federalist* No. 49, at 339 (Madison) (Feb. 2, 1788).

[115] *Federalist* No. 39, at 250 (Madison) (Jan. 16, 1788).

[116] Pierce Butler (So. Carolina.), Federal Convention (July 6, 1787), *in* 1 FARRAND 542 *See also* Pierce Butler (July 9, 1787), *id.*, at 562 (Butler "warmly" urging the necessity of regarding wealth in the determination of representation).

[117] *See* discussion, Chapter 5, 102–104.

[118] Federal Convention (Aug 7, 1787), *in* 2 FARRAND 201–206.

[119] *Id. at 206.* U.S. CONST., Art. I, §2 (requiring voters for House of Representative to have the same qualification as voters for the lower house of the state's legislature).

[120] Federal Convention (Aug. 10, 1787), *in* 2 FARRAND 249. Note at *id.* (Benjamin Franklin opposing the property requirement because of his "dislike of every thing that tended to debase the spirit of the common people").

argued, the Convention reached a republican consensus that government rested on the people.[121] The republican consensus seems to have restrained the more undemocratic impulses of the delegates so as to prevent any shift toward basing political power on wealth.

Once the document went public, the Constitution was sold on strictly democratic grounds. Hamilton argued for ratification not by the state legislatures but by conventions of the people because only the consent of the people is that "pure original fountain of legitimate authority."[122] Madison said the people are the only legimate source of power and that only a government based on representation of the people was consistent with the genius of America.[123] The door to the House of Representatives, Madison boasted, would be "open to merit of every description, whether native or adoptive, whether young or old, and without regard to poverty or wealth, or to any particular profession of religious faith."[124] Madison's boast was exactly the kind of open democracy that shocked Anti-Federalist "Federal Farmer."

Under Federalist philosophy, moreover, the general government rested upon popular sovereignty, and the Anti-Federalists objected to that base. The states were properly not sovereign, the Federalists said, because "[t]he principle of this Constitution [is that] the supreme power resides in the people."[125] The Anti-Federalist position was that the Constitution should be built on the authority of the states alone, and not on the authority of the people.[126] Voting by states, however, as the Anti-Federalists wanted, is not a properly democratic principle because it allows a minority of the people, in small states, to out-vote the will of the popular majority.[127] In the Bill of Rights debate, moreover, the Anti-Federalists argued that Congress would abuse the people and it was the Federalists who parried by pointing out that the Congress was the representative of the people.[128] As Cecilia Kenyon has

[121] WOOD at 567–592.
[122] *Federalist* No. 22, at 146 (Hamilton) (Dec. 18, 1787).
[123] *Federalist* No. 49, at 339 (Madison) (Feb. 2, 1788).
[124] *Federalist* No. 52, at 355 (Madison) (Feb. 8, 1788).
[125] Wilson, Pennsylvania Convention (Dec. 11, 1787), *in* 2 ELLIOT 502.
[126] John Smilie, Pennsylvania Convention (Nov. 28, 1787), *in* 2 DHRC 407, 408–409. *See* discussion, Chapter 5, pp. 102–104.
[127] *See* discussion, Chapter 5, p. 106.
[128] Samuel Stillman, Massachusetts Convention, Feb. 6, 1788, *in* 6 DHRC 1458 (asking "who are the Congress?" and answering "They are ourselves: The men of our own choice… whose interest is inseparabley connected with our own. Why is it then, that gentlemen speak of Congress as some foreign body?"); John Marshall, Virginia Convention (June 10, 1788), *in* 9 DHRC 1118 (responding that "we *were not* represented in Parliament"). *See also* Washington to Jay (Aug. 15, 1786), *in* 3 PJJat 208 (saying that "[t]o be fearful of vesting Congress, constituted as that body is, with ample authorities for national purposes,

very ably argued, the Anti-Federalists were not looking for more democracy, they were looking for state power.[129]

Closely related to the debate over democracy is the debate over whether Anti-Federalists or the Federalists were the true heirs of the Revolutionary ideals. The Anti-Federalists sometimes drew an analogy between the British oppressors before independence and the Federalist proponents of the Constitution. Anti-Federalist Richard Henry Lee of Virginia, for instance, wrote that "'Tis really astonishing that the same people who have just emerged from a long & cruel war in defence of liberty, should now agree to fix an elective despotism upon themselves & their posterity."[130] Philadelphiensis argued that the Constitution would re-institute the same British abuses that instigated the Revolutionary War: It would take away the liberty of conscience, of the press, and of trial jury that "roused the sons of America to oppose Britain."[131] Mercy Otis Warren in Massachusetts argued that those who supported the Constitution sought "to lock the strong chains of domestic despotism on a country, which by the most glorious and successful struggles is but newly emancipated from the sceptre of foreign dominion."[132] Consistently, the Anti-Federalists also claimed that the Articles of Confederation embodied the ideals of the Revolution. Anti-Federalist Gilbert Livingston in

appears to me the very climax of popular absurdity and madness"). *Accord*, James Iredell, North Carolina Convention (July 28, 1788), *in* 4 ELLIOT 148 (saying the right to trial under the Constitution will be left to the discretion of *our own legislature* to act, whereas the British deprivation of trial by jury was the work of a foreign legislature).

[129] Kenyon, *supra* note 88, 12 WM. & MARY Q. 3rd. Ser. at 3.
    Charles Beard thought that the Constitution was anti-democratic primarily because it prohibited the states from issuing paper money, under the philosophy of *Federalist* 10. BEARD 154, 324 (1913). Paper money is discussed in Chapter 9, pp. 202–210, which reject Beard's argument. *See* more generally, James E. Viator, *Give Me That Old-time Historiography: Charles Beard and the Study of the Constitution (part 2)*, 43 LOY. L. REV. 311, 406 (1997) (arguing that Beard got *Federalist* 10 backwards because Madison's theory of the extended republic was seeking to ameliorate the power of economic interests, not to further oppression, by creating a guardian of minority rights at the federal level).

[130] Richard Henry Lee to John Lamb, (June 27, 1788) *in* 18 DHRC 58.

[131] Philadelphiensis VIII, PHILADELPHIA FREEMAN'S JOURNAL (Jan. 23, 1788), *reprinted in* 15 DHRC 461.

[132] A COLUMBIAN PATRIOT (MERCY OTIS WARREN), OBSERVATIONS ON THE CONSTITUTION (Feb. 1788), reprinted in 16 DHRC 272, 277. *See also* STATE GAZETTE OF SOUTH CAROLINA (Jan. 28, 1788), *reprinted in* 15 DHRC 486 (poem saying, *e.g.* "...who have bled in Freedom's sacred cause/Ah, why desert her maxims and her law?/ Who sav'd these realms from Britain's bloody hand/"); *The Federalist's Political Creed*, PHILADELPHIA INDE-PENDENT GAZETTEER (May 10, 1788), *reprinted in* 18 DHRC 5 (giving a satirical portrayal of the Federalists from the Anti-Federalist point of view and saying, *e.g.*, "[t]his [Federalist] political creed however is no new invention: 'tis the old tory system revived by different hands").

New York argued that America had had the resolve to resist the most powerful nation on earth, even unto bloodshed. "What was her aim? Equal liberty and safety. What ideas had she of this equal liberty? Read them in her Articles of Confederation."[133]

The Federalists disagreed, arguing that the Constitution would save the Revolution. The Virginia Legislature, in appointing delegates to the Philadelphia Convention, said that by this meeting the "people of America are to decide the solemn question, whether to reap the just fruits of that Independence...and of that Union which they cemented with so much blood; or whether by giving way to unmanly jealousies and prejudices, they will renounce the Revolution."[134] The war debts, to be paid by the Constitution, were "the price of liberty," for which "the faith of America has been repeatedly pledged."[135] The defaults dishonored the "great cause."[136]

Perhaps the best rebuttal to the Anti-Federalist analogy between British tyranny and the Constitution was the people who endorsed the Constitution. George Washington, the Commander-in-Chief of the Continental Army, and Tom Paine, the author of *Common Sense*, were the closest living embodiments of the cause of independence and of the Republican form of government. Both were ardently pro-Constitution. Both sides claimed to be the true heirs of the Revolution, but the Nationalist side did it more creditably.[137]

C. SLAVERY

The Anti-Federalists were also not particularly democratic on the important issue of slavery. Anti-Federalists were commonly rabidly pro-slavery, and in

---

[133] Gilbert Livingston, New York Convention (June 24, 1787), *in* 2 ELLIOT 287. The Articles of Confederation were not ratified until near the end of the war and almost five years after the Declaration of Independence, but there is undoubtedly some more metaphorical sense in which the Articles expressed the earlier-formed war aims.

[134] Virginia Assembly Resolution on Appointment of Delegates to the Conventions (Nov. 23, 1786), *in* 8 DHRC 540, 541. Madison is the apparent author of the Resolution, 9 JM 163.

[135] Hamilton, Report Relative to a Provision for the Support of Public Credit (Jan. 9, 1790), *in* 6 PAH 51, 69. *See also* Madison, Address to the Nation (April 26, 1783), *in* 24 JCC 283 (saying that the defaults prevented "full reward for the blood, the toils, the care, and the calamities which have purchased it" and that the defaults dishonored the "great cause," Madison said, "the last and fairest experiment in favor of the right of human nature").

[136] Madison, Address to the Nation (April 26, 1783), *in* 24 JCC 283.

[137] *See* James H. Hutson, *The Creation of the Constitution: Scholarship at a Standstill*, 12 REVIEWS IN AMERICAN HISTORY 463, 466–472 (1984) for a good description of the battle of history over whether Constitution is a counter-revolutionary document inconsistent with the Declaration of Independence or is in continuity with the republican aspirations of the Declaration.

the South, the Anti-Federalists claimed they opposed the Constitution to defend their "liberty" to be slaveholders. Patrick Henry in Virginia was riding atop a political economy based on slaveholder plantations and he argued repeatedly and with vigor to his fellow owners in the Virginia Ratification Convention that this Constitution would end slaveholders' rights to their slaves. Patrick Henry said that the Constitution would give Congress the power to end slavery and he was certain that Congress would use it.[138] The Virginia Ratification Convention debated the Constitution clause by clause and Henry could find in almost every clause proof that Congress would end slavery. Congress would use its power over commerce, according to Henry, to end the slave trade after 1808.[139] Congress would use its power over war to say that every black man must fight and then free him.[140] Congress would use its power to provide for the general defense and welfare to pronounce all slaves free[141] and Congress could use its tax power to tax the slaves to manumission.[142] "We ought to posses [slaves] in the manner we have inherited them from our ancestors," Patrick Henry told Virginia, "as their manumission is incompatible with the felicity of the country."[143] For Henry, the liberty of blacks did not count in either the "liberty" or the "felicity of the country." "For some the word liberty may mean for each man to do as he pleases with himself," Lincoln would later say, "while with others the same word may mean for some men to do as they please with other men."[144]

Other Southern Anti-Federalists used preservation of slavery against the Constitution. George Mason had argued in Philadelphia that slavery would bring the judgment of heaven upon the nation "[b]y an inevitable chain of causes & effects [by which] providence punishes national sins."[145] By the time of the Virginia Ratification Convention, however, Mason, with typical inconsistency, was arguing along with Patrick Henry that a reason to oppose the

---

[138] Patrick Henry, Virginia Convention (June 17, 1788), *in* 10 DHRC 1341 (arguing that Congress had implied powers to use against slavery); Patrick Henry, Virginia Convention (June 24, 1788), *in id.*, at 1476 (arguing that they have and will certainly exercise the power to abolish slavery); Patrick Henry, Virginia Convention (June 24, 1788), *in id.*, at 1504 (arguing that "they can emancipate our slaves").

[139] U.S. CONST. art. I, sec. 9, cl. 3.

[140] Patrick Henry, Virginia Convention (June 24, 1788), *in* 10 DHRC 1476.

[141] *Id.*

[142] Patrick Henry, Virginia Convention (June 17, 1788), *in* 10 DHRC 1341 (arguing that Congress might lay such heavy taxes on slaves, amounting to emancipation, such "that this property would be lost in this country").

[143] Patrick Henry, Virginia Convention (June 24, 1788), *in* 3 ELLIOT 591.

[144] Abraham Lincoln, Address at a Sanitary Fair in Baltimore, April 15, 1864, *in* ABRAHAM LINCOLN: HIS SPEECHES AND WRITINGS 478 (Roy Basler, ed. 1946).

[145] Mason, Federal Convention (Aug. 29, 1787), *in* 2 FARRAND 370 (Madison's notes).

Constitution was that the North under it could tax slavery to manumission.[146] In South Carolina, Anti-Federalist Rawlins Lowndes would oppose the Constitution because "Negroes were our wealth, our only natural resource; yet behold how our kind friends in the north were determined soon to tie up our hands, and drain us of what we had!"[147]

The Federalists were commonly better on the slavery issue. Hamilton, for example, a consistent nationalist, detested slavery. In 1776, he had proposed enlisting slaves in the Continental army so as "to give them their freedom with their muskets."[148] The Pennsylvania Quakers, who were the party that supported the Constitution, were the leaders in the fight against slavery.[149] When the Federalists became a minority, mostly northern party after 1800, they became outspoken in opposition to slaveholding.[150]

Even in the South, Federalists were able to oppose the slave trade. Madison had proposed in 1785 that the Kentucky constitution should restrain the legislature from licensing the importation of slaves.[151] James Iredell of North Carolina wrote that he regretted the twenty-year moratorium allowed by the Constitution for the slave trade, but said that South Carolina and Georgia insisted on it and might have opposed the Constitution without it. He then told North Carolina, however, that "[t]he interests of humanity will, however, have gained something by the prohibition of this inhuman trade, though at a distance of twenty odd years."[152] Iredell was a core Federalist. He shows up on 40 percent of the pages of the North Carolina Ratification Convention[153] and became a justice of the U.S. Supreme Court.

---

[146] Mason, Virginia Convention (June 17, 1788), *in* 10 DHRC 1343 (arguing that Federalists misconstrued the apportionment clause and that Congress could choose to enact prohibitively high tax on slaves). Henry's arguments that Congress would tax slaves to emancipation are at *id.*, at 1341–1342, at 1504.

[147] Rawlins Lowndes, South Carolina, Convention (Jan. 16, 1788), *in* 4 ELLIOT 273.

[148] Hamilton to Jay (Mar. 14, 1779), *in* 2 PAH 17–19. *See also* Jay, Extract from an Address to the People of the State of New York, on the Subject of the Federal Constitution, 1787, http://rs6.loc.gov (arguing that the Quakers who have freed their slaves have gained because their Negroes laboured so much more cheerfully and did so much more work as freemen than when slaves).

[149] GARY B. NASH & JEAN R. SODERLUND, FREEDOM BY DEGRESS: EMANCIPATION IN PENNSYLVANIA AND ITS AFTERMATH 53, 78–105 (1991) (describing Quaker anti-slavery efforts).

[150] LINDA KERBER, FEDERALISTS IN DISSENT: IMAGERY AND IDEOLOGY IN JEFFERSONIAN AMERICA 23–66 (1970).

[151] Madison to Caleb Wallace (Aug. 23, 1785) *in* 8 JM 351.

[152] JAMES IREDELL, ANSWER TO MASON'S OBJECTIONS TO THE CONSTITUTION 35, *reprinted in* PAMPHLETS ON THE CONSTITUTION OF THE UNITED STATES (Paul Leicester Ford, ed. 1888).

[153] 4 ELLIOT 4–6, 7, 9, 10–11, 13–15, 27, 28, 32–33, 35–36, 37, 38–42, 73–75, 91–92, 95–101, 105, 106–114, 125–131, 132–134, 144–149, 152, 164–167, 170–172, 176–180, 185–186, 192–198, 217, 218–223, 228–234, 241–242, 247, 248–249.

In the South, however, Federalist opposition to the slave trade was commonly tied with support for continued slavery for slaves already in bondage. Federalist Charles Pinckney, for instance, argued that he would personally vote against the slave trade in his home South Carolina legislature, but still that the sanction given by Greece, Rome, France, England, Holland, "& other modern States" justified slavery.[154]

The dominant Federalist attitude in the North appears to have been to avoid interference. Oliver Ellsworth of Connecticut probably expressed the majority view when he argued that "considered in a moral light we ought to free the slaves," but that intervention would be unnecessary because slavery would inevitably atrophy in competition with free labor. He concluded that the North should not "intermeddle."[155] His colleague, Roger Sherman, told the Convention to "leave the matter as we find it" and "despatch [to our] business."[156]

The Philadelphia Convention was skewed to be sympathetic to slavery. The states missing from the Convention were northern states, Rhode Island and New York and sometimes New Hampshire, and their absence turned a northern majority of seven northern states to six slave states if all had attended[157] into a southern majority of six states to four or five northern states for most of the deliberations. In part because of northern absences and northern indifference, the Constitution has many features tilted in favor of the slave states.[158] The new federal government was to return fugitive slaves[159] and suppress slave insurrections, along with other internal rebellions.[160] The Constitution gave white slave owners extra votes in the U.S. House of Representatives and Electoral College by weighing three-fifths of

---

[154] Charles Pinckney (South Carolina) (Aug. 22, 1787), *in* 2 FARRAND 371.

[155] Oliver Ellsworth, *id*.

[156] Roger Sherman, *id*., at 369–370.

[157] The states with modest slave populations were New Hampshire, Massachusetts, Rhode Island, Connecticut, New York, New Jersey, and Pennsylvania. The states with a third of the population as slaves were Maryland, Virginia, North Carolina, South Carolina, and Georgia. Delaware at one-sixth slave is between the Northern and Southern averages. PETER KOLCHIN, AMERICAN SLAVERY, 1619–1877 242, Table 3 (1993). Delaware voted with the slave states, for instance, voting in the Federal Convention for including slaves, counted at 100%, in determining votes in the House of Representatives. July 11, 1787, 1 FARRAND 581.

[158] James H. Hutson, *The Creation of the Constitution: Scholarship at a Standstill*, 12 REVIEWS IN AMERICAN HISTORY 463, 464 (1984) describes the Abolitionist interpretations of the Constitution as pro-slavery.

[159] U.S. CONST. art. IV, sec. 2, cl. 3.

[160] U.S. CONST. art. IV, sec. 4.

the slaves in the determination of white slaveholders' votes.[161] Congress was prohibited from taxing exports,[162] which is partly just mercantilist economics and partly intended to prevent the slave-raised crops of tobacco, indigo, and later cotton from being taxed.[163]

Notwithstanding the missing states gave the Convention a pro-slave state slant, the slaveholders themselves were not sure whether the Constitution was pro- or anti-slavery. The reaction of slaveholders to the Constitution was mixed, and even inconsistent. In Virginia, the largest slaveholders (owning more than 50 slaves) and least slaveholders (owning 1–5 slaves) were disproportionately Federalists. The tier in between (owning 6–49 slaves) were disproportionately Anti-Federalist. Before concluding that that pattern represents a deep truth, realize that in neighboring Maryland the pattern was reversed. The largest slaveholders (more than 100 slaves) and the least (1–24 slaves) were disproportionately Anti-Federalist, whereas the tier in between (25–99 slaves) were disproportionately Federalist.[164] New England supported the Constitution at a level slightly below the national average (59 percent of the delegates for ratification, as against 65 percent overall weighted by population), but then the South also supported the Constitution (63 percent for ratification) at slightly less than the national average. That confused and inconsistent pattern implies that the Constitution was not perceived to be substantially pro- or anti-slavery at the time, even though by the judgment of eternal morality, the Constitution should have done better.

---

[161] U.S. CONST. art. I, sec. 3, cl. 3 (House of Representatives votes), art. II, sec. 1, cl. 2 (Electoral College gives states votes for president equal to the total number of congressmen, including both senators and representatives).

[162] U.S. CONST. art. 1, sec. 9, cl. 3.

[163] *See, e.g.*, Mason, Federal Convention (Aug. 16, 1787), *in* 2 FARRAND 305–306 (arguing that northern states should not deny the Southern or "staple states" this security). The nationalists, Madison and Gouverneur Morris, opposed the prohibition of tax on exports with a view to allowing Congress to tax tobacco. Madison & Gouverneur Morris, Federal Convention (Aug. 16, 1787), *in* 2 FARRAND 306.

[164] RISJORD at 308, 310.

☆ PART TWO ☆

LESS CONVINCING FACTORS

The Constitution was a revolution that replaced the friendship league of the confederation mode of government with a complete, tri-partite national government, able to raise its own revenue by tax directly, to operate without recourse to the states, and to enact laws supreme over the states.[1] The Constitution replaced supremacy of the states with sovereignty of the people and ended the one-state veto of congressional actions necessary for the common defense or general welfare. It is the thesis of this book that the revolution was caused first by anger at the states for their betrayal of the sacred, united cause, and most urgently by the need to raise revenue for the national defense. Others have suggested that the motivating purpose of the Constitution was to allow Congress to regulate commerce, to suppress insurrection, to umpire territory disputes among the states, or to allow creditors who authored the Constitution to get paid. Those factors, however, upon inspection look peripheral, as explained in the next chapters.

[1]   U.S. CONST., art. I, §8 (Congress may tax), art. VI, §2 (federal law supreme).

CHAPTER EIGHT

The Modest and Mercantile
Commerce Clause

The Constitution gives Congress the power to "regulate Commerce with foreign Nations, and among the several States, and with the Indian tribes."[2] Contemporaries listed regulation of commerce as one of the Constitution's major purposes.[3] Indeed, the commerce clause is even now said to be a "strong impetus for calling the Constitutional Convention."[4] A review of the historical record does not support that view. Regulation of commerce is best seen as a modest, even trivial power. Under the best understanding, it contributed little to the adoption of the Constitution.

"Regulation of commerce" was sometimes a synonym for nationalizing the state imposts to give Congress a source of revenue to restore the public credit.

---

[2] U.S. Const., art. I, §8, cl. 3. This chapter is a short summary of Calvin Johnson, *The Panda's Thumb: The Modest and Mercantilist Original Intent of the Commerce Clause*, 13 Wm & Mary Bill of Rights J. 1 (2004).

[3] Washington's cover letter transmitting the Convention's draft of the Constitution to the old Congress listed five new powers, saying that the desire was for the national government to have the power "to make war, peace, and treaties, levy money and to regulate commerce." [George Washington] the President of the Federal Convention to the President of Congress (Sept. 17, 1787), *in* Documents Illustrative of the Formation of the Union of the American States 1003 (Charles C. Tansill, ed. 1927). *See also* Madison to Jefferson (Mar. 18, 1786), *in* 8 JM 501 (saying that "most of our political evils may be traced to our commercial ones") Anti-Federalist Richard Henry Lee treated the commerce power as the motivation for the Constitution in his letter to George Mason of May 15, 1787, 3 PGM at 877.

> The present causes of complaint seem to be, that Congress cannot command the money necessary for the just purposes of paying debts, or for supporting the federal government; and that they cannot make treaties of commerce, unless power unlimited, of regulating trade be given.

[4] Robert J. Steamer, *Commerce Power* in Oxford Companion to the Supreme Court of the United States 167 (Kermit Hall, ed., 1992).

Nationalizing the impost was indeed important. Federal power over imposts, however, is given by the tax clause, the first clause of the powers of Congress,[5] so that the power to regulate commerce does not add anything for tax. Other than tax, none of the programs espoused at the time under the cover of "regulation of commerce" ever amounted to much.

To understand words of a historical document, one must first understand the core programs that words were written to further.[6] We can understand a vague and malleable phrase like "regulation of commerce" only by seeing through the words to look at the programs that lie under the cover of the phrase. When the Constitution came into effect, Congress chose not to adopt the nontax programs previously mentioned under the words "regulation of commerce" even with the constitutional authorization. The congressional rejection of the defining programs once it had the authority, acts as a referendum or opinion poll, as close to the founding as we can expect, showing that what the programs meant by "regulation of commerce" did not in fact have sufficient political support, once the country had considered the issues more deliberately. Programs without sufficient political support to be enacted, once they were authorized and thought about, cannot be considered strong factors in the adoption of the Constitution.

It is also not uncommon to find the commerce power misdescribed as "a part of the liberal, free trade tradition."[7] In the constitutional debates, however, "regulation of commerce," was a synonym for a set of mercantilist programs that would restrict imports or grant monopoly privileges. Mercantilist economics, which was dominant at the time, held that the wealth of the nation would be improved by government intervention. "Regulation of commerce," meant first nationalizing the state imposts, so as to have an effective tax that would suppress luxurious imports, as it raised revenue. Beyond tax, the proponents of the Constitution meant to allow the federal government to grant monopolies or franchises, protecting American ships and merchants. "Regulation of commerce" was also meant to allow a punitive impost on British ships to convince the British to open up the ports of the British West Indies to American ships. There was no substantial debate or program in 1787–1788 within the category of interstate commerce and the Founders

---

5 U.S. CONST., art. I, §8, cl. 1.

6 *See, e.g.,* Quentin Skinner, *Meaning and Understanding the History of Ideas* in MEANING AND UNDERSTANDING: QUENTIN SKINNER AND HIS CRITICS 3, 55–65, 260 (James Tully, ed., 1988).

7 *See, e.g.,* John O. McGinnis & Mark L. Movsesian, *The World Trade Constitution*, 114 HARV. L. REV. 511, 527 (2000).

saw no substantial burdens on interstate commerce that needed to be liberalized or even discussed.

A. NATIONALIZING THE STATE IMPOSTS

The most common reference of "regulation of commerce" in the constitutional debates was to the program of nationalizing the New York and other state imposts. With federalization, the impost would serve to pay the war debts, and not be used for exclusively state purposes. New York had vetoed a 1783 proposal to give the federal government a tax of its own, the 5 percent impost.[8] New York would veto again if given the chance, it was said, so as to tax her neighbors "by the regulation of her trade."[9] New Jersey repudiated the 1786 requisition based on the argument that New Jersey had paid enough tax already because it received its imports through New York and Philadelphia.[10] New Jersey, placed between Philadelphia and New York without a deep-water harbor of its own, was "a Cask tapped at both ends."[11] In Connecticut, the proponents of the Constitution warned that those "gentlemen in New York who receive large salaries ... know that their offices will be more insecure ... when the expenses of government shall be paid by their constituents, than while paid by us."[12] New York had rendered Connecticut and New Jersey tributary to New York, *Publius* said, by its "commercial regulations."[13]

Regulation of commerce, first, meant collecting tax from it. Collecting revenue from the impost required a uniform tax along the entire coast because when one state tried to increase its rates, a neighboring port could destroy the revenue by undercutting rates to capture more commerce. Only

---

[8] KAMINSKI, CLINTON 89–96 (1993). New York, in form, merely set new conditions on approval, including a New York state officer being appointed to collect the revenue and New York paper money being accepted for the tax, but the conditions were understood on both sides to be tantamount to veto. New York paper would not help pay Dutch or French or Pennsylvania creditors. Any allowance given to New York would mean allowances at least as indulgent for all other states.

[9] Nathaniel Gorham, Federal Convention (July 23, 1787), *in* 2 FARRAND 90.

[10] VOTES AND PROCEEDING OF THE GENERAL ASSEMBLY OF THE STATE OF NEW JERSEY 12, Sess. 10, 2d sitting (1786). *See* RUTH BOGIN, ABRAHAM CLARK AND THE QUEST FOR EQUALITY IN THE REVOLUTIONARY ERA, 1774–1794, at 127–131 (1982).

[11] Madison, Preface to Debates in the Convention of 1787 (c. 1830), *in* 3 FARRAND 542.

[12] *Editorial*, NEW ENGLAND CONNECTICUT COURANT (Dec. 24, 1787), *reprinted in* 15 DHRC 82.

[13] *Federalist* No. 7, at 40 (Hamilton) (Nov. 17, 1787).

the general government could regulate commerce to make it productive of general revenue.[14]

Federal imposts were relatively popular taxes under the mercantilist economics of the time because they would suppress imports. Imports drained specie that would facilitate domestic trades. One "Honestus" blamed New York's economic problems on the unfavorable balance of trade that drew gold and silver out of New York. Merchants were the "bane and pest" of the country, Honestus claimed, because without them, luxuries would not be imported in such huge volume.[15] Imports were a kind of puritan sin. Tench Coxe condemned the "ineffectual" federal government under the Articles for its inability to control the "wonton consumption" of imported luxuries.[16] "Devoid of national power," James Wilson regretted, "we could not prohibit the extravagance of our importations nor could we derive a revenue from their excess."[17] Wise commercial regulations, claimed one Federalist, would reduce imports of foreign luxuries in foreign ships to one-tenth of what they were at the time.[18] We need a controlling Union government to regulate commerce, George Washington wrote, to balance against the "luxury, effiminacy and corruption" introduced by foreign trade.[19]

Clause 1 of Article 1, Section 8 gives Congress the power to tax and lists imposts as one of the taxes that Congress is allowed, provided only that the rates for the impost be uniform across the states. The Constitution also

[14] *See, e.g.*, Charles Carroll's Plan of Government (July 23, 1787), *reprinted in* Philip A. Crowl, AM HIST. REV. 588, 591 (1941) (saying that Congress needs exclusive power over regulation of trade by duties on trade because uniformity in duties on imports from foreign countries is necessary to effectual, nonoppressive collection of the duties); One of the Middle Interest, MASSACHUSETTS GAZETTE Dec. 5, 1787, *reprinted in* 4 DHRC 387 ("For if one State makes a law to prohibit foreign goods of any kind, or to draw a revenue, from an imposition upon such goods, another State is sure to take the advantage, and to admit such goods free of costs. By this means it is well known how the trade of Massachusetts is gone to Connecticut, and that for want of a revenue, our own *State taxes* are increased."); Thomas Dawes, Massachusetts Convention (Jan. 21, 1788), *in* 2 ELLIOT 58 (saying that state imposts drive the trade to neighboring states); "Z," PHILADELPHIA FREEMAN's J. (May 16, 1787), *in* 13 DHRC 99 ("The States individually cannot, with any success pretend to regulate trade. The duties and restrictions which one State imposes, the neighbouring States enable the merchants to elude."); Madison, Preface To Debates in the Convention of 1787 (c. 1830), *in* 3 FARRAND 547 (saying that want of a general congressional power over commerce led to an exercise of this power separately by the States, engendered undercutting rivalry and "vain attempts to supply their respective treasuries by imposts").

[15] Honestus, NEW YORK PACKET (Mar. 27, 1785), *quoted in* KAMINSKI, CLINTON at 99.

[16] TENCH COXE, AN ENQUIRY INTO PRINCIPLES ON WHICH A COMMERCIAL SYSTEM SHOULD BE FOUNDED (1787) (regretting that "ineffectual and disjointed" federal government should not be able to overcome the "wonton" consumption of imported luxuries).

[17] Wilson, Pennsylvania Convention (Nov. 26, 1787), *in* 2 ELLIOT 431.

[18] John Howard to George Thatcher (Feb. 27, 1788), *in* 16 DHRC 230.

[19] *See, e.g.*, Washington to James Warren (Oct. 7, 1785), *in* 3 PGW:CS 298, 299–300.

separately prohibits states from imposing their own imposts, except with the permission of Congress.[20] Although in the usage of the times, "tax" on commerce and "regulation" of commerce were often synonyms, we now also tend to call a tax on imports just a "tax" issue, fully authorized by Clause 1. The power to regulate commerce added nothing as to nationalization of the state imposts to the power that was granted elsewhere.

B. THE NAVIGATION ACTS

"Regulation of commerce" was also commonly a reference to proposals to impose a retaliatory impost or embargo on foreign ships coming into American ports so as to convince foreign powers to open up their ports to American ships.[21] The core grievance was that Great Britain, under the British Navigation Act, granted a monopoly to its own vessels for entry into its West Indies possessions in an attempt to capture the profits of shipping for its own nationals. When the American states were still colonies, the purpose of giving a monopoly to British shipping included American ships within the monopoly and it was quite popular in the colonies. When America was a colony, there was also an active trade between the West Indies and American

---

[20] U.S. CONST., art. 1, §10, cl. 2.
[21] See, e.g., James Monroe to Madison (July 26, 1785), in 8 JM 329 (Virginia congressional delegate explains that Congress has proposed to be granted the power to regulate commerce to obtain reciprocity from other nations); Motion in the Virginia House of Delegates (Nov. 30, 1785), in 1 ELLIOT 114 (proposing to allow Congress to embargo or tax any foreign vessel so as to obtain privileges in foreign ports for U.S. vessels); John Rutledge, Speech at the Federal Convention (Aug. 29, 1787), in 2 FARRAND 452 (saying that gaining access to the West Indies is the "great object" of regulating commerce); Federalist No. 11, at 67 (Hamilton) (Nov. 24, 1787) (advocating a government in America, capable of excluding Great Britain from all ports); Dissent of the Minority of the Pennsylvania Convention (Dec. 18, 1987), in 15 DHRC 14 (Anti-Federalists regretting that "we were suffering from the restrictions of foreign nations, who had shackled our commerce, while we were unable to retaliate"); Randolph, Reasons for not Signing the Constitution (Dec. 27, 1787), in 8 DHRC 260, 265 (saying that the states cannot organize retaliation against foreign nations and what is needed is "exclusion . . . opposed to exclusion and restriction to restriction"); Charles Pinckney, South Carolina House of Representatives (Jan. 16, 1788), in 4 ELLIOT 253–254 (saying that the first great inconvenience of the Confederation was the "destruction of our commerce, occasioned by the restrictions of other nations, whose policy it was not in the power of the general government to counteract"); James Bowdoin, Massachusetts Convention (Jan. 23, 1788), in 2 ELLIOT 83 (saying that trade is in a miserable state because other nations can prohibit our vessels from entering their ports or lay heavy duties on our exports, and we cannot prevent it because Congress has no retaliating or regulating power over their vessels and exports); William R. Davie, North Carolina Convention (July 24, 1788), in 4 ELLIOT 18 (arguing that the United States should be empowered to compel foreign nations into commercial regulations and counter British insults).

ports. Dutch, French, and Spanish traders were blocked out. When America achieved independence, however, Britain decided that there was no reason to let American vessels into its West Indian ports.[22]

The grievance against the British was generalized to include the power to retaliate against France and Spain for similar exclusions. All great trading nations were said to have tried "to secure to themselves the advantages of their carrying trade."[23] John Jay complained that because of American "imbecility," all the empires were imposing "commercial restraints upon us" so that there was "not one English, French or a Spanish island or port in the West-Indies to which an American vessel can carry a cargo of flour for sale."[24]

A retaliatory impost or embargo required a uniform policy for all American ports, just as did a revenue-productive impost. When Massachusetts tried to impose a penalty tax on British ships to force open the ports of the British West Indies, other states undercut Massachusetts by welcoming British ships into their ports.[25] Only a federal-level embargo or impost could prevent neighboring states from giving an easy and free end run around the intended penalties.

The proposal to impose a retaliatory impost against the British, however, came to naught. When Madison proposed a retaliation against the British in the first session of the new Congress, the Senate, led by the New York merchants, stripped the anti-British discrimination features from the 1789 impost bill.[26] Great Britain was allowing American ships into the British home ports without restriction or discrimination and opponents of retaliation reasonably feared that Britain would retaliate in turn if faced with American port restrictions.[27] Madison's

---

[22] LORD SHEFFIELD, OBSERVATIONS ON THE COMMERCE OF THE UNITED STATES 264–265 (6th ed. 1784), *described in* JOHN E. CROWLEY, THE PRIVILEGES OF INDEPENDENCE: NEOMERCANTILISM AND THE AMERICAN REVOLUTION 81–83 (1993) and ELKINS & MCKITRICK 69 (1993).

[23] Thomas Russell, Massachusetts Convention (Feb. 1, 1788), *in* 2 ELLIOT 139.

[24] JAY, ADDRESS TO THE PEOPLE OF THE STATE OF NEW YORK 7 (Sept. 17, 1787), *reprinted in* PAMPHLETS ON THE CONSTITUTION.

[25] Gaspard Joseph Amand Ducher to Comte de la Luzerne (Feb. 2, 1788), *in* 16 DHRC 13 (saying that Massachusetts and New Hampshire had both attempted an exclusion of British ships to punish Britain for its strictness against American commerce, but had suspended the attempt because the competing ports in other states would not join the embargo and so got the advantage of British ships newly attracted to their ports).

[26] ELKINS & MCKITRICK at 766, n. 66 collects the evidence for the New York merchants opposing discrimination.

[27] *Editorial note, in* 12 JM 55. *Cf.* John Laurence, House of Representatives (April 21, 1789), *in* 1 ANNALS 192 (arguing that England does not now discriminate against American vessels coming into England).

plan for discrimination against the British failed to be part of the enacted impost.[28]

A retaliatory impost against British shipping probably never was a good idea. There were not very many British ships coming into American ports against which to retaliate because American shipping was on its way to monopolizing transatlantic shipping by successful competition and good American oak. By 1796, American ships were carrying more than 90 percent of the transatlantic commerce.[29] A penalty against British ships would not have been much of an economic stick, even if it extinguished the last of them. Penalties would also have angered the British, perhaps into retaliation against American ships going into British ports. American shipping could not afford a trade-restriction war with Great Britain that denied access to the British home ports. The British West Indies prohibitions on American ships, moreover, were porous; the islands themselves were happy to encourage evasion around the prohibitions on American ships.[30]

Another set of reference of the phrase, "regulation of commerce," was to proposals to imitate the British Navigation Act and grant American shippers the same privileges that the Framers were objecting to when it was British shippers with the monopoly. An American Navigation Act would have required that all American commodities be exported only on American ships.[31]

---

[28] An Act for Laying Duties on Goods, Wares and Merchandise Imported in the United States, July 4, 1789, 1 STAT. 24–27. May 16 and May 26, 1789, *in* 1 ANNALS 365–366, 409 (5 percent impost passes but discrimination defeated).

[29] ELKINS & MCKITRICK at 414 (93 percent).

[30] *See, e.g., id.*, at 131 (finding a treaty opening West Indies would just confirm what was already accessible informally).

[31] *See, e.g.*, Mason, Federal Convention (Sept. 15, 1787), *in* 2 FARRAND 631 (Madison Notes), 635 (King Notes) (asking for a two-thirds majority for the adoption of Navigation Acts to prevent "a few rich merchants" in New York, Philadelphia, and Boston from monopolizing shipping and reducing the value of southern crops by perhaps one-half); The Landholder VI, CONNECTICUT COURANT (Dec. 10, 1787), *reprinted in* 3 FARRAND 164 (arguing that Mason opposed the Constitution because "a navigation act might otherwise be passed excluding foreign bottoms from carrying American produce to market, and throw a monopoly of the carrying business into the hands of the eastern states who attend to navigation"); Thomas Dawes, Massachusetts Convention (Jan. 21, 1788), *in* 2 ELLIOT 58 (objecting that without the Constitution's regulation of commerce, "a vessel from Roseway or Halifax finds as hearty a welcome with its fish and whalebone at the southern ports, as though it was built, navigated, and freighted from Salem or Boston"); Thomas Russell, Massachusetts Convention (Feb. 1, 1788), *in* 2 ELLIOT 139 (arguing that Congress should confine shipping to American vessels, just as all the great trading nations have benefited "from securing to themselves the advantages of their carrying trade"); Hugh Williamson, Speech at Edenton, North Carolina (Nov. 8, 1787) *printed in* DAILY ADVERTISER (NEW YORK) (Feb. 25–27, 1788), *reprinted in* 2 DEBATE 231 (saying that "[b]y the sundry regulations of commerce, it will be in the power of Government not only to collect a vast revenue for

The Constitution was written long before Adam Smith, laissez faire, and free trade came to dominate economic philosophy.[32] The Founders were arch-mercantilists. In true mercantilist terms, James Madison traced most of our political and moral errors to an absence of regulation of foreign commerce and an unfavorable balance of trade, which drained us of our precious specie.[33] Hamilton denounced the argument that trade would regulate itself as a "wild speculative paradox[]... contrary to the sense of the most enlightened nations."[34] Governor James Bowdoin argued that the well-being of trade depended on the proper regulation of it, and that unregulated trade would ruin rather than enrich those who carry it on.[35] George Washington argued that "it behoves us to place [commerce] in its most convenient channels, under proper regulation – freed as much as possible from those vices which luxury ... naturally introduces."[36] Madison denounced those who were "decoying the people into a belief that trade ought to be left to regulate itself."[37]

"Regulation of commerce" covered other restrictions on competition. In April 1785, a committee of Boston merchants voted to petition to give Congress immediate power to regulate the trade of the United States. The immediate complaint was that British merchants residing in Boston had received large quantities of English goods, which were said to be "calculated to drain us of our currency" and "impoverish this country."[38] The merchants also resolved not to lease or sell warehousing to any British merchant and they asked that Massachusetts naval officers prevent goods destined for the British merchants from being landed. In this case, "regulation of commerce" was meant not so much to deny American consumers access to foreign goods, but to give Boston merchants the full profits from the goods and protect

general benefit of the nation, but to secure the carrying trade in the hands of citizens in preference to strangers"); Hamilton, New York Convention (June 20, 1788), *in* 2 ELLIOT 236 (saying that it was in the interest of the northern states that "they should have full power, by a majority in Congress, to make commercial regulations in favor of their own, and in restraint of the navigation of foreigners").

[32] *See, e.g.*, DOUGLAS IRWIN, AGAINST THE TIDE: AN INTELLECTUAL HISTORY OF FREE TRADE 80 (1996) (Adam Smith's free trade ideas did not begin to get cited as orthodoxy among economists until at least a quarter century after they were published in 1776).

[33] Madison to Jefferson (Mar. 18, 1786), *in* 8 JM 501.

[34] Hamilton, Continentalist V (April 18, 1782), *in* 3 PAH 75, 76.

[35] Debate in the Massachusetts Convention (Feb. 1, 1788), *in* 2 ELLIOT 129.

[36] Washington to Jefferson (Mar. 29, 1784), *in* 1 PGW:CS 239.

[37] Madison to James Monroe (Aug. 20, 1785), *in* 8 JM 102.

[38] *Monthly Chronology for April, 1785*, THE BOSTON MAGAZINE, APRIL 4, 1785, at 155–156.

them from British merchants who had come to our shore to reduce prices to consumers.

In the spirit of mercantilism, Madison had sponsored a port bill in the Virginia Assembly in 1784, which would have required that all trade between Virginians and foreign ports had to be conducted out of a single Virginia port.[39] The monopoly given to one port, later expanded to many ports, was intended to give an incentive to the port city to charge higher prices to be able to develop the port facilities. The port preferences have been said to be the "economic centerpiece" of the Madison's Virginia coalition out of which the constitutional movement arose.[40] Both Thomas Jefferson[41] and George Washington[42] supported the port-monopoly idea.

As with retaliation against the British exclusions, nothing came of the suggestion for adoption of an American Navigation Act or any other of the monopoly restrictions. To Madison's regret, the Constitutional Convention itself rejected port preferences, prohibiting preferences "given by any Regulation of Commerce or Revenue to the Ports of one State over those of another."[43] The Constitution itself also cut the heart out of the idea for an American Navigation Act by prohibiting Congress from imposing any tax on exports.[44] The prohibition on tax on exports meant that Congress could not give a differential tax advantage to American ships in the carrying of southern commodities. Congress would have had to take the far more radical step of banning foreign ships from carrying U.S. exports entirely and Congress never seriously considered a complete prohibition. On the import side, where tax was allowed, Congress did discriminate for a while against imports on foreign ships. The first tonnage fees imposed a tax of six cents per ton on U.S.-owned ships, but fifty cents per ton on foreign-owned

---

[39] Madison to James Monroe (June 21, 1785), *in* 8 JM 306, 307.

[40] BRUCE A. RAGSDALE, A PLANTERS' REPUBLIC: THE SEARCH FOR ECONOMIC INDEPENDENCE IN REVOLUTIONARY VIRGINIA 269 (1996).

[41] Jefferson to Madison (Nov. 11, 1784), *in* 8 JM 127.

[42] RAGSDALE, *supra* note 40, at 149.

[43] U.S. CONST. art. I, sec. 9, cl. 6. *See* Mssrs. Carroll and Luther Martin (Aug. 25, 1787), *in* 2 FARRAND 417 (arguing that Congress might enact port preferences, requiring "vessels belonging or bound to Baltimore, to enter and clear at Norfolk [Virginia]"). Madison to Edmund Pendleton (Oct. 28, 1787), *in* 10 JM 223 (regretting that the port preference prohibition was "dictated by the jealousy of some particular States, and was inserted pretty late in the Session").

[44] U.S. CONST. art. I, sec. 9 cl. 5.

ships.[45] Discrimination was gutted by the Jay Treaty of 1794, however, which obligated the United States and Great Britain to stop putting higher taxes on each other's ships,[46] and it seems to have been ended for all foreign ships in 1799 when general impost rates were raised to 10 percent.[47] The call for a monopoly for American ships to carry American commodities never had enough support even to get debated in Congress. Proposals that came naught by reason of insufficient support, even once permitted, do not add importance to the modest commerce clause.

C. INTERSTATE COMMERCE

The important programs under the commerce clause were deep-water shipping issues, involving the British and American Navigation Acts and the state taxes on imports. The commerce clause, however, also gives Congress the power to regulate commerce with the Indian tribes and among the several states. It is now commonly said that the major purpose of the commerce clause was to prevent protectionist economic policies among the states and to establish a common market with free trade across state borders.[48] That statement is a misdescription because the Founders liked a lot of protectionist policies, and because interstate commerce was not in fact important in the constitutional debates.

Reducing barriers on interstate trade is not an important part of the constitutional debates, mostly because the goal had already been accomplished. The Articles of Confederation had already prohibited any state from imposing a

---

[45] An Act for imposing duties on tonnage, 1st Cong., 1st Sess. ch. 3, 1 Stat. 27 (July 20, 1789) renewed, An Act imposing duties on the tonnage of ships or vessels, ch. 30, 1 Stat. 135 (July 30, 1790).

[46] Treaty of Amity, Commerce and Navigation [Jay Treaty], Art. III, XV (concluded Nov. 124, 1794, ratified Feb. 1795, and promulgated Feb. 29, 1796), *in* SAMUEL FLAGG BEMIS, JAY'S TREATY: A STUDY IN COMMERCE AND DIPLOMACY 333–34 (1921).

[47] An Act to regulate the collection of duties on imports and tonnage, ch. 22, §61 (March 2, 1799) (imposing tax of 10 percent of cost). Imports from beyond the Cape of Good Hope were taxed at 20 percent of cost (*id.*), presumably because they would have a far larger mark up than imports, *e.g.*, from Europe, and the statute was using cost as an estimate of value.

[48] H. P. Hood & Sons, Inc. v. Du Mond, 336 U.S. 525, 533, 535 (1949) (saying that a "chief occasion" of the commerce clause was "the mutual jealousies and aggressions of the States, taking form in customs barriers and other economic retaliation" and that the *sole* purpose for which Virginia initiated the movement that ultimately produced the Constitution was to allow Congress to examine the trade of the states and consider a uniform system of commercial regulation); Winkfield F. Twyman, Jr., *Justice Scalia and Facial Discrimination: Some Notes on Legal Reasoning*, 18 VA. TAX REV. 103, 108 (1998) (arguing that the Articles of Confederation had been unable to stem disruptive protectionism among the several states, thus threatening the life of the infant republic).

"duty, imposition or restriction" on any out-of-state citizens that it did not impose on its own inhabitants.[49] The states seem to have largely followed the norm, well enough that the issue did not make it among the issues the debaters talked about. Consistent with the norm and with the mandate of the Articles, the state imposts almost always exempted American source goods from tax. The New York impost that was a major irritant to its neighbors exempted goods and merchandise of the growth and manufacture of the United States.[50] The Pennsylvania impost, which also drained New Jersey, also had an exemption for goods of the "growth, produce or manufacture of the United States or any of them."[51] The Massachusetts and North Carolina imposts had the same exemption.[52] Virginia had a 2-/12 percent impost on goods from "any port or place whatsoever,"[53] which was a violation of the norm, but Virginia was shamed into giving an exemption for goods of American growth or manufacture in January 1, 1788, at which time it also increased the tax rate to 3 percent.[54] The Virginia impost, before amendment, was a violation of the norms against interstate tolls, but it was repealed by Virginia's shame.

Protecting out-of-state Americans against discrimination by a state was an established and important norm in the debates, but the norm shows up almost entirely outside of the commerce clause. The Constitution prohibits states from issuing paper money, and in the constitutional debates, the prohibition was said to be necessary to prevent "aggressions on the rights of other States"[55] and injury to the citizens of other States.[56] Paper money was a trick, Governeur Morris explained, "by which Citizens of other States may

---

[49] ARTICLES OF CONFEDERATION, art. IV (providing that the people of each state shall have free ingress and regress to and from any other state, and shall enjoy therein "all the privileges of trade and commerce, subject to the same duties, impositions, and restrictions as the inhabitants thereof respectively").

[50] 1 Laws of the State of NY (1774–84), March 22, 1784, p. 599, ch x, II. *See* William Frank Zarnow, *New York Tariff Policies, 1775–1789,* 37 NEW YORK HISTORY: PROCEEDINGS OF THE NEW YORK HISTORICAL ASSOCIATION 40, 47 (1956) (New York exemptions).

[51] Act of December 23, 1780, ch. 190, section 21, First Laws of the Commonwealth of Pennsylvania 427 (1984).

[52] Act and Laws of the Commonwealth of Massachusetts, 1783, ch. 12, p. 17.

[53] 11 Hennings Statutes at Large of Virginia, ch. 38, §14 p. 70 (1781); Act of May 1784, Ch. xiii, section 2, at 8 (raising rate from 1 percent to 2 ½ percent).

[54] 12 HENNINGS STATUTES AT LARGE OF VIRGINIA, ch. 1, §5 p. 416 (1788).

[55] Madison, Vices of the Political System of the United States (April 1787), *in* 9 JM 350.

[56] *Federalist* No. 44, at 301 (Madison) (Jan. 25, 1788) (arguing if states were given the power to issue money "the intercourse among them would be impeded; retrospective alterations in its value might be made, and thus the citizens of other States be injured; and animosities kindled among the States themselves").

be affected."[57] State paper money is also specifically prohibited, outside of the commerce clause.[58] The Continental dollar, in becoming worthless, has stolen from all those who held it, and that alone seems sufficient to explain the ban on paper money.

Hamilton did use the specter of trade barriers to scare voters toward ratification of the Constitution. In *Federalist* Number 22, Hamilton argued that if the Constitution were not ratified, the various states would impose multiple duties on interstate transportation, much as the separate German states imposed tolls on the great rivers that flow through Germany.[59] The thrust of the complaints, however, is not about any existing barriers under the Articles, but rather as a threat of what might happen if the United States fell apart into separate sovereignties. Hamilton's example of interstate barriers came from the German empire, not here. Tolls on interstate commerce would require not just a failure to ratify the Constitution, under Hamilton's argument, but also a repeal of the Articles of Confederation prohibition on interstate barriers, as well as an over-riding of the "genius of the American people."[60] For Hamilton, interstate tolls were a goblin in the closet used to scare undecided voters, but were not a current or eminent threat.

When Madison recorded the Convention's agreeing to the commerce clause, without discussion or opposition, on August 16, 1787, he described the clause as the "[c]lause for regulating commerce with foreign nations and &c."[61] Regulation of commerce between the states and regulation of trade with the Indians share only the space allowed by Madison's "&c." So similarly, Anti-Federalist Agrippa summarized the Federalist case, as he saw it, that "the complaints of the deficiency of the Congressional powers are confined to two articles. They are not able to raise a revenue by taxation, and they have not a complete regulation of the intercourse between us and *foreigners*."[62] There was no issue of interstate intercourse in Agrippa's understanding of the argument in favor of the Constitution. As one superb review of the

---

[57] Gouverneur Morris, Federal Convention (July 17, 1787), *in* 2 FARRAND 26.

[58] U.S. CONST.art. I, §10, cl. 1.

[59] *Federalist* No. 22, at 137 (Hamilton) (Dec. 14, 1787). *Accord*, Publicola, *Address to the Freemen of North Carolina*, STATE GAZETTE OF NORTH CAROLINA (Mar. 27, 1788), *reprinted in* 16 DHRC 495 (saying that if North Carolina did not ratify, then the other states would "treat us as foreigners" and preclude commerce with them or impose imposts that would annihilate trade).

[60] *Id.*

[61] 2 FARRAND 308.

[62] Agrippa VIII, MASSACHUSETTS GAZETTE, Dec. 5, 1787, *reprinted in* 5 DHRC 516 (emphasis added).

evidence put it, "the thing that strikes one's attention in seeking reference to interstate commerce is their paucity."[63] The commerce clause was "a modest little power,"[64] preventing threats that were not plausible and allowing programs the nation did not want.

---

[63] Albert S. Abel, *The Commerce Clause in the Constitutional Convention and in Contemporary Comment*, 25 MINN. L. REV. 470 (1941).

[64] *Id.* at 481.

CHAPTER NINE

Creditors, Territories, and Shaysites

Various scholars of the Constitution have seriously proposed that the motive for the document was to serve the economic interests of creditors by allowing them to collect against hard-pressed debtors, that the purpose of the Constitution was to settle territory disputes among the states, or that the motive for the Constitution was to suppress popular unrest like that of Shays's Rebellion. All of those explanations, however, seem quite minor on examination as a factor in the switch to the new Constitution.

A. CREDITORS[!]

Charles Beard, in his famed *Economic Interpretation of the Constitution*, argued that the Constitution was originated and carried to adoption by a small group of men who held public securities and private debt and who wanted to get paid. Ratification, in Beard's view, was a battle of creditor proponents of the Constitution against an opposition consisting of agricultural interests and honest debtors.[1] The Constitution had two fundamental parts, Beard argued: One part created the national government, and the other part imposed "[r]estrictions on the state legislatures which had been so vigorous in their attacks on capital."[2] Professor Gordon Wood has argued, more recently, that although Beard was strictly wrong on part of his thesis, still the Constitution arose more than anything else from a desire to prevent debtor relief legislation in the states.[3]

---

[1] BEARD 324. *See also* FERGUSON at 337–338, 340–341 (1961) (arguing that as a group creditors supported the Constitution).

[2] BEARD at 154.

[3] Gordon S. Wood, *Interests and Disinterests in the Making of the Constitution, in* BEYOND CONFEDERATION 69.

The Constitution does in fact prohibit the states from issuing paper money and from impairing the obligation of contracts, including contractual debt.[4] Both Hamilton and Madison treat state paper money as an evil that will be fixed by the Constitution.[5] For Madison, the states had been irresponsible both in failing to pay their requisitions, which left the national government impotent and imbecilic, and in enacting debtor relief legislation. The failure to pay war debts and the failure to pay private debts, according to Madison, were parallel blots "on the character of Republican Government" chargeable against the states.[6] Both "excite[d] the disgusts agst the state governments."[7] Both failures were "Vices of the U.S. Political System," both were evils sponsored by Patrick Henry and opposed by Madison in Virginia, and both were to be cured by a strong national government.[8]

Of the two evils, the failure to pay the public debt must be understood as more serious than the defaults on the private debts.[9] Defaults on the public debt would imperil the common defense in the coming war. Revenue to restore the public credit was the most desperate immediate need. It is most closely related to the revolutionary change the Constitution made to replace the federal assembly of sovereign states with a supreme tripartite national government. The problem of private debts does show up in the Constitution: In the ninth phrase of Clause 1 of Section 10 of Article 1, the Constitution prohibits the states from "impairing the obligation of Contracts," which is a remedy to stifle state debtor-relief legislation. The same clause prohibits states from issuing paper money, which would have made fixed debts easier to pay. Still the remedies aimed at private debtor relief seem no more important than their placement deep in the text indicates. The remedy for public debts is reflected by everything in the overall structure. The two defaults were the same kind of evil, however, and both excited disgust against the state governments.

---

4 U.S. Const. art. I, §10, cl. 1.

5 *Federalist* No. 10, at 65 (Madison) (Nov. 22, 1787) (condemning the "rage for paper money" and other "wicked" projects); *Federalist* No. 80, at 537 (Alexander Hamilton) (May 28, 1788) (arguing for federal control of "the fraudulent laws which have been passed in too many of the states").

6 *Federalist* No. 44, at 300 (Madison) (Jan. 25, 1788).

7 Madison to Thomas Jefferson (Sept. 6, 1787), *in* 10 JM 164.

8 *See* discussion, Chapter 2, pp. 51–60.

9 I share with Shlomo Slomin, *Motives at Philadelphia, 1787: Gordon Wood's Neo Beardian Thesis Reexamined*, 16 L. & Hist. Rev. 527 (1998) the conclusion that the state encroachments on individual rights are decidedly secondary, *but see* Madison to Jefferson (Oct. 24, 1787), *in* 10 JM 210 (saying that abuse of rights contributed more to uneasiness than failure of revenue).

Selfish creditor interest does not stand up well as an important contributory cause of the Constitution. The Founders were not creditors seeking payment, but rather debtors trying to restore their credit so that they could borrow again. Madison, Washington, and the Virginia slaveholder-planters who provided the leadership for the Constitution were deeply in debt. They borrowed to plant crops, to buy slaves and land, and to fund their lifestyle.[10] George Washington was a very wealthy man in terms of land and slaves, but he often complained that that he did not know whether his assets matched his obligations.[11] Madison, the most important Framer, held no public debt securities[12] and Madison's heir lost Montpelier to creditors upon the expiration of the widow's life estate held by Dolly Madison.[13] The Virginia leadership for the Constitution was land wealthy, but they were not creditors on net.[14] When the Virginia planters accumulated some excess capital they bought slaves or land, and not public securities.[15]

The creditors served by payment of debts were not generally Virginians. The public, federal-level debt was held outside of Virginia, first by the French and Dutch creditors, who had been willing to extend credit for the new nation to fight the Revolutionary War. In so far as public debt was held domestically, it was held disproportionately in the North, in the merchant and financial centers of Philadelphia and Boston.[16] The domestic security holders were

[10] *See, e.g.*, HERBERT E. SLOAN, PRINCIPLE AND INTEREST: THOMAS JEFFERSON AND THE PROBLEM OF DEBT 26–32, 34–37 (describing the Virginia planters' "thralldom" to debt). *Cf.* T.H. BREEN, TOBACCO CULTURE: THE MENTALITY FO TIDEWATER PLANTERS ON THE EVE OF THE REVOLUTION 84–123 (1985).

[11] RISJORD at 123.

[12] MCDONALD, WE, THE PEOPLE at 73.

[13] After Madison's death and the expiration of his widow's life estate, Madison's manor, Montpelier, was sold to pay the creditors. WILLIAM LEE MILLER, THE BUSINESS OF MAY NEXT: JAMES MADISON AND THE FOUNDING 1 (1992). Madison, however, seems to have been living well within his ample means during the period of the consideration of the Constitution. Editorial Note, Resolutions on Private Debts Owed to British Merchants, *in* 8 JM 58.

[14] *See, e.g.*, ALICE HANSON JONES, WEALTH OF A NATION TO BE : THE AMERICAN COLONIES ON THE EVE OF THE REVOLUTION, Tables 5.1 (1980) (reporting Southern financial liabilities at £8 million in 1774 and Southern financial claims assets at £2 million, but Middle Colony financial liabilities of £6 million and financial claims assets of £8 million).

[15] *See, e.g., id.*, tables 3.1, 5.1, 5.5 (1980) (securities were 27% of value of estates in Middle colonies in 1774, but only 4% of estates in Southern colonies; Southern physical assets were worth £61 million, slaves were worth £20 million, but Southern financial claims were worth only £2 million).

[16] As the "North American" explained, the people hurt by the failure of requisitions were the individuals "in commercial States attached to the American cause who had obeyed the public call" and relied on the "fidelity of their rulers" by holding federal debt. The North American No. 1, PENNSYLVANIA JOURNAL AND WEEKLY ADVERTISER (Sept. 17, 1783), *reprinted in* Irving Brant, *Two Neglected Madison Letters*, 3 WM. & MARY Q. 56, 572, 580 (1946) (attributed to Richard Peters of Philadelphia by *Editorial Note, in* 7 JM 319–363).

also "rather too few in number to serve as the fulcrum upon which to raise a new political structure."[17] The private creditors who lent to Virginians were British.[18] Madison did believe in the principle, with strong emotion, that debt must be paid, and the principle applied to both private or government debts. A Virginia gentleman paid his debts or at least he tried to.[19] Madison and his Virginia allies were not creditors seeking payment, however, but rather debtors trying to restore their credit so that they could borrow again.

Consistently, important national champions outside of Virginia were heavily in debt. Indeed, important Federalists including Robert Morris, James Wilson,[20] and Nathaniel Gorham[21] ended in debtors' prison or at least bankrupt and evading debtors' prison by hiding out. Robert Morris, the chief financial officer of the Congress in the later Confederation, seems to have bet on a decline in the value of federal securities and he was sent to debtor's prison, by reason of the Constitution, when ratification turned out to increase the value of the securities.[22]

Critics of Beard have shown that Federalists and Anti-Federalists were not distinguishable by their creditor holdings nor by their ownership of land. Robert Thomas and Forrest McDonald have shown that in general, the

---

[17]   FERGUSON at 285 (saying, however, that speculators did take advantage of the Constitution after the fact).

[18]   RISJORD at 110.

[19]   Thomas Nelson, who followed Jefferson and preceded Henry (second time) as governor of Virginia was a heavy debtor who publicly declared, "By God, I will pay my debts like an honest man," *quoted in* Emory G. Evans, *The Rise and Decline of the Virginia Aristocracy in the Eighteenth Century: The Nelsons, in* THE OLD DOMINION: ESSAYS FOR THOMAS PERKINS ABERNETHY 77 (Darrett B. Rutman, ed. 1964).

[20]   *James Wilson,* 4 ENCYCLOPEDIA OF THE AMERICAN CONSTITUTION 2067 (1986).

[21]   McDONALD, WE, THE PEOPLE at 43.

[22]   KETCHAM 146–148, McDONALD, HAMILTON 154, and Stanley Elkins & Eric McKitrick, *The Founding Fathers: Young Men of the Revolution,* 76 POL. SCI. Q. 181, 195 (June 1961) all argue that Robert Morris went bankrupt in part because he bet on the *decline* in value of federal "paper, bidding for the purchase of Western land in installments using cheap-to-buy federal paper that was treated at par in their bids." The increase in the value of the federal paper devastated him. James Ferguson, *Review of Forrest McDonald, E Pluribus Unum,* 23 WM. & MARY Q. (3d Series) 148, 150 (1966) contests the argument, saying that purchasers got credit only for the depreciated value of the securities in auctions of land sales. The installment sales, according to Ferguson, were a way by which the federal government redeemed its depreciated securities, paying only low value rather than the contracted-for face amount. Ferguson's argument is not a rebuttal because the buyers bidding the most for land with federal securities would be those most pessimistic about the value of the securities. That Morris "put" the securities to purchase land is fair evidence that Morris, bruised and battered from his hard times as financier for the Revolution, was pessimistic about the value of the securities.

Federalists and Anti-Federalists held the same kinds of property, with the same mix of farmland and debt investments, and the same mix of debtors and creditors.[23] Commonly it is the Anti-Federalist delegates who owned more public debt, and thus were the creditors who should have supported the Constitution in their self-interest.[24] Beard concluded that most of the support for the Constitution came from wealthy planters and security holders, and most of the opposition from small slave-less farmers and debtors, and McDonald found that "the precise opposite is nearer the truth." Public security holders were almost equally divided between support and opposition to the Constitution and the majority of the small farmers supported ratification. The wealthy planters were almost equally divided on ratification, McDonald says, but planter-debtors, and particularly the planters who had brought about the passage of laws preventing the collection of British debts, favored ratification by a substantial margin.[25] The authors of the Constitution, who met in Philadelphia, were overwhelmingly landowners.[26]

Anti-Federalists were also commonly savage to the debtor farmers who were supposed to be the heroes of opposition to the Constitution. George Mason, for example, is one of the most important Anti-Federalists. Mason had been an important ally of Madison's in Virginia in the 1780s insisting on payment of public and private debt.[27] George Mason was also a fervid opponent of book debt. Book debt is the tab that storekeepers kept as they let the farmers or small planters have goods and supplies on credit over the year. In 1779, Mason had convinced the Virginia Legislature to impose a six-month statute of limitations on book debt. The Legislature passed Mason's proposal and then repealed it the next year. Mason opposed the repeal because "excessive Credits ... upon open accounts necessarily tended

---

[23] Robert Thomas, *The Virginia Convention of 1788: A Criticism of Beard's 'An Economic Interpretation of the Constitution'*, 57 AM. HIST. REV. 570 (1952); McDONALD, WE, THE PEOPLE 73, 355–356 (1958). Forrest McDonald confirmed the result, except that he found that farmers from the interior disproportionately *supported* ratification. *Id.*, at 268. *See also* RISJORD at 294, 309 (Virginia west of the Piedmont is disproportionately Federalist).

[24] McDONALD, WE, THE PEOPLE at 350–351 (Anti-Federalist delegates to the Pennsylvania Ratification Convention owned on average twice as many securities as the pro-Constitution delegates, New York Anti-Federalists own more than New York Federalists). *But see, id.*, at 355–356 (Virginia, Massachusetts, and Rhode Island proponents and opponents own securities in about the same proportion).

[25] McDONALD, WE, THE PEOPLE at 283.

[26] James E. Viator, *Give Me That Old-time Historiography: Charles Beard and the Study of the Constitution (part 1)*, 36 LOY. L. REV. 981, 1007 (1991).

[27] *See, e.g.* RISJORD at 87.

to ruin." Mason thought that the book debt had reduced the planters to mere servants in the prewar years[28] and he wanted to end it. In a nation so short of hard currency of any kind, the general rule was that no one could sell except to someone they would give credit to. Book debt tended to be a very long-term debt, renewed over and over again, and managed rather than extinguished by the annual harvest. A six-month statute of limitations, as Mason wanted, would have required the shopkeeper to go to court for collection even before the harvest came in. Ending book debt, carried from year to year, would have been a very large change in the Virginia countryside. George Mason is one of the most important Anti-Federalists anywhere, but Mason is no friend of easy credit, nor of any deeply-in-debt yeoman farmer.

The Constitution does prohibit state issuance of paper money, but the issue does not divide the Federalists and Anti-Federalists.[29] The fall of the Continental dollar meant that the Anti-Federalists did not contest the Constitution's prohibition on issuance of state paper money. In the Virginia Ratification Convention, Patrick Henry found monsters hiding in almost every passage of this Constitution, but not in the prohibition of state paper money. Henry said that the prohibition on state issuance of paper money was wise because "paper money would be the bane of this country. I detest it." He claimed he was "at peace on this subject."[30] His ally William Grayson said that it was unanimously wished that the prohibition on state paper money should not be objected to.[31] Anti-Federalist Richard Henry Lee, outside the convention, expressed his preference for paper money to be issued by Congress only,[32] and Anti-Federalist James Monroe declared "let the individual states also be restrained from exercising improper power, making war, emitting paper bill of credit and the like."[33] Anti-Federalist George Mason had joined Madison in the decade before, passing a resolution that "paper money without backing would be destructive of public and private confidence" and the "virtue which [is] the basis of a republican government."[34] As

[28] A Bill for Discouraging Extensive Credit (Oct. 18, 1789), *in* 2 PGM 578; Fairfax County Petition Protesting Repeal of the Act to Prevent Extensive Credit, 2 *id.* at 786–787.
[29] Cecelia M. Kenyon, *Men of Little Faith: The Anti-Federalists on the Nature of Representative Government*, 12 WM. & MARY Q. 3 (3rd Series 1955) made this argument first.
[30] Patrick Henry, Virginia Convention (June 9, 1788), *in* 9 DHRC 1055.
[31] William Grayson, Virginia Convention (June 9, 1788), *in* 10 DHRC 1447.
[32] THE LETTERS OF RICHARD HENRY LEE 421–422 (J.C. Ballagh ed. 1911–1914).
[33] James Monroe, Some Observations on the Constitution (*c.* May 25, 1788), *in* 9 DHRC 845, 860.
[34] RISJORD at 153–154.

Risjord concludes, there was scarcely a politician anywhere in Virginia willing to advocate paper.[35] Similarly, in the crucial ratification state of New York, in which Anti-Federalist delegates were the initial majority, the Convention passed through discussion of the passages of the Constitution prohibiting state issuance of paper money, "with little or no debate."[36] The prohibition on paper money was not an issue that was contested or that distinguished Federalist and Anti-Federalist in what was otherwise an aggressive anti-ratification campaign.

The consensus against paper money can be attributed to the then recent collapse of the Continental dollar. The federal government had printed more than $200 million before 1780 to finance the war and the printed dollars turned out to be worthless paper.[37] Continental dollars would have held their value if the states had absorbed by taxation the excess of what was needed in trade, but the states, manifesting their wickedness, did not.[38] The collapse of the Continental dollar stole from everyone who touched it. State paper money had been as acceptable in the colonial period as necessary for trades so that the collapse of the Continental dollar seems to be what changed the public consensus.[39] The Constitution prohibition on paper money affects the states and not the federal government that issued the Continental dollar, but it is easy to trace responsibility for the collapse of the Continental dollar back to the sovereign states. The states were required to redeem the Continental dollar in specie or in tax and had utterly failed.[40] From that perspective, the Constitution's ban on paper money should be understood as still another manifestation of the anger of the Founders at the wickedness of the states. The failure of requisitions and failure of the paper dollar are twin instances of the states' dereliction of their duty toward the general welfare and their betrayal of the sacred cause.

---

[35] *Id.*, at 175. Risjord says that there were chronic fears that Patrick Henry would endorse paper money, but that Patrick Henry never publicly or privately did so. *See, however*, John Dawson to Madison (Sept. 28, 1787), *in* 10 JM 173 (saying that Henry "harangued" in favor of Virginia printing paper money).

[36] New York Convention (July 2, 1788), *in* 2 ELLIOT 406.

[37] FERGUSON at 30 ($226 million of old Continental dollar and $1.5 million of the new post-1780 dollar).

[38] *See* discussion, Chapter 1, pp. 33–34.

[39] Mary M. Schweitzer, *State-Issued Currency*, BEYOND CONFEDERATION at 314–315 (citing, for instance, Thomas Paine's change in attitude toward state paper money as due to the collapse of the Continental dollar).

[40] Thomas Jefferson, Notes on Debates on the Continental Congress (July 29, 1775), *in* 2 JCC 221 (resolving that each colony should redeem its share of the dollars by its own means). *See* discussion, Chapter 1, at 33–34 for failure to redeem.

Charles Beard interpreted the Constitution as a conservative economic document written to suppress paper money,[41] but that interpretation has more to do with the hopes and dreads of Beard's experience than with the Constitutional period. The Supreme Court of the 1890s, when Beard's thinking developed, was a conservative court that interpreted the Constitution to preclude government regulation of business.[42] Beard seems to have assumed, with the Court of his time, that the Constitution precluded business regulations and then attributed the pro-capital hobbles to the original founders.[43] Similarly, Beard was reacting to his own time in explaining the Constitution in terms of soft versus sound money. He was assuming, so to speak, that the purpose of the Constitution was to "crucify Mankind upon a Cross of Gold."[44] Soft versus hard money divided the nation in Beard's time, but it was not a divided question in the ratification period.

Ironically, it was Alexander Hamilton and his allies who proved to be the best friends of paper money in the new administration and it was the nascent Jeffersonian party that would oppose it. Among the reasons why the Federalists wanted a National Bank in 1791 was that there was too little specie circulating to accommodate the needs of internal sales and purchases. The Federalists wanted the national bank notes to serve as money as a substitute for gold or silver.[45] Bank notes would not be inflationary, under

---

[41] CHARLES BEARD, at 154, 324. The Beardian tradition continues with surprising strength. *See, e.g.,* JENSEN, NEW NATION 424–425; FERGUSON, at 241–245 (1961) (describing a class warfare between paper and hard money interests); WOOD at 626–627 (1969) (arguing that "the Constitution was in some sense an aristocratic document designed to curb the democratic excesses of the Revolution"); Gordon S. Wood, *Interests and Disinterests in the Making of the Constitution, in* BEYOND CONFEDERATION 69, 72 (saying that the Federalists were elites whose motive in suppressing paper money was to hold down the rising standard of living of the middle class, which threatened the elite status of the Framers).

[42] For an attack on the Constitutional doctrines that Beard was reacting against, *see, e.g.,* ARNOLD PAUL, CONSERVATIVE CRISIS AND THE RULE OF LAW: ATTITUDES OF BAR AND BENCH, 1887–1895 (1960).

[43] John Braeman, *Charles A. Beard: Historian and Progressive, in* CHARLES A. BEARD: AN OBSERVANCE OF THE CENTENNIAL OF HIS BIRTH (Marvin C. Swanson, ed. 1974) (arguing that Beard's interpretation arose out of the prevailing judicial interpretation of the Constitution that appeared to present an insuperable barrier to federal regulation of economic activity); Douglas Adair, *The Tenth Federalist Revisited, in* FAME AND THE FOUNDING FATHERS: ESSAYS BY DOUGLASS ADAIR 75 (1974) (arguing that Beard used *Federalist* No. 10 as a confession of guilt to reduce the legitimacy of the Constitution).

[44] William Jennings Bryan, "Cross of Gold," Democratic National Convention (July 9, 1896), *available at* http://douglass.speech.nwu.edu/brya_a26.htm (accessed Jan. 24, 2002).

[45] *See, e.g.,* Hamilton, Report on Public Credit (Jan. 1790), *in* 6 PAH 51, 70–72 (arguing for public debt as a substitute for money); Hamilton, Report on A National Bank (Dec. 12,

Hamilton's thinking, whereas state paper would be, because a bank would be willing to issue its debt only for credit-worthy borrowers able to repay the bank.[46] Bank-debt paper money would automatically be sound because it would be issued only with a clear expectation of payment. Jefferson opposed the bank and said that Hamilton's paper money was "clearly a demerit" of the bank plan.[47] Jefferson thought Hamilton would "deluge the states with paper money."[48] Anti-Federalism and Jeffersonianism are not the same, except in their common push for decentralization and against the general-level government. Still, if Hamilton defines the cause of the Constitution, then it is Hamilton who is in favor of federal paper money of a kind and Jefferson who actively opposed it. If anyone were to be treated as wanting to crucify mankind upon a cross of gold near the constitutional period, it would have to be Jefferson, not Hamilton.

B. TERRITORY

Historian Peter S. Onuf has argued that the territorial disputes between the states were the reason for the creation of the federal government. The states perceived a need for a strong central government to create harmony among themselves, Professor Onuf argues.[49] The chronic conflict between the states over territorial jurisdiction, combined with their unwillingness to go to war, he says, created a demand for a stronger central government to be an umpire to resolve the conflicts.[50] Professor Onuf argues both that fears of anarchy and of bloodshed were "vitally important in creating a climate favorable to the

---

1791), *in* 7 PAH 311, 320, 321 (saying that federal tax would be payable in bank notes and substitute for gold and silver, and that without money trades would be reduced to barter). *Cf.* Theodore Sedgwick, House of Representatives (Feb. 4, 1791), *in* 1 ANNALS 1963 (arguing that the bank would allow precious metals to be retained in circulation).

[46] Hamilton, Report on a National Bank (Dec. 12, 1791), *in* 7 PAH 322 (saying that bank notes were different from government paper money "bubble" because funds and demand for loan would limit the debt). *See* Editorial note, 7 *id. at* 253 for a discussion of what fraction of its loans the banks would hold in specie.

[47] Jefferson, Opinion on the Constitutionality of a Bill for Establishing a National Bank (Feb. 15, 1791), 19 PTJ 275, 278 (saying that Hamilton's paper money was "clearly a demerit"). *Accord,* Madison, The Bank Bill, House of Representatives (Feb. 29, 1791), *in* 13 JM 373 (opposing bank debt as substitute for specie money). *See also* Letter of Jefferson to Charles Yancey (Jan. 6, 1816), *in* 11 WTJ 494 (characterizing bank notes as like a South Seas speculative bubble and calling for withdrawal of bank notes circulating as paper money).

[48] Jefferson, Memorandum of Conversations with the President (Feb. 29, 1792), *in* 23 PTJ 186 (saying that Hamilton would deluge the states with paper money). *Cf.* Jefferson to Edward Rutledge, Aug. 25, 1791, 22 PTJ 74 (attributing economic ills to paper money).

[49] ONUF at 4 (1983).

[50] *Id.,* at xv, 10.

Constitution" and also that the fears were unfounded: "The very fact that such fears were unfounded demonstrated the defective and diminutive character of early American state power that permitted the institution of a stronger central government."[51] Arguing that the fears were unfounded, however, also leans toward making the Constitution unnecessary and illegitimate.

Territorial disputes do not work very well to explain the adoption of the Constitution. The Confederation Congress was impotent and imbecilic over-all, but it had some success in the area of settlement of territorial disputes. During the Confederation period, for instance, settlers from Connecticut in the Wyoming Valley of northeast Pennsylvania tried to make their land become part of Connecticut. Pennsylvania's authority over the Connecticut settlers was decided in favor of Pennsylvania in 1782, in a decision rendered by a federal court set up under Article IX of the Articles of Confedera-tion to settle land disputes between the states.[52] Professor Onuf says that the Article IX procedure was so complicated that it was used only once, in Wyoming Valley.[53] Still, Wyoming Valley was a dispute that caused blood-shed and needed to be settled, so that it was not a trivial issue. Much of the complexity that Onuf points to in Article IX, moreover, is just that the Articles were setting up a court, when no court existed, and trying to ensure unbiased judges. The details are not especially complicated as court proce-dures go, nor exotic.[54] The court, moreover, worked as written. Indeed, the settlement of the Wyoming Valley dispute tended to legitimate the Confeder-ation Congress, when so much outside of the territorial disputes undercut its legitimacy.

Anti-Federalist James Monroe claimed that there were no existing ter-ritorial controversies between any of the states when the Constitution was considered. "Thus, sir," Monroe said, "this great source of public calamity [has] been terminated without the adoption of this [national] government."[55] Monroe's assessment seems plausible.

The Constitution, as adopted, moreover, reduced the power of Congress over territorial disputes. Decisions of the court set up under Article IX of

---

51 *Id.*, at 5.
52 *Id.*, at 57–58.
53 *Id.*, at 6.
54 Article IX provides if the states who were parties to a territorial dispute could appoint judges by joint consent, then those would be the judges. If the states could not agree, the Congress would name three judges from each state (thirty-nine total) and the parties would alternatively strike a name until the panel got down to thirteen judges. Congress would set whether to have seven or nine judges, and their identities would be chosen by lot out of the final thirteen. The Congress as a whole would then be the court of final appeal. ARTICLES OF CONFEDERATION, Art. IX, 19 JCC 217–219 (March 1, 1781).
55 James Monroe, Virginia Convention (June 10, 1788), *in* 3 ELLIOT 212.

the Articles of Confederation were binding on the parties. The Constitution gives its federal courts jurisdiction to include disputes between states over territory if the dispute can be settled under existing law, but if a dispute between states cannot be resolved under settled law, then Congress must resolve the dispute. When Congress settles the dispute, however, either state that is a party can veto the congressional solution. Under the Constitution, Congress may partition or merge states, only with the consent of the legislatures of the states involved.[56] Professor Onuf calls the Congress an "umpire" on territorial disputes, but true umpires do not need to get the consent of both the batter and the pitcher to call a ball or a strike. The Constitution in general made congressional legislation supreme over the states, but territorial disputes is the one issue in which the Constitution allowed the states to trump a congressional decision. The territorial disputes, the single decentralizing aspect of the Constitution, cannot be used to explain why the Constitution is such a centralizing document.

A second set of disputes adequately settled in the Confederation period was that states with claims to western land ceded their claims to the federal government. Virginia, for example, claimed the entire region northwest from the Ohio River to the Great Lakes under its 1609 charter.[57] Ultimately, both Virginia and New York ceded their claims to western lands to the central government: Virginia in 1784[58] and New York in 1780.[59]

The cession of western lands did a bit to ameliorate the fiscal crisis that caused the Constitution. Sale of western lands could be a source of federal revenue. In the ratification debates, the Federalists sometimes claimed that the new Congress would need revenue from only the 5 percent impost, plus the sale of western lands, except in time of war.[60] Sale of western land would not be a sufficient federal revenue source under any reasonable projections, but cessation of the claims did help a bit, and could not put the Confederation Congress in any worse shape, either fiscally or as a matter of prestige.

One other territorial dispute seems to have made the Constitution an important enemy. Vermont declared independence from New York in 1777 and from then on, the Vermont separationists outraged New York's Governor

---

[56] U.S. Const., art. IV, §3.
[57] *See* Risjord at 219–244.
[58] *Id.*, at 75.
[59] Onuf at 106.
[60] *See, e.g.,* Edward Carrington to Jefferson (April 24, 1788), *in* 9 DHRC 755 (arguing that it was probable that imposts plus the sale of western lands would cover federal needs in peacetime, but not in time of war).

George Clinton.[61] The Vermont dispute was not settled until the new Congress admitted it as a state in 1791. Governor Clinton was among the most formidable opponents of the Constitution. If Clinton became an enemy of the central government because of Congress's insufficient sympathy to New York's side on the Vermont issue, then the dispute was an important impediment to the Constitution's adoption, rather than a cause.

Professor Onuf's argument works better if we view the Constitution not as a text or a specific historical event, but instead as a part of a larger movement toward a strong central government, which started with the first Continental Congress and continued through the Articles and into the Constitution.[62] Still, not all states were implicated in border disputes even over the full period from the stirrings against Britain through to adoption of the Constitution and in none of the states were territorial disputes the most important thing going on. (Territorial disputes were never the cause of the Union as implied by Professor Onuf's title, *The Origins of the Federal Republic*). The colonies came together into a union to fight a long and bloody war for independence and the republican form of government, and not to settle border disputes.

C. SHAYS'S REBELLION

Beginning in the summer of 1786 and continuing into the winter, disgruntled farmers seized the courthouses in five counties in western Massachusetts, demanding debt relief and tax reduction.[63] Daniel Shays, who gave his name to the rebellion, was an unpaid veteran, a former captain in the Continental Army, who had served at Lexington and Saratoga.[64] Shays had been only one member of one county committee, but he apparently did give the order

---

[61] KAMINSKI, CLINTON 63–77 (reporting that Clinton was outraged at Vermont "traitors" and that he considered them to be supported by Congress or at least by Congressional inaction).

[62] That Onuf is thinking in terms of a long-term movement is evidenced, for instance, by his statement that Articles of Confederation "*subsequently* offered a procedure" to settle the Connecticut-Pennsylvania dispute over the Wyoming valley. ONUF at 6. "Subsequently" identifies his viewpoint as before the March 1, 1781, ratification of the Articles, and possibly even as before the first 1776 debates over the Articles.

[63] The narrative of what happened in Shays' Rebellion is from DAVID SZATMARY, SHAYS' REBELLION: THE MAKING OF AN AGRARIAN INSURRECTION 98–119 (1980); *Editorial Note, in* 13 DHRC 93; FORREST MCDONALD, E PLURIBUS UNUM: THE FORMATION OF THE AMERICAN REPUBLIC, 1776–1790, at 244–256 (2d ed. 1979). Jonathan Chu, *Debt and Taxes: Public Finance and Private Economic Behavior in Postrevolutionary Massachusetts, in* ENTREPRENEURS: THE BOSTON BUSINESS COMMUNITY, 1700–1850 (Conrad Edick Wright & Katheryn P. Viens, eds. 1997) describes the farmer's difficulties in paying taxes and debts.

[64] JONATHAN SMITH, THE DEPRESSION OF 1785 AND DANIEL SHAYS' REBELLION (1905), *reprinted in* 5 WM. & MARY Q. 77, 88–89 (3d ser, 1948).

on January 25, 1787, to a force to "March, God Damn you, March" against the Springfield, Massachusetts arsenal. The 500 Massachusetts militiamen inside the arsenal were outnumbered by the 12,000 Shaysites outside, but the militia inside had the advantage of cannon. The militia fired two warning shots into the air and then fired grapeshot into the Rebellion army, killing four and dispersing the rest.[65] Four more Shaysites were killed in scattered incidents over the next week. Then on the bitter cold night of February 3, 1787, General Benjamin Lincoln marched 3,000 Massachusetts militiamen all night for thirty miles to Petersham to surprise 2,000 Shaysites, who scattered escaping into the countryside. Four deaths occurred and thirty were wounded at Sheffield on February 27, where the Shaysites adopted the "barbarous practice" of pushing hostages to their front and firing from behind them; the militia returned the fire.[66] After Springfield, Petersham, and Sheffield, the defeated Shaysites fled to safety across state lines. As late as July 1787, small groups continued to raid Massachusetts from across state lines to manhandle individual storekeepers and tax collectors they could capture, but after Sheffield in February, there was no massed Shaysite army.

The Federalists' first response to Shays's Rebellion was overreaction. In October 1786, Henry Knox, the Secretary of War for the Continental Congress, foresaw a Shaysite army marching on Boston. He wrote to Washington that Shays's was "a formidable rebellion against reason, the principle of all government, and against the very name of liberty" and that the government needed to be "braced, changed, or altered to secure our lives and property."[67] General Henry Lee, in Virginia in October 1786, foresaw that "the contagion will certainly spread and may reach Virginia."[68] Madison wrote his father in November that the tumults in Massachusetts were ultimately aimed at "an abolition of debts public & private, [and] a new division of property."[69]

---

[65] Generals William Shepard and Benjamin Lincoln to Governor James Bowdoin of Massachusetts, Springfield (Jan. 26, 1787), *available at* http://longman.awl.com/history/ primarysource_6_4.htm (fired over their heads and then into them).

[66] George Richard Minot, THE HISTORY OF THE INSURRECTIONS, IN MASSACHUSETTS, IN THE YEAR MDCCLXXXVI, AND THE REBELLION CONSEQUENT THEREON at 149 (1788), Evans Collection Digital Edition #21259; DAVID P. SZARTMARY, *supra* note 63, at 111.

[67] NOAH BROOKS, HENRY KNOX: A SOLDIER OF THE REVOLUTION [1900; reprinted New York, 1974], 194–96, *cited in Editorial Note, in* 13 DHRC 92, 93.

[68] Henry Lee to Madison (Oct. 25, 1786), *in* 11 JM 145 *See also* Henry Lee to Washington (Nov. 19, 1786), *in* 8 LMCC 505–6 (acknowledging that Lee was convinced, without hard evidence, that the Shaysites "contemplate a reunion with G[reat] Britain" if it would mean the elimination of private debts).

[69] Madison to James Madison Sr. (Nov. 1, 1786), *in* 9 JM 154.

The second reaction to Shays's was retribution. In February 1787, Governor James Bowdoin of Massachusetts sought to punish the rebels. Hundreds of rebels were arrested and a dozen leaders were condemned to death. All insurgents were to be denied their civil rights to vote, to hold office, to teach school, and to run taverns.[70] Once the threat had passed, however, attitudes softened. By February 24, 1787, Madison knew that General Lincoln had "effectually dispersed the main body of Shay's rebellion insurgents" and that the rebels had fled to Vermont and Canada.[71] By March, General Lincoln himself found that the rebels he had arrested were "not the most dangerous" and he argued for a generous, lenient policy toward the rebels, as a matter of true republican policy.[72] Washington, by March, could argue for the wisdom of leniency, saying that "measures more generally lenient might have produced equally good an effect without entirely alienating the affections of the people from the government. As it now stands it affects a large body of men, some them perhaps, it deprives of the means of gaining a livelihood."[73] Washington also thought that "disenfranchising those who were aiding or abetting, is pregnant with as much evil as good."[74] By summer, Reverend Bazaleel Howard of Springfield, who had supported the established Massachusetts government during the active rebellion, could nonetheless say that government actions against the Shaysites had been spiteful and malevolent.[75]

The voters of Massachusetts agreed that Governor James Bowdoin had been too harsh. In April 1787, they voted Bowdoin out of office and replaced him with John Hancock, by a margin of three to one. Governor Hancock's policy was for peace and conciliation. Hancock cut the direct land taxes, payable in specie.[76] He also pardoned the leaders. None were executed. The malcontents largely immigrated, off to the banks of the Ohio.[77]

---

[70] Robert Brown, *Shays' Rebellion and the Ratification of the Constitution in Massachusetts, in* Beyond Confederation, 116.

[71] Madison to Edmund Pendleton (Feb. 24, 1787), *in* 9 JM 318.

[72] Brown, *supra* note 70, at 113, 117.

[73] Washington to General Benjamin Lincoln (Mar. 23, 1787), *in* 5 PGW:CS 101.

[74] Washington to Marquis de Lafayette (Mar. 25, 1787), *in* 5 PGW:CS 106.

[75] Richard D. Brown, *Shays' Rebellion and Its Aftermath: A View from Springfield, Massachusetts, 1787,* 40 Wm. & Mary Q. 598, 609–610 (3d series 1983) (reporting of the account attributed to Bazaleel Howard written in the summer of 1788).

[76] Ferguson at 247 (saying that the new Hancock legislation cut direct land taxes from $1 million a year in 1781–1786 to no state land taxes in 1787). By 1790, when the federal government had assumed the Massachusetts war debt, Massachusetts land tax was set at $98,500. *Id.*

[77] Louis Guillaume Otto to Comte de Montmorin (Oct. 23, 1787), *in* 1 DHRC 352–353.

In justice, some Shaysites might well have been hung, especially for instance, for firing from behind a line of hostages at Sheffield. The ultimate leniency shows among other things the basic nonviolent tolerance of George Washington.

It is occasionally argued that the Constitutional Convention was a reaction to Shays's Rebellion[78] or, at least, that the Rebellion played an integral part in the genesis and formation of the Constitution.[79] Thomas Jefferson, out of the loop in far-off Paris, concluded that the Constitutional Convention was an overreaction to Shays's, set up "in the spur of the moment" to construct "a kite to keep the hen yard in order" and he clearly sympathizes with the rebellion side.[80] Plausibly Jefferson never lost that attitude toward the Constitution, on an emotional level. Consistently, some modern commentators have argued that the Federalists consciously exaggerated the threat so as to be able to augment national powers.[81]

The Federalists indeed did argue that Shays's Rebellion proved the need for a stronger central government, to replace the imbecilic congress of the Articles. Washington argued in March 1787 that "[t]hese disorders are the evident work of a defective government."[82] At the Convention, Madison used Shays's Rebellion to criticize Patterson's weak-central-government New Jersey Plan because that plan failed to correct the defects exposed by the insurrections in Massachusetts.[83] Still, Madison and Washington were already well convinced of the imbecility of the Confederation government, without Shays's. They were using Shays's as an illustration in their argument without their having had their minds changed by it.

Shays's did not, for instance, seem to have much of a role in convincing Washington to attend the Philadelphia Convention.[84] In March of 1787, Washington was arguing for leniency for the Shaysites, and also had "authorized no expectations of his attendance [at Philadelphia, nor]

---

[78] "A Little Rebellion Now and Then" (film 1986), *as reviewed in* Daniel B. Smith, *Review*, 73 J. OF AM. HISTORY. 822–823 (1986).

[79] SZATMARY, *supra* note 63, at 120.

[80] Jefferson to William Stephens Smith (Nov. 13, 1787), *in* 12 PTJ 357.

[81] VAN BECK HALL, POLITICS WITHOUT PARTIES: MASSACHUSETTS, 1780–1791, at 257 (1972) (arguing that nationalist General Knox used the rebellion as propaganda to increase national powers).

[82] Washington to Lafayette (Mar. 25, 1787), *in* 5 PGW:CS 106.

[83] Madison, Federal Convention (June 19, 1787), *in* 1 FARRAND 318.

[84] STUART LEIBIGER, FOUNDING FRIENDSHIPS 66–70 (1999) looks at the full course of Washington's letters and concludes that "the impact of Shays' Rebellion on [Washington's] decision must not be exaggerated." *Id.* at 67.

precluded himself absolutely from stepping into that field."[85] Washington wrote to Lafayette in March that the "disorders are evident marks of a defective government" and also that "delegates would meet in at Philadelphia the second Monday in May next in general Convention of the States to revise, and correct the defects."[86] But Washington was not telling Lafayette that Shays's had motivated his going to Philadelphia because in June, when he was in attendance, he wrote Lafayette that "[y]ou will be suprized . . . to receive a letter from me at this place."[87]

Shays's Rebellion, moreover, was also used against the Constitution and to prove the dangers of a central government. Anti-Federalist George Clinton, from neighboring New York, argued that the Rebellion was proof that large governments were unstable and that power needed to be maintained in the smaller state governments.[88] Anti-Federalist Agrippa, writing in Massachusetts itself, argued that the state militia's success in the rebellion provided "decisive evidences of the vigour" of the state.[89] "The state governments," said Melancton Smith in New York, "answer the purposes of preserving the states."[90] If the Constitution had failed to be ratified, we would undoubtedly be counting Shays's Rebellion, just as it happened, as a major reason why we did not have a 1787 Constitution. Shays's Rebellion was a then-current event, useful to illustrate arguments, but it was equally useful to both sides to prove the wisdom of each mutually contradictory position.

Anti-Federalism seems to have had a very mixed assessment of Shays, and counter-intuitively was sometimes on the side of the forces of order. Governor Bowdoin, who suppressed the Rebellion and lost the next election, is commonly the villain of the play. But Mercy Otis Warren, authoritatively described as the most accurate, well-balanced, and shrewd of the Anti-Federalists,[91] describes Bowdoin as a man of unsurpassed "firmness, precision and judgment."[92] Shaysites were not heroes at the core of the Anti-Federalism.

---

[85] Madison to Jefferson (Mar. 19, 1787), *in* 9 JM 318.
[86] Washington to Lafayette (Mar. 25, 1787), *in* 5 PGW:CS 105, 106.
[87] Washington to La Fayette (June 6, 1787), *in* 3 FARRAND 34.
[88] George Clinton, JOURNAL OF THE ASSEMBLY OF THE STATE OF NEW YORK, 10th Sess, at 62 (Jan. 12, 1787).
[89] Agrippa II, MASSACHUSETTS GAZETTE (Nov. 27, 1787), *reprinted in* 4 STORING 72.
[90] A Plebian (Melancton Smith), *An Address to the People of the State of New York* (April 17, 1788), *reprinted in* 17 DHRC 151.
[91] 6 STORING 195 (1981); Charles Warren, *Proceedings*, 64 MASS. HIST. SOC. 157 (1932).
[92] MERCY OTIS WARREN, HISTORY OF THE RISE, PROGRESS AND TERMINATION OF THE AMERICAN REVOLUTION (1805), *excerpted in* 6 STORING 206.

Shays's is said to be a protest against taxes and debts, but it is difficult to see how either protest furthered the constitutional movement.[93] Shays's could not be a protest against any revenue that the federal government saw because the federal government collected only $663 of the 1786 requisition across the whole nation, and none of it from western Massachusetts. None of the Massachusetts taxes helped pay the Dutch or prepare for the next war. Federal assumption of the Massachusetts war debts, under Hamilton's initiative in 1791, in fact proved to produce tax relief in Massachusetts, but federal assumption of state debts was not a forgone or necessary conclusion of the Constitution – Madison himself for instance would oppose assumption. No one at the time could have reasonably foreseen or relied on the federal assumption of Massachusetts war debts. If Shays's was tax rebellion, the Constitution brushed the protests aside, because the purpose of the Constitution was to cure the destitution of the general government by giving it the power to collect some tax. Yet, even if the Constitutional movement brushed aside the protests, it is hard to see how the protests themselves supported the greater federal taxes that the Constitution was written to provide.

Similarly it is hard to see how the Shaysites' protest against debts, if it was a protest against debt, helped the movement toward the Constitution. Deflation was a serious hardship to debtors in the decade before Shays's, although not so much immediately before the Rebellion.[94] As the Continental dollar disappeared from circulation and the states withdrew their "emergency" paper money issuances, prices dropped across the board[95]:

[93] In REQUIEM: VARIATIONS ON EIGHTEENTH-CENTURY THEMES 62–68 (1988), Forrest McDonald argues that the rebellion was primarily tax motivated, because there is only a rough correlation between debtors and Shaysites. McDonald's sample, however, seems to exclude book debt, which is debt owed directly by the farmer to the shopkeeper for supplies from the store. Book debt would have been enforced by shopkeeper threats to cut the farmer off if the debt were not controlled or settled, and a farmer cut off from his access to supplies would probably have been very angry at the shopkeeper. *See, e.g.,* John DeWitt, *Essay* 1, (BOSTON) AMERICAN HERALD (Oct.–Dec. 1787), *reprinted in* 4 STORING 15, 17 (attributing the disturbances to "a pressure of embarrassments, which checked, and in many cases, destroyed that disposition of forbearance, which ought to be exercised towards each other").

McDonald also attributes the rebellion in part to the ignorance by the Shaysites of the West that the nominally high taxes could be paid with depreciated securities. McDONALD, REQUIEM, at 68–71.

[94] RISJORD at 97–98 (pointing to rapid deflation caused by retirement of paper money, which under eighteenth century monetary theory, such as it was, was considered to be a temporary expedient, justified only in a military emergency, and something to be retired as soon as the emergency was over).

[95] All figures from JOHN J. McCUSKER, HOW MUCH IS THAT IN REAL MONEY: A HISTORICAL COMMODITY PRICE INDEX FOR USE AS A DEFLATOR OF MONEY VALUES IN THE ECONOMY

TABLE 9.1. *Price of goods*

Year	1781	1782	1783	1784	1785	1786	1787
Price of commodities	$100	$110	$97	$95	$88	$86	$85

The drop in prices after 1782 is merely an alternative to saying that dollars got more expensive in standard of living terms. Repaying with more expensive dollars is like adding an extra interest rate charge, when the nominal dollars are translated into the real goods and services they can buy. For one-year loans, the deflation was like an added annual interest as a percentage of what was borrowed as illustrated in Table 9.2.[96]

TABLE 9.2. *Extra "deflation" interest; negative is reduction in burden of interest due to inflation*

Year	1782	1783	1784	1785	1786	1787
Extra deflation interest	(10%)	11¾%	2%	7½%	2%	1%

The "deflation" interest would have been on top of whatever contractual interest was required. From 1783 through 1785, deflation would have kicked real interest rates into the usurious range and been very hard on the debtors. The perceptions of the debtors might not have been as fine tuned as a good index, but the indexes measure real phenomena that the debtors would have felt because, for instance, their debts were harder to pay in terms of real prices. The deflation undoubtedly was part of the collective memory in western Massachusetts, even though it had abated by 1785.

If deflation was the telling stress on Shaysite debtors, however, the Framers surely did not try to cure the deflation. The Constitution prohibited state paper money, confirming that the deflation of the 1780s would not be reversed. As noted, the Anti-Federalists in New York and Virginia acquiesced to the prohibitions on state paper money, whereas they acquiesced in almost nothing else about the Constitution. The prohibition on paper money was not a contested issue because the collapse of the Continental dollar had been

OF THE UNITED STATES 52–53 (2d ed. 2001) divided by a factor (0.92) designed to make the base be $100 for 1781.

96 The calculation is (year 1 cost of living – year 2 cost of living)/year 1 cost of living. For example the deflation interest for 1783 is ($110 – 97)/$110, or 11.82 percent. The interest rate is rounded to the nearest .25 percent. The change from 1781 to 1782 is inflation, meaning whatever the nominal interest rate was, it should be reduced by 10 percent of amount borrowed to reflect the change in cost of living.

such a searing experience. The deflation, on the other hand, could not be said to have contributed to the constitutional movement because the Constitution went on in spite of the deflation of the 1780s and in spite of Shays's Rebellion, and not because of either element.

The Shaysites, by attacking tax collectors and shopkeepers, put issues in personal terms, not in abstractions like "deflation." The creditors who the Shaysites attacked were the small shopkeepers who had extended credit to the farmers for plows, hardware, woven goods, and seed. It is difficult to see what justice there was in manhandling the shopkeepers or, for that matter, in destroying the institution of shopkeeper credit upon which the farmers so depended. And yet, it is also difficult to see how the deep anger the farmers had in facing their debts reinforced some idea that debtor relief was inappropriate. George Washington, for example, was deeply sympathetic with the Shaysites once the violence had ended and supported leniency so as not to alienate Shaysites from government. As noted, it is difficult to treat the Constitution as primarily or even significantly a creditor tool. The primary creditors to be benefited by the constitutional movement were the Dutch and French holders of public debt and the British trade creditors whose debts were unenforceable due to the violations of the Treaty of Paris.

The Constitution replaced the sovereignty of the states with the sovereignty of the people, but Shays's Rebellion did not undermine the legitimacy of the states. As "Agrippa" and "A Plebian" argued at the time, Shays's did not show the need for a strong federal army for the common defense because the Massachusetts militia handled the threat handily once it was mobilized. Had the government forces proved inadequate, it might have impugned the potency of the Massachusetts government, but it was not the impotence of the state governments that were at issue in the constitutional debates. The fighting itself was internal to Massachusetts. As Patrick Henry asked the Virginia Ratification debate, "Where is the danger [to Virginia]?"[97] The defeated rebels fled to safety just by crossing state lines. The Rebellion, as it turned out after sober reflection, was not a federal issue.

The Constitution adopted the ideology of neither the Shaysites nor the Anti-Shaysites. Governor Bowdoin was defeated in the next election and even Washington thought he had over-reacted. Leading Anti-Federalist

---

[97] Patrick Henry, Virginia Convention (June 5, 1788), *in* 3 ELLIOT 48 (also asking, "Has there been a single tumult in Virginia? Have not the people of Virginia, when laboring under the severest pressure of accumulated distresses, manifested the most cordial acquiescence in the execution of the laws?"). MORRIS at 264–265 (1987) describes Shaysite protests outside of Massachusetts, but Patrick Henry's assessment seems sound.

Mercy Warren came in on Bowdoin's side. Shays's Rebellion neither implied nor rebutted the need for the new, tripartite, supreme central government able to raise funds and operate beyond the states, so as to pay off the war debts.

Shays's Rebellion could also not be used to rebut Montesquieu. Montesquieu believed that democracy could be maintained only within homogeneous small republics, and the Anti-Federalists therefore loved him. But Montesquieu also allowed "that should a popular insurrection happen in one of the States, the others are able to quell it. Should abuses creep into one part, they are reformed by those that remain sound."[98] Montesquieu allowed the small republics to come together in military alliances, both against an external enemy and also against internal insurrections. The Montesquieian support for the small-republic state governments was impervious to Shays's Rebellion, even had the Rebellion been more threatening across state lines.

The Constitution, as adopted, does not allow federal intervention except at the request of the states. Anti-Federalist Elbridge Gerry of Massachusetts argued in Philadelphia that he was "agst. letting loose the myrmidons of the U. States on a State without its own consent" and that "more blood would have been spilt in Massachusetts if the Genl. authority had intermeddled."[99] The Constitution, with a bend toward that argument, permits the federal government to come to the aid of a state during insurrection only with the application of the state, therefore going[100] less far than Montesquieu would have allowed.

Shays's Rebellion plausibly contributed to the sense of crisis and anger. The constitutional revolution arose from a profound sense of anger at the rogue states that had continuously breached their obligations and betrayed the sacred cause. The proponents' sense of desperation over the situation of an imbecilic and impotent general government, which carried the torch of the Revolutionary cause, was undoubtedly strengthened by Shays's. But on an intellectual level, nothing in the facts of Shays's fits well into a Federalist argument in favor of the Constitution nor rebuts any Anti-Federalist argument against it.

---

[98] *Federalist* No. 43, at 295 (Madison) (Jan. 23, 1788) (saying that among the advantages of a confederate republic enumerated by Montesquieu was that other members of the confederation could quell a popular insurrection.) *See also Federalist* No. 9, at 54 (Hamilton) (Nov. 21, 1787) (*accord*).

[99] Elbridge Gerry, Federal Convention (Aug. 17, 1787), *in* 2 FARRAND 317.

[100] U.S. CONST., art. IV, §3, cl. 2.

The Constitutional movement also arose out of Virginia, by way of Madison's work, to ensure that the public and private debts would be paid, and with sponsorship by Virginians. The Constitutional movement arrived in Massachusetts only much later, when Massachusetts was asked to ratify. Indeed it has been argued that, within Massachusetts, Shays's imperiled ratification because the reaction to the suppression of Shays's Rebellion mobilized the opposition to the Constitution that was sympathetic to Shays's. Because of Shays's, it is argued, Massachusetts's ratification became a close race instead of an easy Federalist victory.[101]

At the Massachusetts Ratification Convention on January 25, 1788, one Smith, a "plain man, who [got] his living by the plow," rose to "talk to other ploughmen." "There was a black cloud," he said, "that arose...last winter when People that used to live peaceably, and were before good neighbors, got distracted, and took up arms against government...

> If you went to speak to them, you had the musket of death presented to your breast. They would rob you of your property; threaten to burn your houses; oblige you to be on your guard night and day; alarms spread from town to town; families were broken up; the tender mother would cry, "O, my son is among them! What shall I do for my child!" Some were taken captive, children taken out of their schools, and carried away. Then we should hear of an action, and the poor prisoners were set in the front, to be killed by their own friends. How dreadful, how distressing was this! Our distress was so great that we should have been glad to snatch at any thing that looked like a government.[102]

Smith's speech to the convention was interrupted by a call to order, asking, "What had the history of last winter to do with the Constitution?" The convention ultimately let Smith "go on in his own way" and finish, but the call to order had merit. What if anything did the Rebellion have to do with the Constitution?[103]

---

[101] Robert D. Brown, *Shays' Rebellion and the Ratification of the Federal Constitution in Massachusetts, in* Beyond Confederation 113.

[102] [John K. or Josiah?] Smith, Massachusetts Convention (Jan. 25, 1788), *in* 2 Elliot 103. There were five Smiths at the Massachusetts convention, and John K. Smith and Josiah Smith voted in favor of ratification. 2 Elliot 180, 181.

[103] Robert A. Feer, *Shays' Rebellion and the Constitution: A Study in Causation*, 42 New Eng. Q. 388 (1969) concludes from the evidence that Shays's probably affected nothing. Had there been no Shays's Rebellion, he argues, the Philadelphia Convention would probably have met at about the same time, drafted substantially the same document and had it ratified just as it was. *Id.* at 393.

CHAPTER TEN

Hamilton's Constitution

The "revolution which has given us the Constitution," said a letter to the editor in 1790, was the default on the public war debts and "the very great embarrassments which attended all concerns on that account."[1] The constitutional revolution is in this sense like the French Revolution. In 1792, a delegate to the French National Assembly announced that "we only made the Revolution to become masters of taxation."[2] The French monarchy of the *ancien regime* had used a tax system so riddled with exemptions, privileges, and *libertés*, and saddled with such a thicket of middle men, that it could not reach the wealth of a prosperous country to solve the financial bankruptcy of the monarchy.[3] Like the French Revolution, one aim of our constitutional revolution was to allow the national government to gain access to the wealth of the nation, that is, to master taxation.

The fiscal crisis that caused the constitutional revolution was solved, however, with quite modest federal taxes. In 1790, Alexander Hamilton, the newly installed Secretary of the Treasury, recommended to Congress a financial package that followed the 5 percent impost proposals of 1781 and 1783. The major difference between the 1790 and the 1781 and 1783 proposals was that the new Constitution allowed Congress to adopt the impost, and then a supplemental whiskey tax, without facing the one-state veto rule of the Articles

[1] *Unsigned letter on Hamilton's funding Proposals*, (NEW YORK, FEB. 3, 1790), MARYLAND JOURNAL AND BALTIMORE ADVERTISER (Feb 12, 1790), *quoted in* FERGUSON xiii.
[2] Quoted in Gail Bassenger, *Taxes*, A CRITICAL DICTIONARY OF THE FRENCH REVOLUTION 589 (Francois Furet & Mona Ozoup, eds. 1993).
[3] *Id.* at 582–583 (concluding that financial weakness of the monarchy led to its collapse). *See also* JAMES MACDONALD, A FREE NATION DEEP IN DEBT: THE FINANCIAL ROOTS OF DEMOCRACY 239–266 (2003) (contrasting France with English eighteenth century finance, and showing that England could outspend France in every war and carry debt almost three times the French debt as a percentage of GNP because of greater reliability of English financial system).

and, indeed, without approval from any state. The revenues from the modest federal taxes were pledged to the payment of the war debts. The tax yield proved sufficient to make it possible for the new government to borrow again and at reasonable rates. Hamilton's modest taxes restored the public credit.

A. THE CURE WITH A PITTANCE

Even before Hamilton was installed as Secretary of the Treasury, Congress adopted the 5 percent impost, following the leadership of James Madison. In the opening days of the new Congress in 1789, James Madison, newly elected as a representative from Virginia, offered an immediate 5 percent impost, nearly identical to the 5 percent impost proposed in 1783. The impost, he argued, would remedy the evils caused by the deficiency in our treasury, without being "oppressive to our constituents."[4] The impost, he said, would allow the new government to pay its debts:

> The union, by the establishment of a more effective government having recovered from the state of imbecility, that heretofore prevented a performance of its duty, ought, in its first act, to revive those principles of honor and honesty that have too long lain dormant.[5]

Establishing a tax for the payment of war debts was Congress's first substantive act under the new Constitution.

Madison imitated the 1783 impost proposal. The impost of 1783 had been approved by all the states, Madison argued, "in some form or other."[6] The argument, although technically correct, avoids the substance. New York had effectively vetoed the impost of 1783 by saying in its approving legislation that the impost could be collected and paid over to the federal government in New York state paper. Specie, however, was needed to pay the federal creditors, foreign or domestic, and neither would have accepted New York paper. Still, the 1783 impost was approved in some form or other in all the states.

Both the 1783 proposal and Madison's 1789 proposal included, on top of the 5 percent baseline or default rate, a schedule of taxes to cover specific items including rum, Madeira wine, tea, sugar, and coffee.[7] Madison left the amount of tax on the schedule blank in his 1789 proposal, but thought that the wisest course would be to adopt more or less the same schedule of the

---

[4] Madison, House of Representatives (April 8, 1789), *in* 12 JM 64, 65.

[5] *Id.*

[6] *Id.*

[7] *Id.* at 66 (1789 proposal). *See* 24 JCC 257–258 for the 1783 proposal.

1783 proposal that had been agreed to before.[8] The first tax program had to be rushed, Madison told the House, because, as every gentleman could see, the prospects of tax from the spring imports were daily vanishing.[9]

The following year, in January 1790, Alexander Hamilton, in his role as the first Secretary of Treasury, delivered a comprehensive, even extraordinary, report to Congress on restoration of the public credit.[10] Hamilton's proposed total taxes of $2.8 million per year relied primarily on the impost.

Hamilton's revenue was a small burden, by comparison with the revolution that its absence had caused. The projected revenue of $2.8 million was only 70 cents per capita, spread across a population of 3.9 million.[11] Workman's wages were only about 40–50 cents a day at the time,[12] so 70 cents per capita was more or less a day and a half's worth of work at the pay level of day labor. Assuming 300 working days in a year, a day and half worth of tax would be tax at a rate of $\frac{1}{2}$ percent at a workingman's level. Under modern minimum wage rates, that would be like a per capita burden of roughly $224–$280 per year.[13] "Tax Freedom Day," when federal tax burdens were fulfilled, would arrive for a single worker at midday on January 2.[14]

Hamilton's taxes were also only on things that were supposed to be discouraged. The impost was a tax on imports. Imports were presumed at the time, as George Washington put it, to be the source of "luxury, effeminacy

---

[8] ELKINS & McKITRICK 65 (1993).

[9] Madison, House of Representatives (April 9, 1789), *in* 12 JM 69, 70.

[10] Hamilton, Report Relative to a Provision for the Support of Public Credit (Jan. 9, 1790), *in* 6 PAH 51.

[11] *Id.*, at 137 (Schedule K); U.S. CENSUS BUREAU, STATISTICAL ABSTRACT OF THE UNITED STATES 7 (Table 1) (2000) (reporting August 1790 population of 3.9 million). $2.8 million/3.9 million = 70 cents.

[12] Richard Morris, *Insurrection in Massachusetts, in* AMERICA IN CRISIS: FOURTEEN CRUCIAL EPISODES IN AMERICAN HISTORY 23 (Daniel Aaron, ed. 1952) (reporting Massachusetts wages at 40 cents a day in 1787). *See also* Robert Morris, Report of the Office of Finance (July 29, 1782), *in* 22 JCC 429, 441 (Aug. 5, 1782) (estimating labor at 50 cents per day in 1782).

[13] The average cost of labor in the year 2000 was on the order of $20 an hour or $160 per day (Table 170, Employer Cost per Hour Worked, *in* BUREAU OF THE CENSUS, STATISTICAL ABSTRACT OF THE UNITED STATES, 2000, (http://www.census.gov/prod/2001pubs/statab/sec13.pdf) (accessed Sept 6, 2001), which is 400 times 40 cents a day or 320 times 50 cents a day.

[14] Phillip J. Greven, Jr. *Average Size of Families and Households* in HOUSEHOLD AND FAMILY IN PAST TIME (Peter Laslett and Richard Wall, eds., 1972) calculates the national average size of households in 1790 at 5.59 free persons per household. The per household tax would be 70 cents times 5.59 or $3.91. If there was only one wage earner for the household, the $3.91 average tax per year would have required between eight and ten days work, which is not quite as dramatic as a day and half, but is still modest.

and corruption."[15] Both proponents and opponents of the Constitution condemned the "wonton consumption" entailed by imported luxuries.[16] Thus the impost, although measured here by wages of the workingman, would fall only on the consumption of frivolous luxuries, understanding that the thinking of the times presumed all imports to be unnecessary luxuries. The impost not only raised revenue but it was a "regulation of commerce" that would constrict corrupting imports.

Nationalizing the impost would also end the abuse of commercial states with good harbors draining noncommercial neighbors by state imposts. Nationalizing the impost would improve administration of the tax as well. A state-level impost could be avoided too easily by smuggling across porous state lines or by diverting ships to a competing harbor. On the federal level, by contrast, the impost could be collected easily just by guarding one side – the Atlantic.[17]

Hamilton also proposed a modest tax on domestic production of distilled whiskey in 1790 – on the order of seven cents per capita per year.[18] Hamilton had told New York in the ratification that revenue might properly be drawn from "ardent spirits,"[19] and as *Publius* he had said that the "single article of ardent spirits...might be made to furnish a considerable revenue."[20] A whiskey tax was a just tax: There "is no article of more general and equal

[15] Washington to James Warren (Oct. 7, 1785), *in* 3 PGW:CS 299–300. *See also* Jefferson, Second Inaugural Address (March 4, 1805), http://etext.virginia.edu/jefferson/texts/(accessed Oct. 16, 2002) (bragging that his first term had repealed internal taxes, so that federal revenue came from tax on foreign articles, "paid cheerfully by those who can afford to add foreign luxuries to domestic comforts"); Wilson, Pennsylvania Convention (Nov. 26, 1787), *in* 2 ELLIOT 431 (regretting the extravagance of our importations);. On the Anti-Federalist side, *see* Mason, Federal Convention (Sept. 13, 1787), *in* 2 FARRAND 606 ("descanting" on the necessity of restricting the "excessive consumption of foreign superfluities"); Robert Lansing, New York Convention (June 20, 1787), *in* 2 ELLIOT 218 (arguing that "we launched into every species of extravagance, and imported European goods to an amount far beyond our ability to pay"); Comte de Moustier to Comte de Montmorin (June 25, 1787), *in* 18 DHRC 190 (reporting that New York Anti-Federalists opposed importation of "luxuries that they must do without to live in the simplicity that befits a newborn State"); John Williams, New York Convention (June 21, 1788), *in* 2 ELLIOT 240 (calling for abandoning all the foreign commodities that have deluged our country and loaded us with debt).

[16] *See* Chapter 8, p. 192.

[17] *Federalist* No. 12, at 77 (Hamilton) (Nov. 27, 1787).

[18] Hamilton, Report Relative to a Provision for the Support of Public Credit (Jan. 9, 1790), *in* 6 PAH 51, 137 (Schedule K under heading of Made in the United States) (reporting tax on domestically distilled liquor at $270,00). The tax amounted to only about 7 cents per capita per year. U.S. CENSUS BUREAU, STATISTICAL ABSTRACT OF THE UNITED STATES 7 (Table 1) (2000) (reporting August 1790 population of 3.9 million). $270,000/3.9 million = 7 cents.

[19] Hamilton, New York Convention, (June 28, 1788) *in* 2 ELLIOT 369.

[20] *Federalist* No. 12, at 78 (Nov. 27, 1787).

consumption than [whiskey]," Hamilton told Washington.[21] Like the impost, the whiskey tax would also be a tax on vice, a means, as Robert Morris put it, "of compelling vice to support the cause of virtue."[22] The taxes would be not only "very productive, but... favorable to the morals of the citizens."[23] Even Madison, who was displaying increasing irritation at the administration, was willing to allow a whiskey tax as a kind of "sumptuary regulation."[24]

The proposed excise was also not on all alcohol, but only on the especially intoxicating, distilled hard liquors, whiskey, rum, and gin. The fermented alcohols, that is, good American beer, hard cider, and domestic wine, bore no tax. The tax on domestic whiskey failed the first time through Congress, but it was approved the following year, because by that time Congress needed the extra revenues to cover the federal government's assumption of the state war debts.[25]

Hamilton's tax package was considerably less intrusive than the 1783 proposals that New York's veto had defeated. The 1783 proposal had been tilted – five-eighths of the whole – toward internal or direct tax by asking for $1,500,000 requisition upon the states, compared with the $900,000 projected to come from its proposed 5 percent impost.[26] The state taxes were primarily wealth taxes on land, so the burden of the requisition would fall primarily on land.[27] The requisition of 1786 proposal did not again recommend federal impost – after New York's single-handed defeat of the 1783 proposal – and it asked for $3.8 million requisition which also would have fallen primarily on land tax if anyone had paid the tax.[28] Hamilton's 1790 package had no tax on land. A tax on land could not be rationalized as discouragement

[21] Hamilton to Washington (Aug. 18, 1792), *in* 12 PAH 228, 235 (emphasis omitted).
[22] Robert Morris, Report of the Office of Finance (July 29, 1782), *in* 22 JCC 442.
[23] Robert Livingston, New York Convention, June 27, 1787, 2 ELLIOT 341 (advocating taxes on wines and malt liquors as well as on brandy, and spirits).
[24] Madison, House of Representatives, *in* 14 DHFFC, 1789–1791 at 195.
[25] Hamilton, Report on the Further Provision of the Public Debt (Dec. 13, 1790), *in* 7 PAH 225 (proposing the whiskey tax); An Act repealing, after last day of June next, duties..., ch. 15, 1 Stat. 203, § 15 (March 3, 1791) (adopting the whiskey tax). William D. Barber, *"Among the Most Techy Articles of Civil Police": Federal Taxation and the Adoption of the Whiskey Excise*, 25 WM. & MARY Q. 58, 77–78 (3rd Ser. 1968) discusses the defeat of the whiskey tax in 1790.
[26] Address to the States, by the United States in Congress Assembled (April 26, 1783), *in* 24 JCC 277, 277–279. The identified author of the Address is a committee consisting of James Madison, Alexander Hamilton, and Oliver Ellsworth, but the manuscript was in Madison's handwriting (24 JCC at 283) and Madison claimed to have written it. *Editorial Note, in* 6 JM 498–499.
[27] *See, e.g.*, the inventory of state taxes in Oliver Wolcott, Jr., *Direct Taxes*, H.R. Doc. No. 100-4 (1796), *in* 1 AMERICAN STATE PAPERS: CLASS III FINANCE 414, 423, 426–27, 431 (Walter Lowrie & Matthew St. Clair Clarke, eds., 1832).
[28] Aug. 2, 1786, *in* 31 JCC 462.

of luxury or vice in the same way that a tax on the vices of whiskey and imports could be. A big land tax would also have required land owners to come up with cash when the land owner might well not have cash, and it would have required appraisals of land value by some means or other. The impost was a less controversial tax, collected by importers from the cash paid for imports by willing buyers who had the cash to pay for the imports.[29] Reliance on the impost also allowed the states to cut their land tax. Massachusetts had been imposing a tax in specie on land for revenue of $1 million a year, but by 1790, Massachusetts dropped its state land tax to under 10 percent of that.[30]

Madison had told Hamilton in November 1789 that a federal tax on land was "an essential branch of national revenue" and advocated a federal land tax "before a preoccupancy by the States becomes an impediment."[31] Henry Lee from Virginia warned Madison that the federal government had better make do with the impost and the sale of western land, "for indeed if [they are not sufficient,] I am at a loss to see what you will or can do."[32] Stephen Higginson from Boston told Hamilton that the only reliable sources of revenue were the imposts and the whiskey taxes. "I have no Idea," Higginson wrote, "that any thing can be drawn from the states by requisition, or direct tax."[33] Madison's advocacy of a federal land tax in November 1789 is the last time Madison was more nationalistic than Hamilton on an important issue.

B. RESTATEMENT OF THE DOMESTIC DEBT

Hamilton would not have been able to restore the public credit while avoiding a substantial land tax, except by giving the domestic creditors less than they

---

[29] *See, e.g.*, Oliver Ellsworth, Connecticut Convention (Jan. 7, 1788), *in* 3 DHRC 549 (arguing that people must be provident by setting aside money to pay direct taxes, but that an impost is paid as people are spending money). Preference for the impost over land taxes on this ground goes back through the full post-war period. *See, e.g.*, Letter of Eliphalet Dyer to Jonathan Trumbull, Sr., April 3, 1783, 20 LDCC 139 (saying that "[d]rye, forced & direct taxes for monies on the body of the people we fear will not answer [for the payment of Congressional debts], but [d]utys & Impost on Trade . . . must be paid in the first Instance by those through whose hands our moneys most frequently Circulate Viz the Merchants, and afterword by those only who Choose it, & without the disagreeable force of a Collector").

[30] FERGUSON, at 247 (saying that the new Hancock legislation cut direct land taxes from $1 million a year in 1781–1786 to no state land taxes in 1787). By 1790, when the federal government had assumed the Massachusetts war debt, Massachusetts land tax was set at $98,500. *Id.*

[31] Madison to Hamilton (Nov. 19, 1789), *in* 12 JM 449, 450.

[32] Henry Lee to Madison (Nov. 25, 1789), *in* 12 JM 466–467, 454–455.

[33] Stephen Higginson to Hamilton (Nov. 11, 1789), *in* 5 PAH 507, 511.

had been promised. Hamilton was helped in avoiding the land tax by the boom in imports since 1783. The 1783 five percent impost had been projected to yield $900,000. The 1790 five percent impost was projected to yield more than $2,500,000.[34] Still, that yield was short of supplying what creditors had been promised. Domestic creditors had been promised 6 percent interest per year, appropriate to an investment with risk, but Hamilton's package reduced the annual payments to just over 4 percent per year. When Congress finished with the package, creditors got less than 4 percent per year.

In rhetoric, Hamilton was a staunch protector of the contractual rights of domestic creditors. Hamilton, first, insisted that current holders of the debt should be paid the full amount promised in specie and not in paper money. He also said that the debt holders were entitled to all accrued interest payments at the full contractual 6 percent and that no distinction could be made between the principal owed originally and the contractual interest accrued thereafter.[35] Interest would not be a second-class debt.

The domestic debt had a fair market value that was much lower than the face or promised amount of the debt in 1789. Congress had stopped payments of interest on the federal debt in 1782 because the failure of the states to pay their requisitions left Congress with nothing to give to domestic creditors. "Loan certificates," which had previously borne a healthy 6 percent interest thereafter dropped in value to 25 cents on the dollar. The Quartermaster and commissary certificates given out for impressed supplies and the final settlement certificates given out to the army for overdue pay dropped in value even further to 10–15 cents on the dollar.[36] When the Constitution neared ratification, the market value of the loan certificates rose toward 50 cents on the dollar, as speculators began to see better hope of collection,[37] but the market value was still far below the face or promised amount.

Hamilton in his report on restoring the public credit asked rhetorically why the federal government should pay a full 100 cents to the dollar to a current holder of the debt who might have paid only 15 or 20 cents on the

---

34 Compare Madison, Ellsworth & Hamilton, Address to the States, *supra* note 26, at 277, 277–279 ($900,000 expected from 5% impost) with Report Relative to a Provision for the Support of Public Credit, *in* 6 PAH 86, 137 ($2,500,000 expected from 5% impost). *See also* Hamilton, Paper III (April 29, 1783), *in* 24 JCC 287 (estimating collections from the 5% impost proposed in 1783 at $915,000).

35 Hamilton, Report Relative to a Provision for the Support of Public Credit, *in* 6 PAH 84 (saying that "arrears of interest have pretensions, at least equal to the principal").

36 FERGUSON at 252–253.

37 BRANT, JAMES MADISON: CONSTITUTIONAL FORMATION 296 (1941–1961).

dollar to purchase the debt,[38] but then he answered his own question by saying that the federal government had received its money's worth for the debt and had promised to pay the contractual amount. The current holder of the debt, Hamilton argued, had paid the prior holder the fair worth of the debt at the time. The prior holders had gotten all that the debt was worth when they had sold it. The purchasers had taken "a hazard which was far from inconsiderable," Hamilton argued, with payment turning on "little less than a revolution in government."[39] Do not censure the Stock-jobbers, Elbridge Gerry had told the Philadelphia Convention: "They keep up the value of the paper. Without them there is no market."[40] The purchasers of debt, Robert Morris had told Congress, in giving the original holder some money, "at least afforded him some relief, which he could not obtain elsewhere and if they are deprived of the expected benefit, they never will afford such relief again."[41] Those who buy up the debts, he added, "shew at least as much confidence in the public faith, as those who sell them."[42]

The decline in value of the debt, moreover, was caused by Congress itself. The debt declined in value because Congress had stopped paying interest on it in 1782: "In case of war who would lend us," one newspaper asked, "if our neglecting seven years to pay the sum borrowed will justify our not paying at all?"[43] Paying only value would be a self-fulfilling prophesy that would destroy value because lenders' pessimistic estimates of how little the promise of repayment was worth would always be confirmed. Much more pragmatically, the Dutch speculators who bought so much of the debt second hand would be the very creditors the country would need to borrow from when war came again.[44] If the Dutch were not to be paid, then the pragmatic reason for paying the debts at all would be lost.

---

[38] Hamilton, Report Relative to a Provision for the Support of Public Credit (Jan. 9, 1790), *in* 6 PAH 51, 73–74.

[39] *Id.*, at 74. *See also* Elbridge Gerry, Federal Convention (Aug. 25, 1787), *in* 2 FARRAND 413 (observing that as the public had received the value of the literal amount, they ought to pay that value to somebody).

[40] Elbridge Gerry, Federal Convention (Aug. 25, 1787), *in* 2 FARRAND 413.

[41] Robert Morris, Report of the Office of Finance (Aug. 5, 1782), *in* 22 JCC 429, 444.

[42] *Id.*

[43] 1 AM. MUSEUM 420 (May 1787), *quoted in* Introductory Note, *in* 6 PAH 64.

[44] James C. Riley, *Foreign Credit and Fiscal Stability: Dutch Investment in the United States, 1781–1794*, 65 J. AMER. HISTORY 654, 672–678 (1978) (discussing Dutch investment in U.S. public securities and the Hamilton plan's dependence on the Dutch investments). FERGUSON at 235; E. James Ferguson, *The Nationalists of 1781–1783 and the Economic Interpretation of the Constitution*, 56 J. OF AMER. HISTORY 241, 256 (1969) (repudiation would have hurt valuable Dutch creditors who had invested in American debt at high prices).

Anti-Federalists were commonly in favor of paying the current holders only the fair market value of the debt, 50 cents on the dollar or less, rather than the full dollar promised, whatever the consequences. In the Philadelphia Convention, Anti-Federalist George Mason had argued that he wished at least to leave the door open for buying up the securities at their market value.[45] In Virginia Patrick Henry had descried that the Constitution by prohibiting impairment of contracts had improperly prevented "scaling" of the debts.[46]

James Madison, in his first open opposition to Hamilton and the Washington Administration, argued that the current holders of the domestic debt should be paid only the highest recent market value of the debt. The remainder would be paid over to the soldiers and suppliers who had first received the debt.[47] Madison's position has to be understood as symbolic, and impractical. In most cases there were no public records of who first received a certificate, on the certificate itself or anywhere else, and no public records of the serial bargains between first and current possessor. It would not be possible to go back to split the redemption proceeds to undo the many bargains as the certificates changed hands at fluctuating market values.[48] Early initial holders with the least faith in payment would have sold the most quickly and for the lowest discount and they might have gotten a windfall from Madison's plan. Madison conceded the administrative difficulties. Getting into the equities as to the intermediate holders would lead, as Madison himself saw, into "a labyrinth, for which it is impossible to find a clue."[49] Splitting the redemption payments according to current market value was "not perfect justice."[50]

Madison's proposal to split the redemption payments represented a turning point. In 1783, Madison had argued with vigor that current holders who had purchased the public debt needed to be paid the full contract price.

45 Mason, Federal Convention (Aug. 25, 1787), *in* 2 FARRAND 413.
46 Patrick Henry, Virginia Convention (June 17, 1788), *in* 3 ELLIOT 475.
47 Madison, House of Representatives (Feb. 11, 1790), *in* 13 JM 34–39. *Compare, e.g.,* FERGUSON at 298 (calling Madison's turn a purely political move, not realistic, but also the point at which Madison turned to state-oriented politics where before he had been a nationalist) *with* ELKINS & McKITRICK, at 139–145 (concluding that Madison was sincere in explaining his opposition as coming from being upset at paying the "stockjobbers" full value when they had paid so little to acquire the debt) and HERBERT E. SLOAN, PRINCIPLE AND INTEREST: THOMAS JEFFERSON AND THE PROBLEM OF DEBT 140–144 (1995) (describing the discrimination battle by emphasizing Virginia opinion that emphatically favored it).
48 RISJORD at 395.
49 Madison, Speech on Discrimination (Feb. 11, 1790), in 13 JM 34, 36.
50 *Id* at 37.

Purchasers, he said, "manifest [the] most confidence in their country"[51] – indeed, usually more confidence than those who sold the debt. "To discriminate [against the later purchasers]," Madison had written in 1783, "would be a task equally unnecessary and invidious."[52]

Madison's stance was more significant because it was a change in the direction of the wind in that Madison worked in opposition to Hamilton and the Washington Administration. In retrospect, we can see that Madison's stance was a tell–tale – the flip in the yarn on the jib sail that tells that the wind has changed.[53] Madison was about to become a jealous sibling convinced that George Washington loved another son better. Madison, however, got only 11 votes out of 66 in the House for his stance, most from his Virginia friends and colleagues.[54] Scaling of the debt was not a politically serious proposal, except in its role as a tell-tale sign of a very serious change in the wind.

Hamilton, having established the principle of full payment of principal and interest to current holders, then talked himself with a bootstrap argument into giving the debt holders only 4 percent annually, and not the contractual 6 percent interest. The domestic debt had no term or date for repayment, so that the creditors, Hamilton decided, had left the outstanding balance of the debt to stay with the debtor if the debtor paid annual interest.[55] The certificates given out in exchange for impressments and final settlements of pay to the army were not negotiated bargains, so that there was no element of creditor consent to any terms. For the loan certificates, however, there would have been a supplier or even lender for specie on the creditor side. It was a right of debtors to buy back the debt, Hamilton decided, when

---

[51] Madison, Address to the States (April 26, 1783), in 24 JCC 277, 282–283. For attribution to Madison *see supra* note 26.

[52] *Id.* at 283.

[53] Just before the turn in the wind, Madison reacted mildly to Hamilton's tax package, which included both full payment to current holders and assumption of state debts, in a letter to his father, by saying that "doubts are entertained whether the plan will meet with the full concurrence of Congress," but saying that he could form no opinion, "the members being generally reserved in communicating their views." Madison to James Madison, Sr. (Jan. 21, 1790), 13 JM 1–2. For Madison to have formed "no opinion" seems itself notable: He is starting to think as an outsider rather than the prime mover.

[54] IRVING BRANT, JAMES MADISON: CONSTITUTIONAL FORMATION 298–99 (1941–1961) describes the Virginia votes with Madison and in favor of discrimination as mostly an accommodation to a colleague. HERBERT E. SLOAN, *supra* note 47, at 140–144 (1995) describes Virginia opinion that emphatically favored discrimination.

[55] Hamilton, Report Relative to a Provision for the Support of Public Credit (Jan. 9, 1790), *in* 6 PAH 51, 85 (saying that "[w]herefore as long as the Unites State should pay the interest of their debt, as it accrued their creditors would have no right to demand the principal").

interest rates dropped, so as to reduce the interest charge. Interest rates would drop, Hamilton then declared, to 5 percent in five years and to 4 percent in fifteen years and creditors could thereafter be bought out. Congress would borrow if needed at the new lower rates to buy out the 6 percent debt and creditors would then get no more than that 4 or 5 percent. Because the federal government could refinance at the new lower interest rates, Hamilton reasoned, creditors could insist on no more than 5 percent after five years and 4 percent after fifteen years.

Hamilton then decided to pay only 4 percent per year to the creditors in specie, starting immediately, plus some sweetener to compensate them for the fifteen years before the alternative interest rates on federal borrowing dropped down to 4 percent. Hamilton offered the creditors six options, the first two of which gave the creditors western land to compensate them for the interest they would have received before interest rates dropped to 4 percent. Although in principle the debt was going to be recognized as the full face value, in the purchase of western land, the debt was going to be recognized only at the value of 20 cents per dollar in recognition of the fact that the debt could be purchased for 15 cents on the dollar not long before Hamilton's proposal.[56] Hamilton also offered holders the option of receiving an annuity for life, under which the government would protect the annuitants against the risk that they might live longer than they expected and run out of pension funds for support, but the interest rate to compute the annuity was only 4 percent and the term of the annuity life had to be over 10 years.[57]

Most of the debt held overseas already bore close to 4 percent interest because the prevailing European interest rate at the time was 3 to 4 percent for safe loans.[58] But some of the debt owed to foreigners paid 5 percent and Hamilton proposed borrowing 12 million dollars at 4 percent so as to buy back the 5 percent foreign debt and some of the domestic debt.[59]

Hamilton also "funded" the domestic debt, meaning that he pledged the federal taxes, now available under the new taxing power, would be directed first to the payments (at 4%) he proposed. The new federal tax power and funding did make the debt more likely to be paid, and 6 percent was a penalty

---

[56] *Id.*, at 90–91.

[57] *Id.*, at 91. Robert M. Jennings, Donald F. Swanson, & Andrew P. Trout, *Alexander Hamilton's Tontine Proposal* 45 Wm & Mary Q. 107 (3rd. Ser., 1988) describe the British origin and logic of Hamilton's proposal to offer an annuity as an option.

[58] Hamilton, Report Relative to a Provision for the Support of Public Credit (Jan. 9, 1790), *in* 6 PAH 51, 89. *See* James C. Riley, *supra* note 44, 65 J. Amer. History at 654.

[59] Hamilton, *supra* note 58, at 107.

or risky rate, which Hamilton was trying to avoid for the future. Hamilton said that creditors would change their old debt for one of the new 4 percent payment options only as a voluntary choice and the choice had to be voluntary in fact as well as name.[60] But the funding pledge consumed the taxes he proposed. Repurchases of the federal debt beyond the taxes would come only out of a sinking fund, funded by revenue growth, successful future borrowing, or the post office.[61] Those creditors who stood by their rights to 6 percent understood that they would be placed at the end of the line and that there was considerable doubt, at the end of the line, about their prospects for payment.[62]

In the end Hamilton's program, although stoutly moralistic in principle, reduced the annual payments to creditors from the promised 6 percent to just more than 4 percent. The $3.8 million revenue called for in the 1786 requisition was reduced to $2.8 million in 1790. Hamilton expressed the drop in interest rate to be paid as if it were of benefit to the creditors, arguing that paying the full 6 percent would "require the extension of taxation to a degree, and to objects which the true interest of the public creditors forbids."[63] The creditors, however, had not been paid anything since 1782 and did not have any alternatives beyond what Hamilton offered.

Still, the creditors got less than their contractual 6 percent and they did not like it. Hamilton was mocked in the papers for his pretense of giving creditors a choice as to whether to reduce interest from 6 percent to 4 percent. Creditors protested that they should get their promised 6 percent and let the federal government redeem them out if and when interest in fact fell to 4 percent.[64] Hamilton was robbing the security holders of half their property,

---

[60] *Id.*, at 66 (saying that "no change in the rights of . . . creditors ought be attempted without their voluntary consent; and . . . this consent ought to be voluntary in fact, as well as in name.") *See also id.*, at 88 (saying that creditors needed to be given "a fair equivalent" for what was given up and "unquestionable security for the remainder.") Creditors should accept the funding plan by "discernment of their own true interest" and their desire to place the new government on a sound footing. *Id.*, at 97.

[61] Donald F. Swanson, Andrew P. Trout, *Alexander Hamilton's Hidden Sinking Fund* 49 WM & MARY Q. 108 (3rd Ser., 1992) discuss Hamilton's plans to redeem back the federal debt.

[62] Ferguson at 285–286, 293–294 (saying that Hamilton offered the public creditors 6% in specie, and included the interest, but funding committed the revenues of the country to those who had elected a funded bond, which carried 4% at best, and those who stood by their rights could expect to be at the end of the line for revenue).

[63] Hamilton, Report Relative to a Provision for the Support of Public Credit (Jan. 9, 1790), *in* 6 PAH 51, 87.

[64] Unsigned, NEW YORK DAILY ADVERTISER, *reprinted in* PENNSYLVANIA PACKET (Feb. 16, 1790), *cited in* FERGUSON at 303.

one "Honestus" said, while maintaining the fiction of observing the sanctity of contract.[65]

Hamilton, however, is probably best understood as trying to raise the real value of the domestic debt to equal the face or promised amount. It was important to Hamilton's overall program that creditors be offered enough that the fair market value of their debts would rise to equal the face amount of the debt because Hamilton wanted the federal debts to serve as money in facilitating exchanges. The Constitution prohibited the states from printing paper money, and paper money anywhere was stigmatized by the collapse of the Continental dollar. Yet there was not enough gold and silver in the country to accommodate the transactions that willing buyers and sellers wanted to make. Barters are impossibly difficult to execute – buyers never have goods that sellers want. The rule in this specie-starved country was that you could never sell to anyone that you were not willing to extend credit to. Given the shortage, the American economy would improve if there were enough money or acceptable substitutes to facilitate the desired trades.[66] Hamilton attributed the decrease in value of land to the scarcity of money.[67] "It is well known that in countries in which the national debt is properly funded, and an object of established confidence," Hamilton wrote, "it answers most of the purposes of money."[68]

To serve as money in transactions and in saving, however, the debt had to have a steady value: "The fluctuation and insecurity incident to an unfounded state," Hamilton argued, "render it a mere commodity, and a precarious one."[69] The federal debt was not going to be paid off any time soon – the country could not afford that. Still, if the interest rate on the debt were sufficient to bring the value up to par, then any creditor could collect fairly just by selling the debt to another for full par and the debt, serving as money, would be a blessing.

If the value of the debt could be raised to par or face amount, moreover, the federal government could benefit from a bootstrap in which both risks and interest rates would drop. If its promises were creditable and its debt

---

65 "Honestus," New York Daily Advertiser (Feb. 3, 1790), *cited in* Ferguson at 303. *See also id.* and McDonald, Hamilton 172–173 for other creditor criticisms of Hamilton's plan.

66 *See* Charles W. Calomiris, *Institutional Failure, Monetary Scarcity, and the Depreciation of the Continental*, 48 J. of Econ. History 47, 48–49 (1988) (increase in money supply to the level needed by commerce can costlessly increase consumer wealth by facilitating trades).

67 Hamilton, Report Relative to a Provision for the Support of Public Credit (Jan. 9, 1790), *in* 6 PAH 51, 72.

68 *Id.*, at 70.

69 *Id.*, at 71.

secure, the federal government could get access to the 3 percent and 4 percent interest rates available for low-risk debt and the drop in its interest rate made it feasible to pay the interest from the available non-controversial revenue sources.[70] The market would be satisfied with 3 percent to 4 percent interest and sure payment, instead of 6 percent and doubts. If the federal debt rose in value to par so that it was not a speculative commodity but stable money, the debt left outstanding would serve a positive economic function as money, and it did not even have to be paid off. The federal government would then not have to pay out money it did not have to redeem the principal. The financial package would lift itself by its own bootstraps to make the package work.

Hamilton's reliance on long-term, readily marketable, and reliable debt to finance government has been called the English or Dutch system. In the French and English wars of the eighteenth century, England with half the gross national product (GNP) of France was able to outspend France and was able to carry debt almost three times higher in relationship to GNP as France could carry. British citizens were willing to lend to the government, through the Bank of England, because British debt was readily marketable, because Britain published its budget, and because the single common instrument for British borrowing traded at a price that illuminated the government's credit rating. British creditors in control of the government ensured that the government raised enough taxes to support the British debt. French monarchs, by contrast, acted in secret and borrowed with a puzzling array of techniques and instruments. French monarchs also defaulted. French interest rates were regularly more than twice the British interest rates. It was the monarch's inability to raise taxes to carry the government debts that ultimately brought down the *ancien regime*. It has been argued, indeed, that democracy arose to allow the government to borrow from its citizens. The hero who brought democracy was the citizen-creditor who was willing to entrust his money to the government only because his government was his agent. Hamilton's imitation of the Dutch and English mode of finance instead of the French, was ultimately adopted even by Jefferson, and Jefferson was skeptical of banks, of all things British, and of long-term finance.[71]

Congress, although it adopted the basic framework of Hamilton's recommendations, gave the domestic creditors even less than Hamilton proposed. The full contract debt was assumed in principle, as Hamilton had said, and simultaneously Congress would pay only 4 percent per year for the foreseeable

[70] *Id.*, at 89 (saying that 3–4% is deemed good interest in some parts of Europe).
[71] JAMES MACDONALD, *supra* note 3 at 7, 273, 289–306, 239–266.

future, as Hamilton had suggested, but Congress abandoned some of the options Hamilton would have offered. The option for creditors to receive western land in compensation for loss of entitled interest and the option to ask for annuities for life were dropped. Holders were simply given 6 percent for two-thirds of their debt – which is just another way of saying they would be given 4 percent per year. Interest would eventually be given for the last third, and at the risk-bearing 6 percent contractual interest rate, but that last 6 percent was set to start only in ten years, that is, 1800.[72] A ten-year lag in payments would reduce their present value, computed at the contractual 6 percent, to just over half of what was promised.[73] If we take Hamilton's projections on drops in interest rate seriously, moreover, Congress would be able to refinance the debt at 5 percent then 4 percent, just at the time that the full 6 percent interest would have come into effect, so that Congress on its internal logic would never have to pay the 6 percent.

Congress was also meaner than Hamilton proposed regarding earned but unpaid interest. Hamilton wanted interest that had accrued but not been paid to be respected equally with the original principal. Congress confirmed the accrued but unpaid interest as due, but the accrued interest was separated out and earned only a 3 percent interest rate for the future, that is, half the promised interest rate.[74] Accrued interest was reduced to a kind of second-class ownership, eligible to earn only half of what was offered on principal.

Even as reduced adversely to the creditors, funding as proposed by Hamilton served the immediate purpose of restoring the public debt to safeguard borrowing in the next war. The highest priority was to make the current payments that would avoid default on the debt owed to Dutch lenders. France was insolvent and not a likely source for future loans. The Dutch were necessary for the next war.[75] Hamilton's plan for funding the debt served the need. American debt became very attractive, reaching a value on the Amsterdam market in excess of its face value.[76] Dutch investors incredibly gave the new America an interest rate that was at the level of 4.1 percent, equal to the

---

[72] An act making provision for [the payment of the] debt of the United States, ch. 34, 1 Stat. 140, § 4 (Aug. 4, 1790). The bracketed "[payment of the]" inserted into the title in Statues at Large is a misnomer because the act did not pay the debt, but merely dedicated some future taxes to it (§5 giving the debt priority).

[73] $\$1/(1+6\%)^{10} = 56$ cents.

[74] An act making provision for [the payment of the] debt of the United States, ch. 34, 1 Stat. 140, § 5 (Aug. 4, 1790).

[75] See text accompanying *supra* note 44.

[76] James C. Riley, *supra* note 44, 65 J. OF AMER. HIST. at 676 (at apex of prices in 1792, U.S. 6% debt was selling at 127% face amount).

best interest rate in Europe.[77] The Dutch helped the process along by self-delusion. The Dutch lenders judged creditworthiness primarily by regularity of payment and they tolerated borrowing just to pay past-due interest. They identified ideologically with the Revolution. The Dutch closed their eyes enough to ignore all the signs of risk and debtor distress in the American debt.[78] American costs of financing, in conclusion, were "ludicrously modest."[79] Hamilton had by marvels restored the public credit.

C. ASSUMPTION OF STATE DEBTS AND THE SPECULATORS

Hamilton also stated as a matter of principle that federal government should assume all the war debts and expenses of the states. The only fair way to settle disputes as to who should pay the various state debts, Hamilton argued, was for the federal government to assume all the debts. All expenses of war would be treated as expenses for the common welfare even if incurred by the states rather than by the Congress: "The objects for which both [federal and state] debt were contracted, are in the main the same."[80] "Admitting, as ought to be the case, that provision must be made in some way or other, for the entire debt," Hamilton argued, "[t]he principal question then must be, whether such a provision cannot be more conveniently and effectually made, by one general plan issuing from one authority, than by different plans originating in different authorities."[81] The states and the federal fisc should not compete for tax on the same revenue sources, he argued,[82] and federal creditors should not be more favored than stated creditors, because both debts were contracted for the same unifying war and the same independence from Britain.[83] States had incurred their debts because the federal government could not pay for the common defense as it was expected. The states had

---

[77] *Id.* at 668 (U.S. was able to borrow at 4.1% whereas France borrowed at 6.4%).

[78] Riley argues that much of America's surprisingly good credit rating was due to Dutch ideological identification with the Revolution (*id.* at 672–675) and to a tendency to assess credit by regularity of payment. America was thus able to borrow to pay interest, which is usually a good sign of insolvency. *Id.* at 661, 664. American tax revenue was in fact not sufficient even to carry the debt until 1796, and the United States government carried an extraordinary debt of twenty-one times its tax revenue. *Id.* at 664–668. By 1796, however, American tax revenue had grown to be able to cover the debt service, and the debt dropped to a more manageable ten times tax revenue. *Id.* at 668.

[79] *Id.*

[80] Hamilton, Report Relative to a Provision for the Support of Public Credit (Jan. 9, 1790), *in* 6 PAH 81.

[81] *Id.*, at 78.

[82] *Id.*, at 79.

[83] *Id.*, at 81.

stepped in to pay the soldiers and interest on the public debt, Elias Boudinot argued on the House floor, when the Congress had been unable to, for lack of funds.[84]

Assumption of the state debts came up in the constitutional adoption but was not resolved. Virginia supported a proposal in 1783 that the Congress should assume the state war debts, but Virginia had been alone for assumption at the time.[85] At the Constitutional Convention, John Rutledge of South Carolina argued that because the federal government was to get the best source of funds, the impost, it should just assume that all state debts were war debts for the common cause and assume them all.[86] In the ratification debates, the proponents of the Constitution celebrated the expectation that the new national government would assume the state debts and reduce the burden on the states.[87] But there was nothing in writing that required it.

1. Speculator Risks

Hamilton's plan to assume the state debts leaked out to Northern speculators. Fast boats filled with specie sailed out of New York and Philadelphia to buy up the highly depreciated state debts of North and South Carolina.[88] The northern speculators knew more about Treasury plans from the leaks than the Carolina holders, but the sellers were just bettors as well – the original holders had largely long since sold out.[89] The buyers were taking risks, even speculations, that might well have gone the other way. First, Hamilton's plan

---

[84] Rep. Elias Boudinot, Speech to the House of Representative (May 25, 1790), *in* 1 ANNALS 1647–1655.

[85] Report of a Congressional Committee to Restore Public Credit (Mar. 20 1783), *in* 24 JCC 197 and *id.* at 257 *n. 1.* (proposing that all reasonable expenses of the states supported by satisfactory proof made in defense against the British or Indians shall be considered as part of the common charges, even if not previously authorized by Congress).

[86] John Rutledge, Motion at the Federal Convention (Aug. 18, 1787), *in* 2 FARRAND 327.

[87] Wilson, Public Meeting in Philadelphia, Oct. 6, 1787, 13 DHRC 343 (saying that when a competent and energetic federal system shall be instituted, "the State will then be discharged from an extraordinary burthen"); Benjamin Rush, Pennsylvania Convention, Dec. 3, 1787 2 DHRC 458 (saying that Pennsylvania "has assumed a great disproportion of the public debt" and that it "must be thrown back on Congress"); Demosthenes Minor, GAZETTE OF THE STATE OF GEORGIA, Nov. 22, 1787 *reprinted in* 3 DHRC 245 (saying that the federal government has the duty "to discharge the debts contracted upon the collective faith of the states"); A State Soldier, VA. INDEPENDENT CHRON., April 2, 1788, *reprinted in* 19 DHRC 650 (saying that a "very first object is to discharge our debts").

[88] Whitney K. Bates, *Northern Speculators and Southern State Debts: 1790,* 19 Wm. & MARY Q. 30, 42 (3rd Series, Jan. 1962) (concluding that the Northern purchases of southern debt "almost outran the [Jeffersonian] accusations").

[89] EDWIN J. PERKINS, AMERICAN PUBLIC FINANCE, 1775–1815 at 225 (1994).

espoused assumption of state debts in principle, but he did not in fact recommend any tax to cover payments on the state debts.[90] Hamilton had to come back at the end of the year, once state assumption was settled, and create a new tax, a federal whiskey tax, to cover the newly assumed state debts.[91] The whiskey tax was defeated when it was first proposed and it turned out to be a controversial tax, to the point of rebellion.[92] Indeed, Hamilton's plan was so far from the functional equivalent of payment that when his *Report on Restoration of the Public Credit* was finally published, the price of public securities dropped in value. The speculators had anticipated something even better.[93]

Assumption of state debts, moreover, was not a forgone political conclusion even once Hamilton proposed it.[94] There were important players on the bear side who needed the value of state certificates to decline in value. They had made bids to buy western land from the states, under arrangements that allowed them to use low-value state debt at face value to satisfy their bids. The rise in the value of state debts hurt those speculators because the rise in value of the state certificates made their original bids for the land unwisely expensive.[95]

James Madison opposed assumption of state debts. In 1783, Madison had supported "a transfer into the common mass ... of all the separate expences

---

[90] Hamilton, Report Relative to a Provision for the Support of Public Credit (Jan. 9, 1790), *in* 6 PAH 97, 98 (providing for interest on the domestic debt of $1.7 million, which is a little over 4% of the federal debt of $40 million, *id.* at 88, and arguing that no taxes had been proposed for state debts because assumption of the state debts was still contingent on consent of the state creditors).

[91] Hamilton, Report on the Further Provision of the Public Debt (Dec. 13, 1790), *in* 7 PAH 225.

[92] On the Whiskey Rebellion, *see, e.g.*, ELKINS & McKITRICK at 461–474.

[93] FERGUSON at 327.

[94] For descriptions of the political battles over discrimination and assumptions of state debts *see, e.g.*, ELKINS & McKITRICK at 136–161 (saying that Madison's plan – "if such it may be called" – would have cost more and hurt American credit); FERGUSON at 203–219, 306–325 (describing generosity of settlement of war debts to the South); RUTLAND, MADISON 76–91 (1987) (saying that opponents found Madison to be a Southerner first); McDONALD, HAMILTON 164–188 (arguing that Hamilton bootstrapped market confidence to raise market value of the debt and that much of his opposition would be hurt by market rises in debt); RISJORD at 366–393 (saying that Virginia opposed assumption because its debts had been largely discharged, but also got the most out of a federal city on the Potomac): HERBERT E. SLOAN, *supra* note 47, at 140–143 (1995) (sympathetically citing Virginia voices that supported Madison's position in favor of discrimination and against assumption); EDWIN PERKINS, *supra* note 89, at 199–234 (emphasizing the continuity from Robert Morris to Hamilton).

[95] McDONALD, HAMILTON at 174 citing, for example, Senators Maclay of Pennsylvania, Gunn of Georgia, Hawkins and Samuel Johnson of North Carolina, and Representatives Hugh Williamson of North Carolina, and Jeremiah van Rensselaer of New York.

incurred by the States in their particular defence."[96] At the Philadelphia Convention he had told Hamilton in a talking walk that they were both of the opinion that assumption of state debts was wise, but that it would be better to make it a matter of administration than an article of constitution, "from the impolicy of multiplying obstacles to [the] reception [of the Constitution] on collateral detail."[97] But in 1790, Madison opposed assumption, saying the speculations had been too much: "there must be something wrong radically & morally & politically wrong, in a system which transfers the reward from those who paid the most valuable of all considerations, to those who scarcely paid any consideration at all."[98] Although assumption of the state war debts and expenses eventually passed, the House of Representatives, led by Madison, defeated the assumption of state debts in the early round.[99] Given Madison's influence, the speculators were taking real risks.

It is said that Madison voted against assumption of state debts because of a turn to favor his home state of Virginia. It is said Madison's home state had paid off its state debts and would be hurt more by the taxes to pay for assumption than it would be helped by the assumption of state debts itself.[100] Virginia, however, looks like it came out a little better than even on assumption. It is fair to assume that the whiskey and imports taxes that would pay the state debts would be borne roughly according to population, and Virginia, it was presumed, had 15 percent of the population. In Congress's list of state certificates to be redeemed, Virginia had 16 percent of the total of all state certificates allocated to Virginia certificates. North and South Carolina, the supposed victims of Hamilton's plans, were the biggest state winners in the assumption, with Carolina certificates representing 27 percent of all certificates, while the Carolina population was only 15 percent of the total.[101]

The South also benefited disproportionately when the settlement boards gave coverage even for expenses that Congress had not authorized and

---

96 Madison, Notes of the Debates (Feb. 26, 1783), *in* 25 JCC 913 n. 1.

97 Hamilton to Edward Carrington (May 26, 1792), *in* 11 PAH 428.

98 Madison to Edward Carrington (Mar. 14, 1790), *in* 13 JM 104.

99 April 12, 1790, *in* 1 ANNALS 1577 (assumption of state debts defeated by 29–31).

100 FERGUSON at 309 (saying Virginia had paid off her state debts); RISJORD at 366–393 (saying that Virginia opposed assumption because its debts had been largely discharged).

101 The state population estimates are from U.S. CONST. art. I, §3 setting the allocation of votes in the House of Representatives before the first census results came in. The Aug. 4, 1790 Act for assumption of state debt set maximum amounts of certificates per state. An Act making provision for the debt of the United States §13, 1 ANNALS 142, 1ST Cong. 2d Sess.

also liberalized the rules for proof of the amount and justification of the expenses.[102] The Articles of Confederation had agreed that "expenses for the common defense and general welfare" approved by Congress would be charged to the common treasury, but the credit to the states were not self-executing, and took a long time to settle. Proof and settlement of the Southern war expenses stretched well into the nineteenth century.[103]

Assumption of state debts also turned out to be more expensive than Hamilton knew. He underestimated the state debts by half, at only $12 million, instead of the roughly $25 million that were ultimately assumed.[104] The original Carolina holders, moreover, might well have been paid off by the states themselves even without assumption, or at least, if we were able to assume that the states were fully responsible actors, then the proposed assumption by the federal government should not have increased the value of those state debts. In the event, assumption might well have increased the probability of payment by some value, but assumption was hardly a sure thing and Hamilton's plan did not turn dross into gold.

Speculators also had to guess right as to which continental security to buy, even given perfect foreknowledge of Hamilton's proposals. Hamilton recommended that Continental dollars be redeemed at the 2 1/2 cents on the dollar, which was the value for the Continental dollar when Congress devalued the dollar in 1780. Congress in fact, however, decided to pay only 1 cent on the Continental dollar, that is, at only 40 percent of what Hamilton proposed.[105] Speculators who bought Continentals

---

[102] FERGUSON at 203–208, 212–214, 218, 324 (saying that the southern states did well by assumption in part because of lax standards for proof of claims). *See also id.*, at 323, 333 (General board in charge of settlement of state expenses settled claims without vouchers generously and destroyed all the records showing how they had calculated allowable charges, for fear of second guessing).

[103] *Id.*, at 309, 324, 332.

[104] *Compare* Hamilton, Report Relative to a Provision for the Support of Public Credit, *supra* note 10, at 87 (Hamilton's $12 million estimate) with ELKINS & MCKITRICK at 121 ("roughly $25 million"). FERGUSON at 333–334 states the numbers as $18 million worth of state debts assumed in 1790 and $55–$65 million worth of state war expenses for which the states were given credit.

[105] FERGUSON at 296. Anti-Federalists generally assumed that the holders of Continental dollars should be stiffed. Mason, Federal Convention (Aug. 25, 1787), *in* 2 FARRAND 413 (worrying that federal assumption of confederate debts "might extend to all the old continental paper"); Patrick Henry, Virginia Convention (June 17, 1788), *in* 3 ELLIOT 471 (arguing that the Constitution's prohibition on impairment of contracts would require that Virginia pay for her share of payment of continental money, "shilling for shilling"); Luther Martin, *Defense of Gerry*, MARYLAND JOURNAL (Jan. 18, 1788), *reprinted in* 3 FARRAND 259 (defending Gerry by saying he had never proposed paying the Continental dollar).

relying on rumors or indeed accurate knowledge of Hamilton's proposals lost badly.

2. Hamilton and Jefferson Settle

Congress ultimately approved of the assumption of state debts in a compromise that gave considerable benefits to the South. In the first grand compromise of the new government, Madison's allies supported assumption only after they achieved siting the capital of the new government on the Potomac River.[106] Thomas Jefferson claimed that he brokered the bargain at a dinner party at his house in June 1790.[107] In the ratification debate the southern Anti-Federalists had treated the capital city as a serious menace to its neighbors – a "sanctuary of the blackest crimes,"[108] a refuge for slaves,[109] a site to prosecute honest editors by trial without a jury,[110] even as a walled city housing thousands of soldiers who would be privileged to plunder the country.[111] Once the new government was established, however, close placement of the Federal City began to look like it might actually be of benefit to its neighbours.

Jefferson was later to say the bargain by which Virginia got the capital on the Potomac and his enemy, Hamilton, got assumption of state debts was the biggest mistake of his political life.[112] At the time, however, Jefferson supported assumption because nine-tenths of the state debts had been incurred in the "general defence" and because if assumption were not adopted the alternatives might be worse.[113] In any event, with the first grand compromise of the new republic, Dutch and northern speculators got paid on the state debts that they held and the states got rid of their war burdens. Given the bargain reached in June of 1790, the dispute was a spat and not the irreconcilable schism. Madison did ultimately join with Jefferson to form a party of

---

[106] FERGUSON at 306–325.

[107] ELKINS & McKITRICK at 155–157.

[108] Mason, Virginia Convention (June 16, 1788), in 3 ELLIOT 331.

[109] John Taylor of Caroline, Virginia Convention (June 17, 1788), in 3 ELLIOT 455; William Grayson, (June 16, 1788), in 3 id. 434.

[110] Mason, Virginia Convention (June 16, 1788), in 3 ELLIOT 442.

[111] McDONALD, WE, THE PEOPLE, at 311. See also KENNETH R. BOWLING, THE CREATION OF WASHINGTON, D.C.: THE IDEA AND THE LOCATION OF THE NATION'S CAPITAL 81–86 (1991) (collecting other Anti-Federalist attacks on Congress being given the power to establish a Federal City).

[112] Jefferson to Washington (Sept. 9, 1792), in 24 PTJ 352.

[113] Jefferson to John Harvie, July 25, 1790, in 17 PTJ 271.

fervent anti-nationalists, but the assumption of state debts and placement of the capital do not seem to be a key cause of the turning.

D. NO REVOLUTION NEEDED TO RESTORE THE PUBLIC CREDIT

Hamilton's primary goal in the constitutional movement is best understood as simply a restoration of the public credit, so that when war came again, the federal government could borrow again. Hamilton's first contributions to the *Federalist* papers warned the nation that it must be prepared to borrow again for the common defense and warned of imminent dangers of war. When Hamilton, as George Washington's most trusted aide, was offered a cabinet post by the first president, he picked treasury. In his first major report as Secretary of Treasury, he gave Congress a comprehensive plan as to how to restore the public credit. A strong federal government generally was fully consistent with Hamilton's aims for preparedness. As a 23-year-old aide to George Washington, Hamilton had stated the need for a stronger general Congress with powers including especially the power to tax on its own. Hamilton's primary goal articulated in public was for a new Constitution that would allow the general government to restore public credit to borrow again in the next war.

Given the pressure that had built up over the years and the length and depth of the crisis, however, the tax cost of restoring the public credit was extraordinarily modest, both in level of the tax – $\frac{1}{2}$ percent of the lowest, workingman's income – and in the kind of tax – on imported "luxuries" and intoxicating distilled liquor, which were supposed to be suppressed. The federal destitution had instigated a revolution that had ended state primacy and created a complete government on the general level, and yet it was solved, once the one-state veto was ended, with a pittance. The public credit, usable in war, could have been restored with modifications that were considerably less revolutionary than what the Constitution in fact effected. Even staunchly Anti-Federalist John Lansing, while opposing the Constitution, allowed that the Congress could "be vested with a power to raise men and money" so as to be able to defend against foreign assault.[114]

Modest modification of the Articles could have produced the modest revenue needed. If Rhode Island and Virginia and then New York had not exercised their one-state veto, the 5 percent impost would have covered

---

[114] *See, e.g.,* John Lansing, New York Convention (June 20, 1788), *in* 2 ELLIOT 217.

much of what Congress needed to keep making payments on the war debts. All that would then be needed would be small supplementary sumptuary taxes. The counter-factual history in which "Rogue Island," wicked New York, and anti-federal Virginia were not so extreme as to exercise their veto power is a very different history: Congress in fact used every desperate plea and entreaty it had to get the wicked states to behave. Still, in retrospect at least, the solution to the crisis was modest – a cure with a pittance.

Restoration of federal credit for the common defense also did not require any change in foundation. It is true that the states were in general supreme under the Articles of Confederation and that Congress was just an assembly of their agents. Still, the Articles had given the Congress the exclusive power to deal with foreign states and to make war. The Articles prohibited the states from raising armies or navies and gave that power to the Congress. The states were prohibited from sending ambassadors to talk to foreign states and Congress was the sole voice on foreign affairs. On issues of war and foreign affairs, Congress already had the exclusive authority. If Congress had the responsibility to defend the nation in war, then it followed, on a philosophical level, that it needed to be given the necessary and proper tools to succeed in that defense. Revenue for the common defense should have followed from the obligation to defend. The philosopher Montesquieu had said that only small city-states could be true republics and that extended states needed to be run by despots to work. Still, even Montesquieu had allowed the small republics to join together in time of war. Giving the general-level Congress the ability to borrow to organize the country in the next war was allowed even by the philosopher of the Confederation. Hamilton's goals did not require a revolutionary abandonment of the confederate mode of government.

Madison's Virginia Plan, by contrast, was a revolution. The righteous anger at the wicked states blocked and building up for a decade finally exploded into the Constitution. Following Madison's work, the Constitution created a complete government on the federal level supreme over the states. The supremacy was reversed between state and federal level. The new government could find revenue on its own without the states. The Constitution adopted in lieu of the 1783 impost gave Congress permanent and plenary power to tax, limited in purpose by no more than that Congress should "provide for the common Defense and general Welfare." After the Constitution, Congress could enact legislation that was supreme over the law and even constitutions of the states. Before the Constitution, Congress was an assembly of agents of the states and the states were sovereigns on domestic issues and able to give short-term orders to their delegates to the Congress. After the Constitution, "We, the People" were sovereign and the Congress no longer rested on the states. Madison's Constitution is the revolutionary document, whereas Hamilton's Constitution, to restore the public credit for war, was not.

PART THREE

THE SPLIT AND THE END OF THE CONSTITUTIONAL MOVEMENT

Within three years of ratification, the movement that had achieved the Constitution divided into two irreconcilable factions. With the accomplishment of its primary goals, the movement lost its drive. By the adoption of the Eleventh Amendment in 1796, the Congress and the states decided that the just war debts of a state were not enforceable. That adoption is a clear line to mark the end of the constitutional movement.

CHAPTER ELEVEN

The Turning of Madison

A. THE GREAT SCHISM

For all of the strength of Madison's nationalism in 1787, Madison later joined with Jefferson in the opposition to Alexander Hamilton and ultimately in forming a stable political party aligned against the Federalists, and in favor of constraining the federal government. Washington invited both Hamilton and Jefferson into his cabinet, assuming that the country could be run like the Army by candid discussions and advice from his staff. Washington was apparently dumbfounded to learn in February 1792, that Thomas Jefferson strongly disliked Alexander Hamilton and his programs and that the government by consensus that Washington wanted to run was splitting apart into irreconcilable factions.[1]

Madison turned against the national government only after the Constitution was ratified. It had been "a primary article of [Madison's] creed" in the period leading up to the Constitution, as Hamilton "knew for a certainty," that the real danger to our system was the subversion of the national authority by a preponderance of the state governments.[2] Madison had been primarily responsible for the core steps in the Virginia Plan, ending the confederate system and creating a national government able to raise funds and operate on

---

[1] *See* McDonald, Hamilton 242–43 (saying Washington must have been dumbfounded). McDonald traces Jefferson's Manichean opposition to Hamilton to a dinner party in the spring of 1791 at which Hamilton revealed his sympathy for the Walpolean finance party in England, whereas Jefferson was a staunch believer in the country gentry Bollingbrokeans. *Id.*, at 212–17. *See also* James Roger Sharp, American Politics in the Early Republic: The New Nation in Crisis (1993) (describing the Founders' traumatic discovery that they were deeply divided about how to implement the powers of the new government).

[2] Hamilton to Edmund Carrington (May 26, 1792), *in* 11 PAH 437.

its own. Madison had been responsible more than any other person for flipping the system from a supremacy of the states over the Congress to supremacy of the Congress over the states. Madison before the turn had comfortably advocated reducing the states to the status of counties, where they might be "subordinately useful."[3] With a passion he had wanted Congress to be able to veto state legislation before it came into effect, in any case whatsoever, so as to stop the "frequent and flagrant" violation by the states of both the national sphere and individual rights.[4] Once Madison turned, Hamilton complained, he was "disposed to narrow the Federal authority" on assumption of state debts, cod subsidies, and a number of lesser issues.[5] By 1791, Madison was serving on the floor of Congress as Jefferson's ally, arguing that the National Bank was outside the very limited powers of the national government.[6] Madison in 1787 had given proof of the superiority of the national government as a guardian of individual rights against the states because it was an extended diverse republic. By 1791, however, Madison was arguing that the states were needed to protect individual rights because the states were homogeneous.[7] In the Kentucky Resolution of 1798, drafted by Madison and Jefferson, Kentucky resolved that national government was only a compact, "under the style and title of a Constitution," and that any state within the compact had an equal right to judge for itself the extent of the powers it had delegated to the national government. A state could declare "nugatory" and "altogether void, and of no force" federal laws that it did not like.[8] Madison's work in 1787 had been to end the compact among the states, the Articles of Confederation, because the states had breached the contract, and replace the compact with a national government supreme over the states and its own

---

3 Madison, Federal Convention (June 28, 1787), *in* 1 FARRAND 446 (small states and individuals would be best protected against encroachments by the bigger states if the states were reduced to the status of counties); Madison (June 21, 1787), *in* 1 FARRAND 356–357 (saying that people would not be despoiled if the states were reduced to a status parallel to that of the counties' status vis-à-vis the states). *Cf.* Madison to Washington (April 16, 1787), *in* 9 JM 383 (arguing for continuation of the states in so far as they are subordinately useful).

4 Madison to Jefferson (Oct. 24, 1787), *in* 10 JM 212.

5 *Id.*

6 James Madison, The Bank Bill, House of Representatives (Feb. 2, 1791), *in* 13 JM 372. *See* discussion, Chapter 9, pp. 209–210.

7 *Contrast, e.g.* Madison, Vices of the Political System of the United States (April 1787), *in* 9 JM 356–357 (saying that enlargement of the sphere will lessen the insecurity of private rights because majority factions are harder to form in larger spheres) with NATIONAL GAZETTE (Sept. 1791, Nov. 1791), *reprinted in* 6 WRITINGS OF JM 68, 81, 114 (calling for small ideologically homogeneous states, like Virginia, to be a check upon the national government).

8 Kentucky Resolutions of 1798 and 1799, *in* 4 ELLIOT 540–541.

base of popular sovereignty.[9] Between the 1780s and the 1790s, Madison had changed.[10]

Hamilton was surprised and hurt by Madison's turn. He was willing to absorb Madison's opposition to paying current holders the full face amount of the federal debts. Madison's turn on discrimination diminished Hamilton's respect for the force of Madison's mind and for the soundness of Madison's judgment, Hamilton said, but Hamilton wrote that his prior respect for the fairness of Madison's character and his prior reliance on Madison's good will carried over, so that he believed that Madison was misguided on discrimination, but sincere.[11] Then Madison became personally unfriendly toward Hamilton. Madison began to drop expressions in Hamilton's presence, "sometimes without sufficient attention to delicacy."[12] In the conversations with others, Madison questioned Hamilton's principles of government with asperity and ill humor and the conversations got back to Hamilton.[13] And Mr. Madison cooperated with Mr. Jefferson.

Jefferson supported the Constitution once the document was accomplished, but he was unpersuaded on many of the core issues.[14] The

---

[9] James Madison, Federal Convention (June 19, 1787), *in* 1 FARRAND 314–315 (states' contract obligations under the Articles had been absolved by breaches by other states in obligation to pay requisitions). *Cf.* Wilson, Pennsylvania Convention (Dec. 11, 1787), *in* 2 ELLIOT 497–498 (saying that "[t]his . . . is not a government founded upon compact; it is founded upon the power of the people").

[10] LANCE BANNING, SACRED FIRE OF LIBERTY 9 (1995) argues that Madison in opposition was not as inconsistent with Madison, the father of the Constitution, as generally believed. That position can be maintained only by understating how radical was the change that Constitution effected in creating a new, self-sufficient government on the national level and in ending the supremacy of the states. More balanced descriptions include John Zvesper, *The Madisonian Systems*, 37 W. POL. Q. 236, 250 (1984): Douglas Jaenick, *Madison v. Madison: the Party Essays v. the Federalist Papers*, *in* REFLECTIONS ON THE CONSTITUTION: THE AMERICAN CONSTITUTION AFTER TWO HUNDRED YEARS 116 (Richard Maindment & John Zverper, eds. 1989), both of which emphasize the contrasts in Madison's position before and after the break with Hamilton.

[11] Hamilton to Edmund Carrington (May 26, 1792), *in* 11 PAH 428. FERGUSON at 298 (1961) concludes that Madison's turn against the administration and in favor of discrimination between current holders and original holders was a purely political move, not realistic, and the turning toward state-oriented politics whereas before he had been a nationalist). *Compare* ELKINS & McKITRICK at 145 (1993) (concluding that Madison was sincere in explaining his opposition as coming from being upset at speculators and at paying speculators full value when they had paid so little for the debt).

[12] Hamilton to Edmund Carrington (May 26, 1792), *in* 11 PAH at 429.

[13] *Id.*, at 436.

[14] JOSEPH J. ELLIS, AMERICAN SPHINX: THE CHARACTER OF THOMAS JEFFERSON 102–105 (1997) argues that Jefferson was soft on the Constitution at best, and probably would have opposed it had he been at home during the ratification.

Constitutional Convention was a hammer and anvil that shaped everyone in attendance. Oliver Ellsworth from Connecticut, for instance, started by arguing that the confederation form of government would have to be continued, and ended by endorsing a powerful government to satisfy all national goals.[15] Jefferson was out of the country as Ambassador to Paris from 1784–1789 and he never joined the discussions in the Convention by which the consensus was formed that the crisis required an independent national government supreme over the rogue states.[16] Jefferson's first reaction to the Constitution was that he was very unpleased with it and that he preferred amendment to the "good, old and venerable fabrick" of the Articles of Confederation.[17] Jefferson was also consistently a conventional Montesquieuan, from before the Constitution through to his inauguration as president, believing in the superiority of small homogenous republics.[18] In his first inaugural address, Jefferson said that a principle of his administration was support of the states because the states gave "the surest bulwarks against anti-republican tendencies."[19] He never came to agree with Madison's argument for the superiority of the diverse extended republic on the federal level, which formed so much of the intellectual backbone for the Constitution.

From before the Constitution through to his inauguration, Jefferson consistently wanted the federal government to stay out of domestic affairs and to confine its power to foreign affairs.[20] On some issues, Jefferson was even

---

[15] Oliver Ellsworth, Federal Convention, June 20, 1787, *in* 1 FARRAND 335 (arguing that the Confederation should be considered as still subsisting and that the Convention's proposal should go out to the state legislature for ratification as an amendment to the Articles of Confederation) *with* Oliver Ellsworth, Connecticut Convention (Jan. 4, 1788), *in* 2 ELLIOT 186, 191 (saying that the Constitution was based on the "the necessity of combining our whole force, and, as to national purposes, becoming one state" and that the national government must be able to command the whole power of the purse because war had become a matter of the purse rather than the sword).

[16] *See, e.g.*, Edward Carrington to Jefferson (June 6, 1787), *in* 11 PTJ 407, 409–410 (arguing that the consensus in favor of federal control of the states is now "far removed from the views which prevailed when you were amongst us"); Madison to Jefferson (Oct. 24, 1787), *in* 10 JM 208 (saying that considering all the difficulties and diversities of opinion, it was impossible to consider the degree of concord which ultimately prevailed as less than a miracle).

[17] Jefferson to John Adams (Nov. 13, 1787), *in* 12 PTJ 349, 350–1.

[18] *See, e.g.*, Jefferson to Madison (Dec. 16, 1786), *in* 10 PTJ 602, 603 (arguing that small states were "the natural order of things" and saying that "a tractable people may be governed in large bodies, but in proportion as they are less than tractable, the extent of their government must also be less").

[19] Thomas Jefferson, 1st Inaugural Address (March 4, 1801), *in* BASIC WRITINGS OF TJ 334.

[20] Jefferson to Madison (Dec. 16, 1786), *in* 9 JM 210, 211 (saying that the proper division between the general and state governments is that national government would have power over foreign concerns and the states would have power over the domestic ones); Jefferson

more anti-national than the Articles of Confederation had been. In 1798, during the false war with France and as military expenses were mounting, he proposed an amendment to the Constitution whereby the national government would be prohibited from borrowing, even for war, and would have to rely on the states to "bid their credit in borrowing quotas."[21] The Articles had technically allowed the Congress to borrow on its own credit, although it could raise funds for repayment only by requisitions upon the states.[22]

Jefferson had waffled on the key issue of whether the federal government should be given direct or internal taxes in the ratification period, and his administration, once elected, repealed all the dry land or internal taxes.[23] If the purpose of the Constitution was to end the impotence of the federal government, then Jefferson had reservations. He seems to have thought of the central government as like the *ancien regime* he was observing in Paris,[24] and he stated that he was opposed to energy in government.[25] In November 1787,

to Gideon Granger (Aug. 13, 1800) *in* 7 WTS 451 (saying that the true theory is that states are independent as to everything within themselves and general government is reduced to foreign concerns only).

[21] Jefferson to John Taylor (Nov. 26, 1798), *in* 8 WTJ 481 (emphasis in original deleted). In 1788, Jefferson had said that good credit is indispensable to the present system of carrying on war, and that "[t]he existence of a nation having not credit is always precarious." Jefferson to Madison (May 2, 1788), 13 PTJ 129–130.

[22] Articles of Confederation, art. VIII (March 1, 1781), *in* 19 JCC 220 (requiring approval by nine of the thirteen states for borrowing on credit of the United States). *Cf.* art. XII, *id.* at 221 (pledging the credit of the United States to all debts contracted under the authority of Congress before the Articles of Confederation).

[23] Jefferson, first, endorsed federal direct tax (Jefferson to Madison (Dec. 20, 1787), *in* 14 DHRC 482 (saying that he liked the power of Congress to raise taxes without a need for "continual recurrence to the state legislatures"); Jefferson to George Washington (Nov. 4, 1787), *in* 14 PTJ at 328). Jefferson then suggested that the federal government should have only the impost and excises (Jefferson to Edward Carrington (Dec. 21, 1787), *in* 8 DHRC 253 n.1 (asking "Would it not have been better to assign to Congress exclusively the article of imposts for federal purposes, [and] to have left *direct taxation* exclusively to the states?")). Then he decided that denial of federal direct tax would be "very mischievous." Jefferson to William Carmichael (Dec. 25, 1787), *in* 14 PTJ 385. Jefferson made a final switch when he became president by successfully calling for the repeal of all internal taxes. *See* Jefferson, *First Annual Message to Congress, in* Basic Writings of TJ 337 (calling for dispensing with internal taxes, comprehending excises, stamp, auction, license, and carriage taxes); Dumas Malone, Jefferson the President: First Term, 1801–1805, at 100–01 (1970) (Jefferson successfully repeals federal internal tax).

[24] Adrienne Koch, Jefferson and Madison: The Great Collaboration 44 (1986) (arguing that Jefferson always associated central government with the tyrannies of the French *ancien regime* and Madison always associated the state governments with the irresponsibilities during the Confederation).

[25] Jefferson to Madison (Dec. 20, 1787), *in* 12 PTJ 442. The Federalists, by contrast, asked why would any man "choose a lame horse, lest a sound one run away with him?" A Citizen of

Jefferson read the proposed document as a conservative ruse against the honest Shaysites set up as "a kite to keep the hen yard in order."[26] Shays's Rebellion, in fact, probably had little or nothing to do with the Constitution.

In December 1787, Jefferson found himself just "nearly a neutral" on the Constitution.[27] When the Constitution was finally ratified, he did tell Madison that he "sincerely rejoice[d] at the acceptance of our new constitution by nine states" but he also even then wanted a bill of rights to "retouch ... the good canvas."[28] That he accepted the office of first Secretary of State showed he could either adapt to or accommodate to what he would not have chosen on his own. Jefferson termed his election in 1800, the Revolution of 1800, saying that it was "as real a revolution in the principles of our government as that of 1776 was in its form."[29]

Once Hamilton had been vanquished, Jefferson as president supported some extraordinary powers for the federal government. Jefferson, for instance, was offered some fine arguments resting on the text of the Constituition for his purchase of the territories and peoples of Louisiana and Florida. But Jefferson rejected the textual arguments[30] and chose instead to justify both acquisitions on the grounds of national necessity.[31] In truth, the grounds he offered for "necessity" far more resembled short-term political expediency than any real necessity or emergency.[32] For Jefferson to go beyond the text of the Constitution and claim power under unstated powers of necessity is quite extraordinary, especially for one who in the bank

---

PHILADELPHIA, REMARKS ON THE ADDRESS OF SIXTEEN MEMBERS (Oct. 18, 1787), *reprinted in* 1 DHRC 301.

[26] Jefferson to William Stephens Smith (Nov. 13, 1787), *in* 12 PTJ 357.

[27] Jefferson to Edward Carrington (Dec. 21, 1787), in 12 PTJ 446.

[28] Jefferson to Madison (July 31, 1788), *in* 13 PTJ 442.

[29] Jefferson to Spencer Roane (Sept. 6, 1819), *in* 10 WTJ 140.

[30] Jefferson to William Gary Nicholas (Sept. 7, 1803), *in* 8 WTJ 247 (deciding that relying on textual powers to justify administering territories and U.S. property and making treaties would make the Constitution "a blank piece of paper by construction"); Jefferson to John Dickenson (Aug. 9, 1803), *in* WTJ 262 (deciding that the Constitution "made no provision for holding foreign territory, & still less for incorporating it into our Union"); *see* DAVID N. MAYER, THE CONSTITUTIONAL THOUGHT OF THOMAS JEFFERSON 244–251 (1994); David Currie, *The Constitution in Congress: Jefferson and the West, 1801–1809*, 39 WM. & MARY L. REV. 1441, 1474 (1998) (concluding that Jefferson had the express power to acquire Louisiana and Florida, saying that "[i]t is very hard today, even for one who shares their general approach to federal authority, to find merit in the remarkably cramped reading that Jefferson in his most self-effacing moment offered of the explicit authorization to make treaties").

[31] Jefferson to John B. Colvin (Sept. 20, 1810), *in* BASIC WRITINGS OF TJ 683.

[32] *See, e.g., id.* at 683 (arguing that John Randolph might defeat the acquisition of Florida in the Senate).

crises had wanted necessity to be so narrowly construed. For a president to claim powers outside of the Constitution has the makings of a coup. Arguably the Louisiana and Florida purchases can be squeezed into issues of foreign concern, where Jefferson thought the national government had a role, but still upon acquisition, the new territories and peoples did become part of the domestic territories and domestic sphere. Given his subsequent coup-like nationalism as president, Jefferson's anti-nationalism in the 1780s might well be understood as political animus, arising from his hatred of Hamilton. Jefferson decided by 1792 that he hated Hamilton, his finances, and his bank.

While Jefferson was in Paris, Madison could be the entrepreneur who built the Constitution, but when Jefferson returned, Madison dropped back into a role as loyal lieutenant. Jefferson and Madison together moved into opposition to Hamilton. The uncompromisable break was over Hamilton's proposal for the National Bank in 1792. Jefferson considered the bank a "species of gambling, destructive of morality."[33] Hamilton's policies had created, he confided to Washington,

> [a] corrupt squadron, deciding the voice of the legislature, [who] have manifested their dispositions to get rid of the limitations imposed by the constitution on the general legislature, limitations, on the faith of which, the states acceded to that instrument; that the ultimate object of all this is to prepare the way for a change, from the present republican form of government, to that of a monarchy, of which the English constitution is to be the model. That this was contemplated in the Convention, is no secret, because its partisans have made none of it. To effect it then was impracticable; but they are still eager after the object, and are predisposing every thing for its ultimate attainment.[34]

Jefferson proposed that the Virginia Assembly should make doing National Bank business in Virginia treason to the sovereignty of Virginia, punishable by death.[35] Jefferson played mean.

Hamilton on his side of the dispute thought that

> [In Jefferson's vocabulary] creditor and enemy appear to be synonymous terms[,] . . . support of public creditor and corruption [have] similar import, and construction of the constitution for the public good and for the maintenance of due energy of the national authority [have]

---

33 Memoranda of Conversations with the President (Mar. 1, 1792), *in* 23 PTJ 184, 186–187. *See also* Jefferson's opposition to bank notes as paper money, Chapter 9, pp. 209–210.

34 Jefferson to Washington (May 23, 1792), *in* 23 PTJ 537.

35 Jefferson to Madison (Oct. 1, 1792), *in* 14 JM 375.

the same meaning with usurpation and a conspiracy to overturn the republican form of government.[36]

By 1792, the coalition that created the Constitution had split into two irreconcilable factions, who talked trash of each other.

B. DID MADISON TURN EARLY?

1. The Malapportioned Senate

A number of commentators have adopted the thesis that Madison turned from nationalist to states' rights advocate because of the Great Compromise in the Convention over the Senate. Professor Drew McCoy, then of Harvard, for instance, argued that Madison became an anti-nationalist when he was required to accede to the principle that votes in the Senate would be equal per state rather than equal per constituent population.[37] Madison biographers Ralph Ketcham and Irving Brant also attribute the turning of Madison in large part to the existence of the Senate.[38] If Madison turned because of the Senate Compromise, it is possible to ignore his nationalist vision in the preparation and early parts of the Convention and say that the written Constitution reflects a new Madison far more like the states' rights fire-eating gentleman of the 1790s, than the barn-burner nationalist of the 1780s. This section questions the soundness of the argument that Madison turned because of the Senate, both because Madison remained an immoderate nationalist after the close of the ratification debates, and because the Senate and House rules for apportionment do not seem to make any difference to Virginia's power.

Madison indeed advocated shifting the foundation of government from the states to popular sovereignty, and consistently favored apportioning congressional votes to population. Madison wrote to Washington and Jefferson before the Convention that the northern states would want the shift because of their present populousness, and the southern states because they expected

---

[36] Hamilton to Washington (Aug. 18, 1792), *in* 12 PAH 248.
[37] Drew McCoy, *James Madison and Visions of American Nationality in the Confederation Period: A Regional Perspective, in* BEYOND CONFEDERATION 226. In agreement with the thesis that the Great Compromise turned Madison, *see* PETER LYNCH, NEGOTIATING THE CONSTITUTION 259 n.25 (1999) (saying that Madison was a committed states' rights advocate after the decision of Convention to grant equality of representation to the states in the Senate).
[38] KETCHAM 215 (saying Madison's nationalism reached its peak in the weeks before the Great Compromise); BRANT, THE FOURTH PRESIDENT 170–174 (saying the Great Compromise "affected at once his attitude toward federal powers").

to become more populous.[39] Madison's argument presumes that the South would grow more rapidly than the northern states, apparently because of an assumption that the western lands across the Appalachians would be settled predominantly from the South.[40]

Governor Edmund Randolph claimed to the Convention and to the Virginia legislature that he had changed his mind and opposed giving power to the federal government because of the Senate Compromise.[41] Randolph was a chameleon, however,[42] and he switched back to becoming a staunch nationalist. His public letter of December 1787 is an articulate defense of the desperate need for the Constitution, one of the best of the entire ratification debate.[43] Randolph was ultimately an ardent and effective speaker in defense of the Constitution in the Virginia Ratification Convention, primarily on the ground the Constitution would preserve the union.[44] Randolph's nationalistic defense of the Constitution seems to be the critical argument that explains why Virginia ultimately ratified the Constitution, and it occurs after the Senate Compromise.

Madison also argued, at least tactically, that he did not know how much power the federal government should be given, until he knew which rule of representation the Constitution would adopt.[45] Madison hated the voting equality of states in the Senate and the Senate Compromise: Equal

---

[39] Madison to Washington (April 16, 1787), *in* 9 JM 383. *Accord* Madison to Jefferson (Mar. 19, 1787), *in* 9 JM 318–319.

[40] *See* McCoy, *supra* note 37, at 228–239 (expanding on the Virginia assumption that Western settlement would be southern in orientation).

[41] Randolph, Federal Convention (July 16, 1787), *in* 2 FARRAND 17; Randolph to the Speaker of the Virginia House of Delegates (Oct. 10, 1787), in 1 ELLIOT 486.

[42] Jefferson to Madison (Aug. 11, 1793), *in* 15 JM 57 (saying that Randolph was "the poorest Camelion I ever saw having no colour of his own, & reflecting that nearest him").

[43] *See* Randolph to Speaker (Dec. 27, 1787), *in* 15 DHRC123 (arguing that the failure of requisitions will be repeated upon the next military threat, that coercion is an indispensable ingredient, but that it cannot be used and that he would agree to the Constitution *without amendment* to preserve the union).

[44] *See, e.g.*, Randolph, Virginia Convention (June 4, 1788), *in* 3 ELLIOT 26 (saying that he would rather have his arm lopped off than have the Union be dissolved); June 6, 1788, *in* 3 ELLIOT 65–71; June 9, 1788, *in* 3 ELLIOT 188–194 (speaking for the preservation of the Union); June 10, 1788, *in* 3 ELLIOT 194–207 (speaking for the preservation of the Union); June 25, 1788, *in* 3 ELLIOT 652 (supporting the Constitution when the single question is "union or no union"). *See also* Virginia Convention (June 24, 1788), *in* 3 ELLIOT 600–601 (defending the deletion of the "expressly delegated" limitation on Congress, so as, for instance, to protect the passport); (June 10, 1788), *in* 3 ELLIOT 206 (defending the necessary and proper clause). *See also* Randolph's nationalism as attorney general, taking the position that the states were subject to suit in federal court on their war debts. Chapter 12, pp. 264–267, 271.

[45] Madison, Federal Convention (July 7, 1787), *in* 1 FARRAND 551 (also saying that equal votes for small states might render the new government as impotent and as short-lived as the old).

votes for small and large states was a "radical vice" of confederation systems. It allowed a minority of the people to become a majority.[46] Still, as with Randolph, the Senate Compromise did not deflect Madison for long. In his explanation of the Convention's Constitution to Jefferson, Madison does say that the Senate Compromise was "very much to the dissatisfaction of [the] large States,"[47] but he gets over it. What upset Madison most, as expressed to Jefferson, was that the Constitution did not give enough power to the national government: "[T]he plan should it be adopted will neither effectively answer its national objects nor prevent the local mischiefs which every where excite disgust agsts the state government."[48] Madison also gave Jefferson an "immoderate digression" on how important it was to have had a congressional negative on all state legislation and he lays out his full theory of the inevitable superiority of the extended and diverse national government. Even after the Senate Compromise, Madison believed that the negative was important for every case because the national government must guard the rights of individuals against the "flagrant and frequent" encroachments by the states.[49] Madison was an ardent nationalist after the Senate Compromise was settled, the Convention was over, and the written Constitution was set.

Even after Virginia and New York had ratified, moreover, effectively ending the battle, Madison was still angry at Anti-Federalist attempts to restrain federal power to lay direct tax. Madison was sure in July 1788 that the real object of the zeal to restrict federal direct tax was "to re-establish the supremacy of the State Legislatures."[50] Madison was against the supremacy of the state legislatures even well after the Senate Compromise.

---

[46] Madison, Federal Convention (June 30, 1787), *in* 1 FARRAND 485 (opposing a motion to give states equal votes in the Senate by saying that the equality of state votes in several confederations was a "radical vice in their structure"); Madison, Federal Convention (July 7, 1787), *in* 1 FARRAND 554 (saying that an equality of votes in the Senate will let a minority hold a majority). *See also* Madison, Federal Convention (June 28, 1787), *in* 1 FARRAND 446 (opposing giving small states equal votes by asking "Would 30 or 40 million of people submit their fortunes into the hands, of a few thousands?"); Madison, Federal Convention (May 30, 1787), *in* 1 FARRAND 37 (opposing giving small states equal votes and suggesting that Delaware might avoid embarrassments by having the vote be taken in committee); Madison (July 9, 1787), *in* 1 FARRAND 562 (saying that the states ought to vote as their citizens do).

[47] Madison to Jefferson (Oct. 24, 1787), *in* 10 JM 215.

[48] Madison to Jefferson (Sept. 6, 1787), *in* 10 JM 163–164.

[49] Madison to Jefferson (Oct. 24, 1787), *in* 10 JM 212.

[50] Madison to Tench Coxe (July 20, 1788), *in* 11 JM 210. *See also* Madison to Hamilton (Nov. 19, 1789), *in* 12 JM 449, 450. New Hampshire, the ninth state necessary under Art. VI for ratification, ratified in 1788.

Although Madison was an ardent foe of the Senate Compromise and an ardent advocate of the negative on state law, he adjusted like the professional he was to his losses. By the time of *Federalist* Number 10 in November 1787,[51] Madison used his theory of the superiority of the diversified extended republic not to justify the negative remedy specifically, but to make a more diffuse case for the superiority of the national level. By the time of *Federalist* Number 39 in January 1788, Madison could describe the Senate Compromise in very positive terms as proving that the Constitution is not an extreme nationalist document aiming for consolidation, as Brutus and Federal Farmer were claiming, but a mixed system, partly national and partly confederal.[52]

Attributing the turning of Madison to the Senate Compromise is also independently not plausible. The Senate Compromise does not make any difference to the important division of power between the North and the South. Article I, Section 3 of the Constitution lays out what the Founders expected the allocation of votes in the House would be, in anticipation of a census that was to be taken in 1790 to settle the issue. As shown by Table 11.1, if you count Delaware as a slave state,[53] then there is no difference – down to the level of four significant digits – between the power of the South in the House and the power of the South in the Senate.

Table 11.1 compares the percentage votes of the thirteen states in the Senate (left columns) and House of Representatives (right columns), starting at the southernmost state and listing the cumulative votes of the states. This table shows that if slave states continue through Delaware, then the slave states, overall, get 46.15 percent of the votes and the North gets a majority at 53.85 percent. It does not matter whether Senate or House rules govern; the slave versus nonslave states balance is the same.

---

[51] *Federalist* No. 10, at 57 (Madison) (Nov. 22, 1787).

[52] *Federalist* No. 39, at 255 (Madison) (Jan. 16, 1788) ("The Senate on the other hand will derive its powers from the States, as political and co-equal societies; and these will be represented on the principle of equality in the Senate, as they now are in the existing Congress. So far the government is *federal*, not *national*."). Accord, *Federalist* No. 62, *id.* at 416 (Feb. 27, 1788) (saying that Constitution creates "a compound republic partaking both of the national and federal character," and in a compound republic, "the government ought to be founded on a mixture of the principles of proportional and equal representation").

[53] Delaware had a slave population of 15% in 1790, far higher than the 2.1% average slave population in the states to Delaware's north, but only half as high as the 33.5% average for the states south of Maryland. PETER KOLCHIN, AMERICAN SLAVERY, 1619–1877, 242, Table 3 (1993). Delaware voted with the slave states, for instance, voting in the Federal Convention for including slaves, counted at 100%, in determining votes in the House of Representatives (July 11, 1787), *in* 1 FARRAND 581.

TABLE 11.1. *Power of slave states in Senate and House*

	(1)	(2)	(3)	(4)	(5)	(6)
	Slave % in 1790 Census[54]	Senate Votes (1/13)	Senate Cumulative Percentage	House Seats[55]	House Percentage	House Cumulative Percentage
Ga.	35.5%	7.69%		3	4.62%	
So. Car.	43%	7.69%		5	7.69%	
N. Car.	25.5%	7.69%		5	7.69%	
Va.	39.5%	7.69%		10	15.38%	
Ma.	32.2%	7.69%	38.46%	6	9.23%	44.61%
Del.	15%	7.69%	46.15%	1	1.54%	46.15%
Pa.		7.69%		8	12.31%	
NJ		7.69%		4	6.15%	
NY		7.69%		6	9.23%	
Conn.		7.69%		5	7.69%	
RI		7.69%		1	1.54%	
Mass.		7.69%		8	12.31%	
NH		7.69%	100%	3	4.62%	100%
North overall	2.10%		53.85%			53.85%

As it turned out, the Senate came to be a better refuge for slave states than the House. The North grew much faster than the South in the antebellum period in population than in number of states and the ratio in the Senate proved more favorable to the South than the ratio in the House.[56] This should have been deducible at the time of the ratification from the premise that the western lands would be predominantly slave settled. The new slave states to the West would have low populations, compared to the Eastern seaboard, and low population states carry an overallocation of votes in the Senate relative to the votes in the House.

If Delaware were considered a nonslave state, then there is a disparity under which the South loses power in the Senate at the time of the Constitution, dropping from 45 percent in the House to 38 percent in the Senate. Delaware is over-represented by four times in the Senate, using the House votes as a base, so if it is considered a free state it puts its extra weight on the northern

---

54 *Id.*
55 U.S. Const., art. I, sec. 3.
56 Counting the border states that did not secede as on the slave state side, the slave states held 43% of the Senate in 1860, but only 32% of the House of Representatives. Bureau of the Census, Historical Statistics of the United States, Colonial times to 1957, at 693 (1960).

side. The slave population in Delaware at 15 percent is halfway between the 33.5 percent average for the slave population of the South as a whole, and the 2.1 percent slave population for the North as a whole.[57] With Delaware treated as nonslave, the South should be preferring the rule of votes in the House over the rule in the Senate, as indeed the argument that the Great Compromise turned Madison would imply, but it is difficult to see how a difference between 45 percent and 38 percent could have been thought to make any material difference to outcomes. The slave states were a minority in both House and Senate under any view and they knew it.[58]

Madison, moreover, had also been a fervent nationalist supporting the Continental Congress under the Articles of Confederation, when the Congress had equal votes for each state.[59] If he had been a nationalist when the whole of the Congress voted by state, why should he abandon his nationalism because half of the Congress continued the status quo and voted by state? It is thus implausible that Madison would have turned to restrict the national government because of the Senate Compromise because there was nothing there worth a turn.

By the time Madison turned, in sum, the Constitution had been finished. The ink had dried and the original meaning had become fixed.

---

[57] Anti-Federalist William Grayson in arguing that this Constitution would allow the Congress to overtax Virginia slaves, and put Delaware on the side of the North. William Grayson, Virginia Ratifying Convention (June 12, 1788), *in* 3 ELLIOT 285.

[58] *See, e.g.*, Mason, Federal Convention (Aug. 29, 1787), *in* 2 FARRAND 451 (asking for two-thirds approval of navigation laws because the South was a minority in both houses and might otherwise be delivered up to its enemies).

[59] *See* discussion, Chapter 1, pp. 20–23.

CHAPTER TWELVE

The End of the Constitutional Movement

The pressing need for which the Constitution was adopted was to re-establish the public credit by making creditable payments on the debts of the Revolutionary War. When war came again, the Congress would need to be able to borrow. The problem of the war debts could not be solved if Rhode Island – and also other miscreant states – were given the veto required by the Articles of Confederation. Given that it was impossible to fix the problem within the context of the Articles, the Framers tore up the Articles and started afresh. Starting afresh, it was easy to conclude with Madison that the confederation form of government always failed for want of power at the center, and so the Constitution created a complete government on the federal level able to operate independent of the states, and supreme over them. Given that new framework, Hamilton as Secretary of the Treasury was able to restore the public credit with modest tax on sinful things such as imports and whiskey. With the addition of a tax on whiskey, Hamilton could even go beyond the mandatory restoration of federal credit and assume the war debts of the states.

Ulimately, however, the drive to pay the war debts ended, and honest creditors who supplied the Army were not paid. We can mark the end of the constitutional movement with Georgia's refusal to pay one Robert Farquhar and with the adoption of the Eleventh Amendment in 1795, which backed up and even constitutionalized Georgia's unrighteous refusal to pay its debt. By 1795, the constitutional movement had accomplished its objectives. By 1795, there was an energetic three-part government on the federal level, supreme over the states, with the ability to borrow. The Founders had split into two partisan camps – one Federalist and one Jeffersonian-Republican – which were never able to cooperate again. Public discussions and politics moved on to other things.

The Eleventh Amendment to the Constitution provides that foreigners or out-of-state citizens cannot sue a state in federal court. The Eleventh Amendment was adopted in reaction to the Supreme Court's 1793 decision in *Chisholm v. Georgia*,[1] which held that under the Constitution, before amendment, the state of Georgia could be sued in federal court to enforce payment of debts incurred for the Revolutionary War.

Chisholm, the plaintiff in the case, was the executor of one Robert Farquhar, a Savannah merchant. In 1777, Farquhar sold $170,000 worth of clothing and supplies to Georgia state commissioners appointed to make the acquisition for the benefit of the American army just outside Savannah. Farquhar was an angel to an army in deep distress. The purchases were called "one of the more fortunate incidences of the times," and a principal means by which Georgia clothed and armed her army "for the battle for freedom."[2] This was a sizable transaction – in 2003 dollars, the sale price would be on the order of $2.9 million.[3]

Committees of the Georgia legislature itself found the claim was meritorious over the years, notwithstanding a fair amount of political pressure to justify Georgia's disowning the debt.[4] The Georgia commissioners seem to have been given continental loan office certificates to turn over to Farquhar, but they had been misdirected or misappropriated and Farquhar never received them.[5] There was also a comprehensive assumption of state debts and state war expenses by the federal government in 1791, and it is a mystery why federal assumption did not cover Farquhar's claim against Georgia.[6]

---

[1] 2 U.S. (2 Dallas) 419 (1793). The facts of *Chisholm v. Georgia* described here are supplemented by Doyle Mathis, *Chisholm v. Georgia: Background and Settlement*, 54 J. OF AM. HIST. 19 (1967).

[2] Christine Desan, *Contesting the Character of the Political Economy in the Early Republic, in* THE HOUSE AND SENATE IN THE 1790S: PETITIONER, LOBBYING AND INSTITUTIONAL DEVELOPMENT 178, 185–186 (2002). Desan herself argues that expectations of the time were that Farquhar should be paid by petition to the legislature, but even she admits that the state of Georgia's first defense, that it had given debt certificates to its own agents who had misappropriated them, was not meritorious.

[3] JOHN J. MCCUSKER, HOW MUCH IS THAT IN REAL MONEY: A HISTORICAL COMMODITY PRICE INDEX FOR USE AS A DEFLATOR OF MONEY VALUES IN THE ECONOMY OF THE UNITED STATES 52, 60 (2d ed. 2001) (commodity index at $2111 for 2002 (est.) and $128 for 1777, so multiplier is 2111/126 or 16.5 and 16.5 times $170,000 = $2.8 million). Inflation from 2002 to 2003 was another 3% (U.S. CENSUS, STATISTICAL ABSTRACT OF THE UNITED STATES, 2004–2005 at 461) and 103% of $2.8 mil. = $2.9 million.

[4] DOYLE MATHIS, *supra* note 1, at 29.

[5] *Id.* at 21.

[6] *See* FERGUSON at 207–208, 212–214, 323, 333 (1961) (federal assumption of Southern debts was generous to South in proof of both amount and authorization).

Farquhar's debt, in any event, was not federalized either in 1777 or in 1791 and it remained unpaid at Farquhar's death. Chisholm, the South Carolina executor of Farquhar, sued the state of Georgia in federal court for payment.

The Supreme Court, four justices to one, held that Chisholm's suit was allowed in the new federal courts both by the letter and the spirit of the Constitution. The Supreme Court's decision in *Chisholm* said that suit against Georgia in the federal court fit within the literal words of the Constitution, was not blocked by the tradition of sovereign immunity, and was justified to prevent state impairment of contracts.

The Attorney General of the United States arguing in support of Chisholm's suit was Edmund Randolph, who had moved from objector to become a very effective spokesman in favor of the Constitution in the Virginia ratification debate, and he remained very effective in *Chisholm* as well. Randolph argued that the suit was covered by the language of Article III, Section 2, of the Constitution, which provides that the power of federal courts "shall extend to controversies between a State and citizens of another State," even when the state is defendant rather than plaintiff.[7] Chisholm was a citizen of "another state" (South Carolina) in comparison to Georgia. In the Virginia Ratification Convention, James Madison and John Marshall had argued that states could not be sued on their war debts in federal court on the ground that Article III would apply only to allow the states to be plaintiffs to sue out-of-state individuals for recovery of state claims.[8] The text of Article III, however, expresses federal jurisdiction in terms of cases in which the state shall be "a party" and the term, "party" includes both defendants and plaintiffs. Justice Blair's opinion, the shortest opinion in *Chisholm*, relied on the plain text argument – the suit was within the language "between a State and citizens of another State" even when the state is the defendant.[9] Chief Justice John Jay also said that the suit fell within the "true sense" of Article III's "controversies between States and citizens of another State."[10]

The Court in *Chisholm* also rejected the British common law rule of sovereign immunity as inapplicable to republican states. Sovereign immunity arose as a corollary of the idea that the sovereign is supreme over the law

---

7 *Id.* at 420. *See also* clause 2 of Article III, section 2, providing that the Supreme Court shall have original, but not exclusive jurisdiction, in all cases "in which a State shall be Party."

8 James Madison and John Marshall, Virginia Ratification Convention (June 20, 1788), *in* 3 ELLIOT 533, 555.

9 2 U.S. at 450–451.

10 *Id.*, at 479.

because the sovereign makes the law. Under Roman law, it has been said, "the emperor is not bound by statutes."[11] "The sovereign of a Commonwealth, be it an assembly or one man," Hobbes wrote in the Leviathan, "is not subject to the civil laws."[12] According to Blackstone, no suit or action could be brought against the king, because giving a court jurisdiction over the king "implies superiority of power."[13] Oliver Wendell Holmes said that a sovereign is exempt from suit "on the logical and practical ground that there can be no legal right as against the authority that makes the law on which the right depends."[14]

The Court in *Chisholm* rejected Georgia's sovereign immunity claim because they rejected the supremacy of the state over individuals. Randolph argued that the states have no immunity because the Framers of the Constitution would never have supposed an individual plaintiff was inferior to a state. "Legislators were not so far sublimed above other men," he said, "as to soar beyond the region of passion."[15] The Constitution replaced the Articles of Confederation, Randolph argued, with a government that "derives its origin immediately from the people; and the people individually are . . . subject to the legislative, executive, and judicial authorities thereby established."[16] The states were liable to process of law, Randolph concluded, "because they were just assemblages of these individuals."[17]

Justice James Wilson agreed with Randolph in *Chisholm*, calling the argument that the king was supreme over law and courts, a branch of "systematic despotism . . . lately formed in England."[18] Chief Justice John Jay also agreed, saying that "[i]n this country there are no inferior[s], for all the citizens being as to civil rights perfectly equal."[19] "By the language, 'We the people of the United States,'" Jay said, "the people established their sovereignty, and the people acting as sovereigns established a Constitution to which the State governments were to be bound."[20]

[11] 1 THE DIGEST OF JUSTINIAN 13 (T. Mommsen & P. Krueger eds., A. Watson transl. 1985), *quoted in* Alden v. Maine, 527 U.S. at 768 n. 6.
[12] LEVIATHAN, ch. 26, p. 130, *quoted in* Alden v. Maine, 527 U.S. at 768.
[13] 1 W. BLACKSTONE, COMMENTARIES ON THE LAWS OF ENGLAND 234–235 (1765), *quoted in* Alden v. Maine, 527 U.S. at 715 (Kennedy, J.).
[14] Kawananakoa v. Polyblank, 205 U.S. 349, 353 (1907).
[15] 2 U.S. at 423.
[16] *Id.*
[17] *Id.*
[18] 2 U.S. at 458.
[19] *Id.* at 471.
[20] *Id. See also* 2 Dall., at 454–458 (Wilson, J.) (state sovereignty inconsistent with the sovereignty of the people established by the Constitution).

Superiority of the sovereign to the law has similarly been said by other courts to be inconsistent with republican ideals. The "bloody paths trod by English monarchs" and the Declaration of Independence, Justice Stevens has argued, made the proposition that the king was above the law unacceptable on this side of the Atlantic.[21] Sovereign immunity does not properly extend to officers of the state, as Justice John Harlan put it, because "[n]o man in this country is so high that he is above the law. No officer of the law may set that law at defiance with impunity. All the officers of the government, from the highest to the lowest, are creatures of the law, and are bound to obey."[22] The superiority of the Crown over the law and the courts may be assumed to have been a tenet of British common law, but the new nation often rejected aspects of British common law that it did not like. The more inconsistent it was with republican ideals, the less likely a British common law rule was to be brought over.[23]

Randolph, finally, argued that Chisholm's suit was necessary to protect individuals from impairment of contract. The Constitution had imposed many prohibitions on states, Randolph argued, including a prohibition on impairing contracts. The prohibitions "announce to the world," Randolph said, "the . . . apprehensions that States may injure individuals in their property, their liberty, and their lives; may oppress sister States; and may act in derogation of the general [i.e., national] sovereignty."[24] The states had no "high privilege of acting thus eminently wrong, without controul," so that a remedy for the wrong would be implied.[25]

Justice James Wilson took up the impairment-of-contract aspect of the argument especially. "What good purpose could [the prohibition on impairment of contract secure]," Wilson asked, "if a State might pass a law impairing the obligation of its own contracts; and be amenable, for such a violation of right, to no controuling judiciary power?[26] A State, like a merchant, makes a contract," Wilson posited.

> A dishonest State, like a dishonest merchant, wilfully refuses to discharge it: The latter is amenable to a Court of Justice: Upon general

---

[21] Seminole Tribe v. Florida, 517 U.S. 44, 95 (Stevens, J., dissenting).

[22] Tindal v. Wesley, 167 U.S. 204, 217 (1897). The author of the opinion is the first of two Justices John Harlan.

[23] *See, e.g.,* Randolph, Virginia Convention (June 17, 1788), *in* 3 ELLIOT 469–470 (arguing that constitutional incorporation of the common law would be "destructive to republican principles."); Madison to Washington (Oct. 18, 1787), in 3 FARRAND 129, 130 (saying that English common law included "a thousand heterogeneous & antirepublican doctrines").

[24] 2 U.S. at 421–422.

[25] *Id.* at 422 (saying that under the common law, an "infraction of a prohibitory law, although an express penalty be omitted, is still punishable").

[26] *Id.* at 465 (Wilson, J.).

principles of right, shall the former when summoned to answer the fair demands of its creditor, be permitted, proteus-like, to assume a new appearance, and to insult him and justice, by declaring I am a Sovereign State?[27]

Impairment of contracts was considered not only a violation of individual rights but also a violation of the comity that the states owed to each other. Using the judiciary power of the United States for such controversies, Randolph argued, would obviate quarrels between states on account of the claims of one of their citizens, which might reach the "crest of war."[28] Chief Justice John Jay took up this aspect of Randolph's argument saying that the legal remedy against Georgia obviates occasions of quarrels between states on account of the claims of their respective citizens.[29]

Justice James Iredell, dissenting, did not reach the constitutional issue, but he was of the opinion that the constitutional provisions were not self-executing without an act of Congress. Given the traditional immunity of the king under common law, Iredell argued, he thought that Congress would have to authorize legal process against Georgia before the federal courts could act: "[I]n respect to the manner of its proceeding," he said, "we must receive our directions from the Legislature in this particular."[30] Iredell did have what he termed a present opinion "in some measure extra-judicial" that creditor suits should not be allowed against a state for recovery of money.[31] Apart from the extra-judicial musings, Iredell simply called for Congress to take the lead and his objections would not have struck down congressional legislation that allowed suits against a state.

Although Georgia lost the case, it resisted payment. Georgia had refused to participate in the argument.[32] Georgia's stated defense was that Farquhar's certificates of indebtedness had been delivered to Georgia agents to give to him, and misappropriated there.[33] Misbehavior by Georgia's own agents is not a legal defense, however, nor indeed a very good equitable defense. Georgia did not exactly repudiate the debt or the Supreme Court's judgment,

[27] *Id.* at 456.
[28] *Id.* at 424 (Attorney General Randolph).
[29] *Id.* at 478.
[30] 2 U.S. at 432 (Iredell, J.) (also saying that the Court got its authority by act of the Legislature only), at 436 (saying "[w]hatever be the true construction of the Constitution in this particular ... the Legislature has in fact proceeded upon the ... supposition [that federal judiciary had only transfer of state judicial powers, which did not include suits against the state]"); *id.* (saying "looking at the act of Congress, which I consider is on this occasion the limit of our authority[,] whatever further might be constitutionally, enacted").
[31] *Id.* at 449–450.
[32] 2 U.S. at 419.
[33] Desan, *supra* note 2, at 190–191.

but the Georgia House of Representatives did propose to hang anyone trying to enforce the judgment in Georgia,[34] and Georgia also did not pay.
Despite a finding by Georgia legislative committees that Farquhar's claim
was meritorious, Georgia did not finally pay the claim until 1847, seventy
years after the goods had been delivered to the desparate American Army
outside Savannah.[35]

The Eleventh Amendment, which takes jurisdiction away from the federal
courts for suits by out-of-state individuals against the states, was proposed in
1794 and ratified in 1795 in reaction to the *Chisholm* decision.[36] On its face,
the Eleventh Amendment does not mean very much. It just denies out-of-
state creditors access to the federal courts for suits against states, perhaps to
give the states a kind of home court advantage to litigate their legal obligations in their own, presumably friendlier courts. The Framers had almost not
allowed lower federal courts to be created at all and within that environment,
an exemption from the jurisdiction of federal courts was not very surprising.
Violations, such as Georgia's, of the impairment-of-contracts prohibition of
Article I, section 10 of the Constitution could have been litigated as a federal issue in state courts and ultimately decided on appeal by the Supreme
Court.[37] Reading the words of the amendment literally as only a forum rule
diminishes the importance of the amendment. Indeed one explanation for
its swift passage is that the Eleventh Amendment is only a small forum rule,
another sop, and does not establish a broader right of states to impair contracts and stiff honest suppliers like Robert Farquahar.[38] Long after passage
of the amendment, however, in 1890, after a completely new set of defaults

---

[34] DAVID CURRIE, THE CONSTITUTION IN CONGRESS: THE FEDERALIST PERIOD 1789–1801
at 196 (1997), *cited by* Alden v. Maine, 527 U.S. at 721 (Kennedy, J.). We seem forced to take
it that execution was an acceptable defense of states rights on money issues at the time. *See*
Jefferson to Madison (Oct. 1, 1792), *cited in* 12 PAH 85n. (proposing that Virginia should
make the signing, issuing, or passing of national bank notes in Virginia an act of Treason,
punishable by death).

[35] MATHIS, *supra* note 2, at 29.

[36] The Eleventh Amendment was proposed by the House on March 4, 1794. Ratification by
the ninth state, necessary to make it effective, was in December, 1794, although President
John Adams did not announce that the Amendment was in effect until 1798. 5 FOUNDERS'
CONSTITUTION 407. John Gibbons, *Eleventh Amendment and State Sovereign Immunity: A
Reinterpretation*, 83 COLUM. L. REV. 1889, 1899–1826 (1983) is the best recent history of
the Amendment.

[37] There is an even narrower reading of the Eleventh Amendment that it takes away only
jurisdiction of federal courts based upon diversity, that is, the fact that Chisholm and Georgia
came from different states, and does not take away jurisdiction to decide federal issues. *See,
e.g.*, William Fletcher, *The Diversity Explanation of the Eleventh Amendment: A Reply to Critics*,
56 U. CHI. L. REV. 1261 (1989).

[38] *See* Gibbons, *supra* note 36 at 1938 (calling the Amendment a tub thrown to a whale).

on state debt unrelated to those of the constitutional era, the Supreme Court held that the states had immunity from suit by their creditors on meritorious claims even within the state courts.[39] Extending sovereign immunity to state courts turns the immunity from a possibly minor forum rule for the site of origin of a suit that would be reviewed by the Supreme Court into a bar that prevents the creditor from recovering at all.

Justice Kennedy recently said that the Eleventh Amendment rather than *Chisholm* represented the "well-understood meaning of the Constitution."[40] That is an overstatement, to say the least. There are statements saying that states would have immunity from suit under the pending Constitution, but they are counterbalanced by creditable evidence that it was also understood that the states could be sued in federal court. The messages are mixed and the understanding was contested. As noted, both James Madison and John Marshall misdescribed the text of the document to the Virginia Ratification Convention, saying that federal court jurisdiction over states as a party would just allow states to appear as plaintiffs to use the federal courts to recover their claims against out-of-staters.[41] In fact the text describes states as "parties" in federal court, and "party" covers states as defendants being sued. Because we have a written Constitution, we can read the writing ourselves, and the misdescriptions of the text by Madison and Marshall can be ignored.

In May, 1788 in *Federalist* Number 81, Hamilton denied any intent to overcome sovereign immunity, saying that there is

> no colour to pretend that the state governments, [would be divested] of the privilege of paying their own debts in their own way, free from every constraint but that which flows from the obligations of good faith. The contracts between a nation and individuals are only binding on the conscience of the sovereign, and have no pretensions to a compulsive force.[42]

39 Hans v. Louisiana, 134 U.S. 1 (1890). *See* Gibbons, *supra* note 36 at 1973–2003 (tracing the history of *Hans v. Louisiana* in the surrounding political situation of Southern state defaults on Reconstruction bonds).

40 Alden v. Maine, 527 U.S. 706, 727 (1999).

41 Madison, Virginia Convention (June 20, 1788), *in* 3 ELLIOT 533 (saying that the Article III language about federal court jurisdiction when the state was a party would apply only to cases in which the state brings the suit, because "[i]t is not in the power of individuals to call any state into court"); John Marshall, Virginia Convention (June 20, 1788), *in* 3 ELLIOT 555 (saying that it is not rational to suppose that the sovereign power should be dragged before a court and that the Article III language was only about the state bringing suit against out-of-state defendants).

42 *Federalist* No. 81, at 549 (Hamilton) (May 28, 1788). It is apparently a slip or error for Hamilton to talk about contracts between the *nation* and individuals or federal sovereign immunity. The passage is otherwise all about state immunity.

Immunity for states in federal courts was, however, as forcefully denied. Edmund Pendleton, a proponent of the Constitution, argued to the Virginia Ratification Convention in favor of legal process against the states in federal court. Pendleton told Virginia that the "impossibility of calling a sovereign state before the jurisdiction of another sovereign state, shows the propriety and necessity of vesting [the federal courts] with the decision of controversies to which a state shall be a party."[43] Pendleton was promising creditors, whose support some would say was necessary to carry the Constitution, that the states would be "called before" the federal jurisdiction. Anti-Federalist George Mason read the Constitution in the Virginia Convention to allow "this state to be brought to the bar of justice like a delinquent individual." He used process against Virginia as a grounds against ratification of the Constitution as a whole because "[i]t would be ludicrous to say that you could put the state's body in jail."[44] Indeed, although Madison eventually decided to misdescribe the text in favor of state immunity, Madison's first response to Mason was that giving jurisdiction to the federal courts in disputes between out-of-state citizens and the state was "wise and salutary."[45] Hamilton and Wilson also defended the federal courts in the ratification debates as the proper place to hear suit by individuals against the states so as to counteract the partiality of state court judges.[46]

State immunity from suit was not understood to be part of the Constitution in North Carolina. The North Carolina Ratification Convention refused to ratify the Constitution on the first round, demanding a series of amendments including

> That Congress shall not, directly or indirectly, either by themselves or through the judiciary, interfere with any one of the states in the redemption of paper money already emitted and now in circulation, or in liquidating and discharging the public securities of any one of the states; but

---

[43] Edmund Pendleton, Virginia Convention (June 20, 1788), *in* 3 ELLIOT 549.

[44] Mason, Virginia Convention (June 18, 1788), *in* 3 ELLIOT 526–527 (also asking "How is the judgment, then, to be enforced?" and arguing that "A power which cannot be executed ought not to be granted").

[45] Madison, Virginia Convention (June 18, 1788), *in* 3 ELLIOT 530. Hamilton and Wilson also defended the federal courts as the proper place to hear suits by individuals against the states so as to secure impartiality.

[46] *Federalist* No. 80, at 538 (Hamilton) (May 28, 1788) (saying that federal court is proper place to hear suit by individuals against states so as to counteract the "strong predilection" of state judges, "to the claims of [their] own government"); Wilson, Pennsylvania Convention (Dec. 7, 1787), *in* 2 ELLIOT 491 (saying that since "[i]mpartiality is the leading feature in this Constitution . . . [w]hen a *citizen* has a controversy with another state, there ought to be a tribunal where both parties may stand on a just and equal footing") (emphasis added).

each and every state shall have the exclusive right of making such laws and regulations, for the above purposes, as they shall think proper.[47]

It was not well understood in North Carolina that the states already had the power to decide how to pay off their paper and public securities without the demanded amendment, even after the Constitution had received the necessary nine states for ratification. North Carolina's proposal, moreover, did not even try to demand that a state's private or contractual debt, such as Georgia's debt to Farqhuar, would benefit from immunity.

Justice James Wilson, who decided *Chisholm*, and Attorney General Edmund Randolph, who argued it, were, moreover, among the most important and influential delegates to the Federal Convention. Only Madison was more influential. *Chisholm* could not have been decided as it was, if it was indeed "well-understood" that the states were to have immunity from suit. The language of Article III, allowing the state to be a "party" in federal court, also fits *Chisholm* rather than the Eleventh Amendment. The results of the Eleventh Amendment could not be extracted from anything in the unamended language of Article III.

Chisholm's judgment in favor of suppliers like Robert Farquhar is also entirely consistent with the ideals that lead to the Constitution as a whole. The primary purpose of the Constitution was to end the impotence of the national government so as to maintain payments on the debts of the Revolutionary War and restore the public credit. The constitutional revolution was made necessary by the wickedness of the states in failing to pay their requisitions and in vetoing federal taxes that would allow the debts to be paid. When war came again, the federal government would need to borrow again. The debt to Farquhar was a just war debt, left in default by the wickedness of Georgia. Georgia's behavior dishonored the great cause of Independence and subjected the friends and patrons of the Republican form of government to "the votaries of tyranny,"[48] just like the other war debts that made the Constitution necessary.

Article I, Section 10 of the Constitution prohibits the states from "impairing contracts." The impairment of contracts prohibited by Section 10 is especially abusive on the rights of creditors when the contract is the state's own promise – as Wilson, Jay, and Randolph said in *Chisholm*. Because of the prohibition on a state's impairing the obligation of contracts in the Constitution,[49] the state does not have the power to modify the *Chisholm* contract.

---

47 North Carolina Convention (Aug. 1, 1788), *in* 4 ELLIOT 247.
48 Madison, Address to the Nation (April 26, 1783), *in* 24 JCC 283.
49 U.S. CONST. art. I, sec. 10, cl 1.

Without the power to modify the contract, a state cannot be supreme over the contract. Even a true sovereign is bound by the laws it creates. According to the Alexander Pope,

> Nature, like liberty, is but restrained
> By the same laws which first herself ordained.[50]

Given the inability to modify, it is difficult to see how Georgia was supreme over the contract, even if the contract arose under its own law.

Georgia, according to Wilson, was a dishonest state that, like a dishonest merchant, refused to discharge its contract[51] and Wilson's righteous anger at the state for its dishonesty is exactly the anger at the states felt by the proponents of the Constitution as a whole. Justice Kennedy has called Wilson a "radical nationalist"[52] but Wilson is the second most influential man at the Philadelphia Convention,[53] echoing Madison's radicalism. Wilson was a radical nationalist in exactly the same way that the Constitution is. Georgia's stiffing of Farquhar and then Chisholm, moreover, was exactly the kind of frequent and flagrant encroachment of individual rights by the states that formed such an important part of Madison's original vision. Madison was more upset at the wicked states' encroachments on the national sphere by failing to pay their requisitions, but the the anger at abuse by the states of individual rights, such as Farquhar's, is reflected in the Constitution in the Article I, Section 10 bar on the impairment of contract. Georgia's behavior is the kind of wickedness that the Constitution, and especially the impairment-of-contract clause, was adopted to end.

The Eleventh Amendment bar to collection of debts is even now not a morally attractive part of the Constitution. The Fifth Amendment bars a government from taking private property without just compensation and the states are bound by that restriction.[54] Allowing Georgia to avoid paying Farquhar for the $170,000 worth of goods Farquhar delivered was not a "taking" or "confiscation," but only because of the paper-thin legal cover that Georgia gave Farquhar a promise to induce him to deliver the goods, and then dishonorably reneged on the promise. The ethical basis for the just

---

[50] Alexander Pope, "An Essay on Criticism" (1711).
[51] 2 U.S. (2 Dallas) at 456, quoted at *supra* note 27.
[52] 527 U.S., at 725.
[53] Robert G. McCloskey, *James Wilson* in 1 THE JUSTICES OF THE UNITED STATES SUPREME COURT 1789–1969 at 79 (Leon Friedman & Fred L. Israel, eds. 1969–1978). *Accord*, MORRIS at 272.
[54] U.S. Const. Amend. V. applied to the states by incorporation into the 14th Amendment due process guarantee by *Chicago, B& Q R.R. Co. v. Chicago*, 166 U.S. 226 (1897) (states required to give just compensation for taking of private property).

compensation requirement for a taking is that it is unfair to lay the burdens of government disproportionately on the single individual or a few individuals that are the target of the taking,[55] and that rationale covers the burden on Farquhar. A tax scheme that taxed only Farquhar would not be ethical.[56] Georgia's action was expropriation from Farquhar except for the fraudulent promise it gave, followed by the legal cover of immunity.

Justice Kennedy has argued that sovereign immunity is necessary to allow the states "to govern in accordance with the will of their citizens . . . to allow the states to allocate resources among competing needs and interests" by the political process, (and to allow "other important needs and worthwhile ends [that] compete for access to the public fisc."[57]) That rationale is merely an equivalent to saying that if the voters of Georgia do not want to pay more taxes to pay for Farquhar's goods and prefer to confiscate the goods and not pay for them, then immunity of the state will allow it. Applying that rationale to a takings problem would allow a state to confiscate any private property and then decide by the political process to allocate its resources to other more "important needs and worthwhile ends [that] compete for access to the public fisc" or just to cut taxes. Our general protection for private property and the things that the state of Georgia did to Farquhar are not consistent.

Notwithstanding that *Chisholm* is consistent with the grand idealism of the historical Constitution, however, there was also room, even within the grand sweep, for a backwash or eddy giving a privileged exemption for state debts, including Georgia's. The important debts that needed to be paid in preparation for the next war were the foreign debts. Default on state debts to domestic suppliers did not threaten the ability to borrow when war came again in quite the same way that defaults on the foreign debt did. The states did not have jurisdictional responsibility for war or foreign affairs under either Articles of Confederation or the Constitution and it might well have been possible to tolerate defaults by the states that did not implicate the federal level. The Dutch in bidding up the value of United States federal debt do not seem to have blamed the United States for Georgia's defaults.

It was not settled before ratification, for example, that the federal government would even assume the state war debts. Both the Continental Congress and the Philadelphia Convention received proposals requiring

---

55 *See, e.g.*, Frank J. Michelman, *Property, Utility, and Fairness: Comments on the Ethical Foundations of "Just Compensation" Law*, 80 Harv. L. Rev. 1165, 1165 (1967) (saying that taking law is essentially "deciding when government may execute public purposes while leaving associated costs disproportionately concentrated upon one or a few persons").

56 *Id.*, at 1169 (saying taking law is deciding whether costs should be paid for by the tax structure or leaving them where they fall).

57 527 U.S. at 751.

federal assumption of the state war debt, but did not adopt them.[58] Madison at the time said that assumption of state debts was good in principle, but that it should not be guaranteed in writing "from the impolicy of multiplying obstacles to [the] reception [of the Constitution] on collateral detail."[59] Even after ratification, assumption of the state war debts was a contested political issue in Congress in 1790. Congress ended up assuming the state debts and expenses of war, but Madison opposed assumption and won against the assumption in early rounds.[60] Even with a broad settlement after 1791, the federal government did not pick up Georgia's debt to Farqhuar for some mysterious reason. Consistent with the constitutional requirements, Congress could have gone the other way after ratification and left the state creditors to the uneven fates of the separate and demonstrably irresponsible states. The state debts could have gone the same way as the Continental dollar, which stole from all who held it. In the end the fact that only Farquhar was caught by the irresponsibility of the states was lucky. The constitutional movement was a movement of grand idealism; that sovereign immunity applied to stiff Farquhar is a miserable little exception to it. Still, the course of any real historical movement is not entirely clear, pure, or overwhelming.

Even if state immunity could have found room within the grand sweep of nationalism of the Constitution, however, that does not mean that Justice Kennedy is justified in saying the Eleventh Amendment rather than *Chisholm* represented the "well-understood meaning of the Constitution."[61] *Chisholm* settled how the Constitution was understood at the time perfectly well as a matter of law. Even Iredell, the dissenter to *Chisholm*, only wanted Congress to give clear directions by statute and that posture means that he would have upheld the constitutionality of federal suits against the states had Congress asked for it. The original text could not be forced to read the result that the proponents of the Eleventh Amendment wanted, which is why, of course, an amendment was needed.

The Eleventh Amendment, moreover, was not part of the original package, but rather part of the backwash or reaction. The Eleventh Amendment was

---

[58] John Rutledge, Motion at the Federal Convention (Aug. 18, 1787), *in* 2 FARRAND 327 (proposing federal assumption of state debts); Report of a Congressional Committee to Restore Public Credit (Mar. 20, 1783), *in* 24 JCC 197 (proposing that all reasonable expenses of the states supported by satisfactory proof made in defense against the British or Indians shall be considered as part of the common charges, even if not previously authorized by Congress).

[59] Hamilton to Edward Carrington (May 26, 1792), *in* 11 PAH 428.

[60] *See* discussion, Chapter 10, pp. 238–243. ELKINS & MCKITTRICK 146–161 (1993); RISJORD, at 363–393, and MCDONALD, HAMILTON 163–188 also describe the fight, issues, and settlement.

[61] Alden v. Maine, 527 U.S. 706, 727 (1999).

proposed in 1794 and adopted in 1795 after Hamilton's marvels had gone into effect. By 1794, the new federal taxes and Hamilton's scheme of funding had cured the fiscal crisis that was the proximate cause of the Constitution and restored the public credit.[62] By 1794, as well, the complete three-part national government supreme over the states was in operation and an overwhelming public success.[63] With the establishment of the national government and the restoration of public credit, the energy of the radical nationalism that made those accomplishments possible was no longer necessary and had begun to dissipate. There was nothing else of major importance that the constitutional movement needed to accomplish.

With the accomplishment of the goals of the constitutional movement, the pendulum had begun to swing. By 1795, Jefferson and Madison had turned against the Washington Administration, and they were organizing the opposition, the Jeffersonian Republican party, founded on the principle that the states and not the extended republic was the better protector of individual rights. Jefferson's Revolution of 1800 – "as real a revolution in the principles of our government," he said, "as that of 1776 was in its form"[64] – would look to the states for all domestic concerns and as the "surest bulwarks against anti-republican tendencies."[65] The Constitution was a vector written to end the imbecility and impotence of the federal level – not to hobble the federal horse, but to get it to run – but Jefferson's election meant that the pendulum's momentum had shifted in the other direction to take power away from the federal government in favor of the states. Whether we interpret the Eleventh Amendment as a sop or as a substantive protection, in any event, it was not part of the nationalizing vector of 1787–1788. The adoption of the Eleventh Amendment to overturn *Chisholm* is indeed a convenient marker, correlated with the rise of the Republican party, that marks the end of the historical constitutional movement. The nationalizing vector that created the Constitution had weakened and dissipated and could no longer pull toward the center.

---

[62] *See* Chapter 10, especially pp. 237–38.
[63] *See* Chapter 6, pp. 130–31.
[64] Jefferson to Spencer Roane (Sept. 6, 1819), *in* 10 WTJ 140. *See generally* DAN SISSON, THE AMERICAN REVOLUTION OF 1800 (1974) describing the history by which Jefferson became President.
[65] Jefferson, First Inaugural Address (March 4, 1801), *in* BASIC WRITINGS OF TJ 334.

Concluding Summary

The purpose of the Constitution was to end the imbecility and impotence of the Confederation Congress. The pressing need was to give the federal government enough revenue to pay enough of the war debts that the federal government could borrow again to the defend the nation against the coming threats. The Constitution is first a tax document, a pro-tax document, written by nationalists to allow the federal government to tax people and things directly without going through the states.

The tax power is a necessary explanation for the Constitution, but it is not enough. Tax did not in fact require the revolutionary changes that the Constitution made. The Hamilton package that restored the public credit asked for a pittance – a day and half of workingman's wages per capita – and taxed only those things that were supposed to be suppressed – imports and hard liquor. Land was not taxed on the federal level, despite Madison's recommendation. Hamilton's package was less burdensome both in terms of revenue and means of tax than the 1783 impost and requisition proposal that New York had vetoed. The 1783 proposal worked within the assumptions of the confederation mode and would have kept Congress as the agent of the sovereign states.

The Constitution ended the supremacy of the states and the confederation mode and replaced it with a complete three-part national government able to walk on its own legs. The sovereignty of the people replaced the sovereignty of the states. The Framers ripped up the existing constitution, the Articles of Confederation, and ignored the instructions that had authorized the Convention. The proposal was ratified, not by each state as the Articles had required, but by the people. Federal law was made supreme over state law and even state constitutions. The national government was able to raise revenue and operate to provide for the common defense and general welfare, without recourse to the states.

The revolution that the Constitution effected is best explained by the welled-up anger of the nationalist Founders at the wickedness of the states. The states had failed to pay their requisitions. They had vetoed the most reasonable solution to the fiscal crisis. Dating back into the Revolution they had betrayed Washington's army and the sacred united cause of the Revolutionary War. The Founders thought that both New York and Rhode Island should rest in hell for their vetoes of the impost proposals. The anger at wicked Rhode Island and evil New York meant that the Framers were willing to go forward with their revolution, ignoring their instructions and the Articles' requirement of unanimous ratification. The states had been supreme under the articles but they had forfeited their sovereignty by failing to pay requisitions and by vetoing the most reasonable alternatives.

The constitutional revolution is James Madison's work to a surprising extent. There is no prior intellectual history and no precursor plans for the revolution, outside of Madison's work. Madison believed that the extended republic, the national government, would end the abuses that the states, especially Patrick Henry's state, inevitably imposed on individual rights. Madison convinced first his Virginia colleagues, then the Convention, and finally the nation that confederations inevitably failed and that the state supremacy needed to be ended. Madison did not get everything he wanted. He lost as to state power in the Senate and he lost on his beloved federal veto of state legislation of any kind. Still he accomplished a nationalist revolution.

Factors other than tax and the welled-up anger are not significant contributory causes to adoption of the Constitution. The Constitution was not written to limit the national government, but to get it to run. Limitation of the federal government beyond the vague standards of "common Defence and general Welfare" was an issue to be faced on another day. The Bill of Rights was a sop, stripped of all the meaningful structural proposals that the Anti-Federalists cared about by a nationalist James Madison and the overwhelmingly nationalist First Congress. The Virginia Founders were debtors trying to restore their credit rating, and not creditors. The creditors of first importance were the Dutch. Shays's Rebellion was a current event, but it reinforced rather than delegitimated the states. Slavery, democracy, and individual rights are extremely important issues, but they do not divide the Nationalists from the Anti-Federalist opposition nor affect the shape or adoption of the Constitution.

The ratification debate was overwhelmingly over the question of whether the state or the federal government should be the superior. The most hard and closely fought issue in the ratification was over whether the federal government could lay direct or dry-land taxes in time of war. The Anti-Federalists did not participate in the drafting of the document and they opposed what they saw. The Constitution was once a weapon used by the nationalists to accomplish nationalist programs. The fence-sitters voted to ratify the Constitution because of their loyalty to the idealism of the Union. "United we stand, divided we fall" represented the highest ideals of the War for Independance and of the republican form of government for which the war was fought. By ratification of the Constitution, the nationalists won the battle. In original intent, in struture and design, the Constitution is a nationalizing vector, written by ardent nationalists to accomplish a program, a new and strong national government for the *United* States of America.

Index

Note: Speakers in the Constitutional debates are identified by state and as Federalists (F) or Anti-Federalists (AF). Quotes surround pseudonyms. Underlined names are subsequent commentators. Italics identifies court cases or authored works. References found only in footnotes are marked by n after page. Beginning prepositions and articles are ignored in alphabetizing.

Hamilton (*cont.*)
  against scaling debt, 229–232
  slavery, against, 184
  state barons, against, 98, 139
  state immunity, for, 269
  state sovereignty, against, 93
  state debts, assumption, 238–243
  tax, *see* Hamilton's tax
  war, fear of, 18–19, 36–39, 72
Hamilton's tax, 25, 89, 223–228, 240
  1783 compared, 75, 227
  day and a half burden, 160, 225
  impost, reliance on, 225–226
  land tax, against, 227–228
  Mass. relief., 218, 228
  modesty, 158, 225–227, 244–246, 262
  to suppress imports, 225
  for whiskey tax, 226–227, 240
Hancock, John (Gov. Mass.), 134n, 220, 228n
Henry, Patrick (ex-Gov. Va. AF)
  anti-Baptist, 60, 164, 174
  anti-Semitism, 167
  Bill of Rights, against, 165–166, 172–173
  British creditors, against, 54–56, 166
  Constitution aimed at, 51–57, 60, 63, 115–116, 203, 277
  for debtor relief, 54–59
  direct tax, against, 159
  for disunion, 141
  on Dutch, 152
  for Episcopal assessments, 51, 60, 64, 144
  for ex post facto law, 166
  federal government a threat to, 139, 141
  intolerance, 167
  Jefferson vs., 52, 143
  Madison vs., 5, 51–69, 143, 174, 277
  paper money, against, 207–208
  paper money, for, 146
  requisitions, defeats, 5, 51
  for scaling public debt, 231
  Senators, appoints Anti-Federalist, 130
  Shays's, not a threat, 220
  slaveholder, 144, 182–183
  tax, against federal, 145
  Virginia, controls, 51
  war threats overblown, 152
  We, the People, against, 95
Higginson, Stephen (Mass. F), 228

Holmes, Abraham (Mass. AF.), 136
"Honestus" (NY), 192, 235
House of Representatives
  Anti-Federalists in First, 130
  Monroe v. Madison, 174
  property requirements, 176
  representing wealth, 102–103, 107–108
  slaveholder representation, 174, 185–186, 259–261
Howell, David (RI Congressman), 27n, 90n, 153
Huntington, Samuel (Gov. Conn. F), 80
Hutson, James H., 178, 182

Imbecility of the Federal, *see also* Impotency of the Federal
  Constitution written to end, 8, 43–50, 276
Impairment of contracts, 116, 235, 266–267, 272
"Impartial Examiner," (Va. AF), 48n, 165n
Impost
  Anti-Federalists on, 153, 155–156
  interstate, 198–199
  New York on, 2, 28–29, 38, 50, 75n, 140
  "regulation of commerce," 191–193
  retaliatory, 193–195
  Rhode Island on, 2, 27–28, 59, 153
  State veto, 2, 26–29, 38, 72, 75, 90, 128, 140, 244–245
  sufficient?, 157–158, 237
  under Constitution, 2, 75, 89, 224–228, 239
Impotency of the federal, 1, 8, 17, 120, 221, 276, *see also* Imbecility of the federal
Impressments, 35–36, 232
Individual rights, 250
  Bill of Rights, 163–175
  Eleventh Amendment, and, 271, 272
  federal protection, 50–60, 115–116
  Henry vs, 51–60, *see also* Henry, Patrick
  judicial review, 115–116
  Madison turn, 250
  Mason against, 146–147
  the negative, 109–112, 115–116
  representation protection, 164–168
  state abuse of, 66, 74
  state protection of, 51–60, 169, 272–273

Slavery, 183–186
  absent Northern states, 185–186
  in Declaration of Independence, 114
  and Negative, 114
  Quakers, 142
  and requisitions, 159
  three-fifths clause, 107–108, 185
  and voting power, 259–261
Smilie, John (Pa. AF)
  anti-Anglican, 144
  anti-tax, 154, 155n
  opposes Sovereignty of the People, 95,
    180n
Smith, Adam
  absent from constitutional debates,
    196
  Federalist no. 10 compared, 71
Smith, (Josiah or John K?) (Mass F), 222
Smith, Melancton (NY AF)
  anti-democrat, 176
  anti-tax, 153, 154
  New York, carried, 161, 171
  against Rhode Island, 27–28
  Shays's Rebellion, 217
  for Union, 161
Soldiers, Revolutionary War
  unpaid debts to, 23–24, 27, 34, 80, 231,
    239
Sovereign immunity, *see* State immunity from
  paying debts
Sovereignty of the People, 2, 4, 74–99, 146,
    177; *see also* Democracy; People, We the;
    Representation; State Sovereignty
  Anti-Federalists opposition to, 64–65,
    95–96, 135, 180
  Founders in favor, 91–94, 180
  Madison responsible, 240, 246
  representation rule, 100–108
  from requisitions, failure of, 4, 103
  use against state sovereignty, 2, 4, 91–93,
    146, 175, 265n, 276
  Shift from State to, 74–99
  in Tenth Amendment draft, 175
  Wilson for, 91–93, 177
Sovereignty of the States, *see* State
  Sovereignty
Spaight, R.D. (NC F), 79
State debts
  assumption of, 218, 238–244
  buy at value? 26, 242
  Carolinas ahead on assumption, 241
  Chisholm v. Georgia, 263–268

didn't need to be paid, 238–239, 240,
    273–274
  fair market value payment?, 26, 241
  immunity from paying, 268–274
  Massachusetts, 218
  stiffing creditors, 272–273
  Virginia broke even on assumption, 241
  whiskey tax to cover, 227, 240
State immunity from paying debts, 268–274
State sovereignty, *see also* People, we the;
    Sovereignty of the People
  bank is capital treason upon, 255, 268
  Constitution ends, 2, 8, 276–277
  direct tax ban would re-establish, 258
  Federal supremacy over, 10, 40, 72–73,
    74–99
  federal tax did not end, 2, 244–246,
    276–277
  federal tax violates, 4, 29, 90
  Founders against, 93–95, 146
  Hamilton plan consistent with, 2,
    244–246, 276–277
  immunity and, 264–265, 272
  impost ends, 4, 90
  impost violates, 27, 90
  judicial review over, 113, 115, 145
  Madison against, 5, 43–50, 77, 240, 258
  Mason against, 146
  Negative over, 112–113
  New York claims, 29, 90
  People sovereignty trump, 4, 265
  Rhode Island claims, 29, 90
  Shays's did not threaten, 219
  shift from, to Sovereignty of the People,
    74–99
  Virginia claims, 28, 90
States, *see also under name of the State*;
    Clinton, George; Henry, Patrick; State
    debts; State sovereignty
  abuses by, 5, 8, 15–39, 43–60, 70, 164,
    171n, 174, 203, 266
  anti-discrimination norm, 199–200
  encroachments on federal sphere, 3, 5,
    15–39, 43–60, 111, 116, 148, 171n, 203n
  Feudal Baronies, 6, 138
  "frequent and flagrant" abuses, 41n, 59,
    70, 114, 115, 250, 258, 272
  "local demagogues," 4, 98, 139
  perversity of, 27, 80
  seize Continental supplies, 36–37
  wicked, 3, 28, 58, 60, 80, 208, 272
  willful, 25–26, 33